SEVENTEENTH CENTURY POETRY

The Schools of Donne and Jonson

Edited by Hugh Kenner

Holt, Rinehart and Winston, Inc.

NEW YORK • CHICAGO • SAN FRANCISCO • ATLANTA • DALLAS
MONTREAL • TORONTO • LONDON • SYDNEY

Library of Congress Catalog Card Number: 64-12614
ISBN: 0-03-026090-6
Printed in the United States of America
89 008 12

Contents

VI. COURTLY WITS 329

VII. MEN OF SENSE AND MEN OF WIT 385

Editor's Note

INNOVATION and renovation, these are the two constant themes in the history of the art of poetry. This book brings together what the student needs for an understanding of the great effort inaugurated by John Donne and Ben Jonson, whose examples presided over the course of English poetry during one of its richest half centuries. It was the time of what came to be called metaphysical poetry, but of much more than that; there was more than one way, even in the heyday of the metaphysicals, for a poet to use his intelligence. For more generally it was a time of great active intelligence, intelligence working its way down into the very capillaries of a poem; and it ended when, by the time of the Restoration, the nature of the intellective process itself had been revalued.

Commentary has been confined to the Introduction and the Headnotes to the various poets; the notes give purely elucidative information. The notes, it goes without saying, lean on generations of scholarship, but notably on the learning of the editors of the standard scholarly editions from which I have taken my texts. I am indebted also to the apparatus contained in Helen Gardner's selection, *The Metaphysical Poets* (London, 1957), and in R. C. Bald's *Seventeenth Century English Poetry* (N.Y., 1959). And I owe an imponderable debt to the conversation of my colleague Alan Stephens, particularly to our discussions of Jonson.

For convenience I have presented the materials poet by poet, but the poets are arranged not in chronological order of birth, but in what seem the most useful groupings for study. The student is encouraged to refer freely to the chronological chart, lest he come to suppose that Donne lived before Jonson, or Marvell before Cowley.

A word on the texts. I have distinguished "u" from "v," "then" from "than," "i" from "j," and replaced the old long "s" with the modern form, but have otherwise retained old spellings. The student who finds getting used to this an effort deserves to be told why.

Modern spelling, essentially a set of printing-house usages imposed by printers, represents a gain not in logic but in consistency.

Consistency, however, is a technologist's virtue, not a rhetorician's, and to impose it on the writings of minds technology had not yet mesmerized can be positively misleading. For Donne, for Jonson, for Carew, for Marvell, the written lines are a speaker's memorandum; when we find in Donne's text,

> . . . Here I unsweare, and overswear them thus . . .

it is the voice that is shaping the utterance, not the printing case. "Sweare" elbows "swear" not out of quaint exuberance but in keeping with a pragmatic conviction that any orthography will suffice that preserves the sounds. It will be for a later age to think of printed words as standardized parts, interchangeable like the cubes of lead from which they are composed, obdurately identical whatever the scheme of rhythm or intonation that courses round them.

Donne's readers, in short, did not feel as we do that a word's identity is inextricable from its spelling; hence the naturalness, in their utterances, of what we uncomfortably feel to be "puns." "Sun" and "son" are for us two different words which sound alike; so are "Donne" and "done"; and we think a writer who exploits the similarity of sound does something brash and a little disreputable. For the seventeenth century Dean of St. Paul's, however, "sunne" was imprimis an *utterance,* vocalic not typographic, which in denoting both the Second Person of God and the fire of heaven touched on a mystery distinctions of spellings might analyze but not resolve; his great "Hymne to God the Father" does not so much play upon words as meditate on such mysteries. To normalize the spellings in such poems is to obscure something essential, their vocalic base; and in making his way through lines which he must sound out because the words look unfamiliar the modern reader is repeating, more closely than he knows, the experience of the readers whose lips first moved in the presence of these pages.

Santa Barbara, California HUGH KENNER
February, 1964

Introduction

THAT man is distinguished from the brutes by speech, that full humanity flows constantly into language, and that to be comprehensively alive to each instant of one's fortunes is to be steadily, resourcefully articulate, these were nearly the sole commonplaces that could go, in Donne's age, without saying. All else must be said. Cleopatra transfigures her suicide with language, the mere act her least concern. A sonnet in antiphon, seemingly improvised on the dance floor, accompanies the first touch of Romeo's hand with Juliet's. Desdemona is won with speech and slain to the beat of words, Othello creating moment by moment, in the act of shaping phrases, his own awareness of what he is about:

> Put out the Light, and then put out the Light:
> If I quench thee, thou flaming Minister,
> I can againe thy former light restore,
> Should I repent me. But once put out thy Light,
> Thou cunning'st Patterne of excelling Nature,
> I know not where is that *Promethaean* heate
> That can thy Light re-Lume.
> When I have pluck'd thy Rose,
> I cannot give it vitall growth againe,
> It needs must wither. Ile smell thee on the Tree.
> (*kisses her*)

He had not known the nature of his own act, he who in past times has dealt so much in killing, until he spread the deed before his own tranced mind, phrased in those words. This language is not "communication" but utterance, and not the mere cry uttered, but the inarticulate inchoate fact rendered articulate, its structure disclosed, intelligible: intelligible to its utterer, for the first time. "Articulated," says the dictionary: "divided into precise and distinct parts." Fully to articulate what we do and suffer is to understand its structure part by part and so fully to experience it; to be incapable of articulation is to be less than human.

So Donne examines and articulates into its parts a depression which he begins by locating in the midwinter night of the year's shortest day:

> Tis the yeares midnight, and it is the dayes,
> *Lucies,* who scarce seaven houres herself unmaskes,
> The Sunne is spent, and now his flasks
> Send forth light squibs, no constant rayes;
> The worlds whole sap is sunke:

The very lines huddle and dwindle, from ten syllables to eight to a mere six; and the poem knows this (the poet is counting), articulation keeping one eye on its own processes. He notes a coincidence of two midnights, to which he will shortly add a third, his own. The day is a person, a saint, named Lucy, for light: its shining, such as it is, is her unmasking. The sun too is a person, but also an alchemical process. The whole world is a vegetative process, gone sapless.

> The general balme th'hydroptique earth hath drunk,
> Whither, as to the beds-feet, life is shrunke,
> Dead and enterr'd;

Earth has absorbed the world's sap as though compelled by the disease now called edema; disease leads to a deathbed and to death; life, notes the mind, still quick in the midst of its own gloom, is quite literally "enterr'd," gone down *in terram;* and its being drawn down is mimed by the huddling of a dying man toward the foot of his bed.

And still Donne claims our attention, as he sets this psychic state into relation with many drear happenings normal in the world. For if life shrunk toward the bed's feet suggests a man, and death an epitaph, the poem will now produce both:

> yet all these seeme to laugh,
> Compar'd with mee, who am their Epitaph.

Dwindle the world, and compared to his state its dwindling will be as gaiety. Yet if he is their Epitaph, it is these laughing things that are dead. We seem to have gone beyond reason: yet if the Epitaph surpasses in mortal weight the universal death itself, that is its proper dignity, since it alone states, judges, and exhorts, being shaped not out of matter but out of speech. And he in his person is this uttered thing, this form of speech, this text:

> Study me then, you who shall lovers bee
> At the next world, that is, at the next Spring.

His dearth has an epitaph's permanence: it will stay for the instruction of future readers. Meanwhile, just as the dead may expect to enter paradise, so there will be a future here, and a spring, and lovers; the earth will be (except him) renewed; and sending his mind up the other side of the year's curve, he locates himself yet more exactly at its bottom.

> For I am every dead thing,
> In whom love wrought new Alchimie.
> For his art did expresse
> A quintessence even from nothingnesse,
> From dull privations, and lean emptinesse:
> He ruin'd mee, and I am re-begot
> Of absence, darknesse, death; things which are not.

That love is an alchemist, transmuting base metals, or extracting a quintessence, the supreme fifth essence, from natural bodies, this is no original notion. Poets paying an ingenious compliment have toyed with it before. Donne here revitalizes this tired figure; or rather, as always when he seems to be refreshing a convention, he preserves its conventional usage, active in his mind and on his page, as a norm for his own experience to transcend, or from which, as here, to be debarred. For lovers undergo love's alchemy, and privations and absences are numbered among the features of lovers' experiences for that alchemy to transmute. But his nothingness, his privations, his lean emptiness, his absence, darkness, death, these are the elements, and these alone, of which love has remade him. They are not the dross that transmutation leaves behind. And they are not the love sonneteer's usual hyperbolas but literal and ghastly absolutes, depending on a stark fact outside convention's compass: "her death."

The poem takes a long and deliberate route to this shocking fact. It is only in the fourth stanza, commencing his fourth venture through the grave symmetries of his meditation, that he reaches it, in its due place in the argument:

> But I am by her death (which word wrongs her)
> Of the first nothing, the Elixer grown.

It is the "first," the prime or quintessential nothing, not the usual nothingness left by something absent. And now he has arrived at defining his plight with some precision. She is absent; he is quintessentially remade in her absence, by the love which remakes most lovers in a presence.

> (All others, from all things, draw all that's good,
> Life, soule, forme, spirit, whence they beeing have).

And he pursues this theme, dwelling with analytic fascination on the descending hierarchies of being, to be any of which, a man, a beast, a plant, a stone, would be somewhat to stir, to long, to exist. Even to be an "ordinary nothing," a shadow, would be to derive from something;

> But I am None; nor will my Sunne renew.

Meanwhile the ordinary sun, which has now entered Capricorn, will return and infect lovers in the spring to come with goatish passions:

> You lovers, for whose sake the lesser Sunne
> At this time to the Goat is runne
> To fetch new lust, and give it you,
> Enjoy your summer all;

"Enjoy your summer all:" it is the shrunken line of the stanza, the same fifth line which affirmed "the worlds whole sap is sunke," or which voiced from the heart of nothing a contracted plentitude ("If I were any beast"), that he now uses to bid them Godspeed; for his mind is coming to rest on a solemn ceremonial that shrinks their sport into ritual grotesquerie:

> Since shee enjoyes her long nights festivall,
> Let mee prepare towards her, and let mee call
> This houre her Vigill, and her Eve, since this
> Both the yeares, and the dayes deep midnight is.

So, by delicate implication, she is canonized, a new saint replacing St. Lucy; and so the "Nocturnall upon St. Lucies Daye" returns to the words that began it, its depression having after some 300 words not altered itself but located and articulated itself.

So much, and our attention has omitted much, will a moan yield when a Donne's intelligence explores it. Seemingly, out of the blank negation itself the effort to piece and define and encompass the negation has risen, attending to the steps of its own ascent, missing no foothold in its own harsh logic, measuring its sentences by the diastole and systole of an elaborate stanza, and scrupulous about the symmetries, likenesses, differences, by which its incomprehensible blankness is comprehended. The poem does not claim to be recollecting in tranquillity. But two centuries later Wordsworth will have nothing whatever to say in the presence of jocund daffodils, and little to think:

> I gazed—and gazed—but little thought
> What wealth the show to me had brought.

For it had come to seem natural by Wordsworth's time that in the mute undergoing of powerful impressions the distinctively human character should be found; and their distinctively poetic character in simply affirming them afterwards, perhaps long afterwards. Yet another century, and part of the poet's work will be to make it seem plausible that any utterance should be going on at all. Mr. Eliot's "Prufrock" begins somewhere in its own epigraph, and we are not sure whether anyone has begun to speak, or when, or to whom. "Prufrock" is a poem arising out of the virtual impossibility of there being a poem. And when Mr. Eliot's Gerontion asserts:

> Here I am, an old man in a dry month,
> Being read to by a boy, waiting for rain,

we learn to see his precipitate affirmative selfhood as a moral flaw. For Mr. Eliot's age, if not for his poetry, full humanity inheres not in speech but in sexual being, or perhaps in simple activity, and speech is but a surrogate for action refused or deferred.

A man ceaselessly speaking out of the midst of what he does and suffers is stuff for the dramatist; and Donne (born 1572, the exact contemporary of Ben Jonson and only eight years Shakespeare's junior) was, an acquaintance wrote, "a great Frequenter of Plays," as well as "a great Visitor of Ladies" and "a great Writer of conceited Verses." [1] His playgoer's ear heard thousands upon thousands of verses tuned to the run of speech, and registered a hundred times the formal theatricalities that sustain, through incidents no matter how intolerably melodramatic, the continuity of copious language.

[1] Donne's college friend Sir Richard Baker, writing six years after Donne's death. "Conceited" means "packed with pregnant conceptions."

For Godsake hold your tongue, and let me love . . .

Such a line is not first of all iambic decasyllabic, but first of all a man speaking.

When by thy scorne, O murdresse, I am dead,
And that thou thinkst thee free
From all solicitation from mee,
Then shall my ghost come to thy bed . . .

This is imagined melodrama with the sting of live speech in it, transfiguring in the manner of the stage the routine desk-bound poets' routine addresses to cruel ladies. And the astonishing sixteenth elegy, "On His Mistris," is a dramatic monologue implying something like the plot of a fantastic play; for their relationship is secret, and he must go abroad, and must dissuade her from accompanying him disguised as his page. He opens it with the tolling formality of a dramatic set piece:

By our first strange and fatal interview,
By all desires which thereof did ensue,
By our long starving hopes, by that remorse
Which my words masculine perswasive force
Begot in thee, and by the memory
Of hurts, which spies and rivals threatned me,
I calmly beg: . . .

In the middle he dwells on harsh practicalities; Frenchmen will know she is a woman and rape her, Italians will not care that she seems a boy. But the end, in forgetting foreign grotesquerie, in imagining her staying at home and cautioning her not to dream aloud, springs suddenly once more into melodrama:

. . . nor in bed fright thy Nurse
With midnight startings, crying out oh, oh
Nurse, ô my love is slaine, I saw him goe
O'r the white Alpes alone; I saw him, I,
Assail'd, fight, taken, stabb'd, bleed, fall, and die.

In a time of public pageantry, public violence, and gratuitous disaster, a time, moreover, in which the overwhelming realities pertained unquestionably to the soul's other world, it was natural to feel all this world as a stage, and so to receive from whatever stuff players might enact a sense not of fantasy but of familiar experience heightened, lurid though the plots might be, excessive though the language. A sensibility trained on drama in such a time ranged readily over every order of happening, finding nothing strange. Donne, writing of a public death, presents us with a scene exceeding Webster:

> . . . Or as sometimes in a beheaded man,
> Though at those two Red seas, which freely ranne,
> One from the Trunke, another from the Head,
> His soule be sail'd, to her eternall bed,
> His eyes will twinckle, and his tongue will roll,
> As though he beckned, and cal'd backe his soule,
> He graspes his hands, and he pulls up his feet,
> And seemes to reach, and to step forth to meet
> His soule; when all these motions which we saw,
> Are but as Ice, which crackles at a thaw: . . .

Yet this was not a literary fancy but something everyone had seen enacted more than once in the London daylight: in fact a wordless play, a ritual death, a public drama mounted on official boards. And almost casually Donne imposes on it another drama, the crossing of the Red Sea to the promised land; and does not fail to note that here there are two Red seas. This is the famous "conceit," which came to be thought of as his trademark: the remorselessly logical handling of the interrelations between image and theme. It is a "conceit" because not plainly seen but by ingenuity conceived; and the style came at last to be called "metaphysical" because of its logic's quality, moving with persuasive or merely fantastic force among unrealities.

The logical justifying of an image was not Donne's innovation. Wyatt, a generation before Donne was born, found something to interest him in Petrarch's 156th sonnet, and in his English version ("The Lover Compareth His State to a Ship in Perilous Storm Tossed on the Sea) is careful to account for the steersman, the oars, the wind (sighs), the rain (tears), the dark cloud (disdain). His technique has the gait of a blackboard demonstration; and even when Shakespeare brings it onto the stage—Juliet's father comparing her little weeping body to a bark, a sea, a wind; Richard II in prison hammering out the analogy between his tormented body and a clock —a static set piece results, useful, Shakespeare's dramatic instinct prompted him, for characterizing a pompous windbag or a prisoner with time to idle in. Donne's innovation was to throw the logical process itself into the foreground of the poem, and present it in the act of discovering, savoring, and testing the taut sensations rigor can bring to analogy.

The process is intensely dramatic, for though he generally starts with some familiar poeticism, we cannot tell where we will be taken once his scrutiny of it commences. At the opening of "The Funerall" we find him recumbent, wearing his mistress' favor, plaited from a little of her hair: for all the world like an expiring Don Quixote:

> Who ever comes to shroud me, do not harme
> Nor question much
> That subtile wreath of haire, which crowns my arme;
> The mystery, the signe you must not touch, . . .

when suddenly another convention, that of lovers as soul mates, intersects this one:

> For 'tis my outward Soule,

and pursuing the logic of the situation, he establishes the relation of that soul to the one he was born with, and reflects that in the presence of a soul the body does not decay:

> . . . my outward Soule,
> Viceroy to that, which then to heaven being gone,
> Will leave this to controule,
> And keepe these limbes, her Provinces, from dissolution.

His method is to take the terms of a convention as actual, and then use his wits. He continues:

> For if the sinewie thread my brain lets fall
> Through every part,
> Can tye those parts, and make mee one of all;
> These hairs which upward grew, and strength and art
> Have from a better braine,
> Can better do'it;

But suddenly he is struck by an alternative explanation; for the lady who gave him the favor has shown no other sign that she intends to prolong his life:

> Except she meant that I
> By this should know my pain,
> As prisoners then are manacled, when they're condemned to die.

Behind these words yet another convention, that of love's prisoner, has asserted itself, but only enough to control the presence at the stanza's end of the familiar grim Elizabethan ribaldry which never tired of denoting by a single word the sexual spasm and death.

There remains one more convention to be invoked; for since he has established that his body will not be corrupted, and since incorruptibility is the prerogative of the bodies of saints, he must invoke his only claim to sainthood: he is, ten thousand bad sonnets give him license to assert, "Love's martyr."

> What ere shee meant by'it, bury it with me,
> For since I am
> Loves martyr, it might breed idolatrie,
> If into others hands these Reliques came.

Here Donne relates the conventional jargon of amorous martyrdom to the actual religious conditions of the 1590's, when so much policy was being devoted to stamping out the usages of the old religion. Then moving back suddenly to unrepentant secularity, and offsetting a spiritual virtue with a worldly one, he addresses his last thirty words straight to the unpersuadable lady herself:

> As 'twas humility
> To afford to it all that a Soule can doe,
> So, 'tis some bravery,
> That since you would save none of mee, I bury some of you.

We can never guess, three lines ahead, where such a poem is going to turn; so, though each of its figures is thoroughly conventional, Donne exacts of us an unremitting attention to which his taut wording answers. Each move is articulated; there are no gaps; yet he was thought difficult in his own time, and is often difficult now. Our difficulties are not those of his contemporaries, however. The puzzled reader of a manuscript in 1595 expected poetry to supply him once again with the old familiar themes, and recognized their terminology on Donne's page: but what was he to make of this agile realism, this tough unsinging rigor of application? John Dryden spoke for several generations of such readers when he blamed Donne for "perplexing the minds of the fair sex with nice speculations of philosophy, when he should engage their hearts and entertain them with the softnesses of love." The twentieth-century reader of old poems in a book, however, is puzzled in a different way. It is not the tone of hard-bitten speech that worries him: he would probably distrust anything else. Nor do the allusions, thanks to modern footnotes, nor the logic, thanks to modern reading habits, really deter him. His difficulty is that he has not the conventions at his fingertips: so that the most troublesome aspects of Donne's invention, for him, are likely to be such notions as love's alchemy, which Donne did not invent at all. He is detained, in short, and irrelevantly preoccupied by, the famous "conceits."

But not only was the habit of elaborately justifying a comparison no innovation of Donne's but part of the tradition he inherited, the comparisons themselves are apt to be, if not traditional, secondhand, bits of machinery employed by a decadent poeticizing. Not even the famous comparison of lovers to compasses is necessarily original: we find it embedded in a madrigal by the Italian poet G. B. Guarini, published in 1598. Donne's poem is said to have been written thirteen years later. We may gather the content of Guarini's poem from Thomas Carew's translation:

> You'le aske perhaps wherefore I stay,
> Loving so much, so long away,
> O doe not thinke t'was I did part,
> It was my body, not my hearte,
> For like a Compasse in your love,
> One foote is fix'd and cannot moove,
> The other may follow her blinde guide
> Of giddy fortune, but not slide
> Beyond your service, nor dares venture
> To wander farre from you the Center.

Carew extracts from Guarini what Guarini extracted from the idea, a graceful singable compliment. If part of him (his body) moves, the other part (his heart) is fixed; and the fixed part controls the moving; and she is to take cheer, for what is fixed is fixed in her love.

Whether or not Donne borrowed the image from Italy, he means our attention to focus not on the image itself, where generations of commentary have tended to fix it, but rather on the details of his dramatic dealing with it. He articulates it into parts, as he does every other figure he employs, and puts it to a use from which irony is not absent. For beneath the graceful quatrains beats the insistent accent of a man talking, steadily talking, to keep the lady from bursting into tears. He is about to leave her and cross the seas; and as in another valediction he had suggested that her lamentations were competing with the tempests on the English Channel—

> Weepe me not dead, in thine armes, but forebeare
> To teach the sea, what it may doe too soone;
> Let not the winde
> Example finde,
> To doe me more harm, than it purposeth;

so in "A Valediction: Forbidding Mourning" he strives to head off "teare-floods" and "sigh-tempests" by fixing her essentially simple attention on all sorts of difficult things he is finding to say: on the death of virtuous men, the moving of the earth, the relation of sense and soul, the expansion of gold leaf; for so long as her mind is "puzzled with metaphysics" she is likely to be quiet, more or less. And having posited that their two souls are one, which is enough of a poetic commonplace to be thin comfort, he quickens attention once more by introducing the famous simile:

> If they be two, they are two so
> As stiffe twin compasses are two.

It is not really an image, but a puzzle: Why are our two souls like a pair of compasses? And he keeps her attention fixed on it, producing not one solution but three:

> Thy soule the fixt foot, makes no show
> To move, but doth, if the'other doe.

[1. The center does not turn.]

> And though it in the center sit,
> Yet when the other far doth rome,
> It leanes, and hearkens after it,
> And growes erect, as that comes home.

[2. If you close the compasses the spraddled legs grow upright.]

> Such wilt thou be to mee, who must
> Like th'other foot, obliquely runne;
> Thy firmnes makes my circle just,
> And makes me end, where I begunne.

[3. The moving foot, when you are drawing a circle, ends where it began, though not, he avoids pointing out, where the stationary foot is.]

"And makes me end, where I begunne." These are the words that ring in her grateful ears at the end. They contain scant comfort if she has been following the logic carefully, but she probably has not, and is unlikely to notice that the circle ends as far from its center as it started. The poem is brilliant, tender in its tone and in its concern, casuistic, a little cynical in its methods, in those final stanzas more than a little meretricious. But there is something meretricious, the gravity of tone succeeds in reminding us, in all attempts at comfort which must seek to wave away some irremediable fact: a death, a parting.

Such is Donne's deep originality, knowing how to extract what can be extracted from the deceptions of poetry, knowing at bottom how little use they are, knowing how desperation and joy alike need them in satisfying the need to speak. He did astonishing things with a hopelessly degenerate poetic habit, the poetic of the 1580's and '90's.

Another man, Donne's equally great contemporary Ben Jonson, preferred to brush the foolish conventions aside. Jonson was what Donne was not, a professional writer, in fact fiercely professional; not a hack, either, like Nashe, but a deliberately self-constituted man of letters, the model for Dryden. He published his *Works,* plays and all, in a 1616 folio, by Jacobean standards scrupulously proofread, challenging by such a format comparison with the masterwork of antiquity. (Donne's poems, by contrast, like Shakespeare's plays, were only posthumously published, which may be the reason for our ingrained reluctance to think of Donne as an Elizabethan.) Jonson, with talents at least equal to his pretensions, setting out to establish the right of the vernacular man of letters to enter the plenum inhabited by Horace, Cicero, Seneca, Martial, Homer himself, had no time for bric-a-brac left over from the vogue of Italian sonnet writers. Civilization was for him something centered, and centered in that commerce of understanding between the lively minds of the present and those lively minds long dead whom one might hope to treat with as equals, and whose writings constituted that which a literate man could claim to know. Since vivacity is timeless, we need not be cowed by their example, and since decorum is equally timeless, we should share their literary manners, their terminology, and their sentiments and figures, without fearing to impair our proper vigor. The highest tribute Jonson could pay to Shakespeare was to call up Aeschylus, Sophocles, Euripides, Seneca, to hear the Shakespearean tragedies, and imply that such a confrontation of the old and the new threatened neither discourtesy nor embarrassment to either party. He adds that in each of Shakespeare's "well-turned and true-filed lines,"

> he seemes to shake a Lance,
> As brandish't at the eyes of Ignorance;

for presumptuous ignorance, against which all learning and all talent unite, is the one thing intolerable.

He went on to praise Shakespeare for doing what he privately believed Shakespeare had done too seldom:

> Yet must I not give Nature all: Thy Art,
> My gentle Shakespeare, must enjoy a part.
> For though the Poet's matter, Nature be,
> His Art doth give the fashion. And, that he,
> Who casts to write a living line, must sweat,
> (Such as thine are) and strike the second heat
> Upon the Muses anvile: turne the same,
> (And himselfe with it) that he thinkes to frame;
> Or for the lawrell, he may gaine a scorne,
> For a good Poet's made, as well as borne.
> And such wert thou.

The racy ease of expression is as typically Jonson's as the studied refusal to invent a new thing to say. The terminology—"Nature" and "Art"—comes straight from Horace's *Ars Poetica,* line 408,

> *Natura fieret laudabile carmen, an arte*
> *Quaesitum est,*

Englished with ingenuous directness. The disinclination to exalt one element above the other echoes Horace again (lines 409–411). The image of the anvil amplifies a Horatian detail (line 441). And the assertion that a good poet is made as well as born reverses, with the implied approval of Horace, a Latin tag (*poeta nascitur, non fit*) which, Jonson hints, if it has the truth of anything ancient, still tells only part of the truth about *good* poets.

These very lines of Jonson's, it is clear, are brandished at the eyes of ignorance. In the book of prose reflections which was published in 1641, five years after his death, Jonson had more to say about the poetic judgments of the ignorant. In these things, he says,

> the unskilfull are naturally deceiv'd, and judging wholly by the bulke, thinke rude things greater than polish'd; and scatter'd more numerous, than compos'd: Nor thinke this only to be true in the sordid multitude, but the neater sort of our *Gallants:* for all are the multitude; only they differ in cloaths, not in judgement or understanding.
>
> *I remember,* the Players have often mentioned it as an honour to *Shakespeare,* that in his writing, (whatsoever he penn'd) hee never blotted out line. My answer hath beene, Would he had blotted a thousand. Which they thought a malevolent speech. I had not told posterity this, but for their ignorance, who chose that circumstance to commend their friend by, wherein he most faulted. And to justifie mine owne candor, (for I lov'd the man, and doe honour his memory (on this side Idolatry) as much as any.) Hee was (indeed) honest, and of an open, and free nature: had an excellent *Phantasie;* brave notions, and gentle expressions: wherein hee flow'd with that facility, that sometime it was necessary he should be stop'd: *Sufflaminandus erat;* as *Augustus* said of *Haterius.* His wit was in his owne power; would the rule of it had beene so too. . . .

If this is Jonson's candor, it is natural to ask why he went out of his way in the commendatory verse to attribute art to the Shakespeare whose want of art distressed him. The reason lies in his careful distinction of genres and occasions. He is writing a preface to the plays, not a memoir of their author; and if these hundreds of folio pages do not contain as much art as he would like, they contain more than their readers are likely to find in other play books. And this is a ceremonial occasion, furthermore, not to be disfigured by autobiographical quarrels. And it is becoming, moreover, on such an occasion, to observe the terminology of the ancients, by way of doing the thing properly.

The ancient writings, Greek and Latin, have this relevance to England in 1623, that they are that which we know. Here some distinctions are necessary. Jonson's classicizing is not a veneration of the primitive: Romanticism was yet to be invented. Nor was it a quest for rules: English Neoclassicism lay two generations ahead. It was a zestful sharing of the springs of articulation with men long dead who earlier had drunk there; or better, since the dead men came to mind less readily than the living words, a tilling of fields where still green grass proved there was water, and a sowing in that tilth of English seeds. The Neoclassicism of Dryden and his successors culminated in a habit, new to the western psyche, of feeling past events stretched out behind one serially in time; if the seventeenth-century epic is *Paradise Lost,* the eighteenth-century epic is *A History of the Decline and Fall of the Roman Empire.* There had been, it grew fashionable to believe, a classical civilization; then a thousand years' darkness; and now an effort to generate a new civilization according to the only available models: hence the fuss about "rules." But this talk of civilizations is post-Jonsonian; his mind runs on *languages.* He claimed for his work only this degree of innovation, that it was built out of English speech as knowingly as others had built out of Athenian speech, or Roman speech.

Though some authors were studied in school and some were not, they were not divided into "standard" and "secondary." Nothing prevented Jonson from reading everything; and it was in the Epistles of Philostratus (now a "minor" author) that he found his imagination quickened, on one occasion, by certain scattered turns of sentiment:

> [33] Pledge me with your eyes alone, with whose lovely cup-bearing owner even Zeus, when he tasted, was smitten. And if you wish, do not waste the wine, but rather dash only water in the cup, put it to your lips, fill it full of kisses, and thus give it to those who need it.
>
> [32] Whenever I see you I am at once athirst, and halt, though unwilling, restraining the cup. I bring it not to my lips; it is rather of you that I know I drink.
>
> [60] And if you drink up, all that is left turns . . . sweeter . . . than nectar. Yes, it goes down . . . as if it had been blended, not with wine, but with kisses.
>
> [2] I have sent you a crown of roses, not honoring you (though this too), but rather showing some favor to the roses themselves, that they might not wilt.
>
> [46] If you wish to comply with love, send what is left of them back, no longer redolent only of roses, but also of you.[2]

And what this became was not a rigid homage to Philostratus, nor a recreation of Greek eroticism, but an English song:

> Drinke to me, onely, with thine eyes,
> And I will pledge with mine;
> Or leave a kisse but in the cup,
> And Ile not looke for wine.
> The thirst, that from the soule doth rise,
> Doth aske a drinke divine:

[2] I owe these translations to my colleague, Keith M. Aldrich.

But might I of *Jove's* Nectar sup,
  I would not change for thine.
I sent thee, late, a rosie wreath,
  Not so much honoring thee,
As giving it a hope, that there
  It could not withered bee.
But thou thereon did'st onely breath,
  And sent'st it backe to mee:
Since when it growes, and smells, I sweare,
  Not of it selfe, but thee.

A century later echoes of standard authors were being employed for the pleasure their resonance could afford the knowing. "Once more, hail and farewell," writes Dryden, and we are meant to feel an enhancement of the occasion in the echo of Catullus' elegy on his brother. This is another use of the ancients with which Jonson's is not to be confused; so far is he from dangling sources before us, that several generations of great scholarly acumen did not chance to trace "Drinke to me, onely, . . ." to Philostratus until a man named Dovaston stumbled on the connection in 1815. So completely does the poem inhabit the English idiom that no one is likely to think of hunting for sources.

Neither sycophant to his reading nor taxidermist, Jonson employs it to guide his shaping of living speech. He intended, he said, from

such wool
As from mere English flocks his Muse can pull

to fashion

a fleece
To match those of Sicily or Greece.

So the English language lends him sweet-sounding names, *Thames, Chelsea, Rumney;* clear native monosyllables, *grass, sands, fields, drops, stars, nights;* liquid sounds, *silver, silent;* a homely openness of syntax, rapidity of declaration, and sure rhymes; and what he can fashion out of these:

. . . All the grasse that Rumney yeelds,
Or the sands in Chelsey fields,
Or the drops in silver Thames,
Or the starres, that guild his streames,
In the silent sommer-nights,
When youths ply their stolne delights . . .

is as much indigenous to a spoken tongue, and achieves as much of a triumph for the shaper, as did the Catullus on which he had one eye:

> *Quam magnus numerus Libyssae arenae . . .*
> *Aut quam sidera multa, cum tacet nox,*
> *Furtivos hominum vident amores. . . .*

English does not lend itself to an encircling syntax, pausing on the numerous stars to make them look down on furtive lovers; its genius, Jonson senses, is to press forward. In a time heavy with reforming pedantries, when inevitably by one means or another English and Latin poetry were going to be brought to some common rule, it was Jonson alone who saw how to align the vernacular's energies with the best of what learned men knew.

This commitment to the spoken tongue saved him from two other traps, the trap of the decorative figure and the trap of the suitable subject. The mind's life being continuous, there are no occasions Jonson's poetic art cannot articulate. A fire has destroyed his papers, and it is natural to introduce Vulcan; but Jonson does not introduce him so as to raise the occasion to poetic stature. He heaps insult upon Vulcan, precisely as though he faced a living man. The verse crackles with innuendo:

> I ne'er attempted, *Vulcan*, 'gainst thy life
> Nor made least line of love to thy loose Wife

[I have not wasted my time writing empty hymns to Venus. But, "thy loose Wife"! It is a blow in the face.]

> Or in remembrance of thy affront and scorne

[And depend upon it, Vulcan remembers how he was cuckolded]

> With Clownes, and Tradesmen, kept thee clos'd in horne.

[He is everyone's laughing-stock, and the horn that shields the lantern's flame proves it. If these are dark sayings, Vulcan will know what is meant, and writhe.]

> . . . Was it because thou wert of old denied
> By Jove to have Minerva for thy Bride

[Another sore point; and she was the goddess of Wisdom, and sprang from Jove's forehead.]

> That since thou tak'st all envious care and paine
> To ruine any issue of the braine?

It is the tone of slam-bang insult, maddeningly superior to the resources of a cloddish forge-tender who can only smart with multiple disgraces, and destroy things. A wit is dressing down a clumsy tradesman, and the locale is a London street, as surely as that of "A Celebration of Charis" is an English garden:

> I beheld her, on a Day
> When her looke out-flourisht May:
> And her dressing did out-brave
> All the Pride the fields then have:
> Farre I was from being stupid,
> For I ran and call'd on *Cupid;*
> Love, if thou wilt ever see
> Marke of glorie, come with me;
> Where's thy Quiver? bend thy Bow:
> Here's a shaft, thou art to slow! . . .

Certainly the opening quatrain adorns no merely conventional occasion: a man who wanted to do no more than that could keep vapidities flowing on for pages without rhyming "stupid" with "Cupid." No, his is a Chaplinesque panic; and no one need be surprised when the lady petrifies him with a glance. Yes, petrifies:

> So that there, I stood a stone,
> Mock'd of all: and call'd of one
> (Which with griefe and wrath I heard)
> *Cupid's* statue with a Beard . . .

He is the eternal oaf who upsets the tea tray; he is also the poet who a few moments later can manage, by way of penance, the exquisite cadences of "Her Triumph" ("Which how Dexterously I doe," he does not forget to alert us, "Heare and make Example too.")

> See the Chariot at hand here of Love
> Wherein my Lady rideth!

The homely iambs have vanished; in a new tension, the verse adjusts, intent, its rapt runs and pauses, creating phrase by phrase the miraculous vision.

> Each that draws, is a Swan, or a Dove,
> And well the Carre Love guideth.

As she goes, all hearts doe duty
Unto her beauty . . .

One intricate ten-line stanza is succeeded by another, doing homage to her eyes, her hair, her forehead, her brows. Then a third stanza, with Jonson's perpetual variation of surface, sets to these by now established rhythms no longer the pure Petrarchan vocabulary of eyes and brows, but a rustic folk-English speech ("smutched"; "bag") transmuted to unimaginable delicacy:

Have you seene but a bright Lillie grow,
Before rude hands have touch'd it?
Ha' you mark'd but the fall o'the Snow
Before the soyle hath smutch'd it?
Ha' you felt the wooll o' the Bever?
Or Swans Downe ever?
Or have smelt o'the bud o' the Brier?
Or the Nard in the fire?
Or have tasted the bag of the Bee?
O so white; O so soft! O so sweet is she!

It is a high moment in the management of our language.

One of those loops with which history delights the contemplative brought that half-forgotten stanza before the mind of another innovating poet three centuries later, leafing a cheap anthology in a concentration camp. So in the summer of 1945 Ezra Pound pencilled into a ruled notebook, across from a page on which he had been drafting a version of Confucius,

. . . This liquid is certainly a
property of the mind
nec accidens est but an element
in the mind's make-up
est agens and functions dust to a fountain pan otherwise
Hast 'ou seen the rose in the steel dust
(or swansdown ever?)
so light is the urging, so ordered the dark petals of iron
we who have passed over Lethe.
(Canto LXXIV)

Earlier on that page he had compared the activity of the mind to a fountain's column tossing a bright ball, and remembered Verlaine (*"les grands jets d'eau sveltes parmi les marbres"*); and the mention of the great rose does homage not only to science classrooms but to Dante. In that habit of calling masters of many tongues into session, so as to purify in their light a barely fledged vernacular, his forty-years' career had had but one great anticipator, Jonson.

There is more light than fancy in this parallel, and as we explore it the neatness of affiliated correspondences grows uncanny. It is worth rehearsing, to impress upon our minds the plight of English verse in the 1590's and the magnitude of Donne's and Jonson's renovation. The English language in the 1590's was as degenerate a poetic instrument as the Anglo-American of the early 1900's, magazine verse answering Petrarchan sonnets, and a few men of serious talent thwarted by the need of a revolution that lay beyond their powers. And John Donne, on whose procedures T. S. Eliot was to model so many of his own, plays the Eliotic role in that revolution, perfecting a learned and essentially dramatic style, exploiting harsh overtones of the language in a poetry dominated by the sometimes cynical, always oracular, voice.

> He ruin'd mee, and I am re-begot
> Of absence, darkness, death; things which are not.

> I an old man,
> A dull head among windy spaces.

Each man is an amateur poet, acclaimed the monarch of wit yet officially engaged at some other work; each guards his privacy; each attracts, by way of the mannerisms that attend the distinguished intelligence, some merely clever imitators and some weighty. Each alters, for a generation or more, the very modes in which poetry is apprehended. (Each ends a great churchman).

And each is but half of the reforming movement in his time. Informally allied with each is a different spirit, a fellow-craftsman of enormous didactic zeal, intent on a public literary career and on reclaiming the dignity due to poets: great eclectics, great classicizers, great transposers of past modes; students of vernacular energy; informal scholars; polymaths; irascible: Jonson, Pound. And it was Jonson like Pound who sought to teach younger poets, insisting on technique, on work, on the power of knowledge to transcend the mere knack.

Such massive reforms perhaps entail bipartite genius; we may tentatively conclude that much, and suppose that the other parallels we may happen on, when we juxtapose the two ages, are of more mnemonic than cognitive importance. It is tempting to notice how Shakespeare resembles Yeats, starting blandly in the old manner, adopting and mastering the new, and managing to emerge as the time's most comprehensive genius.[3] And does not Wyatt hang like Hopkins, some decades too soon, a lonely forerunner, his meters "improved" by Tottel as Bridges improved those of Hopkins? And who is Abraham Cowley but an earlier Auden? Such sketching in the margin of history serves a purpose if it helps the reader to bear in mind how two men of dissimilar genius, Donne and Jonson, made a new start possible, and how it has happened again.

The strength and variety of what Donne and Jonson composed the reader of this book may study in ample detail; and also the brilliant living variousness of the poetry younger men were to compose under their auspices or according to their example. An essay devoted to clarifying their mastery need not attempt to survey their schools, which like all literary schools were to derive for a while incentives and procedures, and patterns of feeling and norms of accomplishment, and lose direction, then cohesion, at last. That venture of the English imagination the reader can assimilate from the poems themselves. The achievement stands. The story of process and decline —not at all the same thing as the achievement—can be briefly summarized.

The new impulse lasted just over half a century, and extraliterary causes, of which the Civil War was the most spectacular, at last so transformed the conditions of discourse that Donne's and Jonson's examples were no longer operative. By that time, however, their traditions themselves had grown decadent. Donne's lesson—how to articulate in poetry the taut discursive intelligence—made possible some memorable work as late as the 1650's. Some of his successors (King, Townshend) wrote memorable isolated poems, and one, George Herbert, was a disciple of genius capable of inventing, certainly in Donne's spirit but without recourse to his mannerisms, a new kind of devotional poetry. There was even a period when, as Crashaw demonstrates, the continental baroque itself could be assimilated without gross exoticism. But gradually—to put a complex matter briefly—changing ideas of what the intelligence was and how it was

[3] See Patrick Cruttwell, *The Shakespearean Moment,* London, 1954, Chapters 1–2.

supposed to work transformed the kind of poet who was interested in Donne into an elaborator of surfaces, and the conceit, as Cleveland's work indicates, into a barren ingenuity. The line of succession from Jonson is less easily traced; his disciples proved not to be the professionals but (Herrick aside) the courtiers, who imitated his vernacular ease. For Herrick poetry was no more than impassioned play. One courtier, Thomas Carew, was as painstaking as the master and as original as Herbert. The others (Lovelace, Waller) standardized and simplified the mode they drew from Ben. Meanwhile Ben himself, overshadowed in drama by Shakespeare and in lyric by Donne, was slowly absorbed into the history of literary ideas, as an interesting precursor of Restoration Neoclassicism.

By the time the Commonwealth had passed away it was possible to look back on a dawn when the unformed language had been mauled by two eccentric originals, and to look forward, under the auspices of new ideals of clarity, to a long civilized time. In 1669 Donne's poems were printed for the last time in the seventeenth century, and Abraham Cowley, "the Muses' Hannibal," had adjusted wit to order, with the aid of safe classical precedent. For words, it was now understood, had meanings, clear and distinct meanings, meanings somehow prescribed for them; and they stood for things; and ideas were the simulacra of things, to be related by either association or antithesis; and there were levels of dignity to which the poetic performance should at all times aspire. So Jonson, who had rhymed "stupid" and "Cupid," could be no longer a viable stylistic model; and Donne, whose words and ideas mime not the agreed truths of nature but an inner drama, was a fantastick indistinguishable from Cleveland, in fact less witty, with furthermore no command of "numbers."

It is pleasant to reflect that before so great an effort at innovation ended one poet, Andrew Marvell, should have been vouchsafed the wit, the poise, and the generosity of imagination to inventory and summarize, memorably, in amber language, each of its modes.

Selected Bibliography

BRIEF MENTION of critical works likely to stimulate or enlighten the serious newcomer may be found just after the introductory paragraphs on most of the poets in this book. For compendious bibliographies see Douglas Bush, *English Literature in the Earlier Seventeenth Century,* 1600–1660, 2nd edition, Oxford, 1962. Our understanding of this poetry has, of course, altered greatly with time. The turning points may be plotted as follows:

(1) Samuel Johnson, *Lives of the Poets,* 1779; see especially the comments on Cowley, Denham, and Waller.

(2) Sir Herbert Grierson's pioneer 2-volume edition of Donne (Oxford, 1912), and his *Metaphysical Lyrics and Poems* (1921), which terminate the century or more during which these poets were regarded as antiquarian curiosities.

(3) T. S. Eliot's essays, "The Metaphysical Poets," "Andrew Marvell," and "John Dryden" (written in the early 1920s, reprinted in his *Selected Essays,* 1932, and elsewhere), the decisive and seminal statements about the relevance of the School of Donne to the modern sensibility.

(4) Eliot's critical successors. F. R. Leavis, *Revaluation,* 1936, is subtly, trenchantly, and profoundly perceptive. George Williamson, *The Donne Tradition,* 1930, is the best of a number of books that deploy Eliot's insights with the aid of systematic scholarship. Alfred Alvarez, *The School of Donne,* 1961, is the most intelligent short compendious book on the period.

SOME GENERAL BOOKS ON THE PERIOD

Jones, Richard Foster, *The Seventeenth Century,* 1951.

Keast, William R., ed., Seventeenth Century English Poetry, 1962. (Twenty-seven essays by various hands).

Martz, Louis, *The Poetry of Meditation: a Study in English Religious Literature of the Seventeenth Century,* 1954.

Nicolson, Marjorie, *The Breaking of the Circle,* 1950.

Sharp, Robert L., *From Donne to Dryden,* 1940.

Tuve, Rosamond, *Elizabethan and Metaphysical Imagery,* 1947.

Wallerstein, Ruth C., *Studies in Seventeenth Century Poetic,* 1950.

White, Helen C., *The Metaphysical Poets,* 1936.

Willey, Basil, *The Seventeenth Century Background,* 1934.

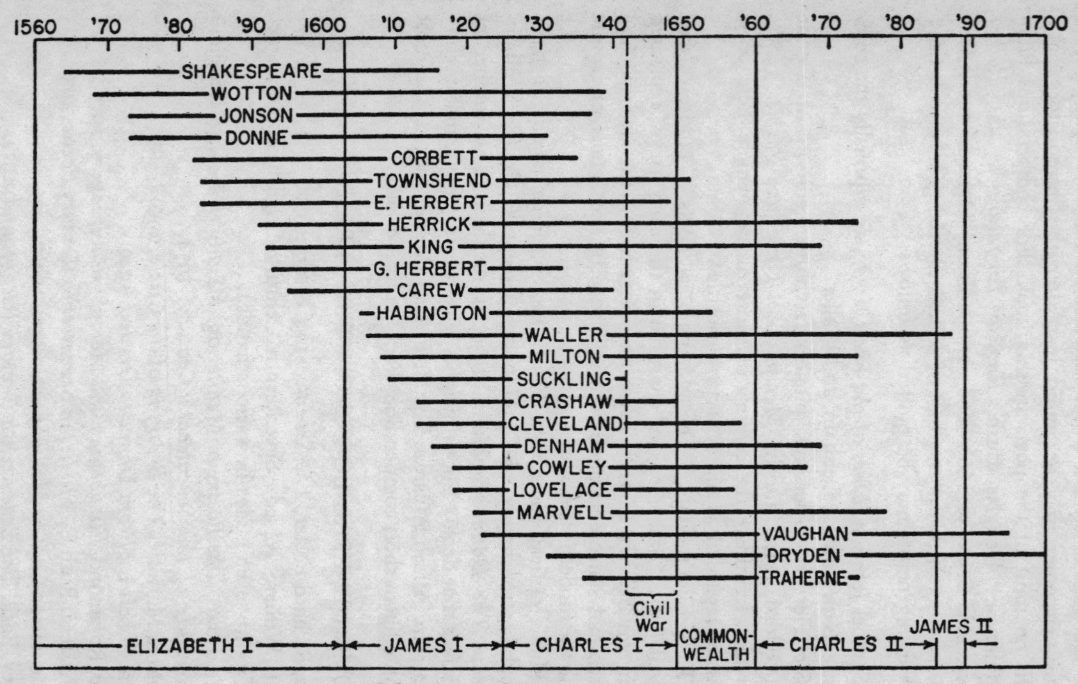

Chronological Chart

I

DONNE AND JONSON

John Donne (1572–1631)
Ben Jonson (1573–1637)

John Donne

(1572–1631)

SHAKESPEARE would have known him, and he must have been rather like Hamlet: morose, magnetic, a University man hankering after order in a disjointed time. His Oxford friends were, like himself, young professional men of marked abilities and decent family. He studied law, took part in foreign wars, acquired a name as poet, wit, and gallant, and secured, at 26, the kind of post that led to the kind of career he clearly expected: one bringing glory and high public responsibility, like Francis Bacon's or Edward Coke's. And an imprudent marriage ruined it all. For the post he had secured was that of secretary to the Lord Keeper of England, Sir Thomas Egerton, who was influential enough to sponsor any ambition; and a niece of Sir Thomas's wife lived in the household; and late in 1601 Jack Donne secretly married her. Anne's father, Sir George More, saw to Donne's dismissal, and even had him imprisoned for two months.

For the next decade he had no prospects. He lived with relatives of his wife's in the country; he moved back to London; he cultivated wealthy ladies and royal favorites; he put his erudition at the disposal of at least one religious polemicist; finally, by composing and publishing an Anniversary elegy on the death of Sir Robert Drury's only child, he secured the Drurys as patrons.

These were stopgap measures; his abilities were entitled to royal preferment. It grew clear, however, that preferment from James I would only come to a churchman; and a churchman, at long last, Donne accordingly became. He was ordained in January 1615, by Henry King's father. Within a year he was one of the royal chaplains, Doctor of Divinity (Cambridge) by special royal command, with at his disposal the revenues of two livings, and by way of status and responsibility the Readership in Divinity at Lincoln's Inn. He was 44, established, and dogged by the poems he had written in his twenties. As part of his solemn determination to remake his life in keeping with his new profession, he endeavored to destroy them, but they were saved for posthumous publication by the enthusiasm of men who circulated copies and in turn recopied them. Today's editors wince at the profusion of manuscript variants.

In 1617 his wife died, having borne him twelve children. By 1621 he was Dean of St. Paul's, a very famous devout man, esteemed as the greatest preacher of his time. In his last days he rose from his deathbed twice: to pose, in his shroud, for his funeral effigy, and to preach, at the court, a Lenten sermon, "Death's Duel," before the king.

Ben Jonson reported in 1619 that "Donne for not keeping of accent deserved hanging," that he was "the first poet in the World in some things," but that "Donne himself for not being understood would perish"; also that he had "written all his best pieces err he was 25 years old." This last statement is probably correct enough. Donne was 25 in 1597, and had by then been living around London six years, studying law and satisfying his "hydroptique immoderate desire of humane learning and languages." These were the years in which his Oxford contemporary Sir Richard Baker recalled Mr. Donne living at the Inns of Court: "not dissolute but very neat; a great visitor of ladies, a great frequenter of plays, a great writer of conceited verses." The latter would have included the Satires and most of the Songs and Sonnets and Elegies. To the bleak decade after his marriage only the two Anniversaries and some Divine Poems are known to belong; to his sixteen years in holy orders, only a few of the Holy Sonnets and three hymns. There was never any question of his setting up as, or being esteemed for, a professional writer. Except for the two Anniversaries, bait for Drury's patronage, and one public Elegy, he always succeeded in keeping his verses out of print; not even the Miscellanies so frequent at the century's turn have anything of his. The poems that were to charge the English language for sixty years with a novel dramatic activity of the embodied intelligence were a young man's amusement, esteemed in circulated copies and imitated, for two more generations, by other young men as aloof from literary professionalism as himself.

TEXT: *Poems*, ed. John Hayward (Penguin). The standard edition, edited by Sir Herbert Grierson (Oxford, 1912) is still unmatched for detailed scholarship, but some of its textual decisions seem no longer defensible. A wholly new edition, edited by Miss Helen Gardner, is in preparation.

COMMENT: All accounts of his life are based on Izaak Walton's *Life of Dr. Donne* (1640, enlarged 1658 and 1675). Curiously, there has been no modern biography since Edmund Gosse's in 1899. T. S. Eliot, "The Metaphysical Poets," in *Selected Essays* (New York, 1950). A. Alvarez, *The School of Donne* (New York, 1961). J. B. Leishman, *The Monarch of Wit* (London, 1951). *John Donne, a Collection of Critical Essays*, ed. Helen Gardner (Englewood Cliffs, N.J., 1962).

SONGS AND SONETS

The Good-Morrow

I wonder by my troth, what thou, and I
Did, till we lov'd? were we not wean'd till then?
But suck'd on countrey pleasures, childishly?
Or snorted we in the seaven sleepers den?
T'was so; But this, all pleasures fancies bee. 5
If ever any beauty I did see,
Which I desir'd, and got, t'was but a dreame of thee.

And now good morrow to our waking soules,
Which watch not one another out of feare;
For love, all love of other sights controules, 10
And makes one little roome, an every where.
Let sea-discoverers to new worlds have gone,
Let Maps to other, worlds on worlds have showne,
Let us possesse one world, each hath one, and is one.

---

5. *But:* except for.
13. *other:* others.

My face in thine eye, thine in mine appeares, 15
And true plaine hearts doe in the faces rest,
Where can we finde two better hemispheares
Without sharpe North, without declining West?
What ever dyes, was not mixt equally;
If our two loves be one, or, thou and I 20
Love so alike, that none doe slacken, none can die.

19. Scholastic doctrine held that only compounds between whose elements there was some "contrariety" could be dissolved.

Song

Goe, and catche a falling starre,
Get with a child a mandrake roote,
Tell me, where all past yeares are,
Or who cleft the Divels foot,
Teach me to heare Mermaides singing, 5
Or to keep off envies stinging,
And finde
What winde
Serves to advance an honest minde.

If thou beest borne to strange sights, 10
Things invisible to see,
Ride ten thousand daies and nights,
Till age snow white haires on thee,
Thou, when thou retorn'st, wilt tell mee
All strange wonders that befell thee, 15
And sweare
No where
Lives a woman true, and faire.

If thou findst one, let mee know,
Such a Pilgrimage were sweet; 20
Yet doe not, I would not goe,
Though at next doore wee might meet,

2. *mandrake roote:* often bifurcated like a woman's lower limbs.

Though shee were true, when you met her,
And last, till you write your letter,
Yet shee 25
Will bee
False, ere I come, to two, or three.

The Sunne Rising

Busie old foole, unruly Sunne,
Why dost thou thus,
Through windowes, and through curtaines call on us?
Must to thy motions lovers seasons run?
Sawcy pedantique wretch, goe chide 5
Late schoole boyes and sowre prentices,
Goe tell Court-huntsmen, that the King will ride,
Call countrey ants to harvest offices;
Love, all alike, no season knowes, nor clyme,
Nor houres, dayes, moneths, which are the rags of time. 10

Thy beames, so reverend, and strong
Why shouldst thou thinke?
I could eclipse and cloud them with a winke,
But that I would not lose her sight so long:
If her eyes have not blinded thine, 15
Looke, and to morrow late, tell mee,
Whether both the'India's of spice and Myne
Be where thou leftst them, or lie here with mee.
Aske for those Kings whom thou saw'st yesterday,
And thou shalt heare, All here in one bed lay. 20

She'is all States, and all Princes, I,
Nothing else is.
Princes doe but play us; compar'd to this,
All honor's mimique; All wealth alchimie.
Thou sunne art halfe as happy'as wee, 25
In that the world's contracted thus;

21. *alchimie:* imposture.

Thine age askes ease, and since thy duties bee
To warme the world, that's done in warming us.
Shine here to us, and thou art every where;
This bed thy center is, these walls, thy spheare. 30

The Canonization

For Godsake hold your tongue, and let me love,
Or chide my palsie, or my gout,
My five gray haires, or ruin'd fortune flout,
With wealth your state, your minde with Arts improve,
Take you a course, get you a place, 5
Observe his honour, or his grace,
Or the Kings reall, or his stamped face
Contemplate, what you will, approve,
So you will let me love.

Alas, alas, who's injur'd by my love? 10
What merchants ships have my sighs drown'd?
Who saies my teares have overflow'd his ground?
When did my colds a forward spring remove?
When did the heats which my veines fill
Adde one more to the plaguie Bill? 15
Soldiers finde warres, and Lawyers finde out still
Litigious men, which quarrels move,
Though she and I do love.

Call us what you will, wee are made such by love;
Call her one, mee another flye, 20
We'are Tapers too, and at our owne cost die,
And wee in us finde the'Eagle and the Dove.
The Phœnix ridle hath more wit
By us, we two being one, are it.

30. *Center* in Donne nearly always means the earth, the center of the pre-Copernican universe. The *spheare* was the crystalline globe to which the sun was attached, and which by revolving carried the sun round the earth.
23–24. The phoenix was unique, and yet it procreated.

So, to one neutrall thing both sexes fit, 25
Wee dye and rise the same, and prove
Mysterious by this love.

Wee can dye by it, if not live by love,
And if unfit for tombes and hearse
Our legend bee, it will be fit for verse; 30
And if no peece of Chronicle wee prove,
We'll build in sonnets pretty roomes;
As well a well wrought urne becomes
The greatest ashes, as halfe-acre tombes,
And by these hymnes, all shall approve 35
Us *Canoniz'd* for Love:

And thus invoke us; You whom reverend love
Made one anothers hermitage;
You, to whom love was peace, that now is rage;
Who did the whole world's soule contract, and drove 40
Into the glasses of your eyes
(So made such mirrors, and such spies,
That they did all to you epitomize,)
Countries, Townes, Courts: Beg from above
A patterne of your love! 45

26, 28. *Dye* has the common Elizabethan sense of sexual climax.
44. *Beg:* saints are expected to relay prayers, not to grant them.

Lovers Infinitenesse

If yet I have not all thy love,
Deare, I shall never have it all,
I cannot breath one other sigh, to move,
Nor can intreat one other teare to fall,
And all my treasure, which should purchase thee, 5
Sighs, teares, and oathes, and letters I have spent.
Yet no more can be due to mee,
Than at the bargaine made was ment,
If then thy gift of love were partiall,

That some to mee, some should to others fall, 10
Deare, I shall never have Thee All.

Or if then thou gavest mee all,
All was but All, which thou hadst then;
But if in thy heart, since, there be or shall,
New love created bee, by other men, 15
Which have their stocks intire, and can in teares,
In sighs, in oathes, and letters outbid mee,
This new love may beget new feares,
For, this love was not vowed by thee.
And yet it was, thy gift being generall, 20
The ground, thy heart is mine, what ever shall
Grow there, deare, I should have it all.

Yet I would not have all yet,
Hee that hath all can have no more,
And since my love doth every day admit 25
New growth, thou shouldst have new rewards in store;
Thou canst not every day give me thy heart,
If thou canst give it, then thou never gavest it:
Loves riddles are, that though thy heart depart,
It stayes at home, and thou with losing savest it: 30
But wee will have a way more liberall,
Than changing hearts, to joyne them, so wee shall
Be one, and one anothers All.

Song

Sweetest love, I do not goe,
For weariness of thee,
Nor in hope the world can show
A fitter Love for mee;
But since that I 5
Must dye at last, 'tis best,
To use my selfe in jest
Thus by fain'd deaths to dye;

Yesternight the Sunne went hence,
  And yet is here to day, 10
He hath no desire nor sense,
  Nor halfe so short a way:
    Then feare not mee,
But beleeve that I shall make
Speedier journeyes, since I take 15
  More wings and spurres than hee.

O how feeble is mans power,
  That if good fortune fall,
Cannot adde another houre,
  Nor a lost houre recall! 20
    But come bad chance,
And wee joyne to'it our strength,
And wee teach it art and length,
  It selfe o'r us to'advance.

When thou sigh'st, thou sigh'st not winde, 25
  But sigh'st my soule away,
When thou weep'st, unkindly kinde,
  My lifes blood doth decay.
    It cannot bee
That thou lov'st mee, as thou say'st, 30
If in thine my life thou waste,
  That art the best of mee.

Let not thy divining heart
  Forethinke me any ill,
Destiny may take thy part, 35
  And may thy feares fulfill;
    But thinke that wee
Are but turn'd aside to sleepe;
They who one another keepe
  Alive, ne'r parted bee. 40

The Legacie

When I dyed last, and, Deare, I dye
As often as from thee I goe,
Though it be but an houre agoe,
And Lovers houres be full eternity,
I can remember yet, that I 5
Something did say, and something did bestow;
Though I be dead, which sent mee, I should be
Mine owne executor and Legacie.

I heard mee say, Tell her anon,
That my selfe, (that is you, not I,) 10
Did kill me, and when I felt mee dye,
I bid mee send my heart, when I was gone,
But I alas could there finde none,
When I had ripp'd me, 'and search'd where hearts did lye;
It kill'd mee againe, that I who still was true, 15
In life, in my last Will should cozen you.

Yet I found something like a heart,
But colours it, and corners had,
It was not good, it was not bad,
It was intire to none, and few had part. 20
As good as could be made by art
It seem'd; and therefore for our losses sad,
I meant to send this heart in stead of mine,
But oh, no man could hold it, for twas thine.

Aire and Angels

Twice or thrice had I loved thee,
Before I knew thy face or name;
So in a voice, so in a shapeless flame,
Angells affect us oft, and worship'd bee;

20. ***intire to none:*** tied to no one lover.

Still when, to where thou wert, I came, 5
Some lovely glorious nothing I did see.
But since my soule, whose child love is,
Takes limmes of flesh, and else could nothing doe,
More subtile than the parent is,
Love must not be, but take a body too, 10
And therefore what thou wert, and who,
I bid Love aske, and now
That it assume thy body, I allow,
And fixe it selfe in thy lip, eye, and brow.

Whilst thus to ballast love, I thought, 15
And so more steddily to have gone,
With wares which would sinke admiration,
I saw, I had loves pinnace overfraught,
Ev'ry thy haire for love to worke upon
Is much too much, some fitter must be sought; 20
For, nor in nothing, nor in things
Extreme, and scatt'ring bright, can love inhere;
Then as an Angell, face, and wings
Of aire, not pure as it, yet pure doth weare,
So thy love may be my loves spheare; 25
Just such disparitie
As is twixt Aire and Angells puritie,
'Twixt womens love, and mens will ever bee.

23–24. Angels assume bodies of air when they appear to men.

The Anniversarie

All Kings, and all their favorites
All glory of honors, beauties, wits,
The Sun it selfe, which makes times, as they passe,
Is elder by a yeare, now, than it was
When thou and I first one another saw: 5
All other things, to their destruction draw,

Only our love hath no decay;
This, no to morrow hath, nor yesterday,
Running it never runs from us away,
But truly keeps his first, last, everlasting day. 10

Two graves must hide thine and my coarse,
If one might, death were no divorce.
Alas, as well as other Princes, wee,
(Who Prince enough in one another bee,)
Must leave at last in death, these eyes, and eares, 15
Oft fed with true oathes, and with sweet salt teares;
But soules where nothing dwells but love
(All other thoughts being inmates) then shall prove
This, or a love increased there above,
When bodies to their graves, soules from their graves remove. 20

And then wee shall be throughly blest,
But wee no more, than all the rest;
Here upon earth, we'are Kings, and none but wee
Can be such Kings, nor of such subjects bee.
Who is so safe as wee? where none can doe 25
Treason to us, except one of us two.
True and false feares let us refraine,
Let us love nobly, and live, and adde againe
Yeares and yeares unto yeares, till we attaine
To write threescore; this is the second of our raigne. 30

11. *coarse:* corpses.
18. *prove:* test, experience.
19. *This:* the love we know now.

Twicknam Garden

Blasted with sighs, and surrounded with teares,
Hither I come to seeke the spring,
And at mine eyes, and at mine eares,

Twickenham: the home from 1608 to 1617 of Lucy, Countess of Bedford, Donne's patron and frequent hostess.

Receive such balmes, as else cure every thing;
  But O, selfe traytor, I do bring 5
The spider love, which transubstantiates all,
  And can convert Manna to gall,
And that this place may thoroughly be thought
  True Paradise, I have the serpent brought.

'Twere wholsomer for mee, that winter did 10
  Benight the glory of this place,
  And that a grave frost did forbid
These trees to laugh, and mocke mee to my face;
  But that I may not this disgrace
Indure, nor yet leave loving, Love let mee 15
  Some senseless peece of this place bee;
Make me a mandrake, so I may groane here,
  Or a stone fountaine weeping out my yeare.

Hither with christall vyals, lovers come,
  And take my teares, which are loves wine, 20
  And try your mistresse Teares at home,
For all are false, that tast not just like mine;
  Alas, hearts do not in eyes shine,
Nor can you more judge womans thoughts by teares,
  Than by her shadow, what she weares. 25
O perverse sexe, where none is true but shee,
  Who's therefore true, because her truth kills mee.

---

17. *mandrake:* the humanoid plant, supposed to shriek when its bifurcated root was pulled from the earth. Donne appears to suppose that even when undisturbed it might groan, like a lover.

The Dreame

Deare love, for nothing lesse than thee
Would I have broke this happy dreame,
    It was a theame
For reason, much too strong for phantasie,

Therefore thou wakd'st me wisely; yet 5
My Dreame thou brok'st not, but continued'st it,
Thou art so truth, that thoughts of thee suffice,
To make dreames truths; and fables histories;
Enter these armes, for since thou thoughtst it best,
Not to dreame all my dreame, let's act the rest. 10

As lightning, or a Tapers light,
Thine eyes, and not thy noise wak'd mee;
Yet I thought thee
(For thou lovest truth) an Angell, at first sight,
But when I saw thou sawest my heart, 15
And knew'st my thoughts, beyond an Angels art,
When thou knew'st what I dreamt, when thou knew'st when
Excesse of joy would wake me, and cam'st then,
I must confesse, it could not chuse but bee
Prophane, to thinke thee any thing but thee. 20

Comming and staying show'd thee, thee,
But rising makes me doubt, that now,
Thou art not thou.
That love is weake, where feare's as strong as hee;
'Tis not all spirit, pure, and brave, 25
If mixture it of *Feare, Shame, Honor,* have.
Perchance as torches which must ready bee,
Men light and put out, so thou deal'st with mee,
Thou cam'st to kindle, goest to come; Then I
Will dreame that hope againe, but else would die. 30

15–17. that is, she has divine, not merely angelic, powers; hence *prophane* in line 20. Compare with line 7.

27–28. Since a fresh torch is difficult to light, they were lit and extinguished to make them easily lit when wanted.

A Valediction: of Weeping

Let me powre forth
My teares before thy face, whil'st I stay here,
For thy face coines them, and thy stampe they beare,
And by this Mintage they are something worth,

For thus they bee 5
Pregnant of thee;
Fruits of much griefe they are, emblems of more,
When a teare falls, that thou falls which it bore,
So thou and I are nothing then, when on a divers shore.

On a round ball 10
A workeman that hath copies by, can lay
An Europe, Afrique, and an Asia,
And quickly make that, which was nothing, *All*:
So doth each teare,
Which thee doth weare, 15
A globe, yea world by that impression grow,
Till thy teares mixt with mine doe overflow
This world, by waters sent from thee, my heaven dissolved so.

O more than Moone,
Draw not up seas to drowne me in thy spheare, 20
Weepe me not dead, in thine armes, but forbeare
To teach the sea, what it may doe too soone;
Let not the winde
Example finde,
To doe me more harme, than it purposeth; 25
Since thou and I sigh one anothers breath,
Who e'r sighes most, is cruellest, and hastes the others death.

3. That is, they bear the image of her face, as a coin did the sovereign's.
22. The farewell is preliminary to a sea voyage.

Loves Alchymie

Some that have deeper digg'd loves Myne than I,
Say, where his centriquè happinesse doth lie:
I have lov'd, and got, and told,
But should I love, get, tell, till I were old,

3. *told:* counted.

I should not finde that hidden mysterie; 5
Oh, 'tis imposture all:
And as no chymique yet th'Elixar got,
But glorifies his pregnant pot,
If by the way to him befall
Some odoriferous thing, or medicinall, 10
So, lovers dreame a rich and long delight,
But get a winter-seeming summers night.

Our ease, our thrift, our honor, and our day,
Shall we, for this vaine Bubles shadow pay?
Ends love in this, that my man, 15
Can be as happy'as I can; If he can
Endure the short scorne of a Bridegroomes play?
That loving wretch that sweares,
'Tis not the bodies marry, but the mindes,
Which he in her Angelique findes, 20
Would sweare as justly, that he heares,
In that dayes rude hoarse minstralsey, the spheares.
Hope not for minde in women; at their best
Sweetness and wit, they'are but *Mummy*, possest.

---

7. *Elixar:* the Elixir Vitae, which heals all disease and indefinitely prolongs life, but which unfortunately no alchemist ever quite succeeded in isolating.
15. *man:* servant.
17. *play:* the horseplay that accompanied a wedding. Compare with line 22.
22. *the spheares:* their quintessential music is audible only to the intellect.
24. Mummy dust was one of the alchemist's preferred ingredients, when he could get it.

The Flea

Marke but this flea, and marke in this,
How little that which thou deny'st me is;
It suck'd me first, and now sucks thee,
And in this flea, our two bloods mingled bee;
Thou know'st that this cannot be said 5

A sinne, nor shame, nor losse of maidenhead,
Yet this enjoyes before it wooe,
And pamper'd swells with one blood made of two,
And this, alas, is more than wee would doe.

Oh stay, three lives in one flea spare, 10
Where wee almost, yea more than maryed are.
This flea is you and I, and this
Our mariage bed, and mariage temple is;
Though parents grudge, and you, w'are met,
And cloysterd in these living walls of Jet. 15
Though use make you apt to kill mee,
Let not to that, selfe murder added bee,
And sacrilege, three sinnes in killing three.

Cruell and sodaine, hast thou since
Purpled thy naile, in blood of innocence? 20
Wherein could this flea guilty bee,
Except in that drop which it suckt from thee?
Yet thou triumph'st, and saist that thou
Find'st not thy selfe, nor mee the weaker now;
'Tis true, then learne how false, feares bee; 25
Just so much honor, when thou yeeld'st to mee,
Will wast, as this flea's death tooke life from thee.

A Nocturnall upon S. Lucies Day,

BEING THE SHORTEST DAY

Tis the yeares midnight, and it is the dayes,
Lucies, who scarce seaven houres herself unmaskes,
The Sunne is spent, and now his flasks
Send forth light squibs, no constant rayes;
The worlds whole sap is sunke: 5
The generall balme th'hydroptique earth hath drunk,
Whither, as to the beds-feet, life is shrunke,

3. ***flasks:*** the stars, which were supposed to store up light from the sun.

Dead and enterr'd; yet all these seeme to laugh,
Compar'd with mee, who am their Epitaph.

Study me then, you who shall lovers bee 10
At the next world, that is, at the next Spring:
For I am every dead thing,
In whom love wrought new Alchimie.
For his art did expresse
A quintessence even from nothingnesse, 15
From dull privations, and leane emptinesse
He ruin'd mee, and I am re-begot
Of absence, darknesse, death; things which are not.

All others, from all things, draw all that's good,
Life, soule, forme, spirit, whence they beeing have; 20
I, by loves limbecke, am the grave
Of all, that's nothing. Oft a flood
Have wee two wept, and so
Drownd the whole world, us two; oft did we grow
To be two Chaosses, when we did show 25
Care to ought else; and often absences
Withdrew our soules, and made us carcasses.

But I am by her death, (which word wrongs her)
Of the first nothing, the Elixer grown;
Were I a man, that I were one, 30
I needs must know; I should preferre,
If I were any beast,
Some ends, some means; Yea plants, yea stones detest,
And love; All, all some properties invest;
If I an ordinary nothing were, 35
As shadow, a light, and body must be here.

---

13. *New* alchemie, because it took nonbeing rather than substance as its point of departure.

21. *limbecke:* alembic, alchemical apparatus used in distilling elixirs and quintessences from less perfect substances.

30–33. A traditional hierarchy. Man's rational soul is self-conscious; the beast's perceptive soul can select ends and means; plants' vegetable souls select and reject what they can and cannot feed on; and some minerals have magnetic powers.

But I am None; nor will my Sunne renew.
You lovers, for whose sake, the lesser Sunne
At this time to the Goat is runne
To fetch new lust, and give it you, 40
Enjoy your summer all;
Since shee enjoyes her long nights festivall,
Let mee prepare towards her, and let mee call
This houre her Vigill, and her Eve, since this
Both the yeares, and the dayes deep midnight is. 45

39. *Goat:* on St. Lucy's day the sun enters Capricorn.

The Apparition

When by thy scorne, O murdresse, I am dead,
And that thou thinkst thee free
From all solicitation from mee,
Then shall my ghost come to thy bed,
And thee, fain'd vestall, in worse armes shall see; 5
Then thy sicke taper will begin to winke,
And he, whose thou art then, being tyr'd before,
Will, if thou stirre, or pinch to wake him, thinke
Thou call'st for more,
And in false sleepe will from thee shrinke, 10
And then poore Aspen wretch, neglected thou
Bath'd in a cold quicksilver sweat wilt lye
A veryer ghost than I;
What I will say, I will not tell thee now,
Lest that preserve thee'; and since my love is spent, 15
I'had rather thou shouldst painfully repent,
Than by my threatenings rest still innocent.

A Valediction: Forbidding Mourning

As virtuous men passe mildly away,
And whisper to their soules, to goe,
Whilst some of their sad friends doe say,
The breath goes now, and some say, no:

So let us melt, and make no noise, 5
  No teare-floods, nor sigh-tempests move,
T'were prophanation of our joyes
  To tell the layetie our love.

Moving of th'earth brings harmes and feares,
  Men reckon what it did and meant, 10
But trepidation of the spheares,
  Though greater farre, is innocent.

Dull sublunary lovers love
  (Whose soule is sense) cannot admit
Absence, because it doth remove 15
  Those things which elemented it.

But we by a love, so much refin'd,
  That our selves know not what it is,
Inter-assured of the mind,
  Care lesse, eyes, lips, and hands to misse. 20

Our two soules therefore, which are one,
  Though I must goe, endure not yet
A breach, but an expansion,
  Like gold to ayery thinnesse beate.

If they be two, they are two so 25
  As stiffe twin compasses are two,
Thy soule the fixt foot, makes no show
  To move, but doth, if the'other doe.

And though it in the center sit,
  Yet when the other far doth rome, 30
It leanes, and hearkens after it,
  And growes erect, as that comes home.

---

11. *trepidation:* the swaying of the Ninth, or Crystalline, sphere, which was supposed to cause the precession of the equinoxes, a phenomenon detectable only by the most sophisticated and prolonged observations.

Such wilt thou be to mee, who must
 Like th'other foot, obliquely runne;
Thy firmnes drawes my circle just, 35
 And makes me end, where I begunne.

The Extasie

Where, like a pillow on a bed,
 A Pregnant banke swel'd up, to rest
The violets reclining head,
 Sat we two, one anothers best.
Our hands were firmely cimented 5
 With a fast balme, which thence did spring,
Our eye-beames twisted, and did thred
 Our eyes, upon one double string;
So to'entergraft our hands, as yet
 Was all the meanes to make us one, 10
And pictures in our eyes to get
 Was all our propagation.
As 'twixt two equall Armies, Fate
 Suspends uncertaine victorie,
Our soules, (which to advance their state, 15
 Were gone out,) hung 'twixt her, and mee.
And whil'st our soules negotiate there,
 Wee like sepulchrall statues lay;
All day, the same our postures were,
 And wee said nothing, all the day. 20
If any, so by love refin'd,
 That he soules language understood,
And by good love were growen all minde,
 Within convenient distance stood,
He (though he knew not which soul spake, 25
 Because both meant, both spake the same)

Ecstasy: literally "standing outside," a condition described by Neo-Platonic philosophers in which the soul moves outside the body in quest of more perfect divine communion. Compare with lines 15–16.
11. *get:* beget.

Might thence a new concoction take,
  And part farre purer than he came.
This Extasie doth unperplex
  (We said) and tell us what we love, 30
Wee see by this, it was not sexe,
  Wee see, we saw not what did move:
But as all severall soules containe
  Mixture of things, they know not what,
Love, these mixt soules, doth mixe againe, 35
  And makes both one, each this and that.
A single violet transplant,
  The strength, the colour, and the size,
(All which before was poore, and scant,)
  Redoubles still, and multiplies. 40
When love, with one another so
  Interinanimates two soules,
That abler soule, which thence doth flow,
  Defects of lonelinesse controules.
Wee then, who are this new soule, know, 45
  Of what we are compos'd, and made,
For, th'Atomies of which we grow,
  Are soules, whom no change can invade.
But O alas, so long, so farre
  Our bodies why doe wee forbeare? 50
They are ours, though they are not wee, Wee are
  The intelligences, they the spheares.
We owe them thankes, because they thus,
  Did us, to us, at first convay,
Yeelded their forces, sense, to us, 55
  Nor are drosse to us, but allay.
On man heavens influence workes not so,

---

27. *concoction:* one of the phases in the alchemical process of transmuting less worthy metals into more worthy.

45. *know:* to hold in the mind that which incorruptibly exists. It would not be possible to "know" the component souls if they had lost their identities in merging.

52. *intelligences:* the powers that revolve the crystalline spheres to which the heavenly bodies are attached.

56. *drosse:* impurity skimmed off and discarded in the process of refining a metal.

But that it first imprints the ayre,
Soe soule into the soule may flow,
Though it to body first repaire. 60
As our blood labours to beget
Spirits, as like soules as it can,
Because such fingers need to knit
That subtile knot, which makes us man:
So must pure lovers soules descend 65
T'affections, and to faculties,
Which sense may reach and apprehend,
Else a great Prince in prison lies.
To our bodies turne wee then, that so
Weake men on love reveal'd may looke; 70
Loves mysteries in soules doe grow,
But yet the body is his booke.
And if some lover, such as wee,
Have heard this dialogue of one,
Let him still marke us, he shall see 75
Small change, when we'are to bodies gone.

---

76. ***bodies:*** atoms.

Loves Deitie

I long to talke with some old lovers ghost,
Who dyed before the god of Love was borne:
I cannot thinke that hee, who then lov'd most,
Sunke so low, as to love one which did scorne.
But since this god produc'd a destinie, 5
And that vice-nature, custome, lets it be;
I must love her, that loves not mee.

Sure, they which made him god, meant not so much,
Nor he, in his young godhead practis'd it.
But when an even flame two hearts did touch, 10
His office was indulgently to fit
Actives to passives. Correspondencie

Only his subject was; It cannot bee
Love, till I love her, that loves mee.

But every moderne god will now extend 15
His vast prerogative, as far as Jove.
To rage, to lust, to write to, to commend,
All is the purlewe of the God of Love.
Oh were wee wak'ned by this Tyrannie
To ungod this child againe, it could not bee 20
I should love her, who loves not mee.

Rebell and Atheist too, why murmure I,
As though I felt the worst that love could doe?
Love might make me leave loving, or might trie
A deeper plague, to make her love mee too, 25
Which, since she loves before, I'am loth to see;
Falshood is worse than hate; and that must bee,
If shee whom I love, should love mee.

The Funerall

Who ever comes to shroud me, do not harme
Nor question much
That subtile wreath of haire, which crowns my arme;
The mystery, the signe you must not touch,
For'tis my outward Soule, 5
Viceroy to that, which then to heaven being gone,
Will leave this to controule,
And keep these limbes, her Provinces, from dissolution.

For if the sinewie thread my braine lets fall
Through every part, 10
Can tye those parts, and make mee one of all;
These haires which upward grew, and strength and art
Have from a better braine,
Can better do'it; Except she meant that I

14. ***Except:*** unless.

By this should know my pain, 15
As prisoners then are manacled, when they'are condemn'd to die.

What ere shee meant by'it, bury it with me,
For since I am
Loves martyr, it might breed idolatrie,
If into others hands these Reliques came; 20
As'twas humility
To afford to it all that a Soule can doe,
So,'tis some bravery,
That since you would save none of mee, I bury some of you.

---

23. *bravery:* bravado, spirit.

The Blossome

Little think'st thou, poore flower,
Whom I have watch'd sixe or seaven dayes,
And seene thy birth, and seene what every houre
Gave to thy growth, thee to this height to raise,
And now dost laugh and triumph on this bough, 5
Little think'st thou
That it will freeze anon, and that I shall
To morrow finde thee falne, or not at all.

Little think'st thou poore heart
That labour'st yet to nestle thee, 10
And think'st by hovering here to get a part
In a forbidden or forbidding tree,
And hop'st her stiffenesse by long siege to bow:
Little think'st thou,
That thou to morrow, ere that Sunne doth wake, 15
Must with this Sunne, and mee a journey take.

But thou which lov'st to bee
Subtile to plague thy selfe, wilt say,
Alas, if you must goe, what's that to mee?

Here lyes my businesse, and here I will stay: 20
You goe to friends, whose love and meanes present
Various content
To your eyes, eares, and tongue, and every part.
If then your body goe, what need you a heart?

Well then, stay here; but know, 25
When thou hast stayd and done thy most;
A naked thinking heart, that makes no show,
Is to a woman, but a kinde of Ghost;
How shall shee know my heart; or having none,
Know thee for one? 30
Practise may make her know some other part,
But take my word, shee doth not know a Heart.

Meet mee at London, then,
Twenty dayes hence, and thou shalt see
Mee fresher, and more fat, by being with men, 35
Than if I had staid still with her and thee.
For Gods sake, if you can, be you so too:
I would give you
There, to another friend, whom wee shall finde
As glad to have my body, as my minde. 40

The Relique

When my grave is broke up againe
Some second ghest to entertaine,
(For graves have learn'd that woman-head
To be to more than one a Bed)
And he that digs it, spies 5
A bracelet of bright haire about the bone,
Will he not let'us alone,
And thinke that there a loving couple lies,

3. *head:* the section of a general discourse (on women) pertaining to this particular characteristic. He is being grimly bookish.

Who thought that this device might be some way
To make their soules, at the last busie day, 10
Meet at this grave, and make a little stay?

If this fall in a time, or land,
Where mis-devotion doth command,
Then, he that digges us up, will bring
Us, to the Bishop, and the King, 15
To make us Reliques; then
Thou shalt be a Mary Magdalen, and I
A something else thereby;
All women shall adore us, and some men;
And since at such time, miracles are sought, 20
I would have that age by this paper taught
What miracles wee harmelesse lovers wrought.

First, we lov'd well and faithfully,
Yet knew not what wee lov'd nor why,
Difference of sex no more wee knew, 25
Than our Guardian Angells doe;
Comming and going, wee
Perchance might kisse, but not between those meales;
Our hands ne'r toucht the seales,
Which nature, injur'd by late law, sets free: 30
These miracles wee did; but now alas,
All measure, and all language, I should passe,
Should I tell what a miracle shee was.

---

17. Painters always depict St. Mary Magdalen with golden hair. Her reputation before she met Jesus was dubious, and she might well be supposed to have given a token to a lover.
24. Compare the idea here with the traditional conception of sexual activity as a mode of knowledge.
27–28. The kiss of salutation and parting, which lasted in some countries until the later eighteenth century.

The Dampe

When I am dead, and Doctors know not why,
    And my friends curiositie
Will have me cut up to survay each part,
When they shall finde your Picture in my heart,
    You thinke a sodaine dampe of love 5
    Will through all their senses move,
And worke on them as mee, and so preferre
Your murder, to the name of Massacre.

Poore victories! But if you dare be brave,
    And pleasure in your conquest have, 10
First kill th'enormous Gyant, your *Disdaine,*
And let th'enchantresse *Honor,* next be slaine,
    And like a Goth and Vandall rize,
    Deface Records, and Histories
Of your owne arts and triumphs over men, 15
And without such advantage kill me then.

For I could muster up as well as you
    My Gyants, and my Witches too,
Which are vast *Constancy,* and *Secretnesse,*
But these I neyther looke for, nor professe; 20
    Kill mee as Woman, let mee die
    As a meere man; doe you but try
Your passive valor, and you shall finde then,
Naked you'have odds enough of any man.

5. *dampe:* noxious exhalation, not necessarily moist.
7. *preferre:* promote.
21. In the jocularities of Donne's time, the verb "kill" is used of the man's act of love, and "die," of the woman's.

The Expiration

So, so, breake off this last lamenting kisse,
    Which sucks two soules, and vapors Both away,

Turne thou ghost that way, and let mee turne this,
  And let our selves benight our happiest day,
We ask'd none leave to love; nor will we owe 5
  Any, so cheape a death, as saying, Goe;

Goe; and if that word have not quite kil'd thee,
  Ease mee with death, by bidding mee goe too.
Oh, if it have, let my word worke on mee,
  And a just office on a murderer doe. 10
Except it be too late, to kill me so,
  Being double dead, going, and bidding, goe.

A Lecture upon the Shadow

Stand still, and I will read to thee
A Lecture, love, in Loves philosophy.
    These three houres that we have spent,
    Walking here, Two shadowes went
Along with us, which we our selves produc'd; 5
But, now the Sunne is just above our head,
    We doe those shadowes tread;
    And to brave clearnesse all things are reduc'd.
  So whilst our infant loves did grow,
  Disguises did, and shadowes, flow, 10
  From us, and our cares; but, now 'tis not so.

That love hath not attain'd the high'st degree,
Which is still diligent lest others see.

Except our loves at this noone stay,
We shall new shadowes make the other way. 15
    As the first were made to blinde
    Others; these which come behinde
Will worke upon our selves, and blind our eyes.
If our loves faint, and westwardly decline;
    To me thou, falsly, thine, 20
    And I to thee mine actions shall disguise.

The morning shadowes weare away,
But these grow longer all the day,
But oh, loves day is short, if love decay.

Love is a growing, or full constant light; 25
And his first minute, after noone, is night.

ELEGIES, SATIRES, AND OTHER POEMS

ELEGIE IV

The Perfume

Once, and but once found in thy company,
All thy suppos'd escapes are laid on mee;
And as a thiefe at barre, is question'd there
By all the men, that have beene rob'd that yeare,
So am I, (by this traiterous meanes surpriz'd) 5
By thy Hydroptique father catechiz'd.
Though he had wont to search with glazed eyes,
As though he came to kill a Cockatrice,
Though hee hath oft sworne, that hee would remove
Thy beauties beautie, and food of our love, 10

---

2. *escapes:* escapades. The word was applied especially to breaches of chastity.
6. *Hydroptique:* having an insatiable thirst (here, for information).
8. *Cockatrice:* this creature killed by a glance of its eye. If *glazed* in line 7 means "staring," he presumably hoped to slay it with its own weapon.

Hope of his goods, if I with thee were seene,
Yet close and secret, as our soules, we'have beene.
Though thy immortall mother which doth lye
Still buried in her bed, yet will not dye,
Takes this advantage to sleepe out day-light, 15
And watch thy entries, and returnes all night,
And, when she takes thy hand, and would seeme kind,
Doth search what rings, and armelets she can finde,
And kissing notes the colour of thy face,
And fearing least thou'art swolne, doth thee embrace; 20
To trie if thou long, doth name strange meates,
And notes thy palenesse, blushing, sighs, and sweats;
And politiquely will to thee confesse
The sinnes of her owne youths ranke lustinesse;
Yet love these Sorceries did remove, and move 25
Thee to gull thine owne mother for my love.
Thy little brethren, which like Faiery Sprights
Oft skipt into our chamber, those sweet nights,
And kist, and ingled on thy fathers knee,
Were brib'd next day, to tell what they did see: 30
The grim eight-foot-high iron-bound serving-man,
That oft names God in oathes, and onely then,
He that to barre the first gate, doth as wide
As the great Rhodian Colossus stride,
Which, if in hell no other paines there were, 35
Makes mee feare hell, because he must be there:
Though by thy father he were hir'd to this,
Could never witnesse any touch or kisse.
But Oh, too common ill, I brought with mee
That, which betray'd mee to my enemie: 40
A loud perfume, which at my entrance cryed
Even at thy fathers nose, so were wee spied.
When, like a tyran King, that in his bed
Smelt gunpowder, the pale wretch shivered.
Had it beene some bad smell, he would have thought 45
That his owne feet, or breath, that smell had wrought.
But as wee in our Ile emprisoned,

---

21. Longing for strange foods was thought a sign of pregnancy.

Where cattell onely,'and diverse dogs are bred,
The pretious Unicornes, strange monsters call,
So thought he good, strange, that had none at all. 50
I taught my silkes, their whistling to forbeare,
Even my opprest shoes, dumbe and speechlesse were,
Onely, thou bitter sweet, whom I had laid
Next mee, mee traiterously hast betraid,
And unsuspected hast invisibly 55
At once fled unto him, and staid with mee.
Base excrement of earth, which dost confound
Sense, from distinguishing the sicke from sound;
By thee the seely Amorous sucks his death
By drawing in a leprous harlots breath; 60
By thee, the greatest staine to mans estate
Falls on us, to be call'd effeminate;
Though you be much lov'd in the Princes hall,
There, things that seeme, exceed substantiall.
Gods, when yee fum'd on altars, were pleas'd well, 65
Because you'were burnt, not that they lik'd your smell;
You'are loathsome all, being taken simply alone,
Shall wee love ill things joyn'd, and hate each one?
If you were good, your good doth soone decay;
And you are rare, that takes the good away. 70
All my perfumes, I give most willingly
To'embalme thy fathers corse; What? will hee die?

ELEGIE VII

Natures lay Ideot, I taught thee to love,
And in that sophistrie, Oh, thou dost prove
Too subtile: Foole, thou didst not understand
The mystique language of the eye nor hand:
Nor couldst thou judge the difference of the aire 5
Of sighes, and say, this lies, this sounds despaire:
Nor by the'eyes water call a maladie
Desperately hot, or changing feaverously.
I had not taught thee then, the Alphabet

1. *lay:* ignorant. *Ideot:* not a mental defective, but simply one not professionally learned: a "layman."

Of flowers, how they devisefully being set 10
And bound up, might with speechlesse secrecie
Deliver errands mutely, and mutually.
Remember since all thy words us'd to bee
To every suitor; *Ay, if my friends agree;*
Since, houshold charmes, thy husbands name to teach, 15
Were all the love trickes, that thy wit could reach;
And since, an houres discourse could scarce have made
One answer in thee, and that ill arraid
In broken proverbs, and torne sentences.
Thou art not by so many duties his, 20
That from the worlds Common having sever'd thee,
Inlaid thee, neither to be seene, nor see,
As mine: who have with amorous delicacies
Refin'd thee'into a blis-full Paradise.
Thy graces and good words my creatures bee; 25
I planted knowledge and lifes tree in thee,
Which Oh, shall strangers taste? Must I alas
Frame and enamell Plate, and drinke in Glasse?
Chafe waxe for others seales? breake a colts force
And leave him then, being made a ready horse? 30

13, 15, 17. *since:* formerly.
22. *Inlaid:* laid away, concealed.
26. Compare with Gen. 2 : 9.
28. *Frame:* fashion. *Plate:* gold or silver vessels.

ELEGIE XVI

On His Mistris

By our first strange and fatall interview,
By all desires which thereof did ensue,
By our long starving hopes, by that remorse
Which my words masculine perswasive force
Begot in thee, and by the memory 5
Of hurts, which spies and rivals threatned me,
I calmly beg: But by thy fathers wrath,
By all paines, which want and divorcement hath,
I conjure thee, and all the oathes which I

And thou have sworne to seale joynt constancy, 10
Here I unsweare, and overswear them thus,
Thou shalt not love by wayes so dangerous.
Temper, ô faire Love, loves impetuous rage,
Be my true Mistris still, not my faign'd Page;
I'll goe, and, by thy kinde leave, leave behinde 15
Thee, onely worthy to nurse in my minde,
Thirst to come backe; ô if thou die before,
My soule from other lands to thee shall soare.
Thy (else Almighty) beautie cannot move
Rage from the Seas, nor thy love teach them love, 20
Nor tame wilde Boreas harshnesse; Thou hast reade
How roughly hee in peeces shivered
Faire Orithea, whom he swore he lov'd.
Fall ill or good, 'tis madnesse to have prov'd
Dangers unurg'd; Feed on this flattery, 25
That absent Lovers one in th'other be.
Dissemble nothing, not a boy, nor change
Thy bodies habite, nor mindes; bee not strange
To thy selfe onely; All will spie in thy face
A blushing womanly discovering grace; 30
Richly cloath'd Apes, are call'd Apes, and as soone
Ecclips'd as bright we call the Moone the Moone.
Men of France, changeable Camelions,
Spittles of diseases, shops of fashions,
Loves fuellers, and the rightest company 35
Of Players, which upon the worlds stage be,
Will quickly know thee, and know thee, and alas!
Th'indifferent Italian, as we passe
His warme land, well content to thinke thee Page,
Will hunt thee with such lust, and hideous rage, 40
As *Lots* faire guests were vext. But none of these
Nor spungy hydroptique Dutch shall thee displease,
If thou stay here. O stay here, for, for thee

14. "In connexion with the general theme of this poem it may be noted that in 1605 Sir Robert Dudley, the illegitimate son of the Earl of Leicester, who like Donne served in the Cadiz and Islands expeditions, left England accompanied by the beautiful Elizabeth Southwell disguised as a page. At this period the most fantastic poetry was never more fantastic than life itself."—Grierson.

England is onely a worthy Gallerie,
To walke in expectation, till from thence 45
Our greatest King call thee to his presence.
When I am gone, dreame me some happinesse,
Nor let thy lookes our long hid love confesse,
Nor praise, nor dispraise me, nor blesse nor curse
Openly loves force, nor in bed fright thy Nurse 50
With midnights startings, crying out, oh, oh
Nurse, ô my love is slaine, I saw him goe
O'er the white Alpes alone; I saw him I,
Assail'd, fight, taken, stabb'd, bleed, fall, and die.
Augure me better chance, except dread *Jove* 55
Thinke it enough for me to'have had thy love.

---

44. *Gallerie:* entrance-hall.

ELEGIE XIX

To His Mistris Going to Bed

Come, Madam, come, all rest my powers defie,
Until I labour, I in labour lie.
The foe oft-times having the foe in sight,
Is tir'd with standing though he never fight.
Off with that girdle, like heavens Zone glistering, 5
But a far fairer world incompassing.
Unpin that spangled breastplate which you wear,
That th'eyes of busie fooles may be stopt there.
Unlace your self, for that harmonious chyme,
Tells me from you, that now it is bed time. 10
Off with that happy busk, which I envie,
That still can be, and still can stand so nigh.
Your gown going off, such beautious state reveals,
As when from flowry meads th'hills shadow steales.
Off with that wyerie Coronet and shew 15
The haiery Diademe which on you doth grow:
Now off with those shooes, and then safely tread
In this loves hallow'd temple, this soft bed.
In such white robes, heaven's Angels us'd to be

Receavd by men; Thou Angel bringst with thee 20
A heaven like Mahomets Paradice; and though
Ill spirits walk in white, we easly know,
By this these Angels from an evil sprite,
Those set our hairs, but these our flesh upright.
  Licence my roaving hands, and let them go, 25
Before, behind, between, above, below.
O my America! my new-found-land,
My kingdome, safeliest when with one man man'd,
My Myne of precious stones, My Emperie,
How blest am I in this discovering thee! 30
To enter in these bonds, is to be free;
Then where my hand is set, my seal shall be.
  Full nakedness! All joyes are due to thee,
As souls unbodied, bodies uncloth'd must be,
To taste whole joyes. Gems which you women use 35
Are like Atlanta's balls, cast in mens views,
That when a fools eye lighteth on a Gem,
His earthly soul may covet theirs, not them.
Like pictures, or like books gay coverings made
For lay-men, are all women thus array'd; 40
Themselves are mystick books, which only wee
(Whom their imputed grace will dignifie)
Must see reveal'd. Then since that I may know;
As liberally, as to a Midwife, shew
Thy self: cast all, yea, this white lynnen hence, 45
Here is no pennance, much less innocence.
  To teach thee, I am naked first; why then
What needst thou have more covering than a man.

---

36. *At[a]lanta's balls* were golden apples. She could not resist stopping to pick them up, and so lost the race, and her virginity.
40. *lay-men:* men unqualified to read technical or sacred books.
46. Penance and innocence are both clothed in white.

Epithalamion Made at Lincolnes Inne

The Sun-beames in the East are spred,
Leave, leave, faire Bride, your solitary bed,
No more shall you returne to it alone,
It nourseth sadnesse, and your bodies print,
Like to a grave, the yielding downe doth dint; 5
You and your other you meet there anon;
Put forth, put forth that warme balme-breathing thigh,
Which when next time you in these sheets will smother,
There it must meet another,
Which never was, but must be, oft, more nigh; 10
Come glad from thence, goe gladder than you came,
To day put on perfection, and a womans name.

Daughters of London, you which bee
Our Golden Mines, and furnish'd Treasurie,
You which are Angels, yet still bring with you 15
Thousands of Angels on your mariage daies,
Help with your presence and devise to praise
These rites, which also unto you grow due:
Conceitedly dresse her, and be assign'd,
By you, fit place for every flower and jewell, 20
Make her for love fit fewell
As gay as Flora, and as rich as Inde;
So may shee faire, rich, glad, and in nothing lame,
To day put on perfection, and a womans name.

And you frolique Patricians, 25
Sonnes of these Senators, wealths deep oceans,
Ye painted courtiers, barrels of others wits,
Yee country men, who but your beasts love none,
Yee of those fellowships whereof hee's one,

Donne became a student at Lincoln's Inn in 1592. It is not known whose marriage the poem celebrates.

17. ***devise:*** not a verb but a noun meaning fancy, invention.

Of study and play made strange Hermaphrodits, 30
Here shine; This Bridegroom to the Temple bring.
Loe, in yon path which store of straw'd flowers graceth,
The sober virgin paceth;
Except my sight faile, 'tis no other thing;
Weep not nor blush, here is no griefe nor shame, 35
To day put on perfection, and a womans name.

Thy two-leav'd gates faire Temple unfold,
And these two in thy sacred bosome hold,
Till, mystically joyn'd, but one they bee;
Then may thy leane and hunger-starved wombe 40
Long time expect their bodies and their tombe,
Long after their owne parents fatten thee.
All elder claimes, and all cold barrennesse,
All yeelding to new loves bee far for ever,
Which might these two dissever, 45
All wayes all th'other may each one possesse;
For, the best Bride, best worthy of praise and fame,
To day puts on perfection, and a womans name.

Oh winter dayes bring much delight,
Not for themselves, but for they soon bring night; 50
Other sweets wait thee than these diverse meats,
Other disports than dancing jollities,
Other love tricks than glancing with the eyes,
But that the Sun still in our halfe Spheare sweates;
Hee flies in winter, but he now stands still. 55
Yet shadowes turne; Noone point he hath attain'd,
His steeds nill bee restrain'd,
But gallop lively downe the Westerne hill;
Thou shalt, when he hath runne the worlds half frame,
To night put on perfection, and a womans name. 60

The amorous evening starre is rose,
Why then should not our amorous starre inclose

---

31. *shine:* this verb shows that *Sonnes* (line 26) also means "suns."

Her selfe in her wish'd bed? Release your strings
Musicians, and dancers take some truce
With these your pleasing labours, for great use 65
As much wearinesse as perfection brings;
You, and not only you, but all toyl'd beasts
Rest duly; at night all their toyles are dispensed;
But in their beds commenced
Are other labours, and more dainty feasts; 70
She goes a maid, who, lest she turne the same,
To night puts on perfection, and a womans name.

Thy virgins girdle now untie,
And in thy nuptiall bed (loves altar) lye
A pleasing sacrifice; now dispossesse 75
Thee of these chaines and robes which were put on
T'adorne the day, not thee; for thou, alone,
Like vertue'and truth, art best in nakednesse;
This bed is onely to virginitie
A grave, but, to a better state, a cradle; 80
Till now thou wast but able
To be what now thou art; then that by thee
No more be said, *I may bee,* but, *I am,*
To night put on perfection, and a womans name.

Even like a faithfull man content, 85
That this life for a better should be spent,
So, shee a mothers rich stile doth preferre,
And at the Bridegroomes wish'd approach doth lye,
Like an appointed lambe, when tenderly
The priest comes on his knees t'embowell her; 90
Now sleep or watch with more joy; and O light
Of heaven, to morrow rise thou hot, and early;
This Sun will love so dearely
Her rest, that long, long we shall want her sight;
Wonders are wrought, for shee which had no maime, 95
To night puts on perfection, and a womans name.

SATYRE III

[ON RELIGION]

Kinde pitty chokes my spleene; brave scorn forbids
Those teares to issue which swell my eye-lids;
I must not laugh, nor weepe sinnes, and be wise,
Can railing then cure these worne maladies?
Is not our Mistresse faire Religion, 5
As worthy of all our Soules devotion,
As vertue was to the first blinded age?
Are not heavens joyes as valiant to asswage
Lusts, as earths honour was to them? Alas,
As wee do them in meanes, shall they surpasse 10
Us in the end, and shall thy fathers spirit
Meete blinde Philosophers in heaven, whose merit
Of strict life may be imputed faith, and heare
Thee, whom hee taught so easie wayes and neare
To follow, damn'd? O if thou dar'st, feare this; 15
This feare great courage, and high valour is.
Dar'st thou ayd mutinous Dutch, and dar'st thou lay
Thee in ships woodden Sepulchers, a prey
To leaders rage, to stormes, to shot, to dearth?
Dar'st thou dive seas, and dungeons of the earth? 20
Hast thou couragious fire to thaw the ice
Of frozen North discoveries? and thrise
Colder than Salamanders, like divine
Children in th'oven, fires of Spaine, and the line,
Whose countries limbecks to our bodies bee, 25
Canst thou for gaine beare? and must every hee
Which cryes not, Goddesse, to thy Mistresse, draw,
Or eate thy poysonous words? courage of straw!
O desperate coward, wilt thou seeme bold, and

---

7. ***the first blinded age:*** the heyday of Greece and Rome, before the Christian revelation was vouchsafed.

9. ***them:*** the great pagans.

25. ***limbecks:*** vessels in which substances are distilled by heat. The ***line*** (line 24) is the equator.

To thy foes and his (who made thee to stand 30
Sentinell in his worlds garrison) thus yeeld,
And for the forbidden warres, leave th'appointed field?
Know thy foes: The foule Devill (whom thou
Strivest to please,) for hate, not love, would allow
Thee faine, his whole Realme to be quit; and as 35
The worlds all parts wither away and passe,
So the worlds selfe, thy other lov'd foe, is
In her decrepit wayne, and thou loving this,
Dost love a withered and worne strumpet; last,
Flesh (it selfes death) and joyes which flesh can taste, 40
Thou lovest; and thy faire goodly soule, which doth
Give this flesh power to taste joy, thou dost loath.
Seeke true religion. O where? Mirreus
Thinking her unhous'd here, and fled from us,
Seekes her at Rome; there, because hee doth know 45
That shee was there a thousand yeares agoe,
He loves her ragges so, as wee here obey
The statecloth where the Prince sate yesterday.
Crantz to such brave Loves will not be inthrall'd,
But loves her onely, who at Geneva is call'd 50
Religion, plaine, simple, sullen, yong,
Contemptuous, yet unhansome; As among
Lecherous humors, there is one that judges
No wenches wholsome, but coarse country drudges.
Graius stayes still at home here, and because 55
Some Preachers, vile ambitious bauds, and lawes
Still new like fashions, bid him thinke that shee
Which dwels with us, is onely perfect, hee
Imbraceth her, whom his Godfathers will
Tender to him, being tender, as Wards still 60
Take such wives as their Guardians offer, or
Pay valewes. Carelesse Phrygius doth abhorre
All, because all cannot be good, as one
Knowing some women whores, dares marry none.
Graccus loves all as one, and thinkes that so 65

---

33. *foes:* the world, the flesh, and the devil.
62. *valewes:* sums paid their guardians by wards who refused arranged marriages: here compared to the fine a recusant paid for not attending his parish church.

As women do in divers countries goe
In divers habits, yet are still one kinde,
So doth, so is Religion; and this blind-
nesse too much light breeds; but unmoved thou
Of force must one, and forc'd but one allow; 70
And the right; aske thy father which is shee,
Let him aske his; though truth and falsehood bee
Neare twins, yet truth a little elder is;
Be busie to seeke her, beleeve mee this,
Hee's not of none, nor worst, that seekes the best. 75
To adore, or scorne an image, or protest,
May all be bad; doubt wisely; in strange way
To stand inquiring right, is not to stray;
To sleepe, or runne wrong, is. On a huge hill,
Cragged, and steep, Truth stands, and hee that will 80
Reach her, about must, and about must goe;
And what the hills suddennes resists, winne so;
Yet strive so, that before age, deaths twilight,
Thy Soule rest, for none can worke in that night.
To will, implyes delay, therefore now doe: 85
Hard deeds, the bodies paines; hard knowledge too
The mindes indeavours reach, and mysteries
Are like the Sunne, dazling, yet plaine to all eyes.
Keepe the truth which thou hast found; men do not stand
In so ill case here, that God hath with his hand 90
Sign'd Kings blanck-charters to kill whom they hate,
Nor are they Vicars, but hangmen to Fate.
Foole and wretch, wilt thou let thy Soule be tyed
To mans lawes, by which she shall not be tryed
At the last day? Oh, will it then boot thee 95
To say a Philip, or a Gregory,
A Harry, or a Martin taught thee this?
Is not this excuse for mere contraries,
Equally strong? cannot both sides say so?
That thou mayest rightly obey power, her bounds know; 100
Those past, her nature, and name is chang'd; to be
Then humble to her is idolatrie.

96–97. Philip of Spain, Henry VIII of England, Martin Luther. *Gregory* is probably Pope Gregory XIII or XIV.

As streames are, Power is; those blest flowers that dwell
At the rough streames calme head, thrive and do well,
But having left their roots, and themselves given 105
To the streames tyrannous rage, alas are driven
Through mills, and rockes, and woods, and at last, almost
Consum'd in going, in the sea are lost:
So perish Soules, which more chuse mens unjust
Power from God claym'd, than God himselfe to trust. 110

To Mr I. L.

Blest are your North parts, for all this long time
My Sun is with you, cold and darke'is our Clime;
Heavens Sun, which staid so long from us this yeare,
Staid in your North (I thinke) for she was there,
And hether by kinde nature drawne from thence, 5
Here rages, chafes, and threatens pestilence;
Yet I, as long as shee from hence doth staie,
Thinke this no South, no Sommer, nor no day.
With thee my kinde and unkinde heart is run,
There sacrifice it to that beauteous Sun: 10
And since thou art in Paradise and need'st crave
No joyes addition, helpe thy friend to save.
So may thy pastures with their flowery feasts,
As suddenly as Lard, fat thy leane beasts;
So may thy woods oft poll'd, yet ever weare 15
A greene, and when thee list, a golden haire;
So may all thy sheepe bring forth Twins; and so
In chace and race may thy horse all out goe;
So may thy love and courage ne'r be cold;
Thy Sonne ne'r Ward; Thy lov'd wife ne'r seem old; 20
But maist thou wish great things, and them attaine,
As thou telst her, and none but her, my paine.

Mr. I. L.'s identity is not known.

Of the Progresse of the Soule: The Second Anniversary

WHEREIN, BY OCCASION OF THE RELIGIOUS DEATH OF MISTRIS ELIZABETH DRURY, THE INCOMMODITIES OF THE SOULE IN THIS LIFE, AND HER EXALTATION IN THE NEXT, ARE CONTEMPLATED.

Nothing could make me sooner to confesse *The entrance.*
That this world had an everlastingnesse,
Then to consider, that a yeare is runne,
Since both this lower world's, and the Sunnes Sunne,
The Lustre, and the vigor of this All, 5
Did set; 'twere blasphemie to say, did fall.
But as a ship which hath strooke saile, doth runne
By force of that force which before, it wonne:
Or as sometimes in a beheaded man,
Though at those two Red seas, which freely ranne, 10
One from the Trunke, another from the Head,
His soule be sail'd, to her eternall bed,
His eyes will twinckle, and his tongue will roll,
As though he beckned, and cal'd backe his soule,
He graspes his hands, and he pulls up his feet, 15
And seemes to reach, and to step forth to meet
His soule; when all these motions which we saw,
Are but as Ice, which crackles at a thaw:
Or as a Lute, which in moist weather, rings
Her knell alone, by cracking of her strings: 20
So struggles this dead world, now shee is gone;
For there is motion in corruption.
As some daies are at the Creation nam'd,

The second (and last) of a projected series of annual meditations on the death in 1610 of Sir Robert Drury's fifteen-year-old daughter. The "First Anniversary" was an "anatomie" of the ruined universe from which she departed.

Before the Sunne, the which fram'd daies, was fram'd,
So after this Sunne's set, some shew appeares, 25
And orderly vicissitude of yeares.
Yet a new Deluge, and of *Lethe* flood,
Hath drown'd us all, All have forgot all good,
Forgetting her, the maine reserve of all.
Yet in this deluge, grosse and generall, 30
Thou seest me strive for life; my life shall bee,
To be hereafter prais'd, for praysing thee;
Immortall Maid, who though thou would'st refuse
The name of Mother, be unto my Muse
A Father, since her chast Ambition is, 35
Yearely to bring forth such a child as this.
These Hymnes may worke on future wits, and so
May great Grand children of thy prayses grow.
And so, though not revive, embalme and spice
The world, which else would putrifie with vice. 40
For thus, Man may extend thy progeny,
Untill man doe but vanish, and not die.
These Hymnes thy issue, may encrease so long,
As till Gods great *Venite* change the song. 44
Thirst for that time, O my insatiate soule, *A just disestimation of this world.*
And serve thy thirst, with Gods safesealing Bowle.
Be thirstie still, and drinke still till thou goe
To th'only Health, to be Hydroptique so.
Forget this rotten world; And unto thee
Let thine owne times as an old storie bee. 50
Be not concern'd: studie not why, nor when;
Doe not so much as not beleeve a man.
For though to erre, be worst, to try truths forth,
Is far more businesse, than this world is worth.
The world is but a carkasse; thou art fed 55

23–24. see Genesis i : 16. The sun was not created until the fourth day.

29. *forgetting her:* to Ben Jonson's remark that only the Virgin Mary could sustain such adulation, Donne retorted "that he described the Idea of a Woman, and not as she was."

36. *Yearely:* only two "anniversaries" were in fact written.

46. *Bowle:* the communion chalice.

By it, but as a worme, that carkasse bred;
And why should'st thou, poore worme, consider more,
When this world will grow better than before,
Than those thy fellow wormes doe thinke upon
That carkasses last resurrection. 60
Forget this world, and scarce thinke of it so,
As of old clothes, cast off a yeare agoe.
To be thus stupid is Alacritie;
Men thus Lethargique have best Memory.
Look upward; that's towards her, whose happy state 65
We now lament not, but congratulate.
Shee, to whom all this world was but a stage,
Where all sat harkning how her youthfull age
Should be emploi'd, because in all shee did,
Some Figure of the Golden times was hid; 70
Who could not lacke, what e'r this world could give,
Because shee was the forme, that made it live;
Nor could complaine, that this world was unfit
To be staid in, then when shee was in it;
Shee that first tried indifferent desires 75
By vertue, and vertue by religious fires,
Shee to whose person Paradise adher'd,
As Courts to Princes, shee whose eyes enspheard
Star-light enough, t'have made the South controule,
(Had shee beene there) the Star-full Northerne Pole, 80
Shee, shee is gone; she is gone; when thou knowest this,
What fragmentary rubbidge this world is
Thou knowest, and that it is not worth a thought;
He honors it too much that thinkes it nought. 84
Thinke then, my soule, that death is but a Groome,
Which brings a Taper to the outward roome,
Whence thou spiest first a little glimmering light,
And after brings it nearer to thy sight:
For such approaches doth heaven make in death.
Thinke thy selfe labouring now with broken breath, 90
And thinke those broken and soft Notes to bee

Contemplation of our state in our death-bed.

75. *tried:* tested.

Division, and thy happyest Harmonie.
Thinke thee laid on thy death-bed, loose and slacke;
And thinke that, but unbinding of a packe,
To take one precious thing, thy soule from thence. 95
Thinke thy selfe parch'd with fevers violence,
Anger thine ague more, by calling it
Thy Physicke; chide the slackness of the fit.
Thinke that thou hear'st thy knell, and think no more,
But that, as Bels cal'd thee to Church before, 100
So this, to the Triumphant Church, calls thee.
Thinke Satans Sergeants round about thee bee,
And thinke that but for Legacies they thrust;
Give one thy Pride, to'another give thy Lust:
Give them those sinnes which they gave thee before, 105
And trust th'immaculate blood to wash thy score.
Thinke thy friends weeping round, and thinke that they
Weepe but because they goe not yet thy way.
Thinke that they close thine eyes, and thinke in this,
That they confesse much in the world, amisse, 110
Who dare not trust a dead mans eye with that,
Which they from God, and Angels cover not.
Thinke that they shroud thee up, and think from thence
They reinvest thee in white innocence.
Thinke that thy body rots, and (if so low, 115
Thy soule exalted so, thy thoughts can goe,)
Think thee a Prince, who of themselves create
Wormes which insensibly devoure their State.
Thinke that they bury thee, and thinke that right
Laies thee to sleepe but a Saint Lucies night. 120
Thinke these things cheerefully: and if thou bee
Drowsie or slacke, remember then that shee,
Shee whose Complexion was so even made,
That which of her Ingredients should invade
The other three, no Feare, no Art could guesse: 125

---

123. *Complexion:* the relative proportion of the four humors (hot, cold, moist, dry) that determined a person's "temperament." (It could be gauged by the color of the face, hence the modern sense of the word.) Illness and mortality were attributed to an imbalance: see "The Good-Morrow," line 19.

So far were all remov'd from more or lesse.
But as in Mithridate, or just perfumes,
Where all good things being met, no one presumes
To governe, or to triumph on the rest,
Only because all were, no part was best. 130
And as, though all doe know, that quantities
Are made of lines, and lines from Points arise,
None can these lines or quantities unjoynt,
And say this is a line, or this a point,
So though the Elements and Humors were 135
In her, one could not say, this governes there.
Whose even constitution might have wonne
Any disease to venter on the Sunne,
Rather than her: and make a spirit feare,
That hee to disuniting subject were. 140
To whose proportions if we would compare
Cubes, th'are unstable; Circles, Angular;
She who was such a chaine as Fate employes
To bring mankinde all Fortunes it enjoyes;
So fast, so even wrought, as one would thinke, 145
No Accident could threaten any linke;
Shee, shee embrac'd a sicknesse, gave it meat,
The purest blood, and breath, that e'r it eate;
And hath taught us, that though a good man hath
Title to heaven, and plead it by his Faith, 150
And though he may pretend a conquest, since
Heaven was content to suffer violence,
Yea though hee plead a long possession too,
(For they're in heaven on earth who heavens workes do)
Though hee had right and power and place, before, 155
Yet Death must usher, and unlocke the doore.
Thinke further on thy selfe, my Soule, and thinke
How thou at first wast made but in a sinke;
Thinke that it argued some infirmitie,
That those two soules, which then thou foundst in me, 160
Thou fedst upon, and drewst into thee, both

Incommodities of the Soule in the Body.

127. *Mithridate:* a universal antidote.
138. *Sunne:* by definition incorruptible, as Spirits (line 139) are indivisible.
152. *violence:* see Matthew 11 : 12.

My second soule of sense, and first of growth.
Thinke but how poore thou wast, how obnoxious;
Whom a small lumpe of flesh could poyson thus.
This curded milke, this poore unlittered whelpe 165
My body, could, beyond escape or helpe,
Infect thee with Originall sinne, and thou
Couldst neither then refuse, nor leave it now.
Thinke that no stubborne sullen Anchorit,
Which fixt to a pillar, or a grave, doth sit 170
Bedded, and bath'd in all his ordures, dwels
So fowly as our Soules in their first-built Cels.
Thinke in how poore a prison thou didst lie
After, enabled but to suck, and crie.
Thinke, when'twas growne to most, 'twas a poore Inne, 175
A Province pack'd up in two yards of skinne,
And that usurp'd or threatned with the rage
Of sicknesses, or their true mother, Age.
But thinke that Death hath now enfranchis'd thee, 179
Thou hast thy'expansion now, and libertie; *Her liberty by death.*
Thinke that a rustie Peece, discharg'd, is flowne
In peeces, and the bullet is his owne,
And freely flies: This to thy Soule allow,
Thinke thy shell broke, thinke thy Soule hatch'd but now.
And think this slow-pac'd soule, which late did cleave 185
To'a body, and went but by the bodies leave,
Twenty, perchance, or thirty mile a day,
Dispatches in a minute all the way
Twixt heaven, and earth; she stayes not in the ayre,
To looke what Meteors there themselves prepare; 190
She carries no desire to know, nor sense,
Whether th'ayres middle region be intense;
For th'Element of fire, she doth not know,
Whether she past by such a place or no;
She baits not at the Moone, nor cares to trie 195
Whether in that new world, men live, and die.
Venus retards her not, to'enquire, how shee
Can, (being one starre) *Hesper,* and *Vesper* bee;
Hee that charm'd *Argus* eyes, sweet *Mercury,*
Workes not on her, who now is growne all eye; 200

Who, if she meet the body of the Sunne,
Goes through, not staying till his course be runne;
Who findes in *Mars* his Campe no corps of Guard;
Nor is by *Jove,* nor by his father barr'd;
But ere she can consider how she went, **205**
At once is at, and through the Firmament.
And as these starres were but so many beads
Strung on one string, speed undistinguish'd leads
Her through those Spheares, as through the beads, a string,
Whose quick succession makes it still one thing: **210**
As doth the pith, which, lest our bodies slacke,
Strings fast the little bones of necke, and backe;
So by the Soule doth death string Heaven and Earth;
For when our Soule enjoyes this her third birth,
(Creation gave her one, a second, grace,) **215**
Heaven is as neare, and present to her face,
As colours are, and objects, in a roome
Where darknesse was before, when Tapers come.
This must, my Soule, thy long-short Progresse bee;
To'advance these thoughts, remember then, that shee, **220**
Shee, whose faire body no such prison was,
But that a Soule might well be pleas'd to passe
An age in her; she whose rich beauty lent
Mintage to other beauties, for they went
But for so much as they were like to her; **225**
Shee, in whose body (if we dare preferre
This low world, to so high a marke as shee,)
The Westerne treasure, Easterne spicerie,
Europe, and Afrique, and the unknowne rest
Were easily found, or what in them was best; **230**
And when w'have made this large discoverie
Of all, in her some one part then will bee
Twenty such parts, whose plenty and riches is
Enough to make twenty such worlds as this;
Shee, whom had they knowne who did first betroth **235**
The Tutelar Angels, and assign'd one, both
To Nations, Cities, and to Companies,

---

204. *his father:* Saturn.

To Functions, Offices, and Dignities,
And to each severall man, to him, and him,
They would have given her one for every limbe; 240
She, of whose soule, if wee may say, 'twas Gold,
Her body was th'Electrum, and did hold
Many degrees of that; wee understood
Her by her sight; her pure, and eloquent blood
Spoke in her cheekes, and so distinctly wrought, 245
That one might almost say, her body thought;
Shee, shee, thus richly and largely hous'd, is gone:
And chides us slow-pac'd snailes who crawle upon
Our prisons prison, earth, nor thinke us well,
Longer, than whil'st wee beare our brittle shell. 250
But 'twere but little to have chang'd our roome,
If, as we were in this our living Tombe
Oppress'd with ignorance, wee still were so.
Poore soule, in this thy flesh what dost thou know?
Thou know'st thy selfe so little, as thou know'st not, 255
How thou didst die, nor how thou wast begot.
Thou neither know'st, how thou at first cam'st in,
Nor how thou took'st the poyson of mans sinne.
Nor dost thou, (though thou know'st, that thou art so)
By what way thou art made immortall, know. 260
Thou art too narrow, wretch, to comprehend
Even thy selfe: yea though thou wouldst but bend
To know thy body. Have not all soules thought
For many ages, that our body'is wrought
Of Ayre, and Fire, and other Elements? 265
And now they thinke of new ingredients,
And one Soule thinkes one, and another way
Another thinkes, and 'tis an even lay.
Knowst thou but how the stone doth enter in
The bladders cave, and never breake the skinne? 270
Know'st thou how blood, which to the heart doth flow,
Doth from one ventricle to th'other goe?
And for the putrid stuffe, which thou dost spit,

Her ignorance in this life and knowledge in the next.

---

242. *Electrum:* not pure gold, but alloyed with a little silver.
271–272. This was written fourteen years before the publication of Harvey's treatise on the circulation of the blood.

Know'st thou how thy lungs have attracted it?
There are no passages, so that there is 275
(For ought thou know'st) piercing of substances.
And of those many opinions which men raise
Of Nailes and Haires, dost thou know which to praise?
What hope have wee to know our selves, when wee
Know not the least things, which for our use be? 280
Wee see in Authors, too stiffe to recant,
A hundred controversies of an Ant;
And yet one watches, starves, freeses, and sweats,
To know but Catechismes and Alphabets
Of unconcerning things, matters of fact; 285
How others on our stage their parts did Act;
What *Caesar* did, yea, and what *Cicero* said.
Why grasse is greene, or why our blood is red,
Are mysteries which none have reach'd unto.
In this low forme, poore soule, what wilt thou doe? 290
When wilt thou shake off this Pedantery,
Of being taught by sense, and Fantasie?
Thou look'st through spectacles; small things seeme great
Below; But up unto the watch-towre get,
And see all things despoyl'd of fallacies: 295
Thou shalt not peepe through lattices of eyes,
Nor heare through Labyrinths of eares, nor learne
By circuit, or collections to discerne.
In heaven thou straight know'st all, concerning it,
And what concernes it not, shalt straight forget. 300
There thou (but in no other schoole) maist bee
Perchance, as learned, and as full, as shee,
Shee who all libraries had thoroughly read
At home in her owne thoughts, and practised
So much good as would make as many more: 305
Shee whose example they must all implore,
Who would or doe, or thinke well, and confesse
That all the vertuous Actions they expresse,
Are but a new, and worse edition
Of her some one thought, or one action: 310

292. *Fantasie:* not fancies, but Aristotle's *phantasmata,* conveyed to the intellect by the senses.

She who in th'art of knowing Heaven, was growne
Here upon earth, to such perfection,
That she hath, ever since to Heaven she came,
(In a far fairer print,) but read the same:
Shee, shee not satisfied with all this waight, 315
(For so much knowledge, as would over-fraight
Another, did but ballast her) is gone
As well t'enjoy, as get perfection.
And cals us after her, in that shee tooke, 319
(Taking her selfe) our best, and worthiest booke.

Of our company in this life, and in the next.

Returne not, my Soule, from this extasie,
And meditation of what thou shalt bee,
To earthly thoughts, till it to thee appeare,
With whom thy conversation must be there.
With whom wilt thou converse? what station 325
Canst thou choose out, free from infection,
That will not give thee theirs, nor drinke in thine?
Shalt thou not finde a spungie slacke Divine
Drinke and sucke in th'instructions of Great men,
And for the word of God, vent them agen? 330
Are there not some Courts (and then, no things bee
So like as Courts) which, in this let us see,
That wits and tongues of Libellers are weake,
Because they do more ill, than these can speake?
The poyson's gone through all, poysons affect 335
Chiefly the chiefest parts, but some effect
In nailes, and haires, yea excrements, will show;
So lyes the poyson of sinne in the most low.
Up, up, my drowsie Soule, where thy new eare
Shall in the Angels songs no discord heare; 340
Where thou shalt see the blessed Mother-maid
Joy in not being that, which men have said.
Where she is exalted more for being good,
Than for her interest of Mother-hood.
Up to those Patriarchs, which did longer sit 345
Expecting Christ, than they'have enjoy'd him yet.
Up to those Prophets, which now gladly see
Their Prophesies growne to be Historie.
Up to th'Apostles, who did bravely runne

All the Suns course, with more light than the Sunne. 350
Up to those Martyrs, who did calmly bleed
Oyle to th'Apostles Lamps, dew to their seed.
Up to those Virgins, who thought, that almost
They made joyntenants with the Holy Ghost,
If they to any should his Temple give. 355
Up, up, for in that squadron there doth live
She, who hath carried thither new degrees
(As to their number) to their dignities.
Shee, who being to her selfe a State, injoy'd
All royalties which any State employ'd; 360
For shee made warres, and triumph'd; reason still
Did not o'rthrow, but rectifie her will:
And she made peace, for no peace is like this,
That beauty, and chastity together kisse:
She did high justice, for she crucified 365
Every first motion of rebellious pride:
And she gave pardons, and was liberall,
For, onely her selfe except, she pardon'd all:
Shee coy'nd, in this, that her impressions gave
To all our actions all the worth they have: 370
She gave protections; the thoughts of her brest
Satans rude Officers could ne'r arrest.
As these prerogatives being met in one,
Made her a soveraigne State; religion
Made her a Church; and these two made her all. 375
She who was all this All, and could not fall
To worse, by company, (for she was still
More Antidote, than all the world was ill,)
Shee, shee doth leave it, and by Death, survive
All this, in Heaven; whither who doth not strive 380
The more, because shees there, he doth not know
That accidentall joyes in Heaven doe grow.
But pause, my soule; And study, ere thou fall
On accidentall joyes, th'essentiall.
Still before Accessories doe abide
A triall, must the principall be tride.
And what essentiall joy can'st thou expect
Here upon earth? what permanent effect

Of essentiall joy in this life and in the next.

Of transitory causes? Dost thou love
Beauty? (And beauty worthy'st is to move) 390
Poore cousened cousenor, *that* she, and *that* thou,
Which did begin to love, are neither now;
You are both fluid, chang'd since yesterday;
Next day repaires, (but ill) last dayes decay.
Nor are, (although the river keepe the name) 395
Yesterdaies waters, and to daies the same.
So flowes her face, and thine eyes, neither now
That Saint, nor Pilgrime, which your loving vow
Concern'd, remaines; but whil'st you thinke you bee
Constant, you'are hourely in inconstancie. 400
Honour may have pretence unto our love,
Because that God did live so long above
Without this Honour, and then lov'd it so,
That he at last made Creatures to bestow
Honour on him; not that he needed it, 405
But that, to his hands, man might grow more fit.
But since all Honours from inferiours flow,
(For they doe give it; Princes doe but shew
Whom they would have so honor'd) and that this
On such opinions, and capacities 410
Is built, as rise and fall, to more and lesse:
Alas, 'tis but a casuall happinesse.
Hath ever any man to'himselfe assign'd
This or that happinesse to'arrest his minde,
But that another man which takes a worse, 415
Thinks him a fool for having tane that course?
They who did labour Babels tower to'erect,
Might have considered, that for that effect,
All this whole solid Earth could not allow
Nor furnish forth materialls enow; 420
And that this Center, to raise such a place,
Was farre too little, to have beene the Base;
No more affords this world, foundation
To erect true joy, were all the meanes in one.
But as the Heathen made them severall gods, 425
Of all Gods Benefits, and all his Rods,
(For as the Wine, and Corne, and Onions are

Gods unto them, so Agues bee, and Warre)
And as by changing that whole precious Gold
To such small Copper coynes, they lost the old, 430
And lost their only God, who ever must
Be sought alone, and not in such a thrust:
So much mankinde true happinesse mistakes;
No Joy enjoyes that man, that many makes.
Then, Soule, to thy first pitch worke up againe; 435
Know that all lines which circles doe containe,
For once that they the Center touch, doe touch
Twice the circumference; and be thou such;
Double on heaven thy thoughts on earth emploid;
All will not serve; Only who have enjoy'd 440
The sight of God, in fulnesse, can thinke it;
For it is both the object, and the wit.
This is essentiall joy, where neither hee
Can suffer diminution, nor wee;
'Tis such a full, and such a filling good, 445
Had th'Angels once look'd on him, they had stood.
To fill the place of one of them, or more,
Shee whom wee celebrate, is gone before.
She, who had Here so much essentiall joy,
As no chance could distract, much lesse destroy; 450
Who with Gods presence was acquainted so,
(Hearing, and speaking to him) as to know
His face in any naturall Stone, or Tree,
Better than when in Images they bee:
Who kept by diligent devotion, 455
Gods Image, in such reparation,
Within her heart, that what decay was growne,
Was her first Parents fault, and not her owne:
Who being solicited to any act,
Still heard God pleading his safe precontract; 460
Who by a faithfull confidence, was here
Betroth'd to God, and now is married there;
Whose twilights were more cleare, than our mid-day;
Who dreamt devoutlier, than most use to pray;
Who being here fil'd with grace, yet strove to bee, 465
Both where more grace, and more capacitie

At once is given: she to Heaven is gone,
Who made this world in some proportion
A heaven, and here, became unto us all,
Joy, (as our joyes admit) essentiall. 470
But could this low world joyes essentiall touch,
Heavens accidentall joyes would passe them much.
How poore and lame, must then our casuall bee?
If thy Prince will his subjects to call thee
My Lord, and this doe swell thee, thou art than, 475
By being greater, growne to bee lesse Man.
When no Physitian of redresse can speake,
A joyfull casuall violence may breake
A dangerous Apostem in thy breast;
And whil'st thou joyest in this, the dangerous rest, 480
The bag may rise up, and so strangle thee.
What e'r was casual, may ever bee.
What should the nature change? Or make the same
Certaine, which was but casuall, when it came?
All casuall joy doth loud and plainly say, 485
Only by comming, that it can away.
Only in Heaven joyes strength is never spent;
And accidentall things are permanent.
Joy of a soules arrivall ne'r decaies;
For that soule ever joyes and ever staies. 490
Joy that their last great Consummation
Approaches in the resurrection;
When earthly bodies more celestiall
Shall be, than Angels were, for they could fall;
This kinde of joy doth every day admit 495
Degrees of growth, but none of losing it.
In this fresh joy, 'tis no small part, that shee,
Shee, in whose goodnesse, he that names degree,
Doth injure her; ('Tis losse to be cal'd best,
There where the stuffe is not such as the rest) 500
Shee, who left such a bodie, as even shee
Only in Heaven could learne, how it can bee
Made better; for shee rather was two soules,

Of accidentall joys in both places.

---

473. *casuall:* fortuitous.
479. *Apostem:* abscess ("imposthume").

Or like to full on both sides written Rols,
Where eyes might reade upon the outward skin, 505
As strong Records for God, as mindes within;
Shee, who by making full perfection grow,
Peeces a Circle, and still keepes it so,
Long'd for, and longing for it, to heaven is gone,
Where shee receives, and gives addition. 510
Here in a place, where mis-devotion frames — ***Conclusion.***
A thousand Prayers to Saints, whose very names
The ancient Church knew not, Heaven knows not yet:
And where, what lawes of Poetry admit,
Lawes of Religion have at least the same, 515
Immortall Maide, I might invoke thy name.
Could any Saint provoke that appetite,
Thou here should'st make me a French convertite.
But thou would'st not; nor would'st thou be content,
To take this, for my second yeares true Rent, 520
Did this Coine beare any other stampe, than his,
That gave thee power to doe, me, to say this.
Since his will is, that to posteritie,
Thou should'st for life, and death, a patterne bee,
And that the world should notice have of this, 525
The purpose, and th'Authoritie is his;
Thou art the Proclamation; and I am
The Trumpet, at whose voyce the people came.

---

511. *here:* France, where Donne was visiting Elizabeth Drury's parents.

DIVINE POEMS

Holy Sonnets

I

Thou hast made me, And shall thy worke decay?
Repaire me now, for now mine end doth haste,

I runne to death, and death meets me as fast,
And all my pleasures are like yesterday;
I dare not move my dimme eyes any way, 5
Despaire behind, and death before doth cast
Such terrour, and my feebled flesh doth waste
By sinne in it, which it t'wards hell doth weigh;
Onely thou art above, and when towards thee
By thy leave I can looke, I rise againe; 10
But our old subtle foe so tempteth me,
That not one houre my selfe I can sustaine;
Thy Grace may wing me to prevent his art,
And thou like Adamant draw mine iron heart.

V

I am a little world made cunningly
Of Elements, and an Angelike spright,
But black sinne hath betraid to endlesse night
My worlds both parts, and (oh) both parts must die.
You which beyond that heaven which was most high 5
Have found new sphears, and of new lands can write,
Powre new seas in mine eyes, that so I might
Drowne my world with my weeping earnestly,
Or wash it if it must be drown'd no more:
But oh it must be burnt! alas the fire 10
Of lust and envie have burnt it heretofore,
And made it fouler; Let their flames retire,
And burne me ô Lord, with a fiery zeale
Of thee and thy house, which doth in eating heale.

VI

This is my playes last scene, here heavens appoint
My pilgrimages last mile; and my race
Idly, yet quickly runne, hath this last pace,
My spans last inch, my minutes latest point,
And gluttonous death, will instantly unjoynt 5
My body, and soule, and I shall sleepe a space,
But my'ever-waking part shall see that face,
Whose feare already shakes my every joynt:
Then, as my soule, to'heaven her first seate, takes flight,

And earth-borne body, in the earth shall dwell, 10
So, fall my sinnes, that all may have their right,
To where they'are bred, and would presse me, to hell.
Impute me righteous, thus purg'd of evill,
For thus I leave the world, the flesh, and devill.

VII

At the round earths imagin'd corners, blow
Your trumpets, Angells, and arise, arise
From death, you numberlesse infinities
Of soules, and to your scattred bodies goe,
All whom the flood did, and fire shall o'erthrow, 5
All whom warre, dearth, age, agues, tyrannies,
Despaire, law, chance, hath slaine, and you whose eyes,
Shall behold God, and never tast deaths woe.
But let them sleepe, Lord, and mee mourne a space,
For, if above all these, my sinnes abound, 10
'Tis late to aske abundance of thy grace,
When wee are there; here on this lowly ground,
Teach mee how to repent; for that's as good
As if thou'hadst seal'd my pardon, with thy blood.

IX

If poysonous mineralls, and if that tree,
Whose fruit threw death on else immortall us,
If lecherous goats, if serpents envious
Cannot be damn'd; Alas; why should I bee?
Why should intent or reason, borne in mee, 5
Make sinnes, else equall, in mee more heinous?
And mercy being easie, and glorious
To God, in his sterne wrath, why threatens hee?
But who am I, that dare dispute with thee?
O God, Oh! of thine onely worthy blood, 10
And my teares, make a heavenly Lethean flood,
And drowne in it my sinnes blacke memorie;
That thou remember them, some claime as debt,
I thinke it mercy, if thou wilt forget.

X

Death be not proud, though some have called thee
Mighty and dreadfull, for, thou art not soe,
For, those, whom thou think'st, thou dost overthrow,
Die not, poore death, nor yet canst thou kill mee.
From rest and sleepe, which but thy pictures bee, 5
Much pleasure, then from thee, much more must flow,
And soonest our best men with thee doe goe,
Rest of their bones, and soules deliverie.
Thou art slave to Fate, Chance, kings, and desperate men,
And dost with poyson, warre, and sicknesse dwell, 10
And poppie, or charmes can make us sleepe as well,
And better than thy stroake; why swell'st thou then?
One short sleepe past, wee wake eternally,
And death shall be no more; death, thou shalt die.

XIV

Batter my heart, three person'd God; for, you
As yet but knocke, breathe, shine, and seeke to mend;
That I may rise, and stand, o'erthrow mee,'and bend
Your force, to breake, blowe, burn and make me new.
I, like an usurpt towne, to'another due, 5
Labour to'admit you, but Oh, to no end,
Reason your viceroy in mee, mee should defend,
But is captiv'd, and proves weake or untrue.
Yet dearly'I love you,'and would be loved faine,
But am betroth'd unto your enemie: 10
Divorce mee,'untie, or breake that knot againe,
Take mee to you, imprison mee, for I
Except you'enthrall mee, never shall be free,
Nor ever chast, except you ravish mee.

Good Friday, 1613. Riding Westward

Let mans Soule be a Spheare, and then, in this,
The intelligence that moves, devotion is,
And as the other Spheares, by being growne
Subject to forraigne motions, lose their owne
And being by others hurried every day, 5
Scarce in a yeare their naturall forme obey:
Pleasure or businesse, so, our Soules admit
For their first mover, and are whirld by it.
Hence is't, that I am carryed towards the West
This day, when my Soules forme bends toward the East. 10
There I should see a Sunne, by rising set,
And by that setting endlesse day beget;
But that Christ on this Crosse, did rise and fall,
Sinne had eternally benighted all.
Yet dare I'almost be glad, I do not see 15
That spectacle of too much weight for mee.
Who sees Gods face, that is selfe life, must dye;
What a death were it then to see God dye?
It made his owne Lieutenant Nature shrinke,
It made his footstoole crack, and the Sunne winke. 20
Could I behold those hands which span the Poles,
And tune all spheares at once, peirc'd with those holes?
Could I behold that endlesse height which is
Zenith to us, and to'our Antipodes,
Humbled below us? or that blood which is 25
The seat of all our Soules, if not of his,
Make durt of dust, or that flesh which was worne
By God, for his apparell, rag'd, and torne?
If on these things I durst not looke, durst I
Upon his miserable mother cast mine eye, 30
Who was Gods partner here, and furnish'd thus
Halfe of that Sacrifice, which ransom'd us?

---

2. *intelligence:* the power who moves a crystalline sphere that carries a planet.
11. *There:* eastward.

Though these things, as I ride, be from mine eye,
They'are present yet unto my memory,
For that looks towards them; and thou look'st towards mee, 35
O Saviour, as thou hang'st upon the tree;
I turne my backe to thee, but to receive
Corrections, till thy mercies bid thee leave.
O thinke mee worth thine anger, punish mee,
Burne off my rusts, and my deformity, 40
Restore thine Image, so much, by thy grace,
That thou may'st know mee, and I'll turne my face.

A Hymne to God the Father

I

Wilt thou forgive that sinne where I begunne,
Which is my sin, though it were done before?
Wilt thou forgive those sinnes, through which I runne,
And do run still: though still I do deplore?
When thou hast done, thou hast not done, 5
For, I have more.

II

Wilt thou forgive that sinne by which I'have wonne
Others to sinne? and, made my sinne their doore?
Wilt thou forgive that sinne which I did shunne
A yeare, or two: but wallowed in, a score? 10
When thou hast done, thou hast not done,
For I have more.

III

I have a sinne of feare, that when I have spunne
My last thred, I shall perish on the shore;

Written during Donne's serious illness in the winter of 1623. The refrain contains a recurrent echo of his name.

1. *that sinne:* the Original Sin of Adam, which darkened the intellect and weakened the will of each of his descendants.

Sweare by thy selfe, that at my death thy sonne 15
Shall shine as he shines now, and heretofore;
And, having done that, Thou haste done,
I feare no more.

15. Here "son" echoes "sun" as in other lines "done" echoes "Donne."

Hymne to God My God, in My Sicknesse

Since I am comming to that Holy roome,
Where, with thy Quire of Saints for evermore,
I shall be made thy Musique; As I come
I tune the Instrument here at the dore,
And what I must doe then, thinke here before. 5

Whilst my Physitians by their love are growne
Cosmographers, and I their Mapp, who lie
Flat on this bed, that by them may be showne
That this is my South-west discoverie
Per fretum febris, by these streights to die, 10

I joy, that in these straits, I see my West;
For, though theire currants yeeld returne to none,
What shall my West hurt me? As West and East
In all flatt Maps (and I am one) are one,
So death doth touch the Resurrection. 15

Is the Pacifique Sea my home? Or are
The Easterne riches? Is *Jerusalem?*
Anyan, and *Magellan*, and *Gibraltare*,
All streights, and none but streights, are wayes to them,
Whether where *Japhet* dwelt, or *Cham*, or *Sem*. 20

Written March 23, 1630–1631, eight days before Donne's death.
10. *Per fretum febris:* through the strait of fever.
18. *Anyan:* Bering Strait, through which the traveller from the fabled Northwest Passage would reach "the easterne riches."
20. *Japhet, Cham, Sem:* the three sons of Noah, whose descendants peopled the earth.

We thinke that *Paradise* and *Calvarie,*
Christs Crosse, and *Adams* tree, stood in one place;
Looke, Lord, and finde both *Adams* met in me;
As the first *Adams* sweat surrounds my face,
May the last *Adams* blood my soule embrace. 25

So, in his purple wrapp'd receive mee Lord,
By these his thornes give me his other Crowne;
And as to others soules I preach'd thy word,
Be this my Text, my Sermon to mine owne.
Therfore that he may raise the Lord throws down. 30

21–22. A common patristic doctrine.

Ben Jonson

(1573–1637)

JONSON had the great William Camden for master at Westminster School. It is not clear how he got there at all, for there was no money in the family, and his withdrawal from school to be apprenticed a bricklayer was thoroughly in keeping with his station. But Camden's precepts stayed by him: not only the injunction to work out his sense in prose before turning it into verse, but the conviction that a man was obliged to acquire all the learning he could master, and the vocation of bringing to the workings of the mind, even its casual or ephemeral workings, whatever analogies were discernible with all that antiquity had thought and said.

He attached himself to a company of actors, began writing plays, got into trouble more than once with the law, even carried to his grave the hangman's brand on his thumb; but never amid the twistings and turnings of a merely picturesque existence lost sight of his self-imposed obligation to reform the English stage according to the best models, and simultaneously to establish, in his own person, the dignity of the profession of letters. By 1616 he had so far succeeded that James I had granted him a pension, chiefly to acknowledge his skill at writing court entertainments. In the same year, with unheard-of coolness, he published his *Works* in folio, challenging by such a format comparison with the masterwork of antiquity. This collection of one man's poems, playscripts, and masques was as much a deed as a book: a gesture of annexation to the English tongue of multiple genres never before so diligently and knowingly practiced: tragedy, comedy, satire, epigram, lyric. Over and over, page after page, in the 1616 Folio and in subsequent work, he proves the amenability, in his hands, of racy and natural English to a discipline of perspicuity without dilution, elegance without ornamentation, ordonnance without cramping, and vigor without looseness.

> Have you seene but a bright Lillie grow
> Before rude hands have touch'd it?

—over running speech the accents fall with elusive cunning.

> And why to me this, thou lame Lord of fire? . . .
> I ne'er attempted, Vulcan, 'gainst thy life,
> Nor made least line of love to thy loose Wife

—the stretched and amplified utterance not of a special domain in which poetry is recited, but of some ideal community of discourse "within which," as Mr. John Hollander puts it, "the literary dialect would be as speech," and Vulcan neither a resuscitated god nor a figure of periphrasis, but rather part of the normal furnishing of the minds of proper men.

Since Jonson there has been no such man of letters. Dryden, with his formal occasions and heroic plays, is pedantic by comparison; Samuel Johnson, one man when he talks, is another, careful of dignity, when he writes; and already indeed by Samuel Johnson's time there was no court, no focus of taste and power worth bothering about.

The 1616 Folio contained the *Epigrammes* and a carefully chosen series of fifteen poems called *The Forrest*. He chose *The Underwood* as the title for a further series of poems but did not live to make the selection, and *The Underwood* became instead in the posthumous 1640 Folio the title for all the uncollected verses its editors were able to find among Jonson's papers, including, presumably, some pieces he had intended for the projected second series of epigrams. It is pointless now to try to extricate from the ruins of his editorial scheme clues to the balance he had intended to establish among its pieces; the student should at least bear in mind that the poems have come to us wearing a more miscellaneous look than their author intended them to have. "A Celebration of Charis, in Ten Lyrick Peeces," though neater in its unity than the longer collection would have been, illustrates his intuitions of order; it is perhaps the earliest *suite* of poems in the language. He made it by prefixing a poem written in his fiftieth year to nine others dating from perhaps ten years before, and incorporating two stanzas sung in one of his plays.

TEXT: Jonson's *Works* were edited in 11 volumes by C. H. Herford and Percy and Evelyn Simpson (Oxford, 1925–1952).

COMMENT: Marchette Chute, *Ben Jonson of Westminster* (New York, 1953), is a popular biography. Most criticism of Jonson concentrates on the plays, but the reader should consult Wesley Trimpi, *Ben Jonson's Poems: a Study of the Plain Style* (Stanford, 1962), Geoffrey Walton, *Metaphysical to Augustan* (London, 1955) and John Hollander's introduction to his selection of Jonson's lyrics (New York, 1961).

THE EPIGRAMS

[PUBLISHED 1616]

XI

On Some-thing, That Walkes Some-where

At court I met it, in clothes brave enough,
To be a courtier; and lookes grave enough,
To seeme a statesman: as I neere it came,
It made me a great face, I ask'd the name.
A lord, it cryed, buried in flesh, and blood, 5
And such from whom let no man hope least good,
For I will doe none: and as little ill,
For I will dare none. Good Lord, walke dead still.

XIII

To Doctor Empirick

When men a dangerous disease did scape,
Of old, they gave a cock to Aesculape;

Let me give two: that doubly am got free,
From my diseases danger, and from thee.

XV

On Court-worme

All men are wormes: But this no man. In silke
'Twas brought to court first wrapt, and white as milke;
Where, afterwards, it grew a butter-flye:
Which was a cater-piller. So t'will dye.

XXII

On My First Daughter

Here lyes to each her parents ruth,
Mary, the daughter of their youth:
Yet, all heavens gifts, being heavens due,
It makes the father, lesse, to rue.
At sixe moneths end, shee parted hence 5
With safetie of her innocence;
Whose soule heavens Queene, (whose name shee beares)
In comfort of her mothers teares,
Hath plac'd amongst her virgin-traine:
Where, while that sever'd doth remaine, 10
This grave partakes the fleshly birth.
Which cover lightly, gentle earth.

XL

On Margaret Ratcliffe

M arble, weepe, for thou dost cover
A dead beautie under-neath thee,
R ich, as nature could bequeath thee:
G rant then, no rude hand remove her.
A ll the gazers on the skies 5
R ead not in faire heavens storie,

E xpresser truth, or truer glorie,
T han they might in her bright eyes.
R are, as wonder, was her wit;
A nd like Nectar ever flowing: 10
T ill time, strong by her bestowing,
C onquer'd hath both life and it.
L ife, whose griefe was out of fashion,
I n these times. Few so have ru'de
F ate, in a brother. To conclude, 15
F or wit, feature, and true passion,
E arth, thou hast not such another.

14–15. She died in 1599, aged twenty-four, of grief over the death of her brother, Sir Alexander Radcliffe, in the Irish war.

XLV

On My First Sonne

Farewell, thou child of my right hand, and joy;
My sinne was too much hope of thee, lov'd boy,
Seven yeeres tho'wert lent to me, and I thee pay,
Exacted by thy fate, on the just day.
O, could I loose all father, now. For why 5
Will man lament the state he should envie?
To have so soone scap'd worlds, and fleshes rage,
And, if no other miserie, yet age?
Rest in soft peace, and, ask'd, say here doth lye
Ben. Jonson his best piece of poetrie. 10
For whose sake, hence-forth, all his vowes be such,
As what he loves may never like too much.

---

1. *child of my right hand:* the Hebrew meaning of "Benjamin." Ben Jr. died in 1603, of plague.
10. *poetrie:* in the literal Greek sense, "something made."

LXXVI

On Lucy Countesse of Bedford

This morning, timely rapt with holy fire,
I thought to forme unto my zealous Muse,
What kinde of creature I could most desire,
To honor, serve, and love; as Poets use.
I meant to make her faire, and free, and wise, 5
Of greatest bloud, and yet more good than great;
I meant the day-starre should not brighter rise,
Nor lend like influence from his lucent seat.
I meant shee should be curteous, facile, sweet,
Hating that solemne vice of greatnesse, pride; 10
I meant each softest vertue, there should meet,
Fit in that softer bosome to reside.
Onely a learned, and a manly soule
I purpos'd her; that should, with even powers,
The rock, the spindle, and the sheeres controule 15
Of destinie, and spin her own free houres.
Such when I meant to faine, and wish'd to see,
My Muse bad, *Bedford* write, and that was shee.

This brilliant court figure and patroness of literary men befriended Jonson, Donne, and other poets.

15. *rock:* distaff. The three Fates of Greek mythology spun the thread of life, determined its length, and cut it off.

XCVI

To John Donne

Who shall doubt, Donne, where I a Poet bee,
When I dare send my Epigrammes to thee?
That so alone canst judge, so'alone dost make:
And, in thy censures, evenly, dost take
As free simplicitie, to dis-avow, 5

---

1. *where:* slurred pronunciation of "whether."

As thou hast best authoritie, t'allow.
Reade all I send: and, if I find but one
Mark'd by thy hand, and with the better stone,
My title's seal'd. Those that for claps doe write,
Let pui'nees, porters, players praise delight, 10
And, till they burst, their backs, like asses load:
A man should seeke great glorie, and not broad.

10. *pui'nees:* juniors. Compare this word with the modern "puny."

CI

Inviting a Friend to Supper

To night, grave sir, both my poore house, and I
Doe equally desire your companie:
Not that we thinke us worthy such a ghest,
But that your worth will dignifie our feast,
With those that come; whose grace may make that seeme 5
Something, which, else, could hope for no esteeme.
It is the faire acceptance, Sir, creates
The entertaynment perfect: not the cates.
Yet shall you have, to rectifie your palate,
An olive, capers, or some better sallade 10
Ushring the mutton; with a short-leg'd hen,
If we can get her, full of egs, and then,
Limmons, and wine for sauce: to these, a coney
Is not to be despair'd of, for our money;
And, though fowle, now, be scarce, yet there are clarkes, 15
The skie not falling, thinke we may have larkes.
Ile tell you more, and lye, so you will come:
Of partrich, pheasant, wood-cock, of which some
May yet be there; and godwit, if we can:
Knat, raile, and ruffe too. How so ere, my man 20
Shall reade a piece of *Virgil, Tacitus,*
Livie, or of some better booke to us,

1. *grave sir:* possibly, since the poem is crammed with classical echoes, Jonson's old schoolmaster Camden.

19–20. *godwit, knat, raile, ruffe:* more names of birds.

Of which wee'll speake our minds, amidst our meate;
And Ile professe no verses to repeate:
To this, if ought appeare, which I not know of, 25
That will the pastrie, not my paper, show of.
Digestive cheese, and fruit there sure will bee;
But that, which most doth take my Muse, and mee,
Is a pure cup of rich Canary-wine,
Which is the Mermaids, now, but shall be mine: 30
Of which had *Horace*, or *Anacreon* tasted,
Their lives, as doe their lines, till now had lasted.
Tabacco, Nectar, or the Thespian spring,
Are all but *Luthers* beere, to this I sing.
Of this we will sup free, but moderately, 35
And we will have no Pooly', or Parrot by;
Nor shall our cups make any guiltie men:
But, at our parting, we will be, as when
We innocently met. No simple word,
That shall be utter'd at our mirthfull boord, 40
Shall make us sad next morning: or affright
The libertie, that wee'll enjoy to night.

---

30. *Mermaid:* the celebrated tavern.
36. *Pooly, Parrot:* notorious spies and informers. Pooly was present at the murder of Marlowe, which occurred after supper.

CII

To William Earle of Pembroke

I doe but name thee Pembroke, and I find
It is an Epigramme, on all man-kind;
Against the bad, but of, and to the good:
Both which are ask'd, to have thee understood.
Nor could the age have mist thee, in this strife 5
Of vice, and vertue; wherin all great life
Almost, is exercis'd: and scarse one knowes,
To which, yet, of the sides himselfe he owes.
They follow vertue, for reward, today:
To morrow vice, if shee give better pay: 10
And are so good, and bad, just at a price,

As nothing else discernes the vertue' or vice.
But thou, whose noblesse keeps one stature still,
And one true posture, though besieg'd with ill
Of what ambition, faction, pride can raise; 15
Whose life, ev'n they, that envie it, must praise;
That art so reverenc'd, as thy comming in,
But in the view, doth interrupt their sinne;
Thou must draw more: and they, that hope to see
The common-wealth still safe, must studie thee. 20

CXX

Epitaph on S.P. a Child of Q. El. Chappel

Weepe with me all you that read
This little storie:
And know, for whom a teare you shed,
Death's selfe is sorry.
'Twas a child, that so did thrive 5
In grace, and feature,
As Heaven and Nature seem'd to strive
Which own'd the creature.
Yeeres he numbred scarse thirteene
When Fates turn'd cruell, 10
Yet three fill'd Zodiackes had he beene
The stages jewell;
And did act (what now we mone)
Old men so duely,
As, sooth, the Parcae thought him one,
He plai'd so truely.
So, by error, to his fate
They all consented;
But viewing him since (alas, too late)
They have repented. 20
And have sought (to give new birth)
In bathes to steepe him;

S. P. (Salomon Pavy) was a boy actor who had played before the queen in Jonson's Masque, *Cynthia's Revels*, in 1600. He died in 1602.
15. *Parcae:* the Fates.

But, being so much too good for earth,
Heaven vowes to keepe him.

CXXIV

Epitaph on Elizabeth, L.H.

Would'st thou heare, what man can say
In a little? Reader, stay.
Under-neath this stone doth lye
As much beautie, as could dye:
Which in life did harbour give 5
To more vertue, than doth live.
If, at all, shee had a fault,
Leave it buryed in this vault.
One name was Elizabeth,
Th'other let it sleepe with death: 10
Fitter, where it dyed, to tell,
Than that it liv'd at all. Farewell.

Elizabeth. Lady Hatton? Her identity cannot be determined.

THE FORREST

[PUBLISHED 1616]

II

To Penshurst

Thou art not, *Penshurst,* built to envious show,
Of touch, or marble; nor canst boast a row

---

1. *Penshurst:* the Sidney family's estate in Kent.
2. *touch:* black marble.

Of polish'd pillars, or a roofe of gold:
Thou has no lantherne, whereof tales are told;
Or stayre, or courts; but stand'st an ancient pile, 5
And these grudg'd at, art reverenc'd the while.
Thou joy'st in better markes, of soyle, of ayre,
Of wood, of water: therein thou art faire.
Thou hast thy walkes for health, as well as sport:
Thy Mount, to which the Dryads doe resort, 10
Where *Pan,* and *Bacchus* their high feasts have made,
Beneath the broad beech, and the chest-nut shade;
That taller tree, which of a nut was set,
At his great birth, where all the Muses met.
There, in the writhed barke, are cut the names 15
Of many a *Sylvane,* taken with his flames.
And thence, the ruddy Satyres oft provoke
The lighter Faunes, to reach thy Ladies oke.
Thy copp's, too, nam'd of *Gamage,* thou hast there,
That never failes to serve thee season'd deere, 20
When thou would'st feast, or exercise thy friends.
The lower land, that to the river bends,
Thy sheepe, thy bullocks, kine, and calves doe feed:
The middle grounds thy mares, and horses breed.
Each banke doth yeeld thee coneyes; and the topps 25
Fertile of wood, *Ashore,* and *Sydney's* copp's,
To crowne thy open table, doth provide
The purpled pheasant, with the speckled side:
The painted partrich lyes in every field,
And, for thy messe, is willing to be kill'd. 30
And if the high swolne Medway faile thy dish,
Thou hast thy ponds, that pay thee tribute fish,
Fat, aged carps, that runne into thy net.
And pikes, now weary their owne kinde to eat,
As loth, the second draught, or cast to stay, 35
Officiously, at first, themselves betray.
Bright eeles, that emulate them, and leape on land,
Before the fisher, or into his hand.

---

14. *his:* Sir Philip Sidney's, in 1554.
19. *Gamage:* Lady Barbara Gamage, Lord Sidney's wife.
36. *officiously:* dutifully, that is, fulfilling their office.

Then hath thy orchard fruit, thy garden flowers,
Fresh as the ayre, and new as are the houres. 40
The earely cherry, with the later plum,
Fig, grape, and quince, each in his time doth come:
The blushing apricot, and wooly peach
Hang on thy walls, that every child may reach.
And though thy walls be of the countrey stone, 45
They'are rear'd with no mans ruine, no mans grone,
There's none, that dwell about them, wish them downe;
But all come in, the farmer, and the clowne:
And no one empty-handed, to salute
Thy lord, and lady, though they have no sute. 50
Some bring a capon, some a rurall cake,
Some nuts, some apples; some that thinke they make
The better cheeses, bring 'hem; or else send
By their ripe daughters, whom they would commend
This way to husbands; and whose baskets beare 55
An embleme of themselves, in plum, or peare.
But what can this (more then expresse their love)
Adde to thy free provisions, farre above
The neede of such? whose liberall boord doth flow,
With all, that hospitalitie doth know! 60
Where comes no guest, but is allow'd to eate,
Without his feare, and of the lords owne meate:
Where the same beere, and bread, and self-same wine,
That is his Lordships, shall be also mine.
And I not faine to sit (as some, this day, 65
At great mens tables) and yet dine away.
Here no man tells my cups; nor, standing by,
A waiter, doth my gluttony envy:
But gives me what I call, and lets me eate,
He knowes, below, he shall finde plentie of meate, 70
Thy tables hoord not up for the next day,
Nor, when I take my lodging, need I pray
For fire, or lights, or livorie: all is there;
As if thou, then, wert mine, or I reign'd here:
There's nothing I can wish, for which I stay. 75

---

67. *tells:* counts.
73. *livorie:* provision.

That found King *James,* when hunting late, this way,
With his brave sonne, the Prince, they saw thy fires
Shine bright on every harth as the desires
Of thy Penates had beene set on flame,
To entertayne them; or the countrey came, 80
With all their zeale, to warme their welcome here.
What (great, I will not say, but) sodayne cheare
Did'st thou, then, make 'hem! and what praise was heap'd
On thy good lady, then! who, therein reap'd
The just reward of her high huswifery, 85
To have her linnen, plate, and all things nigh,
When shee was farre: and not a roome, but drest,
As if it had expected such a guest!
These, *Penshurst,* are thy praise, and yet not all.
Thy lady's noble, fruitfull, chaste withall. 90
His children thy great lord may call his owne:
A fortune, in this age, but rarely knowne.
They are, and have beene taught religion: Thence
Their gentler spirits have suck'd innocence.
Each morne, and even, they are taught to pray, 95
With the whole houshold, and may, every day,
Reade, in their vertuous parents noble parts,
The mysteries of manners, armes, and arts.
Now, *Penshurst,* they that will proportion thee
With other edifices, when they see
Those proud, ambitious heaps, and nothing else,
May say, their lords have built, but thy lord dwells.

---

79. *Penates:* household gods, associated by Romans with the hearth.

IV

To the World

A FAREWELL FOR A GENTLE-WOMAN, VERTUOUS AND NOBLE

False world, good-night: since thou hast brought
That houre upon my morne of age,

Hence-forth I quit thee from my thought,
 My part is ended on thy stage.
Doe not once hope, that thou canst tempt 5
 A spirit so resolv'd to tread
Upon thy throate, and live exempt
 From all the nets that thou canst spread.
I know thy formes are studyed arts,
 Thy subtle wayes, be narrow straits; 10
Thy curtesie but sodaine starts,
 And what thou call'st thy gifts are baits.
I know too, though thou strut, and paint,
 Yet art thou both shrunke up, and old,
That onely fooles make thee a saint, 15
 And all thy good is to be sold.
I know thou whole art but a shop
 Of toyes, and trifles, traps, and snares,
To take the weake, or make them stop:
 Yet art thou falser than thy wares. 20
And, knowing this, should I yet stay,
 Like such as blow away their lives,
And never will redeeme a day,
 Enamor'd of their golden gyves?
Or, having scap'd, shall I returne, 25
 And thrust my necke into the noose,
From whence, so lately, I did burne,
 With all my powers, my selfe to loose?
What bird, or beast, is knowne so dull,
 That fled his cage, or broke his chaine, 30
And tasting ayre, and freedome, wull
 Render his head in there againe?
If these, who have but sense, can shun
 The engines, that have them annoy'd;
Little, for me, had reason done, 35
 If I could not thy ginnes avoyd.
Yes, threaten, doe. Alas I feare
 As little, as I hope from thee:

34. ***engines:*** devices.
35. ***ginnes:*** snares.

I know thou canst nor shew, nor beare
  More hatred, than thou hast to mee. 40
My tender, first, and simple yeeres
  Thou did'st abuse, and then betray;
Since stird'st up jealousies and feares,
  When all the causes were away.
Then, in a soile hast planted me, 45
  Where breathe the basest of thy fooles;
Where envious arts professed be,
  And pride, and ignorance the schooles,
Where nothing is examin'd, weigh'd,
  But, as 'tis rumor'd, so beleev'd: 50
Where every freedome is betray'd,
  And every goodnesse tax'd, or griev'd.
But, what we'are borne for, we must beare:
  Our fraile condition it is such,
That, what to all may happen here, 55
  If't chance to me, I must not grutch.
Else, I my state should much mistake,
  To harbour a divided thought
From all my kinde: that, for my sake,
  There should a miracle be wrought. 60
No, I doe know, that I was borne
  To age, misfortune, sicknesse, griefe:
But I will beare these, with that scorne,
  As shall not need thy false reliefe.
Nor for my peace will I goe farre, 65
  As wandrers doe, that still doe rome,
But make my strengths, such as they are,
  Here in my bosome, and at home.

---

56. *grutch:* complain.

v

Song

TO CELIA

Come my *Celia,* let us prove,
While we may, the sports of love;
Time will not be ours, for ever:
He, at length, our good will sever.
Spend not then his guifts in vaine. 5
Sunnes, that set, may rise againe:
But if once we loose this light,
'Tis, with us, perpetuall night.
Why should we deferre our joyes?
Fame, and rumor are but toyes. 10
Cannot we delude the eyes
Of a few poore houshold spyes?
Or his easier eares beguile,
So removed by our wile?
'Tis no sinne, loves fruit to steale, 15
But the sweet theft to reveale:
To be taken, to be seene,
These have crimes accounted beene.

VI

To the Same

Kisse me, sweet: the warie lover
Can your favours keepe, and cover,
When the common courting jay
All your bounties will betray.
Kisse againe: no creature comes. 5
Kisse, and score up wealthy summes

This and the preceding poem together make up a loose and much expanded translation of Catullus, v (*Vivamus, mea Lesbia atque amemus*), with additions based on Catullus, vii.

On my lips, thus hardly sundred,
While you breath. First give a hundred,
Then a thousand, then another
Hundred, then unto the tother 10
Adde a thousand, and so more:
Till you equall with the store,
All the grasse that Rumney yeelds,
Or the sands in Chelsey fields,
Or the drops in silver Thames, 15
Or the starres, that guild his streames,
In the silent sommer-nights,
When youths ply their stolne delights.
That the curious may not know
How to tell 'hem, as they flow, 20
And the envious, when they find
What their number is, be pin'd.

---

13. ***Rumney:*** this Kentish marsh was famous as a pasture ground for cattle.

VII

Song

THAT WOMEN ARE BUT MENS SHADDOWES

Follow a shaddow, it still flies you;
  Seeme to flye it, it will pursue:
So court a mistris, shee denyes you;
  Let her alone, shee will court you.
Say, are not women truely, then, 5
Stil'd but the shaddowes of us men?
At morne, and even, shades are longest;
  At noone, they are or short, or none:
So men at weakest, they are strongest,
  But grant us perfect, they're not knowne. 10
Say, are not women truely, then,
Stil'd but the shaddowes of us men?

IX

Song. To Celia

Drinke to me, onely, with thine eyes,
  And I will pledge with mine;
Or leave a kisse but in the cup,
  And Ile not looke for wine.
The thirst, that from the soule doth rise, 5
  Doth aske a drinke divine:
But might I of *Jove's* Nectar sup,
  I would not change for thine.
I sent thee, late, a rosie wreath,
  Not so much honoring thee, 10
As giving it a hope, that there
  It could not withered bee.
But thou thereon did'st onely breath,
  And sent'st it backe to mee:
Since when it growes, and smells, I sweare, 15
  Not of it selfe, but thee.

XI

Epode

Not to know vice at all, and keepe true state,
  Is vertue, and not Fate:
Next, to that vertue, is to know vice well,
  And her blacke spight expell.
Which to effect (since no brest is so sure, 5
  Or safe, but shee'll procure
Some way of entrance) we must plant a guard
  Of thoughts to watch, and ward
At th'eye and eare (the ports unto the minde)
  That no strange, or unkinde 10
Object arrive there, but the heart (our spie)
  Give knowledge instantly,

To wakefull reason, our affections king:
    Who (in the'examining)
Will quickly taste the treason, and commit 15
    Close, the close cause of it.
'Tis the securest policie we have,
    To make our sense our slave.
But this true course is not embrac'd by many:
    By many? scarse by any. 20
For either our affections doe rebell,
    Or else the sentinell
(That should ring larum to the heart) doth sleepe,
    Or some great thought doth keepe
Backe the intelligence, and falsely sweares, 25
    Th'are base, and idle feares
Whereof the loyall conscience so complaines.
    Thus, by these subtle traines,
Doe severall passions invade the minde,
    And strike our reason blinde. 30
Of which usurping rancke, some have thought love
    The first; as prone to move
Most frequent tumults, horrors, and unrests,
    In our enflamed brests:
But this doth from the cloud of error grow, 35
    Which thus we over-blow.
The thing, they here call Love, is blinde Desire,
    Arm'd with bow, shafts, and fire;
Inconstant, like the sea, of whence 'tis borne,
    Rough, swelling, like a storme: 40
With whom who sailes, rides on the surge of feare,
    And boyles, as if he were
In a continuall tempest. Now, true Love
    No such effects doth prove;
That is an essence farre more gentle, fine, 45
    Pure, perfect, nay divine;
It is a golden chaine let downe from heaven,
    Whose linkes are bright, and even.
That falls like sleepe on lovers, and combines
    The soft, and sweetest mindes 50

16. *close cause:* secret cause.

In equall knots: This beares no brands, nor darts,
    To murther different hearts,
But, in a calme, and god-like unitie,
    Preserves communitie.
O, who is he, that (in this peace) enjoyes   55
    Th'Elixir of all joyes?
A forme more fresh, than are the Eden bowers,
    And lasting, as her flowers:
Richer than Time, and as Time's vertue, rare.
    Sober, as saddest care: 60
A fixed thought, an eye un-taught to glance;
    Who (blest with such high chance)
Would, at suggestion of a steepe desire,
    Cast himselfe from the spire
Of all his happinesse? But soft: I heare   65
    Some vicious foole draw neare,
That cryes, we dreame, and sweares, there's no such thing,
    As this chaste love we sing.
Peace, Luxurie, thou art like one of those
    Who, being at sea, suppose,   70
Because they move, the continent doth so:
    No, vice, we let thee know
Though thy wild thoughts with sparrowes wings doe flye,
    Turtles can chastly dye;
And yet (in this t'expresse our selves more cleare)   75
    We doe not number, here,
Such spirits as are onely continent,
    Because lust's meanes are spent:
Or those, who doubt the common mouth of fame,
    And for their place, and name,   80
Cannot so safely sinne. Their chastitie
    Is meere necessitie.
Nor meane we those, whom vowes and conscience
    Have fill'd with abstinence:
Though we acknowledge, who can so abstayne,   85
    Makes a most blessed gayne.
He that for love of goodnesse hateth ill,

59. *Time's vertue:* truth, the daughter of Time.
74. *Turtles:* turtledoves, types of masculine constancy.

Is more crowne-worthy still,
Than he, which for sinnes penaltie forbeares.
His heart sinnes, though he feares. 90
But we propose a person like our Dove,
Grac'd with a Phoenix love;
A beautie of that cleere, and sparkling light,
Would make a day of night,
And turne the blackest sorrowes to bright joyes: 95
Whose od'rous breath destroyes
All taste of bitternesse, and makes the ayre
As sweet, as shee is fayre.
A body so harmoniously compos'd,
As if Nature disclos'd 100
All her best symmetrie in that one feature!
O, so divine a creature
Who could be false to? chiefly, when he knowes
How onely shee bestowes
The wealthy treasure of her love on him; 105
Making his fortunes swim
In the full floud of her admir'd perfection?
What savage, brute affection,
Would not be fearefull to offend a dame
Of this excelling frame? 110
Much more a noble, and right generous mind
(To vertuous moods inclin'd)
That knowes the waight of guilt: He will refraine
From thoughts of such a straine.
And to his sense object this sentence ever, 115
Man may securely sinne, but safely never.

116. *securely:* carelessly.

XV

To Heaven

Good, and great *God,* can I not thinke of thee,
But it must, straight, my melancholy bee?

2. *bee:* be interpreted as.

Is it interpreted in me disease,
That, laden with my sinnes, I seeke for ease?
O, be thou witnesse, that the reynes dost know, 5
And hearts of all, if I be sad for show,
And judge me after: if I dare pretend
To ought but grace, or ayme at other end.
As thou art all, so be thou all to mee,
First, midst. and last, converted one, and three; 10
My faith, my hope, my love: and in this state,
My judge, my witnesse, and my advocate.
Where have I beene this while exil'd from thee?
And whither rap'd, now thou but stoup'st to mee?
Dwell, dwell here still: O, being every-where, 15
How can I doubt to finde thee ever, here?
I know my state, both full of shame, and scorne,
Conceiv'd in sinne, and unto labour borne,
Standing with feare, and must with horror fall,
And destin'd unto judgement, after all. 20
I feele my griefes too, and there scarce is ground,
Upon my flesh t'inflict another wound.
Yet dare I not complaine, or wish for death
With holy *Paul,* lest it be thought the breath
Of discontent; or that these prayers bee 25
For wearinesse of life, not love of thee.

---

5. *reynes:* Kidneys. See Ps. 7 : 9.
24. *With holy* Paul: see Rom. 7 : 24.

THE UNDERWOOD

[PUBLISHED 1640]

2. A Hymne to God the Father

Heare mee, O God!
A broken heart
Is my best part:
Use still thy rod,

That I may prove
Therein, thy Love. 5

If thou hadst not
Beene sterne to mee,
But left me free,
I had forgot 10
My selfe and thee.

For, sin's so sweet,
As minds ill bent
Rarely repent,
Untill they meet 15
Their punishment.

Who more can crave
Than thou hast done?
That gav'st a Sonne,
To free a slave, 20
First made of nought;
With all since bought.

Sinne, Death, and Hell,
His glorious Name
Quite overcame, 25
Yet I rebell,
And slight the same.

But, I'le come in,
Before my losse,
Me farther tosse, 30
As sure to win
Under his Crosse.

II

A Celebration of Charis in Ten Lyrick Peeces

I. HIS EXCUSE FOR LOVING

Let it not your wonder move,
Lesse your laughter; that I love.
Though I now write fiftie yeares,
I have had, and have my Peeres;
Poets, though devine are men: 5
Some have lov'd as old agen.
And it is not alwayes face,
Clothes, or Fortune gives the grace;
Or the feature, or the youth:
But the Language, and the Truth, 10
With the Ardor, and the Passion,
Gives the Lover weight, and fashion.
If you then will read the Storie,
First, prepare you to be sorie,
That you never knew till now, 15
Either whom to love, or how:
But be glad, as soone with me,
When you know, that this is she,
Of whose Beautie it was sung,
She shall make the old man young, 20
Keepe the middle age at stay,
And let nothing high decay,
Till she be the reason why,
All the world for love may die.

---

9. *feature:* shape.

2. HOW HE SAW HER

I beheld her, on a Day,
When her looke out-flourisht May:
And her dressing did out-brave

All the Pride the fields then have:
Farre I was from being stupid, 5
For I ran and call'd on *Cupid;*
Love if thou wilt ever see
Marke of glorie, come with me;
Where's thy Quiver? bend thy Bow:
Here's a shaft, thou art to slow! 10
And (withall) I did untie
Every Cloud about his eye;
But, he had not gain'd his sight
Sooner, than he lost his might,
Or his courage; for away 15
Strait hee ran, and durst not stay,
Letting Bow and Arrow fall,
Nor for any threat, or Call,
Could be brought once back to looke.
I foole-hardie, there up tooke 20
Both the Arrow he had quit,
And the Bow: with thought to hit
This my object. But she threw
Such a Lightning (as I drew)
At my face, that tooke my sight, 25
And my motion from me quite;
So that there, I stood a stone,
Mock'd of all: and call'd of one
(Which with griefe and wrath I heard)
Cupids Statue with a Beard, 30
Or else one that plaid his Ape,
In a *Hercules*-his shape.

3. WHAT HEE SUFFERED

After many scornes like these,
Which the prouder Beauties please,
She content was to restore
Eyes and limbes; to hurt me more.
And would on Conditions, be 5
Reconcil'd to Love, and me.
First, that I must kneeling yeeld

Both the Bow, and shaft I held,
Unto her; which Love might take
At her hand, with oath, to make 10
Mee, the scope of his next draught,
Aymed with that selfe-same shaft.
He no sooner heard the Law,
But the Arrow home did draw
And (to gaine her by his Art) 15
Left it sticking in my heart:
Which when she beheld to bleed,
She repented of the deed,
And would faine have chang'd the fate,
But the Pittie comes too late. 20
Looser-like, now, all my wreake
Is, that I have leave to speake,
And in either Prose, or Song,
To revenge me with my Tongue,
Which how Dexterously I doe, 25
Heare and make Example too.

4. HER TRIUMPH

See the Chariot at hand here of Love
  Wherein my Lady rideth!
Each that drawes, is a Swan, or a Dove,
  And well the Carre Love guideth.
As she goes, all hearts doe duty 5
    Unto her beauty;
And enamour'd, doe wish, so they might
    But enjoy such a sight,
That they still were, to run by her side,
Through Swords, through Seas, whether she would ride. 10

Doe but looke on her eyes, they doe light
  All that Loves world compriseth!
Doe but look on her Haire, it is bright
  As Loves starre when it riseth!
Doe but marke her forhead's smoother 15
    Than words that sooth her!

And from her arched browes, such a grace
    Sheds it selfe through the face,
As alone there triumphs to the life
All the Gaine, all the Good, of the Elements strife. 20

Have you seene but a bright Lillie grow,
  Before rude hands have touch'd it?
Ha' you mark'd but the fall o'the Snow
  Before the soyle hath smutch'd it?
Ha' you felt the wooll o' the Bever? 25
    Or Swans Downe ever?
Or have smelt o'the bud o' the Brier?
    Or the Nard in the fire?
Or have tasted the bag of the Bee?
O so white! O so soft! O so sweet is she!

---

28. *Nard:* aromatic balsam.

5. HIS DISCOURSE WITH CUPID

Noblest *Charis,* you that are
Both my fortune, and my Starre!
And doe governe more my blood,
Than the various Moone the flood!
Heare, what late Discourse of you, 5
Love, and I have had; and true.
'Mongst my Muses finding me,
Where he chanc't your name to see
Set, and to this softer straine;
Sure, said he, if I have Braine, 10
This here sung, can be no other
By description, but my Mother!
So hath *Homer* prais'd her haire;
So, *Anacreon* drawne the Ayre
Of her face, and made to rise 15
Just above her sparkling eyes,
Both her Browes, bent like my Bow.
By her lookes I doe her know,

---

12. *my Mother:* Cupid's mother was Venus.

Which you call my Shafts. And see!
Such my Mothers blushes be, 20
As the Bath your verse discloses
In her cheekes, of Milke, and Roses;
Such as oft I wanton in;
And, above her even chin,
Have you plac'd the banke of kisses, 25
Where you say, men gather blisses,
Rip'ned with a breath more sweet,
Than when flowers, and West-winds meet.
Nay, her white and polish'd neck,
With the Lace that doth it deck, 30
Is my Mothers! Hearts of slaine
Lovers, made into a Chaine!
And betweene each rising breast,
Lyes the Valley, cal'd my nest,
Where I sit and proyne my wings 35
After flight; and put new stings
To my shafts! Her very Name,
With my Mothers is the same.
I confesse all, I replide,
And the Glasse hangs by her side, 40
And the Girdle 'bout her waste,
All is *Venus:* save unchaste.
But alas, thou seest the least
Of her good, who is the best
Of her Sex: But could'st thou, *Love,* 45
Call to mind the formes, that strove
For the Apple, and those three
Make in one, the same were shee.
For this Beauty yet doth hide,
Something more then thou hast spi'd. 50
Outward Grace weake love beguiles:
Shee is *Venus,* when she smiles,

---

35. *proyne:* preen.

37–38. Jonson is exploiting one of the many blurred identities in classical myth. A passage in the *Iliad* (xviii, 382) identifies Charis as the wife of Hephaestus, a position usually accorded Aphrodite (Venus).

46. *formes:* Venus, Juno, Minerva.

But shee's *Juno,* when she walkes,
And *Minerva,* when she talkes.

6. CLAYMING A SECOND KISSE BY DESERT

Charis guesse, and doe not misse,
Since I drew a Morning kisse
From your lips, and suck'd an ayre
Thence, as sweet, as you are faire,
What my Muse and I have done: 5
Whether we have lost, or wonne,
If by us, the oddes were laid,
That the Bride (allow'd a Maid)
Look'd not halfe so fresh, and faire,
With th'advantage of her haire, 10
And her Jewels, to the view
Of th'Assembly, as did you!
Or, that did you sit, or walke,
You were more the eye, and talke
Of the Court, to day, than all 15
Else that glister'd in *White-hall;*
So, as those that had your sight,
Wisht the Bride were chang'd to night,
And did thinke, such Rites were due
To no other Grace but you! 20
Or, if you did move to night
In the Daunces, with what spight
Of your Peeres, you were beheld,
That at every motion sweld
So to see a Lady tread, 25
As might all the Graces lead,
And was worthy (being so seene)
To be envi'd of the Queene.
Or if you would yet have stay'd,
Whether any would up-braid 30
To himselfe his losse of Time;
Or have charg'd his sight of Crime,
To have left all sight for you:

Guesse of these, which is the true;
And, if such a verse as this, 35
May not claime another kisse.

7. BEGGING ANOTHER, ON COLOUR OF MENDING THE FORMER

For Loves-sake, kisse me once againe,
I long, and should not beg in vaine,
Here's none to spie, or see;
Why doe you doubt, or stay?
I'le taste as lightly as the Bee, 5
That doth but touch his flower, and flies away.
Once more, and (faith) I will be gone.
Can he that loves, aske lesse than one?
Nay, you may erre in this,
And all your bountie wrong: 10
This could be call'd but halfe a kisse.
What w'are but once to doe, we should doe long.
I will but mend the last, and tell
Where, how it would have relish'd well;
Joyne lip to lip, and try: 15
Each suck others breath.
And whilst our tongues perplexed lie,
Let who will thinke us dead, or wish our death.

On colour of: in pretense of.

8. URGING HER OF A PROMISE

Charis one day in discourse
Had of Love, and of his force,
Lightly promis'd, she would tell
What a man she could love well:
And that promise set on fire 5
All that heard her, with desire.
With the rest, I long expected,
When the worke would be effected:
But we find that cold delay,

And excuse spun every day, 10
As, untill she tell her one,
We all feare, she loveth none.
Therefore, *Charis*, you must do't,
For I will so urge you to't,
You shall neither eat, nor sleepe, 15
No, nor forth your window peepe,
With your emissarie eye,
To fetch in the Formes goe by:
And pronounce, which band, or lace,
Better fits him, than his face; 20
Nay, I will not let you sit
'Fore your Idoll Glasse a whit,
To say over every purle
There; or to reforme a curle;
Or with Secretarie *Sis* 25
To consult, if *Fucus* this
Be as good, as was the last:
All your sweet of life is past,
Make accompt, unlesse you can,
(And that quickly) speake your Man. 30

---

23. *purle:* knitted loop.
25. *Secretarie:* attendant.
26. *Fucus:* a cosmetic.

9. HER MAN DESCRIBED BY HER OWNE DICTAMEN

Of your Trouble, *Ben*, to ease me,
I will tell what Man would please me.
I would have him if I could,
Noble; or of greater Blood:
Titles, I confesse, doe take me; 5
And a woman God did make me,
French to boote, at least in fashion,
And his Manners of that Nation.
Young Il'd have him to, and faire,
Yet a man; with crisped haire 10

Cast in thousand snares, and rings
For *Loves* fingers, and his wings:
Chestnut colour, or more slack
Gold, upon a ground of black.
Venus, and *Minerva's* eyes 15
For he must looke wanton-wise.
Eye-brows bent like *Cupids* bow,
Front, an ample field of snow;
Even nose, and cheeke (withall)
Smooth as is the Billiard Ball: 20
Chin, as woolly as the Peach;
And his lip should kissing teach,
Till he cherish'd too much beard,
And make Love or me afeard.
He would have a hand as soft 25
As the Downe, and shew it oft;
Skin as smooth as any rush,
And so thin to see a blush
Rising through it e're it came;
All his blood should be a flame 30
Quickly fir'd as in beginners
In loves schoole, and yet no sinners.
'Twere to long to speake of all,
What we harmonie doe call
In a body should be there. 35
Well he should his clothes to weare;
Yet no Taylor help to make him;
Drest, you still for man should take him;
And not thinke h'had eat a stake,
Or were set up in a Brake. 40
Valiant he should be as fire,
Shewing danger more than ire;
Bounteous as the clouds to earth;
And as honest as his Birth.
All his actions to be such, 45
As to doe nothing too much:

---

13. *slack:* dull.
40. *Brake:* trap.

Nor o're-praise, nor yet condemne;
Nor out-valew, nor contemne;
Nor doe wrongs, nor wrongs receave;
Nor tie knots, nor knots unweave; 50
And from basenesse to be free,
As he durst love Truth and me.
  Such a man, with every part,
I could give my very heart;
But of one, if short he came, 55
I can rest me where I am.

10. ANOTHER LADYES EXCEPTION PRESENT AT THE HEARING

For his Mind, I doe not care,
That's a Toy, that I could spare:
Let his Title be but great,
His Clothes rich, and band sit neat,
Himselfe young, and face be good,
All I wish is understood.
What you please, you parts may call,
'Tis one good part I'ld lie withall.

IV

A Song

Oh doe not wanton with those eyes,
  Lest I be sick with seeing;
Nor cast them downe, but let them rise,
  Lest shame destroy their being:
O, be not angry with those fires, 5
  For then their threats will kill me;
Nor looke too kind on my desires,
  For then my hopes will spill me;
O, doe not steepe them in thy Teares,
  For so will sorrow slay me; 10
Nor spread them as distract with feares,
  Mine owne enough betray me.

V

In the Person of Woman Kind

A SONG APOLOGETIQUE

Men, if you love us, play no more
  The fooles, or Tyrants with your friends,
To make us still sing o're, and o're,
  Our owne false praises, for your ends:
    Wee have both wits, and fancies too, 5
    And if wee must, let's sing of you.

Nor doe we doubt, but that we can,
  If wee would search with care, and paine,
Find some one good, in some one man;
  So going thorow all your straine: 10
    Wee shall at last, of parcells make
    One good enough for a songs sake.

And as a cunning Painter takes
  In any curious peece you see
More pleasure while the thing he makes 15
  Than when 'tis made, why so will wee.
    And having pleas'd our art, wee'll try
    To make a new, and hang that by.

---

10. *thorow:* through.
11. *parcells:* pieces.

VI

Another. In Defence of Their Inconstancie

A SONG

Hang up those dull, and envious fooles
  That talke abroad of Womans change,

We were not bred to sit on stooles,
  Our proper vertue is to range:
    Take that away, you take our lives, 5
    We are no women then, but wives.

Such as in valour would excell
  Doe change, though man, and often fight,
Which we in love must doe aswell,
  If ever we will love aright. 10
    The frequent varying of the deed,
    Is that which doth perfection breed.

Nor is't inconstancie to change
  For what is better, or to make
(By searching) what before was strange, 15
  Familiar, for the uses sake;
    The good, from bad, is not descride,
    But as 'tis often vext and tri'd.

And this profession of a store
  In love, doth not alone help forth 20
Our pleasure; but preserves us more
  From being forsaken, than doth worth,
    For were the worthiest woman curst
    To love one man, hee'd leave her first.

VIII

The Houre-glasse

Doe but consider this small dust,
  Here running in the Glasse,
    By Atomes mov'd;
  Could you beleeve, that this,
    The body was 5
      Of one that lov'd?
And in his Mistris flame, playing like a flye,
  Turn'd to cinders by her eye?

Yes; and in death, as life unblest,
To have't exprest, 10
Even ashes of lovers find no rest.

IX

My Picture Left in Scotland

I now thinke, *Love* is rather deafe, than blind,
For else it could not be,
That she,
Whom I adore so much, should so slight me,
And cast my love behind: 5
I'm sure my language to her, was as sweet,
And every close did meet
In sentence, of as subtile feet,
As hath the youngest Hee,
That sits in shadow of *Apollo's* tree. 10

Oh, but my conscious feares,
That flie my thoughts betweene,
Tell me that she hath seene
My hundreds of gray haires,
Told seven and fortie yeares, 15
Read so much wast, as she cannot imbrace
My mountaine belly, and my rockie face,
And all these through her eyes, have stopt her eares.

---

7. *close:* cadence.
8. *sentence:* meaning.
15. *told:* counted.
17. *rockie:* pock-marked.

XXIII

An Ode. To Himselfe

Where do'st thou carelesse lie
Buried in ease and sloth?
Knowledge, that sleepes, doth die;

And this Securitie,
It is the common Moath, 5
That eats on wits, and Arts, and oft destroyes them both.

Are all th'*Aonian* springs
Dri'd up? lyes *Thespia* wast?
Doth *Clarius* Harp want strings,
That not a Nymph now sings! 10
Or droop they as disgrac't,
To see their Seats and Bowers by chattring Pies defac't?

If hence thy silence be,
As 'tis too just a cause;
Let this thought quicken thee, 15
Minds that are great and free,
Should not on fortune pause,
'Tis crowne enough to vertue still, her owne applause.

What though the greedie Frie
Be taken with false Baytes 20
Of worded Balladrie,
And thinke it Poesie?
They die with their conceits,
And only pitious scorne, upon their folly waites.

Then take in hand thy Lyre, 25
Strike in thy proper straine,
With *Japhets* lyne, aspire
Sols Chariot for new fire,
To give the world againe:
Who aided him, will thee, the issue of *Joves* braine. 30

And since our Daintie age
Cannot endure reproofe,
Make not thy selfe a Page,

---

9. *Clarius:* Apollo.
12. *Pies:* magpies.
27. *Japhets lyne:* Prometheus, who stole fire from heaven.
30. *issue of* Joves *brain:* Minerva, who abetted Prometheus

To that strumpet the Stage,
But sing high and aloofe, 35
Safe from the wolves black jaw, and the dull Asses hoofe.

XXIX

A Fit of Rime against Rime

Rime, the rack of finest wits,
That expresseth but by fits,
True Conceipt,
Spoyling Senses of their Treasure,
Cosening Judgement with a measure, 5
But false weight.
Wresting words, from their true calling;
Propping Verse, for feare of falling
To the ground.
Joynting Syllabes, drowning Letters, 10
Fastning Vowells, as with fetters
They were bound!
Soone as lazie thou wert knowne,
All good Poetrie hence was flowne,
And Art banish'd. 15
For a thousand yeares together,
All *Parnassus* Greene did wither,
And wit vanish'd.
Pegasus did flie away,
At the Well no Muse did stay, 20
But bewail'd
So to see the Fountaine drie,
And *Apollo's* Musique die,
All light failed!
Starveling rimes did fill the Stage, 25
Not a Poet in an Age,
Worth a crowning;
Not a worke deserving Baies,
Nor a lyne deserving praise,

20. *Well:* Hippocrene, the fountain sacred to the Muses.

Pallas frowning. 30
Greeke was free from Rimes infection,
Happy Greeke, by this protection,
Was not spoyled.
Whilst the Latin, Queene of Tongues,
Is not yet free from Rimes wrongs, 35
But rests foiled.
Scarce the hill againe doth flourish,
Scarce the world a Wit doth nourish,
To restore,
Phoebus to his Crowne againe; 40
And the Muses to their braine;
As before.
Vulgar Languages that want
Words, and sweetnesse, and be scant
Of true measure, 45
Tyran Rime hath so abused,
That they long since have refused
Other ceasure;
He that first invented thee,
May his joynts tormented bee, 50
Cramp'd forever;
Still may Syllabes jarre with time,
Still may reason warre with rime,
Resting never.
May his Sense, when it would meet 55
The cold tumor in his feet,
Grow unsounder;
And his Title be long foole,
That, in rearing such a Schoole,
Was the founder. 60

---

43. *Vulgar:* that is, spoken by the populace, as distinguished from Latin and Greek.
48. *ceasure:* caesura. Jonson refers to the function of rhyme in dividing verses from one another.

XLII

An Elegie

Let me be what I am, as *Virgil* cold;
As *Horace* fat; or as *Anacreon* old;
No Poets verses yet did ever move,
Whose Readers did not thinke he was in love.
Who shall forbid me then in Rithme to bee 5
As light, and Active as the youngest hee
That from the Muses fountaines doth indorse
His lines, and hourely sits the Poets horse?
Put on my Ivy Garland, let me see
Who frownes, who jealous is, who taxeth me. 10
Fathers, and Husbands, I doe claime a right
In all that is call'd lovely: take my sight
Sooner than my affection from the faire.
No face, no hand, proportion, line, or Ayre
Of beautie; but the Muse hath interest in: 15
There is not worne that lace, purle, knot or pin,
But is the Poets matter: And he must,
When he is furious, love, although not lust.
But then consent, your Daughters and your Wives,
(If they be faire and worth it) have their lives 20
Made longer by our praises. Or, if not,
Wish, you had fowle ones, and deformed got;
Curst in their Cradles, or there chang'd by Elves,
So to be sure you doe injoy your selves.
Yet keepe those up in sackcloth too, or lether, 25
For Silke will draw some sneaking Songster thither.
It is a ryming Age, and Verses swarme
At every stall; The Cittie Cap's a charme.
But I who live, and have liv'd twentie yeare
Where I may handle Silke, as free, and neere, 30
As any Mercer; or the whale-bone man

---

30. *where I may handle Silke . . . :* that is, at court. This dates the poem about 1624.

That quilts those bodies, I have leave to span;
Have eaten with the Beauties, and the wits,
And braveries of Court, and felt their fits
Of love, and hate: and came so nigh to know 35
Whether their faces were their owne, or no:
It is not likely I should now looke downe
Upon a Velvet Petticote, or a Gowne,
Whose like I have knowne the Taylors Wife put on
To doe her Husbands rites in, e're 'twere gone 40
Home to the Customer: his Letcherie
Being, the best clothes still to praeoccupie.
Put a Coach-mare in Tissue, must I horse
Her presently? Or leape thy Wife of force,
When by thy sordid bountie she hath on 45
A Gowne of that, was the Caparison?
So I might dote upon thy Chaires, and Stooles,
That are like cloath'd: must I be of those fooles
Of race accompted, that no passion have
But when thy Wife (as thou conceiv'st) is brave? 50
Then ope thy wardrobe, thinke me that poore Groome
That from the Foot-man, when he was become
An Officer there, did make most solemne love,
To ev'ry Petticote he brush'd, and Glove
He did lay up, and would adore the shooe, 55
Or slipper was left off, and kisse it too,
Court every hanging Gowne, and after that,
Lift up some one, and doe, I know not what.
Thou didst tell me; and wert o're-joy'd to peepe
In at a hole, and see these Actions creepe 60
From the poore wretch, which though he play'd in prose,
He would have done in verse, with any of those
Wrung on the Withers, by Lord Loves despight,
Had he'had the facultie to reade, and write!
Such Songsters there are store of; witnesse he 65
That chanc'd the lace, laid on a Smock, to see,
And straight-way spent a Sonnet; with that other
That (in pure Madrigal) unto his Mother
Commended the French-hood, and Scarlet gowne
The Lady Mayresse pass'd in through the Towne, 70

Unto the Spittle Sermon. O, what strange
Varietie of Silkes were on th'Exchange!
Or in Moore-fields, this other night! sings one,
Another answers, 'Lasse, those Silkes are none,
In smiling *L'envoye,* as he would deride 75
Any Comparison had with his Cheap-side.
And vouches both the Pageant, and the Day,
When not the Shops, but windowes doe display
The Stuffes, the Velvets, Plushes, Fringes, Lace,
And all the originall riots of the place: 80
Let the poore fooles enjoy their follies, love
A Goat in Velvet; so some block could move
Under that cover; an old Mid-wives hat!
Or a Close-stoole so cas'd; or any fat
Bawd, in a Velvet scabberd! I envy 85
None of their pleasures! nor will aske thee, why
Thou art jealous of thy Wifes, or Daughters Case:
More than of eithers manners, wit, or face!

71. *the Spittle Sermon:* preached at Easter time before the civic dignitaries of St. Mary's Hospital.

XLIII

An Execration upon Vulcan

And why to me this, thou lame Lord of fire,
What had I done that might call on thine ire?
Or urge thy Greedie flame, thus to devoure
So many my Yeares-labours in an houre?
I ne're attempted, *Vulcan,* 'gainst thy life; 5
Nor made least line of love to thy loose Wife;
Or in remembrance of thy affront, and scorne,
With Clownes, and Tradesmen, kept thee clos'd in horne.

Written late in 1623, after Jonson's library and manuscripts were destroyed by fire.

6. *loose Wife:* Venus, who betrayed him with Mars.
8. *horne:* the cuckold's emblematic horns. By line 10 they have become flamboyantly public. The flame in a lantern was protected by a thin sheet of horn.

'Twas *Jupiter* that hurl'd thee headlong downe,
And *Mars,* that gave thee a Lanthorne for a Crowne: 10
Was it because thou wert of old denied
By *Jove* to have *Minerva* for thy Bride,
That since thou tak'st all envious care and paine,
To ruine any issue of the braine?
Had I wrote treason there, or heresie, 15
Imposture, witchcraft, charmes, or blasphemie,
I had deserv'd, then, thy consuming lookes,
Perhaps, to have been burned with my bookes.
But, on thy malice, tell me, didst thou spie
Any, least loose, or scurrile paper, lie 20
Conceal'd, or kept there, that was fit to be,
By thy owne vote, a sacrifice to thee?
Did I there wound the honours of the Crowne?
Or taxe the Glories of the Church, and Gowne?
Itch to defame the State? or brand the Times? 25
And my selfe most, in some selfe-boasting Rimes?
If none of these, then why this fire? Or find
A cause before; or leave me one behind.
Had I compil'd from *Amadis de Gaule,*
Th'*Esplandians, Arthurs, Palmerins,* and all 30
The learned Librarie of Don Quixote;
And so some goodlier monster had begot,
Or spun out Riddles, and weav'd fiftie tomes
Of *Logogriphes,* and curious *Palindromes,*
Or pomp'd for those hard trifles *Anagrams,* 35
Or *Eteostichs,* or those finer flammes
Of Egges, and Halberds, Cradles, and a Herse,
A paire of Scisars, and a Combe in verse;

---

31. *Librarie of Don Quixote:* it contained 100 folio volumes of such romances as those cited in lines 29–30.
34. *Logogriphes:* word puzzles.
Palindromes: phrases that can be read in either direction, like "Niagara, O roar again."
36. *Eteostichs:* encoded dates, for example, LorD haVe MerCIe Vpon Vs (L + D + V + M + C + I + V + V = 1666).
37–38: apparently "shaped" poems, like Herbert's "Easter Wings."

Acrostichs, and *Telestichs,* on jumpe names,
Thou then hadst had some colour for thy flames, 40
On such my serious follies; But, thou'lt say,
There were some pieces of as base allay,
And as false stampe there; parcels of a Play,
Fitter to see the fire-light, than the day;
Adulterate moneys, such as might not goe: 45
Thou should'st have stay'd, till publike fame said so.
Shee is the Judge, Thou Executioner:
Or if thou needs would'st trench upon her power,
Thou mightst have yet enjoy'd thy crueltie
With some more thrift, and more varietie: 50
Thou mightst have had me perish, piece, by piece,
To light Tobacco, or save roasted Geese;
Sindge Capons, or poore Pigges, dropping their eyes;
Condemn'd me to the Ovens with the pies;
And so, have kept me dying a whole age, 55
Not ravish'd all hence in a minutes rage.
But that's a marke, whereof thy Rites doe boast,
To make consumption, ever where thou go'st;
Had I fore-knowne of this thy least desire
T'have held a Triumph, or a feast of fire, 60
Especially in paper; that, that steame
Had tickled your large Nosthrill: many a Reame,
To redeeme mine, I had sent in; enough,
Thou should'st have cry'd, and all beene proper stuffe.
The *Talmud,* and the *Alcoran* had come, 65
With pieces of the *Legend;* The whole summe
Of errant Knight-hood, with the Dames, and Dwarfes;
The charmed Boates, and the inchanted Wharfes,
The *Tristrams, Lanc'lots, Turpins,* and the *Peers,*
All the madde *Rolands,* and sweet *Oliveers;* 70
To *Merlins* Marvailes, and his *Caballs* losse,
With the Chimaera of the *Rosie-Crosse,*
Their Seales, their Characters, Hermetique rings,

---

39. *Acrostichs* spell a name with the initial letters of the lines, *telestichs* with the final letters.
66. *the* Legend: a thirteenth-century collections of saints' lives.

Their Jemme of Riches, and bright Stone, that brings
Invisibilitie, and strength, and tongues:
The art of kindling the true Coale, by lungs;
With *Nicholas Pasquill's,* Meddle with your match,
And the strong lines, that so the time doe catch,
Or Captaine *Pamphlets* horse, and foot; that sallie
Upon th'Exchange, still out of Popes-head-Alley, 80
The weekly Corrants, with *Pauls* Seale; and all
Th'admir'd discourses of the Prophet *Ball:*
These, had'st thou pleas'd either to dine, or sup,
Had made a meale for *Vulcan* to lick up.
But in my Deske, what was there to accite 85
So ravenous, and vast an appetite?
I dare not say a body, but some parts
There were of search, and mastry in the Arts.
All the old *Venusine,* in Poetrie,
And lighted by the *Stagerite,* could spie, 90
Was there made English: with the Grammar too,
To teach some that, their Nurses could not doe,
The puritie of Language; and among
The rest, my journey into *Scotland* sung,
With all th'adventures; Three bookes not afraid 95
To speake the fate of the *Sicilian* Maid
To our owne Ladyes; and in storie there
Of our fift *Henry,* eight of his nine yeare;
Wherein was oyle, beside the succour spent,
Which noble *Carew, Cotton, Selden* lent: 100
And twice-twelve-yeares stor'd up humanitie,
With humble Gleanings in Divinitie;
After the Fathers, and those wiser Guides
Whom Faction had not drawne to studie sides.

77–82: these lines enumerate sundry pamphlets, newsletters, and tip-sheets.

89–90: his translation of the *Ars Poetica,* which the scholarship of his day supposed Horace to have derived from "the Stagirite," Aristotle.

96. Sicilian *Maid:* the heroine of an allegory of European politics which Jonson had translated at James I's behest.

100. Richard Carew, Sir Robert Cotton, John Selden, eminent antiquarians. Some source materials on Henry V lent Jonson by Cotton were destroyed in the fire.

How in these ruines, *Vulcan,* thou dost lurke, 105
All soote, and embers! odious, as thy worke!
I now begin to doubt, if ever Grace,
Or Goddesse, could be patient of thy face.
Thou woo *Minerva!* or to wit aspire!
'Cause thou canst halt, with us, in Arts, and Fire! 110
Sonne of the Wind! for so thy mother gone
With lust conceiv'd thee; Father thou hadst none:
When thou wert borne, and that thou look'st at best,
She durst not kisse, but flung thee from her brest.
And so did *Jove,* who ne're meant thee his Cup: 115
No mar'le the Clownes of *Lemnos* tooke thee up,
For none but Smiths would have made thee a God.
Some Alchimist there may yet be, or odde
Squire of the Squibs, against the Pageant day,
May to thy name a *Vulcanale* say; 120
And for it lose his eyes with Gun-powder,
As th'other may his braines with Quicksilver.
Well-fare the Wise-men yet, on the *Banckside,*
My friends, the Watermen! They could provide
Against thy furie, when to serve their needs, 125
They made a *Vulcan* of a sheafe of Reedes,
Whom they durst handle in their holy-day coates,
And safely trust to dresse, not burne their Boates.
But, O those Reeds! thy meere disdaine of them
Made thee beget that cruell Stratagem, 130
(Which, some are pleas'd to stile but thy madde pranck)
Against the *Globe,* the Glory of the *Banke,*
Which, though it were the Fort of the whole Parish,
Flank'd with a Ditch, and forc'd out of a Marish,
I saw with two poore Chambers taken in 135
And raz'd; e're thought could urge, this might have beene!

---

111. To explain ancient statements that Vulcan was Juno's unfathered son, Jonson with studied tactlessness invokes the belief that mares could be impregnated by wind.
116. *mar'le:* marvel, wonder.
132. *Globe:* Shakespeare's theatre, burned in 1613.
135. *Chambers:* cannon. The disaster was caused by ceremonial gunfire during a performance of *Henry VIII.*

See the worlds Ruines! nothing but the piles
Left! and wit since to cover it with Tiles.
The Brethren, they streight nois'd it out for Newes,
'Twas verily some Relique of the Stewes: 140
And this a Sparkle of that fire let loose
That was lock'd up in the *Winchestrian* Goose
Bred on the *Banck,* in time of Poperie,
When Venus there maintain'd the Misterie.
But, others fell, with that conceipt by the eares, 145
And cry'd, it was a threatning to the beares;
And that accursed ground, the *Parish-Garden:*
Nay, (sigh'd a Sister) 'twas the Nun, *Kate Arden,*
Kindled the fire! But, then did one returne,
No Foole would his owne harvest spoile, or burne! 150
If that were so, thou rather wouldst advance
The place, that was thy Wives inheritance.
O no, cry'd all. *Fortune,* for being a whore,
Scap'd not his Justice any jot the more:
He burnt that Idoll of the Revels too: 155
Nay, let *White-Hall* with Revels have to doe,
Though but in daunces, it shall know his power;
There was a Judgement shew'n too in an houre.
Hee is true *Vulcan* still! He did not spare
Troy, though it were so much his *Venus* care. 160
Foole, wilt thou let that in example come?
Did she not save from thence, to build a *Rome?*
And what hast thou done in these pettie spights,
More then advanc'd the houses, and their rites?
I will not argue thee, from those of guilt, 165
For they were burnt, but to the better built.

---

138. The Globe was rebuilt the next year, but not with a thatched roof.

142. *Winchestrian Goose:* venereal disease. Jonson reflects Puritan surmise that the fire was a judgment on the district's playgoing, immorality, and episcopacy. The Bishop of Winchester's property, on the Bankside, included the brothels of Southwark.

147. *Parish-Garden:* site of the bear pits, near the Globe.

148. *Nun:* a whore. Kate Arden was a notorious one.

153. The Fortune theatre also burned down, in 1621. Dame Fortune is often represented as a whore.

156. *Whitehall:* the banquet hall there was burned down in 1618.

'Tis true, that in thy wish they were destroy'd,
Which thou hast only vented, not enjoy'd.
So would'st th'have run upon the *Rolls* by stealth,
And didst invade part of the Common-wealth, 170
In those Records, which were all Chronicles gone,
Will be remembered by *Six Clerkes*, to one.
But, say all sixe, Good Men, what answer yee?
Lyes there no Writ, out of the *Chancerie*,
Against this *Vulcan*? No Injunction? 175
No order? no Decree? Though we be gone
At *Common-Law*: Me thinkes in his despight
A Court of Equitie should doe us right:
But to confine him to the Brew-houses,
The Glasse-house, Dye-fats, and their Fornaces; 180
To live in Sea-coale, and goe forth in smoake;
Or lest that vapour might the Citie choake,
Condemne him to the Brick-kills, or some Hill-
Foot (out in *Sussex*) to an iron Mill;
Or in small Fagots have him blaze about 185
Vile Tavernes, and the Drunkards pisse him out;
Or in the *Bell*-Mans Lanthorne, like a spie,
Burne to a snuffe, and then stinke out, and die:
I could invent a sentence, yet were worse;
But I'le conclude all in a civill curse. 190
Pox on your flameship, Vulcan; if it be
To all as fatall as't hath beene to me,
And to *Pauls-Steeple;* which was unto us
'Bove all your Fire-workes had at *Ephesus*,
Or *Alexandria;* and though a Divine 195
Losse remaines yet, as unrepair'd as mine.
Would you had kept your Forge, at *Aetna* still,
And there made Swords, Bills, Glaves, and Armes your fill.
Maintain'd the trade at *Bilbo;* or else-where;

169–172. the Six Clerk's Office in Chancery Lane, burned in 1621.
193. *Pauls-Steeple:* the steeple of old St. Paul's Cathedral, burned in 1561.
194. *Ephesus:* site of the Temple of Diana, burned down in 356 B.C.
195. *Alexandria:* the burning of the library here, in A.D. 640, was one of history's irreparable cultural disasters.
199. *Bilbo:* Balboa, in Spain, source of the best blades. Jonson intimates that Vulcan should stick to his legitimate trade, blacksmithing.

Strooke in at *Millan* with the Cutlers there; 200
Or stay'd but where the Fryar, and you first met,
Who from the Divels-Arse did Guns beget;
Or fixt in the *Low-Countrey's,* where you might
On both sides doe your mischiefes with delight;
Blow up, and ruine, myne, and countermyne, 205
Make your Petards, and Granats, all your fine
Engines of Murder, and receive the praise
Of massacring Man-kind so many wayes.
We aske your absence here, we all love peace,
And pray the fruites thereof, and the increase; 210
So doth the *King,* and most of the *Kings men*
That have good places: therefore once agen,
Pox on thee, *Vulcan,* thy *Pandora's* pox,
And all the Evils that flew out of her box
Light on thee: Or if those plagues will not doo, 215
Thy Wives pox on thee, and *Bess Braughtons* too.

---

201. *the Fryar:* Roger Bacon, supposed inventor of gunpowder.
216. *Bess Braughton:* once a fabulously expensive courtesan (hence Jonson's implied comparison with Venus), she ended her career wretched and syphilitic.

LXX

To the Immortall Memorie, and Friendship of That Noble Paire, Sir Lucius Cary, and Sir H. Morison

THE TURNE

Brave Infant of *Saguntum,* cleare
Thy comming forth in that great yeare,

The names of the parts of this poem translate the strophe, antistrophe and epode of which Greek "Pindaric" ode was built.

Sir Lucius Cary's friend and contemporary, Sir Henry Morison, died in 1629, aged about twenty.

1. *Infant of Saguntum:* Jonson's source, Pliny, gives even less detail about this affrighted child than does Jonson.

When the Prodigious *Hannibal* did crowne
His rage, with razing your immortall Towne.
Thou, looking then about, 5
E're thou wert halfe got out,
Wise child, did'st hastily returne,
And mad'st thy Mothers wombe thine urne.
How summ'd a circle didst thou leave man-kind
Of deepest lore, could we the Center find! 10

THE COUNTER-TURNE

Did wiser Nature draw thee back,
From out the horrour of that sack,
Where shame, faith, honour, and regard of right
Lay trampled on; the deeds of death, and night,
Urg'd, hurried forth, and horld 15
Upon th'affrighted world:
Sword, fire, and famine, with fell fury met;
And all on utmost ruine set;
As, could they but lifes miseries fore-see,
No doubt all Infants would returne like thee? 20

THE STAND

For, what is life, if measur'd by the space,
Not by the act?
Or masked man, if valu'd by his face,
Above his fact?
Here's one out-liv'd his Peeres, 25
And told forth fourescore yeares;
He vexed time, and busied the whole State;
Troubled both foes, and friends;
But ever to no ends:
What did this Stirrer, but die late? 30
How well at twentie had he falne, or stood!
For three of his foure-score, he did no good.

THE TURNE

Hee entred well, by vertuous parts,
Got up and thriv'd with honest arts:
He purchas'd friends, and fame, and honours then, 35
And had his noble name advanc'd with men:
But weary of that flight,
Hee stoop'd in all mens sight
To sordid flatteries, acts of strife,
And sunke in that dead sea of life 40
So deep, as he did then death's waters sup;
But that the Corke of Title boy'd him up.

THE COUNTER-TURNE

Alas, but *Morison* fell young:
Hee never fell, thou fall'st, my tongue.
Hee stood, a Souldier to the last right end, 45
A perfect Patriot, and a noble friend,
But most, a vertuous Sonne.
All Offices were done
By him, so ample, full, and round,
In weight, in measure, number, sound, 50
As though his age imperfect might appeare,
His life was of Humanitie the Spheare.

THE STAND

Goe now, and tell out dayes summ'd up with feares,
And make them yeares;
Produce thy masse of miseries on the Stage, 55
To swell thine age;
Repeat of things a throng,
To shew thou hast beene long,
Not liv'd; for Life doth her great actions spell,
By what was done and wrought 60
In season, and so brought
To light: her measures are, how well

Each syllab'e answer'd, and was form'd, how faire;
These make the lines of life, and that's her ayre.

THE TURNE

It is not growing like a tree 65
In bulke, doth make man better bee;
Or standing long an Oake, three hundred yeare,
To fall a logge at last, dry, bald, and seare:
A Lillie of a Day,
Is fairer farre, in May, 70
Although it fall, and die that night;
It was the Plant, and flowre of light.
In small proportions, we just beautie see:
And in short measures, life may perfect bee.

THE COUNTER-TURNE

Call, noble *Lucius,* then for Wine, 75
And let thy lookes with gladnesse shine:
Accept this garland, plant it on thy head,
And thinke, nay know, thy *Morison's* not dead.
Hee leap'd the present age,
Possest with holy rage, 80
To see that bright eternall Day:
Of which we *Priests,* and *Poets* say
Such truths, as we expect for happy men,
And there he lives with memorie: and *Ben*

THE STAND

Jonson, who sung this of him, e're he went 85
Himselfe to rest,
Or taste a part of that full joy he meant
To have exprest,
In this bright *Asterisme:*
Where it were friendships schisme, 90
(Were not his *Lucius* long with us to tarry)

89. *Asterisme:* a constellation.

To separate these twi-
Lights, the *Dioscuri;*
And keepe the one halfe from his *Harry.*
But fate doth so alternate the designe, 95
Whilst that in heav'n, this light on earth must shine.

THE TURNE

And shine as you exalted are;
Two names of friendship, but one Starre:
Of hearts the union. And those not by chance
Made, or indenture, or leas'd out t'advance 100
The profits for a time.
No pleasures vaine did chime,
Of rimes, or ryots, at your feasts,
Orgies of drinke, or fain'd protests:
But simple love of greatnesse, and of good; 105
That knits brave minds, and manners, more than blood.

THE COUNTER-TURNE

This made you first to know the Why
You lik'd, then after, to apply
That liking; and approach so one the tother,
Till either grew a portion of the other: 110
Each stiled by his end,
The Copie of his friend.
You liv'd to be the great surnames,
And titles, by which all made claimes
Unto the Vertue. Nothing perfect done, 115
But as a *Cary,* or a *Morison.*

THE STAND

And such a force the faire example had,
As they that saw

---

93. *Dioscuri:* the Greek twins Castor and Pollux, identified with the constellation Gemini.

The good, and durst not practise it, were glad
That such a Law 120
Was left yet to Man-kind;
Where they might read, and find
Friendship, in deed, was written, not in words:
And with the heart, not pen,
Of two so early men, 125
Whose lines her rowles were, and records,
Who, e're the first downe bloomed on the chin,
Had sow'd these fruits, and got the harvest in.

Lxxix

New yeares, expect new gifts: Sister, your Harpe,
  Lute, Lyre, Theorbo, all are call'd to day,
Your change of Notes, the flat, the meane, the sharpe,
  To shew the rites, and t'usher forth the way
Of the New Yeare, in a new silken warpe, 5
    To fit the softnesse of our Yeares-gift: When
    We sing the best of Monarchs, Masters, Men;
For, had we here said lesse, we had sung nothing then.

A New-Yeares-Gift Sung to King Charles, 1635

Rector To day old Janus opens the new yeare,
Chorus And shuts the old. Haste, haste, all loyall Swaines, 10
That know the times, and seasons when t'appeare,
  And offer your just service on these plaines;
  Best Kings expect first-fruits of your glad gaines.

1. Pan is the great Preserver of our bounds.
2. To him we owe all profits of our grounds, 15
3. Our milke, 4. Our fells, 5. Our fleeces,
    6. and first Lambs,
7. Our teeming Ewes, 8. and lustie-mounting Rammes.

9. See where he walkes with Mira by his side.
Chorus Sound, sound his praises loud, and with his hers divide.

Shepherd Of Pan wee sing, the best of Hunters, Pan, 20
That drives the Hart to seeke unused wayes,
And in the chase, more then Sylvanus can,
Chorus Heare, O you Groves, and, Hills, resound his praise.

Nymph Of brightest Mira, doe we raise our Song,
Sister of Pan, and glory of the Spring: 25
Who walkes on Earth as May still went along.
Chorus Rivers, and Vallies, Eccho what wee sing.

Shepherd Of Pan wee sing, the Chiefe of Leaders, Pan,
That leades our flocks and us, and calls both forth
To better Pastures then great Pales can: 30
Chorus Heare, O you Groves, and, Hills, resound his worth.

Nymph Of brightest Mira, is our Song; the grace
Of all that Nature, yet, to life did bring;
And were shee lost, could best supply her place.
Chorus Rivers, and Valleys, Eccho what we sing. 35

1. Where ere they tread th'enamour'd ground,
The Fairest flowers are alwayes found;
2. As if the beauties of the yeare
Still waited on 'hem where they were.
1. Hee is the Father of our peace; 40
2. She, to the Crowne, hath brought encrease.
1. Wee know no other power than his,
Pan only our great Shep'ard is,
Chorus Our great, our good. Where one's so drest
In truth of colours, both are best. 45
Haste, haste you hither, all you gentler Swaines,
That have a Flock, or Herd, upon these plaines;
This is the great Preserver of our bounds,
To whom you owe all duties of your grounds;
Your Milkes, your Fells, your Fleeces, and first Lambes, 50
Your teeming Ewes, as well as mounting Rammes;
Whose praises let's report unto the Woods,

---

30. ***Pales:*** early Italian shepherd-goddess.

That they may take it eccho'd by the Floods.
'Tis hee, 'tis hee, in singing hee,
And hunting, Pan, exceedeth thee. 55
Hee gives all plentie, and encrease,
Hee is the author of our peace.

Where e're he goes upon the ground,
The better grasse, and flowers are found.
To sweeter Pastures lead hee can, 60
Then ever Pales could, or Pan;
Hee drives diseases from our Folds,
The theefe from spoyle, his presence holds.
Pan knowes no other power than his,
This only the great Shep'ard is. 65
'Tis hee, 'tis hee, &c.

LXXXIII

An Elegie on the Lady Jane Pawlet, Marchion: of Winton

What gentle Ghost, besprent with *April* deaw,
Hayles me, so solemnly, to yonder Yewgh?
And beckning wooes me, from the fatall tree
To pluck a Garland, for her selfe, or mee?
I doe obey you, Beautie! for in death, 5
You seeme a faire one! O that you had breath,
To give your shade a name! Stay, stay, I feele
A horrour in mee! all my blood is steele!
Stiffe! starke! my joynts 'gainst one another knock!
Whose Daughter? ha? Great *Savage* of the Rock? 10
Hee's good, as great. I am almost a stone!
And e're I can aske more of her shee's gone!
Alas, I am all Marble! write the rest
Thou wouldst have written, Fame, upon my brest:
It is a large faire table, and a true, 15
And the disposure will be something new,

---

10. Her father was Viscount Savage, of Rock Savage in Cheshire.

When I, who would the Poet have become,
At least may beare th'inscription to her Tombe.
Shee was the Lady *Jane,* and *Marchionisse*
Of *Winchester;* the Heralds can tell this. 20
Earle *Rivers* Grand-Child—serve not formes, good Fame,
Sound thou her Vertues, give her soule a Name.
Had I a thousand Mouthes, as many Tongues,
And voyce to raise them from my brazen Lungs,
I durst not aime at that: The dotes were such 25
Thereof, no notion can expresse how much
Their Carract was! I, or my trump must breake,
But rather I, should I of that part speake!
It is too neere of kin to Heaven, the Soule,
To be describ'd! Fames fingers are too foule 30
To touch these Mysteries! We may admire
The blaze, and splendor, but not handle fire!
What she did here, by great example, well,
T'inlive posteritie, her Fame may tell!
And, calling truth to witnesse, make that good 35
From the inherent Graces in her blood!
Else, who doth praise a person by a new,
But a fain'd way, doth rob it of the true.
Her Sweetnesse, Softnesse, her fair Curtesie,
Her wary guardes, her wise simplicitie, 40
Were like a ring of Vertues, 'bout her set,
And pietie the Center, where all met.
A reverend State she had, an awfull Eye,
A dazling, yet inviting, Majestie:
What Nature, Fortune, Institution, Fact 45
Could summe to a perfection, was her Act!
How did she leave the world? with what contempt?
Just as she in it liv'd! and so exempt
From all affection! when they urg'd the Cure
Of her disease, how did her soule assure 50
Her suffrings, as the body had beene away!
And to the Torturers (her Doctors) say,
Stick on your Cupping-glasses, feare not, put

---

25. *dotes:* endowments.
27. *carract:* carat, that is, worth.

Your hottest Causticks to, burne, lance, or cut:
'Tis but a body which you can torment, 55
And I, into the world, all Soule, was sent!
Then comforted her Lord! and blest her Sonne!
Chear'd her faire Sisters in her race to runne!
With gladnesse temper'd her sad Parents teares!
Made her friends joyes, to get above their feares! 60
And, in her last act, taught the Standers-by,
With admiration, and applause to die!
Let Angels sing her glories, who did call
Her spirit home, to her originall!
Who saw the way was made it! and were sent 65
To carry, and conduct the Complement
'Twixt death and life! Where her mortalitie
Became her Birth-day to Eternitie!
And now, through circumfused light, she lookes
On Natures secrets, there, as her owne bookes: 70
Speakes Heavens Language, and discourses free
To every *Order*, ev'ry *Hierarchie!*
Beholds her Maker! and, in him, doth see
What the beginnings of all beauties be;
And all beatitudes, that thence doe flow: 75
Which they that have the Crowne are sure to know!
Goe now, her happy Parents, and be sad
If you not understand, what Child you had,
If you dare grude at Heaven, and repent
T'have paid againe a blessing was but lent, 80
And trusted so, as it deposited lay
At pleasure, to be call'd for, every day!
If you can envie your owne Daughters blisse,
And wish her state lesse happie than it is!
If you can cast about your either eye, 85
And see all dead here, or about to dye!
The Starres, that are the Jewels of the Night,
And Day, deceasing! with the Prince of light,
The Sunne! great Kings! and mightiest Kingdomes fall!
Whole Nations! nay, Mankind! the World, with all 90

52–54. She died, aged twenty-four, after doctors lanced an abscess on her cheek.

That ever had beginning there, to'ave end!
With what injustice should one soule pretend
T'escape this common knowne necessitie,
When we were all borne, we began to die;
And, but for that Contention, and brave strife 95
The Christian hath t'enjoy the future life,
Hee were the wretched'st of the race of men:
But as he soares at that, he bruiseth then
The Serpents head: Gets above Death, and Sinne,
And, sure of Heaven, rides triumphing in. 100

LXXXV

The Praises of a Countrie Life. (Horace, Epode 2)

Happie is he, that from all Businesse cleere,
As the old race of Mankind were,
With his owne Oxen tills his Sires left lands,
And is not in the Usurers bands:
Nor Souldier-like started with rough alarmes, 5
Nor dreads the Seas inraged harmes:
But flees the Barre and Courts, with the proud bords,
And waiting Chambers of great Lords.
The Poplar tall, he then doth marrying twine
With the growne issue of the Vine; 10
And with his hooke lops off the fruitless race,
And sets more happy in the place:
Or in the bending Vale beholds a-farre
The lowing herds there grazing are:
Or the prest honey in pure pots doth keepe 15
Of Earth, and sheares the tender Sheepe:
Or when that Autumne, through the fields lifts round
His head, with mellow Apples crown'd,
How plucking Peares, his owne hand grafted had,
And purple-matching Grapes, hee's glad! 20
With which, Priapus, he may thanke thy hands,
And, Sylvane, thine that keptst his Lands!

---

21. *Priapus:* the god who protected gardens.
22. *Sylvane:* Sylvanus, protector of landmarks.

Then now beneath some ancient Oke he may,
  Now in the rooted Grasse him lay,
Whilst from the higher Bankes doe slide the floods, 25
  The soft birds quarrell in the Woods,
The Fountaines murmure as the streames doe creepe,
  And all invite to easie sleepe.
Then when the thundring Jove his Snow and showres
  Are gathering by the Wintry houres; 30
Or hence, or thence, he drives with many a Hound
  Wild Bores into his toyles pitch'd round:
Or straines on his small forke his subtill nets
  For th'eating Thrush, or Pit-falls sets:
And snares the fearfull Hare, and new-come Crane, 35
  And 'counts them sweet rewards so ta'en.
Who (amongst these delights) would not forget
  Loves cares so evill, and so great?
But if, to boot with these, a chaste Wife meet
  For houshold aid, and Children sweet; 40
Such as the Sabines, or a Sun-burnt-blowse,
  Some lustie quick Apulians spouse,
To deck the hallow'd Harth with old wood fir'd
  Against the Husband comes home tir'd;
That penning the glad flock in hurdles by, 45
  Their swelling udders doth draw dry:
And from the sweet Tub Wine of this yeare takes,
  And unbought viands ready makes:
Not Lucrine Oysters I could then more prize,
  Nor Turbot, nor bright Golden eyes: 50
If with bright floods, the Winter troubled much,
  Into our Seas send any such:
Th'Ionian God-wit, nor the Ginny hen
  Could not goe downe my belly then
More sweet than Olives, that new gather'd be 55
  From fattest branches of the Tree:
Or the herb Sorrell, that loves Meadows still,
  Or Mallowes loosing bodyes ill:
Or at the Feast of Bounds, the Lambe then slaine,
  Or Kid forc't from the Wolfe againe. 60
Among these Cates how glad the sight doth come

Of the fed flocks approaching home!
To view the weary Oxen draw, with bare
And fainting necks, the turned Share!
The wealthy houshold swarme of bondmen met, 65
And 'bout the steeming Chimney set!
These thoughts when Usurer Alphius, now about
To turne mere farmer, had spoke out,
'Gainst th'Ides, his moneys he gets in with paine,
At th'Calends, puts all out againe. 70

69–70. The Calends and Ides were days for settlement of debts in Rome.

MISCELLANEOUS POEMS

Hymn to Diana

FROM CYNTHIA'S REVELS

Queene, and Huntresse, chaste, and faire,
Now the Sunne is laid to sleepe,
Seated, in thy silver chaire,
State in wonted manner keepe:
Hesperus intreats thy light, 5
Goddesse, excellently bright.

Earth, let not thy envious shade
Dare it selfe to interpose;
Cynthias shining orbe was made
Heaven to cleere, when day did close: 10
Blesse us then with wished sight,
Goddesse, excellently bright.

Lay thy bow of pearle apart,
And thy cristall-shining quiver;

Give unto the flying hart 15
Space to breathe, how short soever:
Thou that mak'st a day of night,
Goddesse, excellently bright.

Clerimont's Song

FROM EPICENE, OR THE SILENT WOMAN

Still to be neat, still to be drest,
As, you were going to a feast;
Still to be pou'dred, still perfum'd:
Lady, it is to be presum'd,
Though arts hid causes are not found, 5
All is not sweet, all is not sound.

Give me a looke, give me a face,
That makes simplicitie a grace;
Robes loosely flowing, haire as free:
Such sweet neglect more taketh me, 10
Than all th'adulteries of art.
They strike mine eyes, but not my heart.

To the Memory of my Beloved, the Author, Mr. William Shakespeare: And What He Hath Left Us

To draw no envy (*Shakespeare*) on thy name,
Am I thus ample to thy Booke, and Fame:
While I confesse thy writings to be such,
As neither *Man,* nor *Muse,* can praise too much.
'Tis true, and all mens suffrage. But these wayes 5

Written for incorporation in the Shakespeare First Folio, 1623.

Were not the paths I meant unto thy praise:
For seeliest Ignorance on these may light,
Which, when it sounds at best, but eccho's right;
Or blinde Affection, which doth ne're advance
The truth, but gropes, and urgeth all by chance; 10
Or crafty Malice, might pretend this praise,
And thinke to ruine, where it seem'd to raise.
These are, as some infamous Baud, or Whore,
Should praise a Matron. What could hurt her more?
But thou art proofe against them, and indeed 15
Above th'ill fortune of them, or the need.
I therefore will begin. Soule of the Age!
The applause! delight! the wonder of our Stage!
My *Shakespeare,* rise; I will not lodge thee by
Chaucer, or *Spenser,* or bid *Beaumont* lye 20
A little further, to make thee a roome:
Thou art a Moniment, without a tombe,
And art alive still, while thy Booke doth live,
And we have wits to read, and praise to give.
That I not mixe thee so, my braine excuses; 25
I meane with great, but disproportion'd *Muses:*
For, if I thought my judgement were of yeeres,
I should commit thee surely with thy peeres,
And tell, how farre thou didst our *Lily* out-shine,
Or sporting *Kid,* or *Marlowes* mighty line. 30
And though thou hadst small *Latine,* and lesse *Greeke,*
From thence to honour thee, I would not seeke
For names; but call forth thund'ring *Aeschilus,*
Euripides, and *Sophocles* to us,
Paccuvius, Accius, him of *Cordova* dead, 35
To life againe, to heare thy Buskin tread,
And shake a Stage: Or, when thy Sockes were on,
Leave thee alone, for the comparison
Of all, that insolent *Greece,* or haughtie *Rome*

---

35. Horace mentions the dramatists Paccuvius and Accius. "Him of Cordova" in Seneca, whose tragedies were vastly influential in the Elizabethan era.
36. *Buskin:* the high boots worn by Roman tragic actors.
37. *Sockes:* the low-heeled shoes worn for comedy.

Sent forth, or since did from their ashes come. 40
Triumph, my *Britaine,* thou hast one to showe,
To whom all Scenes of *Europe* homage owe.
He was not of an age, but for all time!
And all the *Muses* still were in their prime,
When like *Apollo* he came forth to warme 45
Our eares, or like a *Mercury* to charme!
Nature her selfe was proud of his designes,
And joy'd to weare the dressing of his lines!
Which were so richly spun, and woven so fit,
As, since, she will vouchsafe no other Wit. 50
The merry *Greeke,* tart *Aristophanes,*
Neat *Terrence,* witty *Plautus,* now not please;
But antiquated, and deserted lye
As they were not of Natures family.
Yet must I not give Nature all: Thy Art, 55
My gentle *Shakespeare,* must enjoy a part
For though the *Poets* matter, Nature be,
His Art doth give the fashion. And, that he,
Who casts to write a living line, must sweat,
(Such as thine are) and strike the second heat 60
Upon the *Muses* anvile: turne the same,
(And himselfe with it) that he thinkes to frame;
Or for the lawrell, he may gaine a scorne,
For a good *Poet's* made, as well as borne.
And such wert thou. Looke how the fathers face 65
Lives in his issue, even so, the race
Of *Shakespeares* minde, and manners brightly shines
In his well torned, and true-filed lines:
In each of which, he seemes to shake a Lance,
As brandish't at the eyes of Ignorance. 70
Sweet Swan of *Avon!* what a sight it were
To see thee in our waters yet appeare,
And make those flights upon the bankes of *Thames,*
That so did take *Eliza,* and our *James!*
But stay, I see thee in the *Hemisphere* 75
Advanc'd, and made a Constellation there!
Shine forth, thou Starre of *Poets,* and with rage,

Or influence, chide, or cheere the drooping Stage;
Which, since thy flight from hence, hath mourn'd like night,
And despaires day, but for thy Volumes light. 80

Ode to Himselfe

Come leave the loathed Stage,
And the more loathsome Age,
Where pride and impudence in faction knit,
Usurpe the Chaire of wit:
Inditing and arraigning every day, 5
Something they call a Play.
Let their fastidious vaine
Commission of the braine,
Runne on, and rage, sweat, censure, and condemn,
They were not made for thee, lesse thou for them. 10

Say that thou pour'st'hem wheat,
And they would Akornes eat:
'Twere simple fury, still thy selfe to wast
On such as have no taste:
To offer them a surfeit of pure bread, 15
Whose appetites are dead:
No, give them Graines their fill,
Huskes, Draffe to drinke, and swill:
If they love Lees, and leave the lusty Wine,
Envy them not, their pallat's with the Swine. 20

No doubt a mouldy Tale,
Like *Pericles,* and stale
As the Shrives crusts, and nasty as his Fish,
Scraps out of every Dish,
Throwne forth and rak'd into the common Tub, 25
May keep up the Play Club.

Written after the failure of Jonson's play *The New Inn* (1629).

Broomes sweepings doe as well
There, as his Masters meale:
For who the relish of these guests will fit,
Needs set them but the Almes-basket of wit. 30

And much good do't yee then,
Brave Plush and Velvet men
Can feed on Orts; and safe in your scoene cloaths,
Dare quit upon your Oathes
The Stagers, and the stage-writes too; your Peers, 35
Of stuffing your large eares
With rage of Commicke socks,
Wrought upon twenty Blocks;
Which, if they're torne, and foule, and patch'd enough,
The Gamsters share your gilt, and you their stuffe. 40

Leave things so prostitute,
And take th'*Alcaike* Lute;
Or thine owne *Horace*, or *Anacreons* Lyre;
Warme thee by *Pindars* fire:
And though thy Nerves be shrunke, and blood be cold, 45
Ere years have made thee old,
Strike that disdainfull heat
Throughout, to their defeat:
As curious fooles, and envious of thy straine,
May blushing sweare, no Palsi's in thy braine. 50

But when they heare thee sing
The glories of thy King;
His zeale to God, and his just awe of men,
They may be blood-shaken, then
Feele such a flesh-quake to possesse their powers, 55
That no tun'd Harpe like ours,
In sound of Peace or Warres,
Shall truely hit the Starres

27–28. Richard Brome had been Jonson's apprentice.
33. *Orts:* scraps.
37. *socks:* the low shoes worn by Roman comic actors.

When they shall read the Acts of *Charles* his Reigne,
And see his Chariot triumph 'bove his Waine. 60

60. Charles' Wain (wagon) was the name of the big dipper.

Song

FROM THE SAD SHEPHERD

Though I am young, and cannot tell,
Either what Death, or Love is well
Yet I have heard, they both beare darts,
And both doe ayme at humane hearts:
And then againe, I have been told, 5
Love wounds with heat, as Death with cold;
So that I feare, they doe but bring
Extreames to touch, and meane one thing.

As in a ruine, we it call
One thing to be blowne up, or fall; 10
Or to our end, like way may have,
By a flash of lightning, or a wave:
So Loves inflamed shaft, or brand,
May kill as soone as Deaths cold hand;
Except Loves fires the vertue have 15
To fright the frost out of the grave.

Song

FROM CYNTHIA'S REVELS

Slow, slow, fresh fount, keepe time with my salt teares;
Yet slower, yet, ô faintly gentle springs:
List to the heavy part the musique beares,
Woe weepes out her division, when shee sings.

Droupe hearbs, and flowres; 5
Fall griefe in showres;
Our beauties are not ours:
O, I could still
(Like melting snow upon some craggie hill,)
drop, drop, drop, drop,
Since natures pride is, now, a wither'd daffodill. 10

Francis Beaumont's Letter from the Country to Jonson

The Sun which doth the greatest comfort bringe
To absent friends, because the self same thinge
They know, they see, howe ever absent; is
Here our best Hay-maker (forgive mee this,
It is our Countrey style). In this warme shine 5
I lye, a Dreame of your full Mermaide wine:
O wee have water mixt with Claret Lees,
Drinke apt to bringe in dryer heresies
Than beere; Good only for a Sonnett straine
With fustian Metaphors to stuff the Braine, 10
So mixt, that given to the thirstiest one
T'will not prove Almes, unless he have the stone:
Tis sould by Puritans, mixt with intent
To make it serve for either Sacrament.
I thinke with one Draught mans Invention fades, 15
Twoe Cupps had quite marr'd Homers Iliades.
T'is licquor that will find out Sutcliffs witt,
Lye where it will, & make him write worse yet.
Fill'd with such moisture in a grievous qualme
Did Robert Wisdome write his singing Psalme. 20
And soe I must doe this, and yet I thinke
It is a Potion sent us downe to drinke

Written between 1609 and 1613. Francis Beaumont (1584–1616) wrote popular dramas in collaboration with Fletcher.

6. *Mermaid:* the celebrated tavern, frequented by Jonson and other wits.
17. *Sutcliff:* a dull controversialist.
20. *Robert Wisdome:* contributor to a metrical version of the Psalms.

By speciall Providence, keeps us from fights,
Makes us not laugh, when wee make leggs to Knights;
T'is this that keepes our minds fitt for our states, 25
A Med'cine to obey our Magistrates,
For wee doe live more free, than you; noe hate,
Noe envie of anothers happie state
Moves us, wee are all equall, every whitt:
Of land, that God gives men here, is their witt 30
If wee consider fully; for our best
And Gravest man, will with his Maine-house-jest
Scarce please you; we want subtilty to doe
The Cittie tricks, Lye, Hate, and flatter too:
Here are none that can beare a fained showe, 35
Strike when you winke, and then lament the blowe;
Whoe like Mills, sett the right way for to grinde
Can make their gaines alike with every winde.
Only some fellow with the subtlest pate
Amongst us, may perchance Equivocate 40
At selling of a horse, and that's the most.
Mee thinkes the litle witt I had is lost
Since I saw you; for witt is like a Rest
Held upp at Tennis, which men doe the best
With the best Gamsters. What things have wee seene 45
Done at the Mermaide? heard words that have beene
Soe nimble, & soe full of subtill flame
As if that every one from whom they came
Had meant to putt his whole witt in a Jest
And had resolved to live a foole the rest 50
Of his dull life; then, when there hath been throwne
Witt able enough to justifie the Towne
For three dayes past; witt that might warrant bee
For the whole Citty to talk foolishly
Till that were Cancell'd, & when wee were gone 55
Wee lefte an Aire behind, which was alone
Able to make the two next Companies
Right witty, though they were down-right Cockneyes.

---

24. *make leggs:* bow. The plethora of knights created by James I was a common theme for jest.
43. *Rest:* rally.

When I remember this, & see that nowe
The Countrey gentlemen begin t'allowe 60
My witt for drye bobbs, then I needs must crye
I see my dayes of Ballating are nigh:
I can already Riddle, and can sing
Catches, sell Bargaines, & I feare shall bring
My selfe to speak the hardest words I finde 65
Over, as fast as any with one winde,
That takes no medicines; but one thought of thee
Makes mee remember all these things to bee
The witt of our young men, fellowes that showe
Noe part of good, yet utter all they knowe: 70
Who like trees of the Guard, have growing soules
Only; Strong Destiny, which all Controules
I hope hath lefte a better fate in store
For mee thy friend, than to live evermore
Bannisht unto this home; twill once againe
Bring mee to thee, who wilt make smooth, and plaine
The way of knowledge for mee, and then I
Who'have noe good in mee, but simplicitie,
Knowe that it will my greatest comfort bee
T'acknowledge all the rest to Come from thee.

---

61. *drye bobbs:* coarse jokes.

62–67. An inventory of the country's intellectual diversions; the orthodox Horatian doctrine of lines 27–41 is by now losing its allure.

II

THE DONNE CIRCLE

Edward, Lord Herbert of Cherbury (1583–1648)

Sir Henry Wotton (1568–1639)

Aurelian Townshend (1583–1651)

Richard Corbett (1582–1635)

Henry King (1591–1669)

Townshend was on the periphery of the circle; Corbett is inserted for contrast. The other three were close to Donne.

II

THE DONNE CIRCLE

Edward, Lord Herbert of Cherbury (1583–1648)

Sir Henry Wotton (1568–1639)

Aurelian Townshend ([illegible])

Thomas Carew ([illegible])

Henry King (1592–1669)

[illegible]
[illegible]
[illegible]

Edward, Lord Herbert of Cherbury

(1583-1648)

Magdalen Herbert was Donne's friend and patron; her fifth son, George, was the most original of his immediate disciples; her eldest son, Edward, though eleven years Donne's junior, is the senior member of his School. Like Donne a man of affairs for whom poetry was an incidental accomplishment, he had not Donne's ill luck in the world of affairs, and managed, without spectacular accomplishment, to accumulate the substance of an autobiography in which he appears very well pleased with himself. In this book, incidentally, his poems are not once mentioned: so little, for a nonprofessional, did the literary life require taking account of. Horseman, duelist, lover, amateur of medical remedies, later an amateur of philosophical speculations: that was the figure he chose to cut. Aurelian Townshend accompanied him to France in 1608; Carew was his secretary on his embassy to France in 1619; of such paths, crossing and recrossing with little reference to common literary interests, is the map of Donne's influence made.

Though Herbert knew Jonson, his verse seems little affected by Jonson's colloquial vigor or fierce professionalism. Donne was of more use to him, and specifically Donne the logician. The man who wrote a treatise *De Veritate,* and published it after (he tells us) a sign from heaven, and had his head filled with the taste of Platonism is unremittingly interested in the framework of proof; and proof required, as in "A Description," the detailed tallying of microcosmic detail against macrocosmic, or else, as in "Parted Souls," a show of deducing stanza from stanza with much machinery of "but" and "so." The language that receives this dialectical impress is not, in detail, arresting; its texture is that of Sidney or even Spenser, the Elizabethan poetical, its talk of "eyes" and "souls" unaffected by Donne's restless radicalism. All that Lord Herbert has added is an enquiring rigor of structure. "To a Lady Who Did Sing Excellently" never thinks to question the ravishing effect, but concerns itself, in a long, superbly articulated single sentence, with the process by which so many gracious details enter into a cognizable harmony. And the "Ode upon a question mov'd . . .", indebted though it is to Donne's "Extasie," yet takes up its stance a little outside the ecstatic union, and in establishing the immortality of love takes for its framework a well-mannered discussion, whose personae, being not persons but dialectical figments, are disarmingly named Melander and Celinda. Herbert's is an Elizabethan poetry which has learned from Donne the use of reason; his conceits are not dramatic gestures but phases in a tranquil analytic process.

TEXT: *Poems,* ed. G. C. Moore Smith (Oxford, 1923).

A Sinner's Lament

Lord, thus I sin, repent, and sin again,
As if Repentance only were, in me,
Leave for new Sin; thus do I entertain
My short time, and thy Grace, abusing thee,
And thy long-suffering; which though it be 5
Ne'r overcome by Sin, yet were in vain,
If tempted oft: thus we our Errours see

Before our Punishment, and so remain
Without Excuse; and, Lord, in them 'tis true,
Thy laws are just, but why dost thou distrain 10
Ought else for life, save life? That is thy due:
The rest thou mak'st us owe, and mayst to us
As well forgive; But oh! my sins renew,
Whil'st I do talk with my Creator thus.

A Description

I Sing her worth and praises hy,
  Of whom a Poet cannot ly,
* The little World the Great shall blaze;
Sea, Earth, her Body; Heaven, her Face;
Her Hair, Sun-beams; whose every part 5
Lightens, enflames, each Lover's Heart:
That thus you prove the *Axiom true,
Whilst the Sun help'd Nature in you.
  Her Front, the White and Azure Sky,
In Light and Glory raised hy, 10
Being o'recast by a Cloudy frown,
All Hearts and Eyes dejecteth down.
  Her each Brow a Cœlestial Bow,
Which through this Sky her Light doth show,
Which doubled, if it strange appear, 15
The Sun's likewise is doubled there.
  Her either Cheek a Blushing Morn,
Which, on the Wings of Beauty born,
Doth never set, but only fair
Shineth, exalted in her hair. 20
  Within her Mouth, Heavens Heav'n, reside
Her Words, the Soul's there Glorifi'd.
  Her Nose th' *Æquator* of this Globe,
Where Nakedness, Beauties best Robe,
Presents a form all Hearts to win. 25
  Last Nature made that dainty Chin;
Which that it might in every fashion
Answer the rest, a Constellation,

* μικρόκοσμος, μακρόκοσμος.

* *Sol et homo generant hominem.*

---

3. *blaze:* blazon.
3–4. The marginal Greek words name the microcosm and macrocosm.
4–5. Sea, earth, heaven, sun are water, earth, air, fire, the four elements: hence the world.
7. *the Axiom:* "Man's parents are man and the Sun."
9. *Front:* forehead.

Like to a Desk, she there did place,
To write the Wonders of her Face. 30
  In this Cœlestial Frontispiece,
Where Happiness eternal lies;
First aranged stand three Senses,
This Heavens Intelligences.
Whose several Motions, sweet combin'd, 35
Come from the first Mover, her Mind.
  The weight of this harmonique Sphere,
The *Atlas* of her Neck doth bear;
Whose Favours Day to Us imparts,
When Frowns make Night in Lovers Hearts. 40
  Two foming Billows are her Breasts,
That carry, rais'd upon their Crests,
The *Tyrian* Fish: More white's their Fome,
Then that, whence *Venus* once did come:
  Here take her by the Hand, my Muse, 45
With that sweet Foe, to make my Truce,
To compact Manna, best compar'd,
Whose dewy inside's not full hard.
  Her Waste's an envers'd Pyramis,
Upon whose Cone Love's Trophee is: 50
  Her Belly is that Magazine,
At whose peep Nature did resigne
That pretious Mould, by which alone,
There can be framed such a One:
  At th' entrance of which hidden Treasure, 55
Happy making above measure,
Two Alabaster Pillars stand,
To warn all passage from that Land;
At foot whereof engraved is,
The sad *Non Ultra* of Mans Bliss: 60
  The Back of this most pretious Frame
Holds up in Majesty the same:

---

34. *Intelligences:* the spirits whose office was to impart motion to the heavenly bodies.
57. The Pillars of Hercules were placed by the hero as a warning to mariners against venturing into the open Atlantic.
60. *Non ultra:* no further.

Where, to make Musick to all Hearts,
Love bound the descant of her parts:
  Though all this Beauties Temple be, 65
There's known within no Deity
Save Vertues, shrin'd within her Will:
As I began, so say I still,
I sing her Worth and Praises hy,
Of whom a Poet cannot ly. 70

Loves End

Thus ends my Love, but this doth grieve me most,
  That so it ends, but that ends too, this yet,
Besides the Wishes, hopes and time I lost,
  Troubles my mind awhile, that I am set
Free, worse than deny'd: I can neither boast 5
  Choice nor success, as my Case is, nor get
Pardon from my self, that I loved not
  A better Mistress, or her worse; this Debt
Only's her due, still, that she be forgot
Ere chang'd, lest I love none; this done, the taint 10
  Of foul Inconstancy is clear'd at least
In me, there only rests but to unpaint
  Her form in my mind, that so dispossest
It be a Temple, but without a Saint.

2. *that:* the antecedent is "grief." "This," three words later, is the subject of "troubles" in line 4.

Parted Souls

I Must depart, but like to his last breath
  That leaves the seat of life, for liberty
I go, but dying, and in this our death,
  Where soul and soul is parted, it is I

The deader part that fly away, 5
While she alas, in whom before
I liv'd, dyes her own death and more,
I feeling mine too much, and her own stay.

But since I must depart, and that our love
Springing at first but in an earthly mould, 10
Transplanted to our souls, now doth remove
Earthly effects, what time and distance would,
Nothing now can our loves allay,
Though as the better Spirits will
That both love us and know our ill, 15
We do not either all the good we may.

Thus when our souls that must immortal be,
For our loves cannot dye, nor we, (unless
We dye not both together) shall be free
Unto their open and eternal peace, 20
Sleep, Death's Embassadour, and best
Image, doth yours often so show,
That I thereby must plainly know,
Death unto us must be freedom and rest.

May 1608.

The poem seems remotely to echo Donne's "A Valediction: Forbidding Mourning," though Donne is said to have given that poem to his wife in November 1611, on the eve of a journey to France. But since Donne may have written it earlier, for another occasion, and since on the other hand he is known to have emulated Herbert at least once, it is impossible to be sure which way the influence, if any, ran.

Madrigal

How should I love my best?
What though my love unto that height be grown,
That taking joy in you alone
I utterly this world detest,
Should I not love it yet as th' only place 5

Where Beauty hath his perfect grace,
And is possest?

But I beauties despise,
You, universal beauty seem to me,
Giving and shewing form and degree 10
To all the rest, in your fair eyes,
Yet should I not love them as parts whereon
Your beauty, their perfection
And top, doth rise?

But ev'n my self I hate, 15
So far my love is from the least delight
That at my very self I spite,
Sensless of any happy state,
Yet may I not with justest reason fear
How hating hers, I truly her 20
Can celebrate?

Thus unresolved still
Although world, life, nay what is fair beside
I cannot for your sake abide,
Methinks I love not to my fill, 25
Yet if a greater love you can devise,
In loving you some otherwise,
Believe't, I will.

Epitaph. Cæcil. Boulstr. *quæ post languescentem morbum non sine inquietudine spiritus & conscientiæ obiit.**

Methinks Death like one laughing lyes,
Shewing his teeth, shutting his eyes,
Only thus to have found her here
He did with so much reason fear,
And she despise. 5

*Intelligitur de figura mortis præfigenda.***

* ". . . who died after a wasting illness, in some disturbance of spirit."
** "To be understood of a frontispiece showing Death."

For barring all the gates of sin,
Death's open wayes to enter in,
She was with a strict siege beset,
So what by force he could not get,
By time to win. 10

This mighty Warrior was deceived yet,
For what he, mutin in her powers, thought
Was but their zeal,
And what by their excess might have been wrought,
Her fasts did heal. 15

Till that her noble soul, by these, as wings,
Transcending the low pitch of earthly things,
As b'ing reliev'd by God, and set at large,
And grown by this worthy a higher charge,
Triumphing over Death, to Heaven fled, 20
And did not dye, but left her body dead.

July 1609.

---

12. *mutin:* mutiny.

In a Glass-Window for Inconstancy

Love, of this clearest, frailest Glass,
Divide the properties, so as
In the division may appear
Clearness for me, frailty for her.

A Vision

A Lady combing her hair.

Within an *open curled Sea of Gold* — *The hair.*
A *Bark of Ivory,* one day, I saw, — *The Comb*
Which striking with his *Oars* did seem to draw — *The teeth of the Comb.*
Tow'rds a fair *Coast,* wch I then did behold. — *Her side.*

A Lady held the Stern, while her white hand — 5
Whiter than either Ivory or *Sail,* — *The Cuff or smock sleeve.*
Over the surging Waves did so prevail,
That she had now approached near the *Land.* — *Her shoulder.*

When suddenly, as if she fear'd some wrack,
And yet the Sky was fair, and Air was clear, — 10
And neither *Rock,* nor *Monster* did appear, — *Wart / Lice.*
Doubting the Point, which spi'd, she turned back.

Then with a *Second course* I saw her steer — *Combing in another place.*
As if she meant to reach some other Bay,
Where being approach'd she likewise turn'd away, — 15
Though in the Bark some *Waves* now entred were. — *Hairs in the Comb.*

Thus varying oft her course, at last I found,
While I in quest of the Adventure go,
The Sail took down, and Oars had ceas'd to row, — *She had given over combing.*
And that the Bark it self was run aground. — 20

Wherewith *Earths fairest Creature* I beheld, — *Her face.*
For which both *Bark and Sea I gladly lost.* — *Her hair put up, and Comb cast away.*
Let no Philosopher of Knowledge boast,
Unless that he my Vision can unfold.

This bagatelle reverses the common Renaissance practice of explicating in moral sentences a pictured emblem, by obfuscating with riddling emblems an erotic scene.

Tears, Flow No More

Tears, flow no more, or if you needs must flow,
Fall yet more flow,
Do not the world invade,
From smaller springs than yours rivers have grown,
And they again a Sea have made, 5
Brackish like you, and which like you hath flown.

Ebb to my heart, and on the burning fires
Of my desires,
O let your torrents fall,
From smaller heate than theirs such sparks arise 10
As into flame converting all,
This world might be but my love's sacrifice.

Yet if the tempests of my sighs so blow
You both must flow,
And my desires still burn, 15
Since that in vain all help my love requires,
Why may not yet their rages turn
To dry those tears, and to blow out those fires?

Italy 1614.

To a Lady Who Did Sing Excellently

1.

When our rude & unfashion'd words, that long
A being in their elements enjoy'd,
Sensless and void,
Come at last to be formed by thy tongue,
And from thy breath receive that life and place, 5
And perfect grace,

That now thy power diffus'd through all their parts
Are able to remove
All the obstructions of the hardest hearts,
And teach the most unwilling how to love; 10

2.

When they again, exalted by thy voice,
Tun'd by thy soul, dismiss'd into the air,
To us repair,
A living, moving, and harmonious noise,
Able to give the love they do create 15
A second state,
And charm not only all his griefs away,
And his defects restore,
But make him perfect, who, the Poets say,
Made all was ever yet made heretofore; 20

3.

When again all these rare perfections meet,
Composed in the circle of thy face,
As in their place,
So to make up of all one perfect sweet,
Who is not then so ravish'd with delight 25
Ev'n of thy sight,
That he can be assur'd his sense is true,
Or that he die, or live,
Or that he do enjoy himself, or you,
Or only the delights, which you did give? 30

1618

To His Mistress for Her True Picture

Death, my lifes Mistress, and the soveraign Queen
Of all that ever breath'd, though yet unseen,
My heart doth love you best, yet I confess,
Your picture I beheld, which doth express

No such eye-taking beauty, you seem lean, 5
Unless you'r mended since. Sure he did mean
No honour to you, that did draw you so;
Therefore I think it false: Besides, I know
The picture, Nature drew, (which sure's the best)
Doth figure you by sleep and sweetest rest: 10
Sleep, nurse of our life, care's best reposer,
Natures high'st rapture, and the vision giver:
Sleep, which when it doth seize us, souls go play,
And make Man equal as he was first day.
Yet some will say, Can pictures have more life 15
Than the original? To end this strife,
Sweet Mistress come, and shew your self to me,
In your true form, while then I think to see
Some beauty Angelick, that comes t' unlock
My bodies prison, and from life unyoke 20
My well divorced soul, and set it free,
To liberty eternal: Thus you see,
I find the Painters error, and protect
Your absent beauties, ill drawn, by th' effect:
For grant it were your work, and not the Graves, 25
Draw Love by Madness then, Tyrants by Slaves,
Because they make men such. Dear Mistress, then
If you would not be seen by owl-ey'd Men,
Appear at noon i'th' Air, with so much light,
The Sun may be a Moon, the Day a Night, 30
Clear to my Soul, but dark'ning the weak sense
Of those, the other Worlds Cimmeriens,
And in your fatal Robe, imbroidered
With Starr-characters, teaching me to read
The destiny of Mortals, while your clear brow 35
Presents a Majesty, to instruct me how
To love or dread nought else: May your bright hair,
Which are the threds of life, fair crown'd appear
With that your Crown of Immortality:
In your right hand the Keys of Heaven be; 40

---

32. *Cimmeriens:* inhabitants of a land whose mists, according to Homer, the sun never penetrated. It was there that Odysseus had access to the spirits of the dead.

In th' other those of the Infernal Pit,
Whence none retires, if once he enter it.
And here let me complain, how few are those
Whose souls you shall from earth's vast dungeon lose
To endless happiness! few that attend 45
You, the true Guide, unto their journeys end:
And if of old Vertue's way narrow were,
'Tis rugged now, having no passenger.
Our life is but a dark and stormy night,
To which sense yields a weak and glimmering light; 50
While wandring Man thinks he discerneth all,
By that which makes him but mistake and fall:
He sees enough, who doth his darkness see;
These are great lights, by which less dark'ned be.
Shine then Sun-brighter through my senses vail, 55
A day-star of the light doth never fail;
Shew me that Goodness which compounds the strife
'Twixt a long sickness and a weary life.
Set forth that Justice which keeps all in aw,
Certain and equal more than any Law. 60
Figure that happy and eternal Rest,
Which till Man do enjoy, he is not blest.
Come and appear then, dear Soul-ravisher,
Heavens-Light-Usher, Man's deliverer,
And do not think, when I new beauties see, 65
They can withdraw my settled love from thee.
Flesh-beauty strikes me not at all, I know,
When thou do'st leave them to the grave, they show
Worse, than they now show thee: they shal not move
In me the least part of delight, or love, 70
But as they teach your power: Be she nut-brown,
The loveliest colour which the flesh doth crown:
I'll think her like a Nut, a fair outside,
Within which Worms and rottenness abide:
If fair, then like the Worm it self to be; 75
If painted, like their slime and sluttery.
If any yet will think their beauties best,
And will, against you, spite of all, contest,
Seize them with Age: so in themselves they'l hate

What they scorn'd in your picture, and too late 80
See their fault, and the Painters: Yet if this,
Which their great'st plague and wrinkled torture is,
Please not, you may to the more wicked sort,
Or such as of your praises make a sport,
Denounce an open warr, send chosen bands 85
Of Worms, your souldiers, to their fairest hands,
And make them lep'rous-scabb'd: upon their face
Let those your Pioners, Ring-worms, take their place,
And safely near with strong approaches got
Intrench it round, while their teeths rampire rot 90
With other Worms, may with a damp inbred
Stink to their senses, which they shall not dead:
And thus may all that e'r they prided in,
Confound them now: As for the parts within,
Send Gut-worms, which may undermine a way 95
Unto their vital parts, and so display
That your pale Ensign on the walls: then let
Those Worms, your Veteranes, which never yet
Did fail, enter *Pel mel,* and ransack all,
Just as they see the well-rais'd building fall: 100
While they do this, your Forragers command,
The Caterpillars, to devour their land;
And with them Wasps, your wing'd-worm-horsmen, bring,
To charge, in troop, those Rebels, with their sting:
All this, unless your beauty they confess. 105

And now, sweet Mistress, let m' a while digress,
T' admire these noble Worms, whom I invoke,
And not the Muses: You that eat through Oak
And bark, will you spare Paper, and my verse,
Because your praises they do here reherse? 110

Brave Legions then, sprung from the mighty race
Of Man corrupted, and which hold the place
Of his undoubted Issue; you that are
Brain-born, *Minerva*-like, and like her warr,
Well-arm'd compleat-maile-jointed Souldiers, 115
Whose force *Herculean* links in pieces tears;

To you the vengeance of all spill-bloods falls,
Beast-eating Men, Men-eating Cannibals.
Death-priviledg'd, were you in sunder smit
You do not lose your life, but double it: 120
Best framed types of the immortal Soul,
Which in your selves, and in each part are whole:
Last-living Creatures, heirs of all the earth,
For when all men are dead, it is your birth:
When you dy, your brave self-kill'd Generall 125
(For nothing else can kill him) doth end all.
What vermine-breeding body then thinks scorn,
His flesh should be by your brave fury torn?

Willing, to you, this Carkass I submit,
A gift so free, I do not care for it: 130
Which yet you shall not take, untill I see
My Mistress first reveal her self to me.

Mean while, Great Mistress, whom my soul admires,
Grant me your true picture, who it desires,
That he your matchless beauty might maintain 135
'Gainst all men that will quarrels entertain
For a Flesh-Mistress; the worst I can do,
Is but to keep the way that leads to you,
And howsoever the event doth prove,
To have Revenge below, Reward above; 140
Hear, from my bodies prison, this my Call,
Who from my mouth-grate, and eye-window bawl.

An Ode upon a Question Moved, Whether Love Should Continue for Ever?

Having interr'd her Infant-birth,
The watry ground that late did mourn,
Was strew'd with flow'rs for the return
Of the wish'd Bridegroom of the earth.

The well accorded Birds did sing 5
  Their hymns unto the pleasant time,
  And in a sweet consorted chime
Did welcom in the chearful Spring.

To which, soft whistles of the Wind,
  And warbling murmurs of a Brook, 10
  And vari'd notes of leaves that shook,
An harmony of parts did bind.

While doubling joy unto each other,
  All in so rare concent was shown,
  No happiness that came alone, 15
Nor pleasure that was not another.

When with a love none can express,
  That mutually happy pair,
  Melander and *Celinda* fair,
The season with their loves did bless. 20

Walking thus towards a pleasant Grove,
  Which did, it seem'd, in new delight
  The pleasures of the time unite,
To give a triumph to their love,

They stay'd at last, and on the Grass 25
  Reposed so, as o'r his breast
  She bow'd her gracious head to rest,
Such a weight as no burden was.

While over eithers compass'd waste
  Their folded arms were so compos'd, 30
  As if in straitest bonds inclos'd,
They suffer'd for joys they did taste.

Long their fixt eyes to Heaven bent,
  Unchanged, they did never move,
  As if so great and pure a love 35
No Glass but it could represent.

When with a sweet, though troubled look,
  She first brake silence, saying, Dear friend,
  O that our love might take no end,
Or never had beginning took! 40

I speak not this with a false heart,
  (Wherewith his hand she gently strain'd)
  Or that would change a love maintain'd
With so much faith on either part.

Nay, I protest, though Death with his 45
  Worst Counsel should divide us here,
  His terrors could not make me fear,
To come where your lov'd presence is.

Only if loves fire with the breath
  Of life be kindled, I doubt, 50
  With our last air 'twill be breath'd out,
And quenched with the cold of death.

That if affection be a line,
  Which is clos'd up in our last hour;
  Oh how 'twould grieve me, any pow'r 55
Could force so dear a love as mine!

She scarce had done, when his shut eyes
  An inward joy did represent,
  To hear *Celinda* thus intent
To a love he so much did prize. 60

Then with a look, it seem'd, deny'd
  All earthly pow'r but hers, yet so,
  As if to her breath he did ow
This borrow'd life, he thus repli'd;

O you, wherein, they say, Souls rest, 65
  Till they descend pure heavenly fires,

66. Plato said souls before their human birth were in the stars: see line 135.

Shall lustful and corrupt desires
With your immortal seed be blest?

And shall our Love, so far beyond
That low and dying appetite, 70
And which so chast desires unite,
Not hold in an eternal bond?

Is it, because we should decline,
And wholly from our thoughts exclude
Objects that may the sense delude, 75
And study only the Divine?

No sure, for if none can ascend
Ev'n to the visible degree
Of things created, how should we
The invisible comprehend? 80

Or rather since that Pow'r exprest
His greatness in his works alone,
B'ing here best in his Creatures known,
Why is he not lov'd in them best?

But is't not true, which you pretend, 85
That since our love and knowledge here,
Only as parts of life appear,
So they with it should take their end.

O no, Belov'd, I am most sure,
Those vertuous habits we acquire, 90
As being with the Soul intire,
Must with it evermore endure.

For if where sins and vice reside,
We find so foul a guilt remain,
As never dying in his stain, 95
Still punish'd in the Soul doth bide,

Much more that true and real joy,
  Which in a vertuous love is found,
  Must be more solid in its ground,
Than Fate or Death can e'r destroy. 100

Else should our Souls in vain elect,
  And vainer yet were Heavens laws,
  When to an everlasting Cause
They gave a perishing Effect.

Nor here on earth then, nor above, 105
  Our good affection can impair,
  For where God doth admit the fair,
Think you that he excludeth Love?

These eyes again then, eyes shall see,
  And hands again these hands enfold, 110
  And all chast pleasures can be told
Shall with us everlasting be.

For if no use of sense remain
  When bodies once this life forsake,
  Or they could no delight partake, 115
Why should they ever rise again?

And if every imperfect mind
  Make love the end of knowledge here,
  How perfect will our love be, where
All imperfection is refin'd? 120

Let then no doubt, *Celinda,* touch,
  Much less your fairest mind invade,
  Were not our souls immortal made,
Our equal loves can make them such.

So when one wing can make no way, 125
  Two joyned can themselves dilate,
  So can two persons propagate,
When singly either would decay.

So when from hence we shall be gone,
And be no more, nor you, nor I, 130
As one anothers mystery,
Each shall be both, yet both but one.

This said, in her up-lifted face,
Her eyes which did that beauty crown,
Were like two starrs, that having faln down, 135
Look up again to find their place:

While such a moveless silent peace
Did seize on their becalmed sense,
One would have thought some Influence
Their ravish'd spirits did possess. 140

---

135. See the note on line 65.

Sir Henry Wotton

(1568–1639)

Wotton, Donne's Oxford friend, was later remembered by a common acquaintance as exemplary in the realm for learning and tact.

> This gentleman was employed by King James in embassage to Venice; and indeed the Kingdom afforded no fitter man for matching the capaciousness of Italian wits; a man of so able dexterity with his pen, that he hath done himself much wrong, and the Kingdom more, in leaving no more of his writings behind him.

What little he left was collected by Izaak Walton, and published in 1651 as *Reliquiae Wottonianae.* He was Donne's lifelong friend, the recipient of several of his verse letters, and was to have been his biographer had not death prevented him. His poems, the occasional work of a man of affairs, serve to indicate the intellectual quality of what Donne could regard as normal professional circles: the circles in which Donne's own poems circulated in manuscript.

Upon the Sudden Restraint of the Earle of Somerset, Then Falling from Favor

Dazel'd thus with height of place,
Whilst our hopes our wits beguile,
No man markes the narrow space
'Twixt a prison, and a smile.

The Earl, favorite of James I, was arrested late in 1615 and tried, with his wife, for the murder of Sir Thomas Overbury.

Then, since fortune's favours fade, 5
You, that in her armes doe sleep,
Learne to swim, and not to wade;
For the Hearts of Kings are deepe.

But, if Greatness be so blind
As to trust in towers of Aire, 10
Let it be with Goodness lin'd,
That at least, the Fall be faire.

Then, though darkned, you shall say,
When Friends faile, and Princes frowne,
Vertue is the roughest way, 15
But proves at night a *Bed of Downe.*

On His Mistris, the Queen of Bohemia

You meaner *Beauties* of the *Night,*
That poorly satisfie our *Eies*
More by your *number* than your *light,*
You *Common-people* of the *Skies,*
What are you when the *Moon* shall rise? 5

You curious Chanters of the Wood,
That warble forth *Dame Nature's* layes,
Thinking your *Passions* understood
By your weake *accents,* what's your praise
When *Philomell* her voyce shal raise? 10

You *Violets,* that first appeare,
By your *pure purpel mantels* knowne,
Like the proud *Virgins* of the *yeare,*
As if the *Spring* were all your own,
What are you when the *Rose is blowne?* 15

The Queen of Bohemia was Elizabeth, daughter of James I. Wotton was employed in several embassies on her behalf.

So when my *Mistris* shal be *seene*
  In *form* and *Beauty* of her *mind,*
By *Vertue* first, then *Choyce,* a *Queen,*
  Tell me, if *she* were not design'd
  Th' *Eclypse* and *Glory* of her kind? 20

Tears at the Grave of Sir Albertus Morton

(WHO WAS BURIED AT SOUTHAMPTON) WEPT
BY SIR H. WOTTON

Silence, in truth, would speak my sorrow best,
  For deepest wounds can least their feelings tel;
Yet let me borrow from mine own unrest
  But time to bid him, whom I lov'd, farwel.

O my unhappy lines! you that before 5
  Have serv'd my youth to vent some wanton cries,
And now, congeal'd with grief, can scarce implore
  Strength to accent,—here my Albertus lies.

This is the sable stone, this is the cave,
  And womb of earth that doth his corps imbrace: 10
While others sing his praise, let me engrave
  These bleeding numbers to adorn the place.

Here will I paint the characters of woe,
  Here will I pay my tribute to the dead,
And here my faithfull tears in showrs shal flow 15
  To humanize the flints whereon I tread.

Where, though I mourn my matchlesse losse alone,
  And none between my weaknesse judge and me,

Sir Albertus Morton, Wotton's nephew and sometime secretary, was one of the secretaries of state when he died in 1625, aged forty-one.

Yet even these gentle walles allow my mone,
  Whose doleful echoes to my plaints agree. 20

But is he gon? and live I ryming here,
  As if some Muse would listen to my lay,
When all distun'd sit wailing for their dear,
  And bathe the banks where he was wont to play?

Dwell thou in endlesse light, discharged soul, 25
  Freed now from nature's and from Fortune's trust;
While on this fluent globe my glasse shall role,
  And run the rest of my remaining dust.

Upon the Death of Sir Albertus Morton's Wife

He first deceas'd: she for a little tri'd
To live without Him: lik'd it not, and di'd.

On a *Banck* as I Sate a *Fishing*

A DESCRIPTION OF THE SPRING

And now all *Nature* seem'd in *Love,*
The lusty *Sap* began to move;
New *Juice* did stirre th'embracing *Vines*;
And *Birds* had drawne their *Valentines*:
The *jealous Trout,* that low did lie, 5
Rose at a wel-dissembled *Flie*:
There stood my friend, with patient Skill
Attending of his trembling *quill.*
Already were the *Eaves* possest
With the swift *Pilgrims* daubed nest. 10
The *Groves* already did rejoyce
In *Philomels* triumphing *voyce.*
  The *showers* were short; the *weather* mild;

The *Morning* fresh; the *Evening* smil'd.
Jone takes her neat-rub'd paile, and now 15
She trips to milke the Sand-red *Cow*;
Where, for some sturdy foot-ball *Swaine,*
Jone strokes a *sillibub,* or twaine.
The *Fields* and *Gardens* were beset
With *Tulip, Crocus, Violet.* 20
And now, though late, the *Modest Rose*
Did more then halfe a blush disclose.
Thus all look't *gay,* all full of *Chear,*
To welcome the *New-liveri'd yeare.*

Aurelian Townshend

(c. 1583–c. 1650)

The friend of Carew and the friend of Sir Edward Herbert; perhaps an acquaintance of Jonson's though Jonson had reason to dislike him; an elusive figure in letters, memoirs, and state documents, his very dates unknown; author of no book of poems, no play (except two court masques), and but sparsely represented in manuscript collections: Townshend recedes behind a few delicate accomplishments which unite the internal rigor of the School of Donne with a tradition of graceful unreality, part Elizabethan, part Continental, in such a way as to earn T. S. Eliot's admiring reference to his "faint, pleasing tinkle."

He seems never to have been at home in the great world, which he perhaps began by mistaking for Arcadia. Before he was twenty the great Robert Cecil took his education in hand, proposing to have him trained on the continent to be young William Cecil's companion. He made a hash of the opportunity and was back in three years. At about twenty-five he spent a year as Sir Edward Herbert's companion in France, being "a gentleman that spoke the languages of French, Italian and Spanish in great perfection." But not having the born courtier's capacity for continuous visibility, he is heard of no more until 1632, when he briefly succeeds Ben Jonson as Inigo Jones' librettist. His datable poems, now that he has entered the world of letters, belong to the next five years. By 1643 he was living in poverty (". . . a poore & pocky Poett, [who] would bee glad to sell an 100 verses now at sixepence a piece, 50 shillinges an 100 verses") and appealing to the House of Lords for protection against a creditor; and a few years later he has dropped from sight.

There were many such careers; what distinguishes Townshend's is the poise which a few times joined literary convention with a gentle tenacity of intelligence, to shape a few poems unlike anyone else's. They are as formal and musical as masques, as spare as virginal tunes. The pastoral of "Pure Simple Love" is a way of miming innocence, not of positing a convention about which to be knowing; and the logic that plays, in "A Paradox," with the familiar identification of lovers with saints is content to maintain, by playing, its own appealing tautness rather than seize rhetorical opportunities. In demonstrating that such effects are possible within the tradition of Donne, and with such freedom from fuss, Townshend helps make Marvell's achievement intelligible.

TEXT: *Aurelian Townshend's Poems and Masks,* ed. E. K. Chambers (London: Clarendon Press, 1912).

To the Countesse of Salisbury

Victorious beauty, though your eyes
  Are able to subdue an hoast,
  And therefore are unlike to boast
The taking of a little prize,
Do not a single heart dispise. 5

It came alone, but yet so arm'd
  With former love, I durst have sworne
  That where a privy coat was worne,
With characters of beauty charm'd,
Thereby it might have scapt unharm'd. 10

But neither steele nor stony breast
  Are proofe against those lookes of thine,
  Nor can a Beauty lesse divine
Of any heart be long possest,
Where thou pretend'st an interest. 15

Thy Conquest in regard of me
  Alasse is small, but in respect

The Countess was the daughter-in-law of Townshend's patron.

Of her that did my Love protect,
Were it divulged, deserv'd to be
Recorded for a Victory. **20**

And such a one, as some that view
Her lovely face perhaps may say,
Though you have stolen my heart away,
If all your servants prove not true,
May steale a heart or two from you. **25**

Youth and Beauty

Thou art so fair, and yong withall,
Thou kindl'st yong desires in me,
Restoreing life to leaves that fall,
And sight to Eyes that hardly see
Halfe those fresh Beauties bloom in thee. **5**

Those, under sev'rall Hearbs and Flowr's
Disguis'd, were all *Medea* gave,
When she recal'd Times flying howrs,
And aged *Æson* from his grave,
For Beauty can both kill and save. **10**

Youth it enflames, but age it cheers,
I would go back, but not return
To twenty but to twice those yeers;
Not blaze, but ever constant burn,
For fear my Cradle prove my Urn. **15**

9. ***Aeson:*** **Medea restored him to youth with a cauldron of magical herbs.**

A Dialogue betwixt Time and a Pilgrime

Pilgrim Aged man, that mowes these fields.
Time Pilgrime speak, what is thy will?

Pilgrim Whose soile is this that such sweet Pasture yields?
Or who art thou whose Foot stand never still?
Or where am I? *Time.* In love. 5
Pilgrim His Lordship lies above.
Time Yes and below, and round about
Where in all sorts of flow'rs are growing
Which as the early Spring puts out,
Time fals as fast a mowing. 10
Pilgrim If thou art Time, these Flow'rs have Lives,
And then I fear,
Under some Lilly she I love
May now be growing there.
Time And in some Thistle or some spyre of grasse, 15
My syth thy stalk before hers come may passe.
Pilgrim Wilt thou provide it may. *Time.* No. *Pilgr.* Alleage the cause.
Time Because Time cannot alter but obey Fates laws.
Chorus Then happy those whom Fate, that is the stronger,
Together twists their threads, & yet draws hers the longer. 20

Pure Simple Love

Hide not thy love and myne shal bee
Open and free;
No mask dooth well upon thy face.
Lett those that meane more hurt provide
Love of a guide, 5
Or of some close retyring place.
A harmles kisse would make us thinck
Love hath no Nectar else to drinck.

Our loves are not of age to will
Both good and ill, 10
For thine, alas, is but new borne,
And myne is yett to yonge to speake.
How can they breake

---

5. *of*: with.

Or hold Loves civill Lawes in skorne?
Wee might go naked if some spie, 15
Apt to traduce us, stood not by.

Had wee been that created paire,
Eve half so faire,
Or Adam lov'd but half so well,
The Serpent could have found no charme 20
To doe us harme,
Or had so much as tyme to tell
His tale to thee, or I to view
An apple where such cherries grew.

Yett had hee ledd mee to thy brest, 25
That waye was best
To have seduct mee from thy lipp.
Those apples tempt mee most; They bee
Fruit of that Tree,
That made our first forefathers slipp. 30
I dare not touch them least I dye
The death thou threatnest with thyne Eye.

Yett hee that meanes not to transgres
Needes fearr the lesse,
For what hath Justice heere to doe 35
But with her skales? Her sword may lye
As Useles by,
When shee comes downe to Judge us twoe;
For no persuations can infect
Thyne innocence or my respect. 40

If all the stings of envy laye
Strewde in our waye,
And tongues to tell of all wee did,
As our affection waxeth old,
Shall itt growe cold? 45
Loves Elementall fire forbid
Such frost and snowe, for past all doubt,
If our sparks dye, his fire will out.

Though thanckfull hands and eyes may prove
Cyphers of love, 50
Yett, till some figure bee prefixt,
As oos, by thousands or alone,
Stand all for none,
So, till our lookes and smiles bee mixt
With further meaning, they amount 55
To nothing by a just account.

How golden was that age that lett,
When Couples mett,
Theire lips and hands doe what they woulde,
Left out theire haires and more skinn bare, 60
Then now they dare;
For libertie misunderstood
Is counted lightnes, and when twoe
Maie doe amise, tis thought they doe.

Yett since there bee some people still, 65
That meane no ill,
The worlde is not so full of sinne,
Butt that wee maie finde some place yett
Proper and fitt
To act our mutuall friendship in, 70
And some Spectators to allowe
Of our old loving fashion now.

Then will I lay my cheeke to thyne,
And thou shalt twyne
Thy maiden armes about my neck, 75
And I will compas in thy waste
With arms as chaste,
And one anothers eyes bedeck
With little babies which shall bee
Our unpolluted progenee. 80

Besides weele doe such childish things,
Though Love have wings,
Hee shal bee lothe to fly awaye;

And restles tyme, as lothe to passe
By with his glase, 85
Shall offer everie foote to staie;
One spinn, the next draw out our yeeres,
And the third Fate lett fall her sheeres.

If anie Lovers of one sort
Hether resort, 90
They'll fitt them with our modest sceanes,
And prompted by a wanton eye
Quicklie discrye
Wee know not what such action meanes,
Butt runn awaye and leave the Stage 95
To them and this corrupted age.

And if her eyes, clearest and best
Of all the rest,
Surveigh theise Lynes tract with Loves dart,
Presume to ask her, ere you go, 100
Whether or no
Shee wilbe pleasd to act her part;
Which if shee be ashamd to doe,
Intreat her to excuse mee toe.

---

88. *the third Fate:* her normal duty was to cut the thread of life, which was spun by the first and measured by the second.
99. *tract:* traced.

A Paradox

There is no Lover hee or shee,
That ever was or can be false.
Tis passion or symplycitie
Or some Apostacie that calls
Those votaries, those dead folke soe; 5
For if we goe
To vowes, to prayers, to paines, to all

The penuries Monasticall,
No bare foote man,
Rock Hermitt or Carthusian, 10
Can in a course of life survive
More strict or more contemplative.

For till that sparke of fyre be out,
As holy men are not allow'd
Among the Saints nor goe aboute 15
To prove them selves in sufferance proud,
Soe was there never Lover found
But under ground;
And if he tooke the style before,
And name uncanonized wore, 20
People might say,
This Saint hath nere a holliday,
But like a bold, unbidden Guest,
Intrudes uppon anothers feaste.

What desperate challenger is he, 25
Before he vanish in his flame,
What ere his paines or patience be,
That dares assume a Martyrs name;
For all the way he goes he 's none,
Till he be gone. 30
'Tis death, not dyeing, that must doe
This right to them and Lovers too,
Which they approve,
That make and marr the Lawes of love.
Yet better cheape can none acquire 35
This Crowne of thornes, this Robe of fire.

'Tis not a yeare will serve to trye
How weake ones faith is or how strong;
In this austere Societye
Probation lasts a whole life long. 40

---

16. A saint is canonized only after his death.
22. *holliday:* holy day, that is, saint's day.

No observation singlie vowd
Is here allow'd.
Two heartes must joyne and then those two
Must both alike beleeve and doe;
But as a twynn, 45
This colledge takes no fellow in;
At home, abroade, in all affaires,
They live, they dye, they goe, by payres.

And as two Turtells that have pearcht
And interchanged their fervent eyes, 50
When each in others bosome searcht,
If either Male or Female dyes
And the live Bird survyvith still
To prune and bill,
Not only this that never pynde 55
Is thought of some forgettfull kynde,
But that 's denyde
To be a Turtle true that died;
So fares it here that past all doubt
Th' instinct of Love findes Lovers out. 60

Hard happ when death cannot assure
What our whole lives have deerely bought,
But we must Relatives procure
To Answer every Loving thought.
'Tis much to dye; 'tis more to fynde 65
Two of my minde.

An Elegie Made by Mr. Aurelian Townshend in Remembrance of the Ladie Venetia Digby

What Travellers of matchlesse Venice say,
Is true of thee, admir'd Venetia;
Hee that ner'e saw thee, wants beliefe to reach
Halfe those perfections, thy first sight would teach.

Imagination can noe shape create 5
Aëry enough thy forme to imitate;
Nor bedds of Roses, Damask, red, and white,
Render like thee a sweetnes to the sight.
Thou wer't eye-Musike, and no single part,
But beauties concert; Not one onely dart, 10
But loves whole quiver; no provinciall face,
But universall; Best in every place.
Thow wert not borne, as other women be,
To need the help of heightning Poesie,
But to make Poets. Hee, that could present 15
Thee like thy glasse, were superexcellent.
Witnesse that Pen which, prompted by thy parts
Of minde and bodie, caught as many heartes
With every line, as thou with every looke;
Which wee conceive was both his baite and hooke. 20
His Stile before, though it were perfect steele,
Strong, smooth, and sharp, and so could make us feele
His love or anger, Witneses agree,
Could not attract, till it was toucht by thee.
Magneticke then, Hee was for heighth of style 25
Suppos'd in heaven; And so he was, the while
He sate and drewe thy beauties by the life,
Visible Angell, both as maide and wife.
In which estate thou did'st so little stay,
Thy noone and morning made but halfe a day; 30
Or halfe a yeare, or halfe of such an age
As thy complexion sweetly did presage,
An houre before those cheerfull beames were sett,
Made all men loosers, to paye Natures debt;
And him the greatest, that had most to doe, 35
Thy friend, companion, and copartner too,
Whose head since hanging on his pensive brest
Makes him looke just like one had bin possest
Of the whole world, and now hath lost it all.
Doctors to Cordialls, freinds to counsel fall. 40
He that all med'cines can exactly make,
And freely give them, wanting power to take,
Sitts and such Doses howerly doth dispense,

A man unlearn'd may rise a Doctor thence.
I that delight most in unusuall waies, 45
Seeke to asswage his sorrowe with thy praise,
Which if at first it swell him up with greife,
At last may drawe, and minister releife;
Or at the least, attempting it, expresse
For an old debt a freindly thanckfulnesse. 50
I am no Herald! So ye can expect
From me no Crests or Scutcheons, that reflect
With brave Memorialls on her great Allyes;
Out of my reach that tree would quickly rise.
I onely stryve to doe her Fame som Right, 55
And walke her Mourner, in this Black and Whight.

Richard Corbett

(1582–1635)

CORBETT's high poetic reputation in his lifetime, among churchmen and academicians it is true, is most charitably explicable on the (unlikely) assumption that his better work has not survived. His life is not undiverting. It is intelligible that the author of "The Faeryes Farewell" should have been fond of practical jokes and a fine amateur ballad singer, and edifying to know that an implacable place-hunter, whom a well-timed poetical epistle to Buckingham's secretary made Dean of Christ Church in 1620, should have forgotten the thread of a sermon before James I while toying with a ring the king had given him; but from the fact that he was "one of the most fashionable minor poets in the reign of Charles I" one can learn only that there have been in most times parallel fashions.

He probably knew John Donne, and certainly knew Ben Jonson, whose acquaintance he owed to the same highly placed Oxford friends who saw to his ecclesiastical advancement. His poems illustrate not the value of either acquaintance, but the qualities for which, in the early seventeenth century, an unpretentious writer did not need to work: cohesion, adequacy of diction, and the ease conferred by membership in a society, both learned and vulgar, in which articulateness was nothing remarkable.

TEXT: *Poems,* ed. J. A. W. Bennett and H. R. Trevor-Roper (Oxford, 1955).

Certain True Woords Spoken Concerning One Benet Corbett after Her Death

SHE DYED OCTOBER THE SECOND
ANNO 1634

Here, or not many feet from hence
The virtue lies call'd Patience.
Sickness and Death did do her honour
By loosing paine and feare upon her.
Tis true they forst her to a grave, 5
That's all the triumph that they have,—
A silly one; retreat o'er night
Proves conquest in a morning fight.
She will rise up against them both;
All sleep, believe it, is not sloth. 10
 And thou that read'st her elegie,
Take something of her historie:
She had one husband and one sonne;
Ask who they were, and thou hast done.

Benet Corbett was the poet's mother.

A PROPER NEW

Ballad

INTITULED

The Faeryes Farewell:
or
God-A-Mercy Will:

To be sung or whistled to the Tune of the MEDDOW BROW *by the Learned; by the unlearned; To the Tune of* FORTUNE

Farewell, Rewards & *Faeries,*
  Good Houswives now may say;
For now foule Slutts in Daries
  Doe fare as well as they;
And though they sweepe theyr Hearths no less   5
  Than Maydes were wont to doe,
Yet who of late for Cleaneliness
  Finds *sixe-pence* in her Shoe?

Lament, lament, old Abbies,
  The *Faries* lost Command: 10
They did but change Priests *Babies,*
  But some have changd your *Land*;
And all your Children sprung from thence
  Are now growne *Puritanes*:
Who live as *Changelings* ever since   15
  For love of your Demaines.

At Morning & at Evening both
  You merry were & glad,

So little Care of Sleepe or Sloth
  These Prettie ladies had. 20
When *Tom* came home from labour,
  Or *Ciss* to Milking rose,
Then merrily, merrily went theyre Tabor,
  And nimbly went theyre Toes.

Wittness those Rings & Roundelayes 25
  Of theirs, which yet remaine,
Were footed in Queene *Maries* dayes
  On many a Grassy Playne;
But, since of late *Elizabeth,*
  And later *James,* came in, 30
They never daunc'd on any heath
  As *when the Time hath bin.*

By which wee note the *Faries*
  Were of the old Profession;
Theyre Songs were *Ave Maryes,* 35
  Theyre Daunces were *Procession.*
But now, alas, they all are dead,
  Or gone beyond the Seas,
Or Farther for Religion fled,
  Or elce they take theyre Ease. 40

A Tell-tale in theyre Company
  They never could endure,
And whoe so kept not secretly
  Theyre Mirth, was punisht sure.
It was a just & Christian Deed 45
  To pinch such blacke & blew.
O, how the Common welth doth need
  Such Justices as you!

Now they have left our Quarters
  A *Register* they have, 50
Who looketh to theyre Charters,
  A Man both *Wise* & *Grave*;
An hundred of thyre merry Prancks

By one that I could name
Are kept in Store, conn twenty Thanks 55
To *William* for the same.

I marvell who his Cloake would turne
When *Puck* had led him round,
Or where those Walking Fires would burne,
Where *Cureton* would be found; 60
How *Broker* would appeare to be,
For whom this Age doth mourne;
But that theyre Sp[i]ritts live in Thee,
In Thee, old *William Chourne.*

To *William Chourne* of Stafford Shire 65
Give Laud & Prayses due,
Who every Meale can mend your Cheare
With Tales both old & true.
To *William* all give Audience,
And pray yee for his Noddle, 70
For all the *Faries* Evidence
Were lost, if that were Addle.

---

55. *conn:* offer.
56. *William:* see line 65. He was the servant of Corbett's friend Dr. Leonard Hutton.
59. *Walking Fires: ignes fatui,* will o' the wisps.
60, 61. *Cureton, Broker:* apparently deceased rustics whose firsthand experience of fairies is preserved in William Chourne's reminiscences.

Henry King

(1592–1669)

HENRY KING was twenty years the junior of Donne, whom he knew chiefly as an eminent divine. His father, Bishop John King, ordained Donne priest, and Henry, after long and admiring intimacy with Dean Donne of St. Paul's, served as one of his executors. By 1642 he had risen in his turn to the bishopric of Chichester and the friendship of Charles I, and he lived to see Charles II restored to the throne.

Like Edward Herbert no more than an amateur of poetry, King practiced verses in emulation of his fellow-divine Dr. Donne, and having so schooled an unpretentious talent, called on it from time to time when solemn occasions, chiefly mortuary, demanded a shaped eloquence. Except for the outright imitations of Donne, almost his whole *oeuvre* consists of elegies; and one of these, the "Exequy" upon his young dead wife, is as fine a secondary poem as the seventeenth century can show. To the grave and disciplined feeling, so actual that King feels no need to strain his way to the summit of an occasion, Donne's example brought an articulate intelligence, suffusing with calm ceremony what is never far from the active intimacy of speech.

> Accept thou Shrine of my dead Saint
> Instead of Dirges this complaint; . . .

A speaking, not a declaiming rhythm guides the poem's dealings with figures upon whose mere ingenious fitness it never thinks of dwelling. In "The Departure," by contrast, we see similar figures straining to meet a rhetorical obligation.

TEXT: *Poems of Henry King,* ed. Lawrence Mason (New Haven, Conn., 1914).

Sonnet: The Double Rock

Since thou hast view'd some Gorgon, and art grown
A solid stone:
To bring again to softness thy hard heart
Is past my art.
Ice may relent to water in a thaw; 5
But stone made flesh Loves Chymistry ne're saw.

Therefore by thinking on thy hardness, I
Will petrify;
And so within our double Quarryes Wombe,
Dig our Loves Tombe. 10
Thus strangely will our difference agree;
And, with our selves, amaze the world, to see
How both Revenge, and Sympathy consent
To make two Rocks each others Monument.

Sonnet

Tell me no more how fair she is,
I have no minde to hear
The story of that distant bliss
I never shall come near:
By sad experience I have found 5
That her perfection is my wound.

And tell me not how fond I am
To tempt a daring Fate,
From whence no triumph ever came,
But to repent too late: 10
There is some hope ere long I may
In silence dote my self away.

I ask no pity (Love) from thee,
  Nor will thy justice blame,
So that thou wilt not envy mee — 15
  The glory of my flame:
Which crowns my heart when ere it dyes,
In that it falls her sacrifice.

The Exequy. To His Matchlesse Never To Be Forgotten Freind

Accept thou Shrine of my dead Saint,
Insteed of Dirges this complaint;
And for sweet flowres to crown thy hearse,
Receive a strew of weeping verse
From thy griev'd friend, whom thou might'st see — 5
Quite melted into tears for thee.

  Dear loss! since thy untimely fate
My task hath been to meditate
On thee, on thee: thou art the book,
The library whereon I look — 10
Though almost blind. For thee (lov'd clay)
I languish out not live the day,
Using no other exercise
But what I practise with mine eyes:
By which wet glasses I find out — 15
How lazily time creeps about
To one that mourns: this, onely this
My exercise and bus'ness is:
So I compute the weary houres
With sighs dissolved into showres. — 20

The poem commemorates his wife Anne, who died in 1624, seven years after their marriage.

2. *complaint:* an intensive form of "plaint"; the word had not yet its modern connotation of faultfinding.

Nor wonder if my time go thus
Backward and most preposterous;
Thou hast benighted me, thy set
This Eve of blackness did beget,
Who was't my day, (though overcast 25
Before thou had'st thy Noon-tide past)
And I remember must in tears,
Thou scarce had'st seen so many years
As Day tells houres. By thy cleer Sun
My love and fortune first did run; 30
But thou wilt never more appear
Folded within my Hemisphear,
Since both thy light and motion
Like a fled Star is fall'n and gon,
And twixt me and my soules dear wish 35
The earth now interposed is,
Which such a strange eclipse doth make
As ne're was read in Almanake.

I could allow thee for a time
To darken me and my sad Clime, 40
Were it a month, a year, or ten,
I would thy exile live till then;
And all that space my mirth adjourn,
So thou wouldst promise to return;
And putting off thy ashy shrowd 45
At length disperse this sorrows cloud.

But woe is me! the longest date
Too narrow is to calculate
These empty hopes: never shall I
Be so much blest as to descry 50
A glimpse of thee, till that day come
Which shall the earth to cinders doome,
And a fierce Feaver must calcine
The body of this world like thine,
(My Little World!) that fit of fire 55
Once off, our bodies shall aspire

To our soules bliss: then we shall rise,
And view our selves with cleerer eyes
In that calm Region, where no night
Can hide us from each others sight. 60

Mean time, thou hast her earth: much good
May my harm do thee. Since it stood
With Heavens will I might not call
Her longer mine, I give thee all
My short-liv'd right and interest 65
In her, whom living I lov'd best:
With a most free and bounteous grief,
I give thee what I could not keep.
Be kind to her, and prethee look
Thou write into thy Dooms-day book 70
Each parcell of this Rarity
Which in thy Casket shrin'd doth ly:
See that thou make thy reck'ning streight,
And yield her back again by weight;
For thou must audit on thy trust 75
Each graine and atome of this dust,
As thou wilt answer *Him* that lent,
Not gave thee my dear Monument.

So close the ground, and 'bout her shade
Black curtains draw, my *Bride* is laid. 80

Sleep on my *Love* in thy cold bed
Never to be disquieted!
My last good night! Thou wilt not wake
Till I thy fatē shall overtake:
Till age, or grief, or sickness must 85
Marry my body to that dust
It so much loves; and fill the room
My heart keeps empty in thy Tomb.
Stay for me there; I will not faile
To meet thee in that hollow Vale. 90

And think not much of my delay;
I am already on the way,
And follow thee with all the speed
Desire can make, or sorrows breed.
Each minute is a short degree, 95
And ev'ry houre a step towards thee.
At night when I betake to rest,
Next morn I rise neerer my West
Of life, almost by eight houres saile,
Then when sleep breath'd his drowsie gale. 100

Thus from the Sun my Bottom stears,
And my dayes Compass downward bears:
Nor labour I to stemme the tide
Through which to *Thee* I swiftly glide.

'Tis true, with shame and grief I yield, 105
Thou like the *Vann* first took'st the field,
And gotten hast the victory
In thus adventuring to dy
Before me, whose more years might crave
A just precedence in the grave. 110
But heark! My pulse like a soft Drum
Beats my approch, tells *Thee* I come;
And slow howere my marches be,
I shall at last sit down by *Thee.*

The thought of this bids me go on, 115
And wait my dissolution
With hope and comfort. *Dear* (forgive
The crime) I am content to live
Divided, with but half a heart,
Till we shall meet and never part. 120

101. *Bottom:* ship.

The Departure

AN ELEGY

Were I to leave no more than a good friend,
Or but to hear the summons to my end,
(Which I have long'd for) I could then with ease
Attire my grief in words, and so appease
That passion in my bosom, which outgrowes 5
The language of strict verse or largest prose.
But here I am quite lost; writing to you
All that I pen or think, is forc't and new.
My faculties run cross, and prove as weak
T'indite this melancholly task, as speak: 10
Indeed all words are vain, well might I spare
This rendring of my tortur'd thoughts in ayre,
Or sighing paper. My infectious grief
Strikes inward, and affords me no relief.
But still a deeper wound, to lose a sight 15
More lov'd than health, and dearer than the light.
But all of us were not at the same time
Brought forth, nor are we billited in one clime.
Nature hath pitch't mankind at several rates,
Making our places diverse as our fates. 20
Unto that universal law I bow,
Though with unwilling knee; and do allow
Her cruell justice, which dispos'd us so
That we must counter to our wishes go.
'Twas part of mans first curse, which order'd well 25
We should not alway with our likings dwell.

'Tis onely the Triumphant Church where we
Shall in unsever'd Neighbourhood agree.

Go then best soul, and where You must appear
Restore the Day to that dull Hemisphear. 30

Nere may the hapless Night You leave behind
Darken the comforts of Your purer mind.
May all the blessings Wishes can invent
Enrich your dayes, and crown them with content.
And though You travel down into the West, 35
May Your lifes Sun stand fixed in the East,
Far from the weeping set; nor may my ear
Take in that killing whisper, *You once were.*

Thus kiss I your fair hands, taking my leave
As Prisoners at the Bar their doom receive. 40
All joyes go with You: let sweet peace attend
You on the way, and wait Your journeys end.
But let Your discontents, and sowrer fate
Remain with me, born off in my Retrait.
Might all your crosses in that sheet of lead 45
Which folds my heavy heart lie buried:
'Tis the last service I would do You, and the best
My wishes ever meant, or tongue profest.
Once more I take my leave. And once for all,
Our parting shews so like a funerall, 50
It strikes my soul, which hath most right to be
Chief Mourner at this sad solemnitie.

And think not, Dearest, 'cause this parting knell
Is rung in verses, that at Your farewell
I onely mourn in Poetry and Ink: 55
No, my Pens melancholy Plommets sink
So low, they dive where th'hid affections sit,
Blotting that Paper where my mirth was writ.

Believ't that sorrow truest is which lies
Deep in the breast, not floating in the eies: 60
And he with saddest circumstance doth part,
Who seals his farewell with a bleeding heart.

To My Dead Friend Ben: Johnson

I see that wreath which doth the wearer arm
'Gainst the quick strokes of thunder, is no charm
To keep off deaths pale dart. For, *Johnson* then
Thou hadst been number'd still with living men.
Times sithe had fear'd thy Lawrel to invade, 5
Nor thee this subject of our sorrow made.

Amongst those many votaries who come
To offer up their Garlands at thy Tombe;
Whil'st some more lofty pens in their bright verse
(Like glorious Tapers flaming on thy herse) 10
Shall light the dull and thankless world to see,
How great a maim it suffers wanting thee;
Let not thy learned shadow scorn, that I
Pay meaner Rites unto thy memory:
And since I nought can adde but in desire, 15
Restore some sparks which leapt from thine own fire.

What ends soever others quills invite,
I can protest, it was no itch to write,
Nor any vain ambition to be read,
But meerly Love and Justice to the dead 20
Which rais'd my fameless Muse; and caus'd her bring
These drops, as tribute thrown into that spring,
To whose most rich and fruitful head we ow
The purest streams of language which can flow.

For 'tis but truth, thou taught'st the ruder age 25
To speake by Grammar, and reform'dst the Stage:
Thy Comick Sock induc'd such purged sence,

---

1. *that wreath:* the laurel, which not only made crowns for poets but according to another Greek tradition, warded off lightning.
27. *Sock:* the low shoe worn by Athenian comic actors; hence the emblem of comedy as the platform shoe ("buskin") was of tragedy.

A *Lucrece* might have heard without offence.
Amongst those soaring wits that did dilate
Our English, and advance it to the rate 30
And value it now holds, thy self was one
Helpt lift it up to such proportion.
That thus refin'd and roab'd, it shall not spare
With the full *Greek* or *Latine* to compare.
For what tongue ever durst, but ours, translate 35
Great *Tully's* Eloquence, or *Homers* State?
Both which in their unblemisht lustre shine,
From *Chapmans* pen, and from thy *Catiline.*
All I would ask for thee, in recompence
Of thy successful toyl and times expence, 40
Is onely this poor Boon: that those who can
Perhaps read *French,* or talk *Italian,*
Or do the lofty *Spaniard* affect;
To shew their skill in Forrein Dialect,
Prove not themselves so unnaturally wise, 45
They therefore should their *Mother-tongue* despise.
(As if her Poets both for style and wit
Not equall'd, or not pass'd their best that writ)
Untill by studying *Johnson* they have known
The height and strength and plenty of their own. 50

Thus in what low earth or neglected room
Soere thou sleep'st, *thy book* shall be thy tomb.
Thou wilt go down a happy Coarse, bestrew'd
With thine own Flowres; and feel thy self renew'd,
Whil'st thy immortal never-with'ring Bayes 55
Shall yearly flourish in thy Readers praise.
And when more spreading Titles are forgot,
Or spight of all their Lead and Sear-cloth rot,
Thou wrapt and Shrin'd in *thine own sheets,* wilt ly
A Relick fam'd by all Posterity. 60

---

28. *Lucrece:* Roman matron famous for her chastity.
37. *Tully:* Marcus Tullius Cicero, now better known by his third name.
38. *Catiline:* Jonson's 1611 play on the anarchist conspiracy which Cicero put down.

Upon the Death of My Ever Desired Friend Doctor Donne Dean of Pauls

To have liv'd eminent in a degree
Beyond our lofty'st flights, that is like thee;
Or t'have had too much merit is not safe;
For such excesses find no Epitaph.
At common graves we have Poetick eyes 5
Can melt themselves in easie Elegies;
Each quill can drop his tributary verse,
And pin it with the Hatchments, to the Herse:
But at thine, Poem or inscription
(Rich Soul of wit and language:) we have none; 10
Indeed a silence does that Tomb befit
Where is no Herald left to blazon it.
Widdow'd invention justly doth forbear
To come abroad knowing thou art not here,
Late her great Patron; whose prerogative 15
Maintain'd and cloth'd her so, as none alive
Must now presume to keep her at thy rate,
Though he the Indies for her dowre estate:
Or else that awful fire, which once did burn
In thy clear brain, now fall'n into thy Urn, 20
Lives there to fright rude Empericks from thence,
Which might profane thee by their ignorance:
Who ever writes of thee, and in a style
Unworthy such a Theme, does but revile
Thy precious dust, and wake a learned spirit 25
Which may revenge his rapes upon thy merit.
For all a low-pitcht fancie can devise,
Will prove at best but hallow'd injuries.

8\. *Hatchments:* the armorial bearings of the deceased.

13\. *invention:* rhetoricians' term for the art of devising things to say, prior to arranging and articulating them.

21\. *Empericks:* workers who trust to luck, knack, or experience instead of solid learning.

Thou, like the dying Swan, didst lately sing
Thy mournful Dirge in audience of the King; 30
When pale looks, and faint accents of thy breath,
Presented so to life that piece of death,
That it was fear'd and prophesi'd by all
Thou thither cam'st to preach thy Funerall.
O! hadst thou in an Elegiack knell 35
Rung out unto the world thine own farewell;
And in thy high victorious numbers beat
The solemn measure of thy griev'd retreat:
Thou might'st the Poets service now have mist,
As well as then thou didst prevent the Priest: 40
And never to the world beholden be,
So much as for an Epitaph for thee.

I do not like the office. Nor is't fit
Thou, who didst lend our age such summes of wit,
Should'st now reborrow from her Bankrupt Mine 45
That Ore to bury thee, which once was thine.
Rather still leave us in thy debt; and know
(Exalted Soul!) More glory 'tis to ow
Unto thy Herse what we can never pay,
Than with embased coin those Rites defray. 50

Commit we then Thee to Thy self: nor blame
Our drooping loves, which thus to thine own fame
Leave Thee Executour: since but thy own
No pen could do Thee Justice, nor Bayes crown
Thy vast desert; save that we nothing can 55
Depute to be thy ashes Guardian.

So Jewellers no Art or Metal trust
To form the Diamond, but the Diamonds dust.

29–42. Donne rose from his deathbed to preach his last sermon.
40. *prevent:* anticipate.

Sic Vita

Like to the falling of a Starre;
Or as the flights of Eagles are;
Or like the fresh springs gawdy hew;
Or silver drops of morning dew;
Or like a wind that chafes the flood; 5
Or bubbles which on water stood;
Even such is man, whose borrow'd light
Is streight call'd in, and paid to night.

The wind blowes out; the Bubble dies;
The Spring entomb'd in Autumn lies; 10
The Dew dries up; the Starre is shot;
The Flight is past; and Man forgot.

This is King's contribution to a fashion for poems in this pattern.

A Contemplation upon Flowers

Brave flowers, that I could gallant it like you
and be as little vaine,
you come abroad, and make a harmless shew,
and to your bedds of Earth againe;
you are not proud, you know your birth 5
for your Embroiderd garments are from Earth:

You doe obey your moneths, and times, but I
would have it ever springe,
my fate would know noe winter, never dye
nor thinke of such a thing; 10
Oh that I could my bed of Earth but view
and Smile, and looke as chearefully as you:

Oh teach me to see death, and not to feare
but rather to take truce;
how often have I seene you at a Beere, 15
and there looke fresh and spruce;
you fragrant flowers then teach me that my breath
Like yours may sweeten, and perfume my death.

III

THE DIVINE POET

George Herbert (1593–1633)

George Herbert

(1593–1633)

George Herbert, Edward Herbert's youngest brother, was possibly Donne's most original disciple; he saw beneath the mannerisms to the compression and force, and out of these qualities created a mode of devotional poetry to which Crashaw, Vaughan, Traherne, were to be inextricably indebted.

Though he is remembered as a country clergyman, his poetic achievement depends not on an act of secession from the public world but on an unusually fruitful relationship to it. The ancient myth of retirement from the great world, which Horace and the Latin pastoral poets had handled and Christianity reshaped, became in the seventeenth century, when the court disappointed so many expectations and the Civil War so many more, a topic capable of engrossing a lifetime's experience; it is, for instance, Andrew Marvell's principal theme. For the secluded man, if he is guided by Christian and classical tradition, does not forget about the world where ambition's goals are visible and language is rather a practical than a contemplative instrument; he reshapes and relives, in a new context, that world's values; no amputation has occurred. T. S. Eliot's famous statement about "metaphysical" wit, that it implies, in the expression of every experience, a recognition of other kinds of experience which are possible, is nowhere more strikingly applicable than to such poems as "The Pearl," which counterpoints its devotional refrain against a taut and generous inventory of the ways of learning, honor, pleasure: none of which Herbert has forgotten, nor chosen to forget.

He had had a brilliant career at Cambridge, and risen to an academic post from which, involving as it did official contact with the great men of the realm, his two predecessors in turn had gone to be secretaries of state. But the death of James I in 1625 ended his own hopes of a court appointment. He turned, in long spiritual anguish, toward the church; was offered the rectory of Bemerton in Salisbury; accepted, and was ordained late in 1630; and died within three years.

With tact, with spareness, with a taut give-and-take of homely dialogue, he articulates in disarmingly social metaphors the devout man's intercourse with God.

> But quick-ey'd love, observing me grow slack
> From my first entrance in
> Drew nearer to me, sweetly questioning
> If I lack'd any thing.

This is neither quaint nor rhetorical; they are host and guest, in a mannerly relationship that sublimates but does not abandon the world's manners.

> Whereas my birth and spirit rather took
> The way that takes the town;
> Thou didst betray me to a lingering book
> And wrap me in a gown.

"Betray" is just, when we think of his former expectations; yet the "lingering" is poised against a journeying which that former way would have exacted; if the town "takes" that way, it may also find that way meretriciously "taking"; and he is "wrapped" now. His quiet is never insipid, nor are his contrasts resentful. He has chosen —been chosen for—the life he has chosen. These delicate discriminations, undervaluing nothing, Donne could not have managed; nor, in a poetry that had not undergone Donne's discipline of intent compression, would they have been possible.

TEXT: *Works*, ed. F. E. Hutchinson (Oxford, 1941).

COMMENT: L. C. Knights, *Explorations* (London, 1946).

Superliminare

Thou, whom the former precepts have
Sprinkled and taught, how to behave
Thy self in church; approach, and taste
The churches mysticall repast.

Avoid, Profanenesse; come not here: 5
Nothing but holy, pure, and cleare,
Or that which groneth to be so,
May at his perill further go.

Superliminare: (Lat.) threshold. This little poem mediates between a long introductory exhortation, *The Church Porch,* and the remainder of the volume, *The Church.*

The Altar

A broken ALTAR, Lord, thy servant reares,
Made of a heart, and cemented with teares:
Whose parts are as thy hand did frame;
No workmans tool hath touch'd the same.
A HEART alone 5
Is such a stone,
As nothing but
Thy pow'r doth cut.
Wherefore each part
Of my hard heart 10
Meets in this frame,
To praise thy Name:
That, if I chance to hold my peace,
These stones to praise thee may not cease.
O let thy blessed SACRIFICE be mine, 15
And sanctifie this ALTAR to be thine.

Easter-wings

Lord, who createdst man in wealth and store,
Though foolishly he lost the same,
Decaying more and more,
Till he became
Most poore: 5
With thee
O let me rise
As larks, harmoniously,
And sing this day thy victories:
Then shall the fall further the flight in me. 10

My tender age in sorrow did beginne:
And still with sicknesses and shame
Thou didst so punish sinne,
That I became
Most thinne.
With thee
Let me combine
And feel this day thy victorie:
For, if I imp my wing on thine,
Affliction shall advance the flight in me. 20

19. *imp:* to engraft feathers in a damaged wing, so as to restore or improve the powers of flight.

Redemption

Having been tenant long to a rich Lord,
Not thriving, I resolved to be bold,
And make a suit unto him, to afford
A new small-rented lease, and cancell th' old.
In heaven at his manour I him sought: 5

They told me there, that he was lately gone
About some land, which he had dearly bought
Long since on earth, to take possession.
I straight return'd, and knowing his great birth,
Sought him accordingly in great resorts; 10
In cities, theatres, gardens, parks, and courts:
At length I heard a ragged noise and mirth
Of theeves and murderers: there I him espied,
Who straight, *Your suit is granted,* said, & died.

Affliction (I)

When first thou didst entice to thee my heart,
I thought the service brave:
So many joyes I writ down for my part,
Besides what I might have
Out of my stock of natural delights, 5
Augmented with thy gracious benefits.

I looked on thy furniture so fine,
And made it fine to me:
Thy glorious houshold-stuffe did me entwine,
And 'tice me unto thee. 10
Such starres I counted mine: both heav'n and earth
Payd me my wages in a world of mirth.

What pleasures could I want, whose King I served,
Where joyes my fellows were?
Thus argu'd into hopes, my thoughts reserved 15
No place for grief or fear.
Therefore my sudden soul caught at the place,
And made her youth and fiercenesse seek thy face.

At first thou gav'st me milk and sweetnesses;
I had my wish and way: 20
My dayes were straw'd with flow'rs and happinesse;
There was no moneth but May.

But with my yeares sorrow did twist and grow,
And made a partie unawares for wo.

My flesh began unto my soul in pain, 25
    Sicknesses cleave my bones;
Consuming agues dwell in ev'ry vein,
    And tune my breath to grones.
Sorrow was all my soul; I scarce beleeved,
Till grief did tell me roundly, that I lived. 30

When I got health, thou took'st away my life,
    And more; for my friends die:
My mirth and edge was lost; a blunted knife
    Was of more use then I.
Thus thinne and lean without a fence or friend, 35
I was blown through with ev'ry storm and winde.

Whereas my birth and spirit rather took
    The way that takes the town;
Thou didst betray me to a lingring book,
    And wrap me in a gown. 40
I was entangled in the world of strife,
Before I had the power to change my life.

Yet, for I threatned oft the siege to raise,
    Not simpring all mine age,
Thou often didst with Academick praise 45
    Melt and dissolve my rage.
I took thy sweetned pill, till I came where
I could not go away, nor persevere.

Yet lest perchance I should too happie be
    In my unhappinesse, 50
Turning my purge to food, thou throwest me
    Into more sicknesses.
Thus doth thy power crosse-bias me, not making
Thine own gift good, yet me from my wayes taking.

Now I am here, what thou wilt do with me 55
None of my books will show:
I reade, and sigh, and wish I were a tree;
For sure then I should grow
To fruit or shade: at least some bird would trust
Her houshold to me, and I should be just. 60

Yet, though thou troublest me, I must be meek;
In weaknesse must be stout.
Well, I will change the service, and go seek
Some other master out.
Ah my deare God! though I am clean forgot, 65
Let me not love thee, if I love thee not.

Jordan (I)

Who sayes that fictions onely and false hair
Become a verse? Is there in truth no beautie?
Is all good structure in a winding stair?
May no lines passe, except they do their dutie
Not to a true, but painted chair? 5

Is it no verse, except enchanted groves
And sudden arbours shadow course-spunne lines?
Must purling streams refresh a lovers loves?
Must all be vail'd, while he that reades, divines,
Catching the sense at two removes? 10

Shepherds are honest people; let them sing:
Riddle who list, for me, and pull for Prime:
I envie no mans nightingale or spring;

The title suggests a baptized poetry, enrolled in the service of reality.
5. See Plato, *Republic,* X, for the artist as imitator of imitations. Herbert's *chair* echoes the famous bed of Plato's example.
12. *pull for Prime:* draw cards in the game called *Primers.*

Nor let them punish me with losse of rime,
Who plainly say, *My God, My King.* 15

The Windows

Lord, how can man preach thy eternall word?
He is a brittle crazie glasse:
Yet in thy temple thou dost him afford
This glorious and transcendent place,
To be a window, through thy grace. 5

But when thou dost anneal in glasse thy storie,
Making thy life to shine within
The holy Preachers; then the light and glorie
More rev'rend grows, & more doth win:
Which else shows watrish, bleak, & thin. 10

Doctrine and life, colours and light, in one
When they combine and mingle, bring
A strong regard and aw: but speech alone
Doth vanish like a flaring thing,
And in the eare, not conscience ring. 15

2. *crazie:* cracked, flawed.

Employment (II)

He that is weary, let him sit.
My soul would stirre
And trade in courtesies and wit,
Quitting the furre
To cold complexions needing it. 5

Man is no starre, but a quick coal
Of mortall fire:

Who blows it not, nor doth controll
A faint desire,
Lets his own ashes choke his soul. 20

When th' elements did for place contest
With him, whose will
Ordain'd the highest to be best;
The earth sat still,
And by the others is opprest. 15

Life is a businesse, not good cheer;
Ever in warres.
The sunne still shineth there or here,
Whereas the starres
Watch an advantage to appeare. 20

Oh that I were an Orenge-tree,
That busie plant!
Then should I ever laden be,
And never want
Some fruit for him that dressed me. 25

But we are still too young or old;
The Man is gone,
Before we do our wares unfold:
So we freeze on,
Untill the grave increase our cold. 30

Vertue

Sweet day, so cool, so calm, so bright,
The bridall of the earth and skie:
The dew shall weep thy fall to night;
For thou must die.

Sweet rose, whose hue angrie and brave 5
Bids the rash gazer wipe his eye:

Thy root is ever in its grave,
And thou must die.

Sweet spring, full of sweet dayes and roses,
A box where sweets compacted lie; 10
My musick shows ye have your closes,
And all must die.

Onely a sweet and vertuous soul,
Like season'd timber, never gives;
But though the whole world turn to coal, 15
Then chiefly lives.

11. *closes:* in music, concluding cadences.

The Pearl

MATTH. 13. 45

I know the wayes of Learning; both the head
And pipes that feed the presse, and make it runne;
What reason hath from nature borrowed,
Or of it self, like a good huswife, spunne
In laws and policie; what the starres conspire, 5
What willing nature speaks, what forc'd by fire;
Both th' old discoveries, and the new-found seas,
The stock and surplus, cause and historie:
All these stand open, or I have the keyes:
Yet I love thee. 10

I know the wayes of Honour, what maintains
The quick returns of courtesie and wit:
In vies of favours whether partie gains,
When glorie swells the heart, and moldeth it
To all expressions both of hand and eye, 15

6. *by fire:* by the chemist's furnace.

Which on the world a true-love-knot may tie,
And bear the bundle, wheresoe're it goes:
How many drammes of spirit there must be
To sell my life unto my friends or foes:
Yet I love thee. 20

I know the wayes of Pleasure, the sweet strains,
The lullings and the relishes of it;
The propositions of hot bloud and brains;
What mirth and musick mean; what love and wit
Have done these twentie hundred yeares, and more: 25
I know the projects of unbridled store:
My stuffe is flesh, not brasse; my senses live,
And grumble oft, that they have more in me
Then he that curbs them, being but one to five:
Yet I love thee. 30

I know all these, and have them in my hand:
Therefore not sealed, but with open eyes
I flie to thee, and fully understand
Both the main sale, and the commodities;
And at what rate and price I have thy love; 35
With all the circumstances that may move:
Yet through these labyrinths, not my groveling wit,
But thy silk twist let down from heav'n to me,
Did both conduct and teach me, how by it
To climbe to thee. 40

32. ***sealed:*** eyes sewn shut, like a young hawk's, to ensure its undistracted return to the trainer.
34. ***commodities:*** goods offered in addition.

Man

My God, I heard this day,
That none doth build a stately habitation,
But he that means to dwell therein.

What house more stately hath there been,
Or can be, than is Man? to whose creation 5
All things are in decay.

For Man is ev'ry thing,
And more: He is a tree, yet bears more fruit;
A beast, yet is, or should be more:
Reason and speech we onely bring. 10
Parrats may thank us, if they are not mute,
They go upon the score.

Man is all symmetrie,
Full of proportions, one limbe to another,
And all to all the world besides: 15
Each part may call the furthest, brother:
For head with foot hath private amitie,
And both with moons and tides.

Nothing hath got so farre,
But Man hath caught and kept it, as his prey. 20
His eyes dismount the highest starre:
He is in little all the sphere.
Herbs gladly cure our flesh; because that they
Finde their acquaintance there.

For us the windes do blow, 25
The earth doth rest, heav'n move, and fountains flow.
Nothing we see, but means our good,
As our delight, or as our treasure:
The whole is, either our cupboard of food,
Or cabinet of pleasure. 30

The starres have us to bed;
Night draws the curtain, which the sunne withdraws;
Musick and light attend our head.
All things unto our flesh are kinde
In their descent and being; to our minde 35
In their ascent and cause.

Each thing is full of dutie:
Waters united are our navigation;
Distinguished, our habitation;
Below, our drink; above, our meat; 40
Both are our cleanlinesse. Hath one such beautie?
Then how are all things neat?

More servants wait on Man,
Than he'l take notice of: in ev'ry path
He treads down that which doth befriend him, 45
When sicknesse makes him pale and wan.
Oh mightie love! Man is one world, and hath
Another to attend him.

Since then, my God, thou hast
So brave a Palace built; O dwell in it, 50
That it may dwell with thee at last!
Till then, afford us so much wit;
That, as the world serves us, we may serve thee,
And both thy servants be.

---

41. *one:* one element (water).

Life

I made a posie, while the day ran by:
Here will I smell my remnant out, and tie
My life within this band.
But Time did becken to the flowers, and they
By noon most cunningly did steal away, 5
And wither'd in my hand.

My hand was next to them, and then my heart:
I took, without more thinking, in good part
Times gentle admonition:
Who did so sweetly deaths sad taste convey, 10

Making my minde to smell my fatall day;
        Yet sugring the suspicion.

Farewell deare flowers, sweetly your time ye spent,
Fit, while ye liv'd, for smell or ornament,
        And after death for cures. 15
I follow straight without complaints or grief,
Since if my sent be good, I care not if
        It be as short as yours.

Mortification

    How soon doth man decay!
When clothes are taken from a chest of sweets
  To swaddle infants, whose young breath
    Scarce knows the way;
  Those clouts are little winding sheets, 5
Which do consigne and send them unto death.

    When boyes go first to bed,
They step into their voluntarie graves,
  Sleep bindes them fast; onely their breath
    Makes them not dead: 10
  Successive nights, like rolling waves,
Convey them quickly, who are bound for death.

    When youth is frank and free,
And calls for musick, while his veins do swell,
  All day exchanging mirth and breath 15
    In companie;
  That musick summons to the knell,
Which shall befriend him at the houre of death.

    When man grows staid and wise,
Getting a house and home, where he may move 20
  Within the circle of his breath,
    Schooling his eyes;

That dumbe inclosure maketh love
Unto the coffin, that attends his death.

When age grows low and weak,
Marking his grave, and thawing ev'ry yeare,
Till all do melt, and drown his breath
When he would speak;
A hair or litter shows the biere,
Which shall convey him to the house of death. 30

Man, ere he is aware,
Hath put together a solemnitie,
And drest his herse, while he has breath
As yet to spare:
Yet Lord, instruct us so to die, 35
That all these dyings may be life in death.

Decay

Sweet were the dayes, when thou didst lodge with Lot,
Struggle with Jacob, sit with Gideon,
Advise with Abraham, when thy power could not
Encounter Moses strong complaints and mone:
The words were then, *Let me alone.* 5

One might have sought and found thee presently
At some fair oak, or bush, or cave, or well:
Is my God this way? No, they would reply:
He is to Sinai gone, as we heard tell:
List, ye may heare great Aarons bell. 10

But now thou dost thy self immure and close
In some one corner of a feeble heart:
Where yet both Sinne and Satan, thy old foes,
Do pinch and straiten thee, and use much art
To gain thy thirds and little part. 15

I see the world grows old, when as the heat
Of thy great love, once spread, as in an urn
Doth closet up it self, and still retreat,
Cold Sinne still forcing it, till it return,
And calling *Justice,* all things burn. 20

Jordan (II)

When first my lines of heav'nly joyes made mention,
Such was their lustre, they did so excell,
That I sought out quaint words, and trim invention;
My thoughts began to burnish, sprout, and swell,
Curling with metaphors a plain intention, 5
Decking the sense, as if it were to sell.

Thousands of notions in my brain did runne,
Off'ring their service, if I were not sped:
I often blotted what I had begunne;
This was not quick enough, and that was dead. 10
Nothing could seem too rich to clothe the sunne,
Much lesse those joyes which trample on his head.

As flames do work and winde, when they ascend,
So did I weave my self into the sense.
But while I bustled, I might heare a friend 15
Whisper, *How wide is all this long pretence!*
There is in love a sweetnesse readie penn'd:
Copie out onely that, and save expense.

The Quip

The merrie world did on a day
With his train-bands and mates agree
To meet together, where I lay,
And all in sport to geere at me.

First, Beautie crept into a rose, 5
Which when I pluckt not, Sir, said she,
Tell me, I pray, Whose hands are those?
But thou shalt answer, Lord, for me.

Then Money came, and chinking still,
What tune is this, poore man? said he: 10
I heard in Musick you had skill.
But thou shalt answer, Lord, for me.

Then came brave Glorie puffing by
In silks that whistled, who but he?
He scarce allow'd me half an eie. 15
But thou shalt answer, Lord, for me.

Then came quick Wit and Conversation,
And he would needs a comfort be,
And, to be short, make an Oration.
But thou shalt answer, Lord, for me. 20

Yet when the houre of thy designe
To answer these fine things shall come;
Speak not at large; say, I am thine:
And then they have their answer home.

Paradise

I blesse thee, Lord, because I GROW
Among thy trees, which in a ROW
To thee both fruit and order OW.

What open force, or hidden CHARM
Can blast my fruit, or bring me HARM, 5
While the inclosure is thine ARM?

Inclose me still for fear I START.
Be to me rather sharp and TART,
Than let me want thy hand & ART.

When thou dost greater judgments SPARE, 10
And with thy knife but prune and PARE,
Ev'n fruitfull trees more fruitfull ARE.

Such sharpnes shows the sweetest FREND:
Such cuttings rather heal then REND:
And such beginnings touch their END. 15

The Bag

Away despair! my gracious Lord doth heare.
Though windes and waves assault my keel,
He doth preserve it: he doth steer,
Ev'n when the boat seems most to reel.
Storms are the triumph of his art: 5
Well may he close his eyes, but not his heart.

Hast thou not heard, that my Lord JESUS di'd?
Then let me tell thee a strange storie.
The God of power, as he did ride
In his majestick robes of glorie, 10
Resolv'd to light; and so one day
He did descend, undressing all the way.

The starres his tire of light and rings obtain'd,
The cloud his bow, the fire his spear,
The sky his azure mantle gain'd. 15
And when they ask'd what he would wear;
He smil'd and said as he did go,
He had new clothes a making here below.

When he was come, as travellers are wont,
He did repair unto an inne. 20
Both then, and after, many a brunt
He did endure to cancell sinne:
And having giv'n the rest before,
Here he gave up his life to pay our score.

But as he was returning, there came one 25
That ran upon him with a spear.
He, who came hither all alone,
Bringing nor man, nor arms, nor fear,
Receiv'd the blow upon his side,
And straight he turn'd, and to his brethren cry'd, 30

If ye have any thing to send or write,
I have no bag, but here is room:
Unto my Fathers hands and sight,
Beleeve me, it shall safely come.
That I shall minde, what you impart, 35
Look, you may put it very neare my heart.

Or if hereafter any of my friends
Will use me in this kinde, the doore
Shall still be open; what he sends
I will present, and somewhat more, 40
Not to his hurt. Sighs will convey
Any thing to me. Harke, Despair away.

The Collar

I struck the board, and cry'd, No more.
I will abroad.
What? shall I ever sigh and pine?
My lines and life are free; free as the rode,
Loose as the winde, as large as store. 5
Shall I be still in suit?
Have I no harvest but a thorn
To let me bloud, and not restore
What I have lost with cordiall fruit?
Sure there was wine 10
Before my sighs did drie it: there was corn
Before my tears did drown it.
Is the yeare onely lost to me?
Have I no bayes to crown it?

No flowers, no garlands gay? all blasted? 15
All wasted?
Not so, my heart: but there is fruit,
And thou hast hands.
Recover all thy sigh-blown age
On double pleasures: leave thy cold dispute 20
Of what is fit, and not. Forsake thy cage,
Thy rope of sands,
Which pettie thoughts have made, and made to thee
Good cable, to enforce and draw,
And be thy law, 25
While thou didst wink and wouldst not see.
Away; take heed:
I will abroad.
Call in thy deaths head there: tie up thy fears.
He that forbears 30
To suit and serve his need,
Deserves his load.
But as I rav'd and grew more fierce and wilde
At every word,
Me thoughts I heard one calling, *Child!* 35
And I reply'd, *My Lord.*

The Pulley

When God at first made man,
Having a glasse of blessings standing by;
Let us (said he) poure on him all we can:
Let the worlds riches, which dispersed lie,
Contract into a span. 5

So strength first made a way;
Then beautie flow'd, then wisdome, honour, pleasure:
When almost all was out, God made a stay,
Perceiving that alone of all his treasure
Rest in the bottome lay. 10

For if I should (said he)
Bestow this jewell also on my creature,
He would adore my gifts in stead of me,
And rest in Nature, not the God of Nature:
So both should losers be. 15

Yet let him keep the rest,
But keep them with repining restlesnesse:
Let him be rich and wearie, that at least,
If goodnesse leade him not, yet wearinesse
May tosse him to my breast. 20

The Flower

How fresh, O Lord, how sweet and clean
Are thy returns! ev'n as the flowers in spring;
To which, besides their own demean,
The late-past frosts tributes of pleasure bring.
Grief melts away 5
Like snow in May,
As if there were no such cold thing.

Who would have thought my shrivel'd heart
Could have recover'd greennesse? It was gone
Quite under ground; as flowers depart 10
To see their mother-root, when they have blown;
Where they together
All the hard weather,
Dead to the world, keep house unknown.

These are thy wonders, Lord of power, 15
Killing and quickning, bringing down to hell
And up to heaven in an houre;
Making a chiming of a passing-bell.
We say amisse,
This or that is: 20
Thy word is all, if we could spell.

O that I once past changing were,
Fast in thy Paradise, where no flower can wither!
Many a spring I shoot up fair,
Offring at heav'n, growing and groning thither: 25
Nor doth my flower
Want a spring-showre,
My sinnes and I joining together.

But while I grow in a straight line,
Still upwards bent, as if heav'n were mine own, 30
Thy anger comes, and I decline:
What frost to that? what pole is not the zone,
Where all things burn,
When thou dost turn,
And the least frown of thine is shown? 35

And now in age I bud again,
After so many deaths I live and write;
I once more smell the dew and rain,
And relish versing: O my onely light,
It cannot be 40
That I am he
On whom thy tempests fell all night.

These are thy wonders, Lord of love,
To make us see we are but flowers that glide:
Which when we once can finde and prove, 45
Thou hast a garden for us, where to bide.
Who would be more,
Swelling through store,
Forfeit their Paradise by their pride.

The Sonne

Let forrain nations of their language boast,
What fine varietie each tongue affords:
I like our language, as our men and coast:

Who cannot dresse it well, want wit, not words.
How neatly doe we give one onely name 5
To parents issue and the sunnes bright starre!
A sonne is light and fruit; a fruitfull flame
Chasing the fathers dimnesse, carri'd farre
From the first man in th' East, to fresh and new
Western discov'ries of posteritie. 10
So in one word our Lords humilitie
We turn upon him in a sense most true:
  For what Christ once in humblenesse began,
  We him in glorie call, *The Sonne of Man.*

A Wreath

A wreathed garland of deserved praise,
Of praise deserved, unto thee I give,
I give to thee, who knowest all my wayes,
My crooked winding wayes, wherein I live,
Wherein I die, not live: for life is straight, 5
Straight as a line, and ever tends to thee,
To thee, who art more farre above deceit,
Than deceit seems above simplicitie.
Give me simplicitie, that I may live,
So live and like, that I may know, thy wayes, 10
Know them and practise them: then shall I give
For this poor wreath, give thee a crown of praise.

1–12. The linking of line to line, and of the last line to the first, imitates the wreathing of a garland.

Death

Death, thou wast once an uncouth hideous thing,
        Nothing but bones,
    The sad effect of sadder grones:
Thy mouth was open, but thou couldst not sing.

For we consider'd thee as at some six 5
Or ten yeares hence,
After the losse of life and sense,
Flesh being turn'd to dust, and bones to sticks.

We lookt on this side of thee, shooting short;
Where we did finde 10
The shells of fledge souls left behinde,
Dry dust, which shed no tears, but may extort.

But since our Saviours death did put some bloud
Into thy face;
Thou art grown fair and full of grace, 15
Much in request, much sought for as a good.

For we do now behold thee gay and glad,
As at dooms-day;
When souls shall wear their new aray,
And all thy bones with beautie shall be clad. 20

Therefore we can go die as sleep, and trust
Half that we have
Unto an honest faithfull grave;
Making our pillows either down, or dust.

---

11. *fledge:* plumed and ready for flight.

Dooms-day

Come away,
Make no delay.
Summon all the dust to rise,
Till it stirre, and rubbe the eyes;
While this member jogs the other, 5
Each one whispring, *Live you brother?*

Come away,
Make this the day.

Dust, alas, no musick feels,
But thy trumpet: then it kneels, 10
As peculiar notes and strains
Cure Tarantulas raging pains.

Come away,
O make no stay!
Let the graves make their confession, 15
Lest at length they plead possession:
Fleshes stubbornnesse may have
Read that lesson to the grave.

Come away,
Thy flock doth stray. 20
Some to windes their bodie lend,
And in them may drown a friend:
Some in noisome vapours grow
To a plague and publick wo.

Come away, 25
Help our decay.
Man is out of order hurl'd,
Parcel'd out to all the world.
Lord, thy broken consort raise,
And the musick shall be praise. 30

Judgement

Almightie Judge, how shall poore wretches brook
Thy dreadfull look,
Able a heart of iron to appall,
When thou shalt call
For ev'ry mans peculiar book? 5

What others mean to do, I know not well;
Yet I heare tell,

That some will turn thee to some leaves therein
So void of sinne,
That they in merit shall excell. 10

But I resolve, when thou shalt call for mine,
That to decline,
And thrust a Testament into thy hand:
Let that be scann'd.
There thou shalt finde my faults are thine. 15

Heaven

O who will show me those delights on high?
Echo I.
Thou Echo, thou art mortall, all men know.
Echo No.
Wert thou not born among the trees and leaves? 5
Echo Leaves.
And are there any leaves, that still abide?
Echo Bide.
What leaves are they? impart the matter wholly.
Echo Holy. 10
Are holy leaves the Echo then of blisse?
Echo Yes.
Then tell me, what is that supreme delight?
Echo Light.
Light to the minde: what shall the will enjoy? 15
Echo Joy.
But are there cares and businesse with the pleasure?
Echo Leisure.
Light, joy, and leisure; but shall they persever?
Echo Ever. 20

Love (III)

Love bade me welcome: yet my soul drew back,
    Guiltie of dust and sinne.
But quick-ey'd Love, observing me grow slack
    From my first entrance in,
Drew nearer to me, sweetly questioning, 5
    If I lack'd any thing.

A guest, I answer'd, worthy to be here:
    Love said, You shall be he.
I the unkinde, ungratefull? Ah my deare,
    I cannot look on thee. 10
Love took my hand, and smiling did reply,
    Who made the eyes but I?

Truth Lord, but I have marr'd them: let my shame
    Go where it doth deserve.
And know you not, sayes Love, who bore the blame? 15
    My deare, then I will serve.
You must sit down, sayes Love, and taste my meat:
    So I did sit and eat.

FINIS

Glory be to God *on high*
And on earth peace
Good will towards men.

Love (III)

Love bade me welcome: yet my soul drew back,
    Guiltie of dust and sinne.
But quick-ey'd Love, observing me grow slack
    From my first entrance in,
Drew nearer to me, sweetly questioning,
    If I lack'd any thing.

A guest, I answer'd, worthy to be here:
    Love said, You shall be he.
I the unkinde, ungratefull? Ah my deare,
    I cannot look on thee.
Love took my hand, and smiling did reply,
    Who made the eyes but I?

Truth Lord, but I have marr'd them: let my shame
    Go where it doth deserve.
And know you not, sayes Love, who bore the blame?
    My deare, then I will serve.
You must sit down, sayes Love, and taste my meat:
    So I did sit and eat.

FINIS.

Glorie be to God on high
And on earth peace
Good will towards men.

IV

THE SUCCESSORS OF HERBERT

Richard Crashaw (1613–1649)
Henry Vaughan (1622–1695)
Thomas Traherne (1637–1674)

Richard Crashaw

(1613–1649)

EACH POEM of Crashaw's is a great *performance;* Mr. Eliot has suggested an analogy with the interior of St. Peter's. His invention is as unflagging as his logic; by the sixth stanza of "A Teare" a pillow will be brought to save Mary's tear from laying its head in the dust, and the pillow will be "Stuft with Downe of Angels wing," and on it the tear will be borne (where else?) aloft. In "Musicks Duell" we see his technical faculties at stretch, surpassing, hyperbole upon hyperbole, his own imitations of performance after performance, the lutanist's, the bird's, the lutanist's again, the bird's again, in variety so amazingly sustained that when the bird dies in a last effort at emulation the poet seems barely to have begun. In this unflagging fecundity of elaboration there is none of Donne's dialectical discipline, none of Herbert's responsibility to the devotional occasion. Though he clearly admired both, and named his chief book, in compliment to Herbert, "Steps to the Temple," it is more to the point to relate him, as his best critics have, to the continental baroque, and perhaps incidentally to recall his friendship with Cowley.

He was a Puritan divine's son who disclosed High Church leanings at Cambridge, and Catholic ones a dozen years later. By 1645 he was in Paris, iconoclastic Puritanism being rampant in England; by 1646 in Rome, bearing a letter of introduction to the Pope from the exiled queen of England, to whom Cowley had introduced him. But Rome is a city of delays, and the canonry at Loretto fell to his lot only a few months before his death at thirty-seven.

Both editions of *Steps to the Temple* were published after he left England, and the *Carmen Deo Nostro,* which contains revised versions of many of the earlier poems as well as some new ones, appeared in Paris after his death. Their fulsome Marianism, it is true, would have roused the Commonwealth censors; but wars aside, there is nothing inappropriate in continental publication for this least native of English devotional poets. The point is not that he was a Catholic (Chaucer was a Catholic), nor even that he is rhetorical (Milton is rhetorical). But he is alien to the normal workings of the English sensibility in his penchant for developing headlong any ornament his theme may incur, not playfully nor with humorous ingenuity, but in generous rich language with the full force of his collected attention. And he does not simply run where his first thoughts lead him. He rewrote many poems, and improved them, and never altered their essential nature. He justifies by logic every extravagance, even to showing that Magdalene's weeping eyes are "Portable, & compendious oceans." Donne's lady is "more than Moone" and her tears are worlds, but Donne's hyperbole, with less show of logic, appeals to a dramatic, Crashaw's to a purely emotional justification. For that logic of his comes alive at the bidding of feelings which his friends would have called devout and a historian baroque, and which to a casual reader may seem, but are never really, hysterical.

TEXT: *Poems, English Latin and Greek*, ed. L. C. Martin (Oxford, 1957).

COMMENT: Austin Warren, *Richard Crashaw; a Study in Baroque Sensibility* (Ann Arbor, Michigan, 1939).

The Teare

1 What bright soft thing is this?
Sweet *Mary* thy faire Eyes expence?
A moist sparke it is,
A watry Diamond; from whence
The very Terme, I think, was found 5
The water of a *Diamond*.

2 O 'tis not a Teare,
'Tis a starre about to drop

From thine eye its spheare;
The Sunne will stoope and take it up. 10
Proud will his sister be to weare
This thine eyes Jewell in her Eare.

3 O 'tis a Teare,
Too true a Teare; for no sad eyne,
How sad so e're 15
Raine so true a Teare as thine;
Each Drop leaving a place so deare,
Weeps for it selfe, is its owne Teare.

4 Such a Pearle as this is,
(Slipt from *Aurora's* dewy Brest) 20
The Rose buds sweet lip kisses;
And such the Rose its selfe when vext
With ungentle flames, does shed,
Sweating in too warme a Bed.

5 Such the Maiden Gemme 25
By the wanton Spring put on,
Peeps from her Parent stemme,
And blushes on the manly Sun:
This watry Blossome of thy Eyne
Ripe, will make the richer Wine. 30

6 Faire drop, why quak'st thou so?
'Cause thou streight must lay thy Head
In the Dust? ô no;
The Dust shall never bee thy Bed:
A pillow for thee will I bring, 35
Stuft with Downe of Angels wing.

7 Thus carryed up on high,
(For to Heaven thou must goe)
Sweetly shalt thou lye,
And in soft slumbers bath thy woe; 40
Till the singing Orbes awake thee,
And one of their bright *Chorus* make thee.

8 There thy selfe shalt bee
An eye, but not a weeping one,
Yet I doubt of thee, 45
Whither th'hadst rather there have shone
An eye of Heaven; or still shine here
In th'Heaven of *Mary's* eye, a *Teare.*

Musicks Duell

Now Westward *Sol* had spent the richest Beames
Of Noons high Glory, when hard by the streams
Of *Tiber,* on the sceane of a greene plat,
Under protection of an Oake; there sate
A sweet Lutes-master: in whose gentle aires 5
Hee lost the Dayes heat, and his owne hot cares.
Close in the covert of the leaves there stood
A Nightingale, come from the neighbouring wood:
(The sweet inhabitant of each glad Tree,
Their Muse, their *Syren.* harmlesse *Syren* shee) 10
There stood she listning, and did entertaine
The Musicks soft report: and mold the same
In her owne murmures, that what ever mood
His curious fingers lent, her voyce made good:
The man perceiv'd his Rivall, and her Art, 15
Dispos'd to give the light-foot Lady sport
Awakes his Lute, and 'gainst the fight to come
Informes it, in a sweet *Prœludium*
Of closer straines, and ere the warre begin,
Hee lightly skirmishes on every string 20
Charg'd with a flying touch: and streightway shee
Carves out her dainty voyce as readily,
Into a thousand sweet distinguish'd Tones,
And reckons up in soft divisions,
Quicke volumes of wild Notes; to let him know 25
By that shrill taste, shee could doe something too.
His nimble hands instinct then taught each string
A capring cheerfullnesse; and made them sing

To their owne dance; now negligently rash
Hee throwes his Arme, and with a long drawne dash 30
Blends all together; then distinctly tripps
From this to that; then quicke returning skipps
And snatches this againe, and pauses there.
Shee measures every measure, every where
Meets art with art; sometimes as if in doubt 35
Not perfect yet, and fearing to bee out
Trayles her playne Ditty in one long-spun note,
Through the sleeke passage of her open throat:
A cleare unwrinckled song, then doth shee point it
With tender accents, and severely joynt it 40
By short diminutives, that being rear'd
In controverting warbles evenly shar'd,
With her sweet selfe shee wrangles; Hee amazed
That from so small a channell should be rais'd
The torrent of a voyce, whose melody 45
Could melt into such sweet variety
Straines higher yet; that tickled with rare art
The tatling strings (each breathing in his part)
Most kindly doe fall out; the grumbling Base
In surly groanes disdaines the Trebles Grace. 50
The high-perch't treble chirps at this, and chides,
Untill his finger (Moderatour) hides
And closes the sweet quarrell, rowsing all
Hoarce, shrill, at once; as when the Trumpets call
Hot Mars to th' Harvest of Deaths field, and woo 55
Mens hearts into their hands; this lesson too
Shee gives him backe; her supple Brest thrills out
Sharpe Aires, and staggers in a warbling doubt
Of dallying sweetnesse, hovers ore her skill,
And folds in wav'd notes with a trembling bill, 60
The plyant Series of her slippery song.
Then starts shee suddenly into a Throng
Of short thicke sobs, whose thundring volleyes float,
And roule themselves over her lubricke throat
In panting murmurs, still'd out of her Breast 65
That ever-bubling spring; the sugred Nest
Of her delicious soule, that there does lye

Bathing in streames of liquid Melodie;
Musicks best seed-plot, whence in ripend Aires
A Golden-headed Harvest fairely reares 70
His Honey-dropping tops, plow'd by her breath
Which there reciprocally laboureth
In that sweet soyle. It seemes a holy quire
Founded to th' Name of great *Apollo's* lyre.
Whose sylver-roofe rings with the sprightly notes 75
Of sweet-lipp'd Angell-Imps, that swill their throats
In creame of Morning *Helicon,* and then
Preferre soft Anthems to the Eares of men,
To woo them from their Beds, still murmuring
That men can sleepe while they their Mattens sing: 80
(Most divine service) whose so early lay,
Prevents the Eye-lidds of the blushing day.
There might you heare her kindle her soft voyce,
In the close murmur of a sparkling noyse.
And lay the ground-worke of her hopeful song, 85
Still keeping in the forward streame, so long
Till a sweet whirle-wind (striving to gett out)
Heaves her soft Bosome, wanders round about,
And makes a pretty Earthquake in her Breast,
Till the fledg'd Notes at length forsake their Nest; 90
Fluttering in wanton shoales, and to the Sky
Wing'd with their owne wild Eccho's pratling fly.
Shee opes the floodgate, and lets loose a Tide
Of streaming sweetnesse, which in state doth ride
On the wav'd backe of every swelling straine, 95
Rising and falling in a pompous traine.
And while shee thus discharges a shrill peale
Of flashing Aires; shee qualifies their zeale
With the coole Epode of a graver Noat,
Thus high, thus low, as if her silver throat 100
Would reach the brasen voyce of warr's hoarce Bird;
Her little soule is ravisht: and so pour'd
Into loose extasies that shee is plac't
Above her selfe, Musicks *Enthusiast.*
  Shame now and anger mixt a double staine 105
In the Musitians face; yet once againe

(Mistresse) I come; now reach a straine my Lute
Above her mocke, or bee for ever mute.
Or tune a song of victory to mee,
Or to thy selfe, sing thine owne Obsequie; 110
So said, his hands sprightly as fire hee flings,
And with a quavering coynesse tasts the strings.
The sweet-lip't sisters musically frighted,
Singing their feares are fearfully delighted.
Trembling as when *Appollo's* golden haires 115
Are fan'd and frizled, in the wanton ayres
Of his owne breath: which marryed to his lyre
Doth tune the *Sphæares,* and make Heavens selfe looke higher.
From this to that, from that to this hee flyes
Feeles Musicks pulse in all her Arteryes, 120
Caught in a net which there *Appollo* spreads,
His fingers struggle with the vocall threads,
Following those little rills, hee sinkes into
A Sea of *Helicon;* his hand does goe
Those parts of sweetnesse which with *Nectar* drop, 125
Softer than that which pants in *Hebe's* cup.
The humourous strings expound his learned touch,
By various Glosses; now they seeme to grutch,
And murmur in a buzzing dinne, then gingle
In shrill tongu'd accents: striving to bee single. 130
Every smooth turne, every delicious stroake
Gives life to some new Grace; thus doth h'invoke
Sweetnesse by all her Names; thus, bravely thus
(Fraught with a fury so harmonious)
The Lutes light *Genius* now does proudly rise, 135
Heav'd on the surges of swolne Rapsodyes.
Whose flourish (Meteor-like) doth curle the aire
With flash of high-borne fancyes: here and there
Dancing in lofty measures, and anon
Creeps on the soft touch of a tender tone: 140
Whose trembling murmurs melting in wild aires
Runs to and fro, complaining his sweet cares
Because those pretious mysteryes that dwell,
In musick's ravish't soule hee dare not tell,
But whisper to the world: thus doe they vary 145

Each string his Note, as if they meant to carry
Their Masters blest soule (snacht out at his Eares
By a strong Extasy) through all the sphæares
Of Musicks heaven; and seat it there on high
In th' *Empyræum* of pure Harmony. 150
At length (after so long, so loud a strife
Of all the strings, still breathing the best life
Of blest variety attending on
His fingers fairest revolution
In many a sweet rise, many as sweet a fall) 155
A full-mouth *Diapason* swallowes all.
This done, hee lists what shee would say to this,
And shee although her Breath's late exercise
Had dealt too roughly with her tender throate,
Yet summons all her sweet powers for a Noate 160
Alas! in vaine! for while (sweet soule) shee tryes
To measure all those wild diversities
Of chatt'ring stringes, by the small size of one
Poore simple voyce, rais'd in a Naturall Tone;
Shee failes, and failing grieves, and grieving dyes. 165
Shee dyes; and leaves her life the Victors prise,
Falling upon his Lute; ô fit to have
(That liv'd so sweetly) dead, so sweet a Grave!

Upon *Venus* Putting on *Mars* His Armes

What? *Mars* his sword? faire *Cytherea* say,
Why art thou arm'd so desperately to day?
Mars thou hast beaten naked, and ô then
What need'st thou put on armes against poore men?

Wishes

TO HIS (SUPPOSED) MISTRESSE

Who ere shee bee,
That not impossible shee
That shall command my heart and mee;

Where ere shee lye,
Lock't up from mortall Eye, 5
In shady leaves of Destiny:

Till that ripe Birth
Of studied fate stand forth,
And teach her faire steps to our Earth;

Till that Divine 10
Idæa, take a shrine
Of Chrystall flesh, through which to shine:

Meet you her my wishes,
Bespeake her to my blisses,
And bee yee call'd my absent kisses. 15

I wish her Beauty,
That owes not all his Duty
To gaudy Tire, or glistring shoo-ty.

Something more than
Taffata or Tissew can, 20
Or rampant feather, or rich fan.

More than the spoyle
Of shop, or silkewormes Toyle
Or a bought blush, or a set smile.

A face thats best 25
By its owne beauty drest,
And can alone commend the rest.

A face made up
Out of no other shop,
Than what natures white hand sets ope. 30

A cheeke where Youth,
And Blood, with Pen of Truth
Write, what the Reader sweetly ru'th.

A Cheeke where growes
More then a Morning Rose: 35
Which to no Boxe his being owes.

Lipps, where all Day
A lovers kisse may play,
Yet carry nothing thence away.

Lookes that oppresse 40
Their richest Tires but dresse
And cloath their simplest Nakednesse.

Eyes, that displaces
The Neighbour Diamond, and out faces
That Sunshine by their owne sweet Graces. 45

Tresses, that weare
Jewells, but to declare
How much themselves more pretious are.

Whose native Ray,
Can tame the wanton Day 50
Of Gems, that in their bright shades play.

Each Ruby there,
Or Pearle that dare appeare,
Bee its owne blush, bee its owne Teare.

A well tam'd Heart, 55
For whose more noble smart,
Love may bee long chusing a Dart.

Eyes, that bestow
Full quivers on loves Bow;
Yet pay lesse Arrowes than they owe. 60

Smiles, that can warme
The blood, yet teach a charme,
That Chastity shall take no harme.

Blushes, that bin
The burnish of no sin, 65
Nor flames of ought too hot within.

Joyes, that confesse,
Vertue their Mistresse,
And have no other head to dresse.

Feares, fond and flight, 70
As the coy Brides, when Night
First does the longing lover right.

Teares, quickly fled,
And vaine, as those are shed
For a dying Maydenhead. 75

Dayes, that need borrow,
No part of their good Morrow,
From a fore spent night of sorrow.

Dayes, that in spight
Of Darkenesse, by the Light 80
Of a cleere mind are Day all Night.

Nights, sweet as they,
Made short by lovers play,
Yet long by th'absence of the Day.

Life, that dares send 85
A challenge to his end,
And when it comes say *Welcome Friend.*

Sydnæan showers
Of sweet discourse, whose powers
Can Crowne old Winters head with flowers, 90

Soft silken Houres,
Open sunnes; shady Bowers,
Bove all; Nothing within that lowres.

What ere Delight
Can make Dayes forehead bright; 95
Or give Downe to the Wings of Night.

In her whole frame,
Have Nature all the Name,
Art and ornament the shame.

Her flattery, 100
Picture and Poesy,
Her counsell her owne vertue bee.

I wish, her store
Of worth, may leave her poore
Of wishes; And I wish——No more. 105

Now if Time knowes
That her whose radiant Browes,
Weave them a Garland of my vowes;

Her whose just Bayes,
My future hopes can raise, 110
A trophie to her present praise;

Her that dares bee,
What these Lines wish to see:
I seeke no further, it is shee.

'Tis shee, and heere 115
Lo I uncloath and cleare,
My wishes cloudy Character.

May shee enjoy it,
Whose merit dare apply it,
But Modesty dares still deny it. 120

Such worth as this is,
Shall fixe my flying wishes,
And determine them to kisses.

Let her full Glory,
My fancyes, fly before yee, 125
Bee ye my fictions; But her story.

Upon the Bleeding Crucifix

A SONG

I

Jesu, no more! It is full tide.
From thy head & from thy feet,
From thy hands & from thy side
All the purple Rivers meet.

II

What need thy fair head bear a part 5
In showres, as if thine eyes had none?
What need They help to drown thy heart,
That strives in torrents of it's own?

III

Thy restlesse feet now cannot goe
For us & our eternall good, 10

As they were ever wont. What though?
They swimme. Alas, in their own floud.

IV

Thy hands to give, thou canst not lift;
Yet will thy hand still giving be.
It gives but ô, it self's the gift. 15
It gives though bound; though bound 'tis free.

V

But ô thy side, thy deep-digg'd side!
That hath a double Nilus going.
Nor ever was the pharian tide
Half so fruitfull, half so flowing. 20

VI

No hair so small, but payes his river
To this red sea of thy blood
Their little channells can deliver
Somthing to the Generall floud.

VII

But while I speak, whither are run 25
All the rivers nam'd before?
I counted wrong. There is but one;
But ô that one is one all ore.

VIII

Rain-swoln rivers may rise proud,
Bent all to drown & overflow. 30
But when indeed all 's overflow'd
They themselves are drowned too.

IX

This thy blood's deluge, a dire chance
Dear LORD to thee, to us is found

A deluge of Deliverance; 35
A deluge least we should be drown'd.

N'ere wast thou in a sense so sadly true,
The WELL of living WATERS, Lord, till now.

Upon the Body of Our Bl. Lord, Naked and Bloody

They 'have left thee naked, LORD, O that they had!
This garment too I would they had deny'd.

Thee with thy self they have too richly clad;
Opening the purple wardrobe in thy side.

O never could there be garment too good 5
For thee to wear, But this, of thine own Blood.

The Weeper

I

Hail, sister springs!
Parents of sylver-footed rills!
Ever bubling things!
Thawing crystall! snowy hills,
Still spending, never spent! I mean 5
Thy fair eyes, sweet MAGDALENE!

II

Heavens thy fair eyes be;
Heavens of ever-falling starres.
'Tis seed-time still with thee
And starres thou sow'st, whose harvest dares 10
Promise the earth to counter shine
Whatever makes heavn's forhead fine.

III

But we'are deceived all.
Starres indeed they are too true;
For they but seem to fall, 15
As Heavn's other spangles doe.
It is not for our earth & us
To shine in Things so pretious.

IV

Upwards thou dost weep.
Heavn's bosome drinks the gentle stream. 20
Where th'milky rivers creep,
Thine floates above; & is the cream.
Waters above th' Heavns, what they be
We' are taught best by thy TEARES & thee.

V

Every morn from hence 25
A brisk Cherub something sippes
Whose sacred influence
Addes sweetnes to his sweetest Lippes.
Then to his musick. And his song
Tasts of this Breakfast all day long. 30

VI

Not in the evening's eyes
When they Red with weeping are
For the Sun that dyes,
Sitts sorrow with a face so fair,
No where but here did ever meet 35
Sweetnesse so sad, sadnesse so sweet.

VII

When sorrow would be seen
In her brightest majesty
(For she is a Queen)
Then is she drest by none but thee. 40

Then, & only then, she weares
Her proudest pearles; I mean, thy TEARES.

VIII

The deaw no more will weep
The primrose's pale cheek to deck,
The deaw no more will sleep 45
Nuzzl'd in the lilly's neck;
Much reather would it be thy TEAR,
And leave them Both to tremble here.

IX

There 's no need at all
That the balsom-sweating bough 50
So coyly should let fall
His med'cinable teares; for now
Nature hath learn't to'extract a deaw
More soveraign & sweet from you.

X

Yet let the poore drops weep 55
(Weeping is the ease of woe)
Softly let them creep,
Sad that they are vanquish't so.
They, though to others no releife,
Balsom maybe, for their own greife. 60

XI

Such the maiden gemme
By the purpling vine put on,
Peeps from her parent stemme
And blushes at the bridegroome sun.
This watry Blossom of thy eyn, 65
Ripe, will make the richer wine.

XII

When some new bright Guest
Takes up among the starres a room,

And Heavn will make a feast,
Angels with crystall violls come 70
And draw from these full eyes of thine
Their master's Water: their own Wine.

XIII

Golden though he be,
Golden Tagus murmures tho;
Were his way by thee, 75
Content & quiet he would goe.
So much more rich would he esteem
Thy sylver, than his golden stream.

XIV

Well does the May that lyes
Smiling in thy cheeks, confesse 80
The April in thine eyes.
Mutuall sweetnesse they expresse.
No April ere lent kinder showres,
Nor May return'd more faithfull flowres.

XV

O cheeks! Bedds of chast loves 85
By your own showres seasonably dash't
Eyes! nests of milky doves
In your own wells decently washt,
O wit of love! that thus could place
Fountain & Garden in one face. 90

XVI

O sweet Contest; of woes
With loves, of teares with smiles disputing!
O fair, & Freindly Foes,
Each other kissing & confuting!
While rain & sunshine, Cheekes & Eyes 95
Close in kind contrarietyes.

---

74. *Tagus:* the Iberian river.

XVII

But can these fair Flouds be
Freinds with the bosom fires that fill thee
Can so great flames agree
Æternall Teares should thus distill thee! 100
O flouds, o fires! o suns ô showres!
Mixt & made freinds by love's sweet powres.

XVIII

Twas his well-pointed dart
That digg'd these wells, & drest this Vine;
And taught the wounded HEART 105
The way into these weeping Eyn.
Vain loves avant! bold hands forbear!
The lamb hath dipp't his white foot here.

XIX

And now where're he strayes,
Among the Galilean mountaines, 110
Or more unwellcome wayes,
He's follow'd by two faithfull fountaines;
Two walking baths; two weeping motions;
Portable, & compendious oceans.

XX

O Thou, thy lord's fair store! 115
In thy so rich & rare expenses,
Even when he show'd most poor,
He might provoke the wealth of Princes.
What Prince's wanton'st pride e're could
Wash with Sylver, wipe with Gold. 120

XXI

Who is that King, but he
Who calls't his Crown to be call'd thine,
That thus can boast to be
Waited on by a wandring mine,

A voluntary mint, that strowes 125
Warm sylver shoures where're he goes!

XXII

O pretious Prodigall!
Fair spend-thrift of thy self! thy measure
(Mercilesse love!) is all.
Even to the last Pearle in thy treasure. 130
All places, Times, & objects be
Thy teare's sweet opportunity.

XXIII

Does the day-starre rise?
Still thy starres doe fall & fall
Does day close his eyes? 135
Still the FOUNTAIN weeps for all.
Let night or day doe what they will,
Thou hast thy task; thou weepest still.

XXIV

Does thy song lull the air?
Thy falling teares keep faith full time. 140
Does thy sweet-breath'd praire
Up in clouds of incense climb?
Still at each sigh, that is, each stop,
A bead, that is, A TEAR, does drop.

XXV

At these thy weeping gates, 145
(Watching their watry motion)
Each winged moment waits,
Takes his TEAR, & gets him gone.
By thine Ey's tinct enobled thus
Time layes him up; he's pretious. 150

XXVI

Not, so long she lived,
Shall thy tomb report of thee;
But, so long she greived,

Thus must we date thy memory.
Others by moments, months, & yeares 155
Measure their ages; thou, by TEARES.

XXVII

So doe perfumes expire.
So sigh tormented sweets, opprest
With proud unpittying fire.
Such Teares the suffring Rose that 's vext 160
With ungentle flames does shed,
Sweating in a too warm bed.

XXVIII

Say, ye bright brothers,
The fugitive sons of those fair Eyes
Your fruitfull mothers! 165
What make you here? what hopes can tice
You to be born? what cause can borrow
You from Those nests of noble sorrow?

XXIX

Whither away so fast?
For sure the sordid earth 170
Your Sweetnes cannot tast
Nor does the dust deserve your birth.
Sweet, whither hast you then? o say
Why you trip so fast away?

XXX

We goe not to seek, 175
The darlings of Auroras bed,
The rose's modest Cheek
Nor the violet's humble head.
Though the Feild's eyes too WEEPERS be
Because they want such TEARES as we. 180

XXXI

Much lesse mean we to trace
The Fortune of inferior gemmes,

Preferr'd to some proud face
Or pertch't upon fear'd Diadems.
Crown'd Heads are toyes. We goe to meet 185
A worthy object, our lord's FEET.

A Letter to the Countess of Denbigh

AGAINST IRRESOLUTION AND DELAY IN MATTERS OF RELIGION

What Heav'n-besieged Heart is this
Stands Trembling at the Gate of Blisse:
Holds fast the Door, yet dares not venture
Fairly to open and to enter?
Whose Definition is, A Doubt 5
'Twixt Life and Death, 'twixt In and Out.
Ah! linger not, lov'd Soul: A slow
And late Consent was a long No.
Who grants at last, a great while try'de,
And did his best to have Deny'de. 10
What Magick-Bolts, what mystick Barrs
Maintain the Will in these strange Warrs?
What Fatall, yet fantastick, Bands
Keep the free Heart from his own Hands?
Say, lingring Fair, why comes the Birth 15
Of your brave Soul so slowly forth?
Plead your Pretences, (O you strong
In weaknesse) why you chuse so long
In Labour of your self to ly,
Not daring quite to Live nor Die. 20
So when the Year takes cold we see
Poor Waters their own Prisoners be:
Fetter'd and lock'd up fast they lie
In a cold self-captivity.
Th'astonish'd Nymphs their Floud's strange Fate deplore, 25
To find themselves their own severer Shoar.
Love, that lends haste to heaviest things,
In you alone hath lost his wings.
Look round and reade the World's wide face,

The field of Nature or of Grace; 30
Where can you fix, to find Excuse
Or Pattern for the Pace you use?
Mark with what Faith Fruits answer Flowers,
And know the Call of Heav'n's kind showers:
Each mindfull Plant hasts to make good 35
The hope and promise of his Bud.
Seed-time's not all; there should be Harvest too.
Alas! and has the Year no Spring for you?
Both Winds and Waters urge their way,
And murmure if they meet a stay. 40
Mark how the curl'd Waves work and wind,
All hating to be left behind.
Each bigge with businesse thrusts the other,
And seems to say, Make haste, my Brother.
The aiery nation of neat Doves, 45
That draw the Chariot of chast Loves,
Chide your delay: yea those dull things,
Whose wayes have least to doe with wings,
Make wings at least of their own Weight,
And by their Love controll their Fate. 50
So lumpish Steel, untaught to move,
Learn'd first his Lightnesse by his Love.
What e're Love's matter be, he moves
By th'even wings of his own Doves,
Lives by his own Laws, and does hold 35
In grossest Metalls his own Gold.
All things swear friends to Fair and Good,
Yea Suitours; Man alone is wo'ed,
Tediously wo'ed, and hardly wone:
Only not slow to be undone. 60
As if the Bargain had been driven
So hardly betwixt Earth and Heaven;
Our God would thrive too fast, and be
Too much a gainer by't, should we
Our purchas'd selves too soon bestow 65
On him, who has not lov'd us so.
When love of Us call'd Him to see
If wee'd vouchsafe his company,

He left his Father's Court, and came
Lightly as a Lambent Flame, 70
Leaping upon the Hills, to be
The Humble King of You and Me.
Nor can the cares of his whole Crown
(When one poor Sigh sends for him down)
Detain him, but he leaves behind 75
The late wings of the lazy Wind,
Spurns the tame Laws of Time and Place,
And breaks through all ten Heav'ns to our embrace.
Yield to his Siege, wise Soul, and see
Your Triumph in his Victory. 80
Disband dull Feares, give Faith the day:
To save your Life, kill your Delay.
'Tis Cowardise that keeps this Field;
And want of Courage not to Yield.
Yield then, O yield, that Love may win 85
The Fort at last, and let Life in.
Yield quickly, lest perhaps you prove
Death's Prey, before the Prize of Love.
This Fort of your Fair Self if't be not wone,
He is repuls'd indeed, but You'r undone. 90

An Epitaph upon a Young Married Couple

DEAD AND BURYED TOGETHER

To these, whom Death again did wed,
This Grave's their second Marriage-bed.
For though the hand of fate could force
'Twixt Soul & Body a Divorce,
It could not sunder man & Wife, 5
'Cause They Both lived but one life.
Peace, good Reader. Doe not weep.
Peace, The Lovers are asleep.
They, sweet Turtles, folded ly
In the last knott love could ty. 10

And though they ly as they were dead,
Their Pillow stone, their sheetes of lead,
(Pillow hard, & sheetes not warm)
Love made the bed; They'l take no harm
Let them sleep: let them sleep on. 15
Till this stormy night be gone,
Till the' Æternall morrow dawn;
Then the curtaines will be drawn
And they wake into a light,
Whose day shall never dy in Night. 20

Death's Lecture at the Funeral of a Young Gentleman

Dear Reliques of a dislodg'd Soul, whose lack
Makes many a mourning paper put on black!
O stay a while, ere thou draw in thy head
And wind thy self up close in thy cold bed.
Stay but a little while, untill I call 5
A summons worthy of thy funerall.
Come then, Youth, Beauty, & blood!
    All ye soft powres,
Whose sylken flatteryes swell a few fond howres
Into a false æternity. Come man; 10
Hyperbolized Nothing! know thy span;
Take thine own measure here: down, down, & bow
Before thy self in thine idæa; thou
Huge emptynes! contract thy self; & shrinke
All thy Wild circle to a Point. O sink 15
Lower & lower yet; till thy leane size
Call heavn to look on thee with narrow eyes.
Lesser & lesser yet; till thou begin
To show a face, fitt to confesse thy Kin,
Thy neigbourhood to Nothing. 20
Proud lookes, & lofty eyliddes, here putt on
Your selves in your unfaign'd reflexion,

Here, gallant ladyes! this unpartiall glasse
(Though you be painted) showes you your true face.
These death-seal'd lippes are they dare give the ly 25
To the lowd Boasts of poor Mortality
These curtain'd windows, this retired eye
Outstares the liddes of larg-look't tyranny.
This posture is the brave one this that lyes
Thus low, stands up (me thinkes,) thus & defies 30
The world. All-daring dust & ashes! only you
Of all interpreters read Nature True.

Henry Vaughan

(1622–1695)

"THERE IS NO EXAMPLE in English literature," writes Herbert's editor commenting on Vaughan, "of one poet adopting another poet's works so extensively." For, "He follows only too closely Herbert's subjects and titles, and incorporates into his verse a number, past reckoning, of quotations, conscious and unconscious, from the *Temple* poems." He began (see "To Amoret") by subjecting fashionable secular poets to a similar process; had we only *Poems 1646* to go by we would be safe in dismissing him as an elegant pasticheur. But in *Silex Scintillans, or Sacred Poems* (1650; second part, 1655), we have not only a religious and poetic conversion, which his preface explicitly attributes to Herbert, but an intermittent personal intensity which the decorum borrowed from Herbert both offsets and releases. Like Blake, whom he resembles in his isolation, his eccentric studies, and his cantankerousness, he will happen as though inadvertently on the piercingly accurate word:

O knit me, that am crumbled dust!

neither justifying his *trouvaille* in the larger context of the poem (when Herbert called man "a brittle crazie glass," his whole poem was about church windows) nor even, seemingly, aware that anyone may want it justified. He is an innocent. Herbert's decorous forms blend with a larger decorum, public and social, within which the private act of worship takes place; Vaughan imitates from those forms, almost to the extent of plagiarism, the routine business of organizing a poem, slipping rhythms and locutions through his fingers like beads, intent on his detailed originalities. Like Herbert he will posit a controlling image, but his attention is not on it in Herbert's way. Mr. Alvarez has noted that without the title one would hardly know what "The Timber" is about; Vaughan has not started from timbering but from his own feelings. Similarly,

> 'Twas so, I saw thy birth: That drowsie Lake
> From her faint bosom breath'd thee, the disease
> Of her sick waters, and Infectious Ease.
>   But, now at even
>   Too gross for heaven,
> Thou fall'st in tears, and weep'st for thy mistake.

This starts from disgust with the self, a diseased exhalation of Nature; we need the title, "The Showre," to be sure he is developing a formal analogy ("Ah! it is so with me") rather than generating a symbolist poem twenty-five decades ahead of schedule.

He was an Oxford man, a student of law, an ardent royalist, and for the last forty years of his life a country doctor, given to dabbling in Hermetic philosophy.

TEXT: *Works*, ed. L. C. Martin (Oxford, 1914).

To Amoret

OF THE DIFFERENCE 'TWIXT HIM, AND OTHER LOVERS, AND WHAT TRUE LOVE IS

Marke, when the Evenings cooler wings
  Fanne the afflicted ayre, how the faint Sunne,
    Leaving undone,
    What he begunne,
Those spurious flames suckt up from slime, and earth 5
    To their first, low birth,
    Resignes, and brings.

They shoot their tinsill beames, and vanities,
  Thredding with those false fires their way;
    But as you stay 10
    And see them stray,
You loose the flaming track, and subt'ly they
    Languish away,
    And cheate your Eyes.

Just so base, Sublunarie Lovers hearts 15
Fed on loose prophane desires,
May for an Eye,
Or face comply:
But those removed, they will as soone depart,
And shew their Art, 20
And painted fires.

Whil'st I by pow'rfull Love, so much refin'd,
That my absent soule the same is,
Carelesse to misse,
A glaunce, or kisse, 25
Can with those Elements of lust and sence,
Freely dispence,
And court the mind.

Thus to the North the Loadstones move,
And thus to them th' enamour'd steel aspires: 30
Thus, *Amoret*,
I doe affect;
And thus by winged beames, and mutuall fire,
Spirits and Stars conspire,
And this is L O V E. 35

15-28. Here Vaughan (who published this poem at twenty-four) makes obvious use of Donne's *A Valediction Forbidding Mourning.*

The Search

'Tis now cleare day: I see a Rose
Bud in the bright East, and disclose
The Pilgrim-Sunne; all night have I
Spent in a roving Extasie
To find my Saviour; I have been 5
As far as *Bethlem,* and have seen
His Inne, and Cradle; Being there
I met the *Wise-men,* askt them where
He might be found, or what starre can

Now point him out, grown up a Man? 10
To *Egypt* hence I fled, ran o're
All her parcht bosome to *Nile's* shore
Her yearly nurse; came back, enquir'd
Amongst the *Doctors,* and desir'd
To see the *Temple,* but was shown 15
A little dust, and for the Town
A heap of ashes, where some sed
A small bright sparkle was a bed,
Which would one day (beneath the pole,)
Awake, and then refine the whole. 20
Tyr'd here, I come to *Sychar;* hence
To *Jacobs wel,* bequeathed since
Unto his sonnes, (where often they
In those calme, golden Evenings lay
Watring their flocks, and having spent 25
Those white dayes drove home to the Tent
Their *well-fleec'd* traine;) And here (O fate!)
I sit, where once my Saviour sate;
The angry Spring in bubbles swell'd
Which broke in sighes still, as they fill'd, 30
And whisper'd, *Jesus had been there*
But *Jacobs children would not heare.*
Loath hence to part, at last I rise
But with the fountain in my Eyes,
And here a fresh search is decreed 35
He must be found, where he did bleed;
I walke the garden, and there see
Idæa's of his Agonie,
And moving anguishments that set
His blest face in a bloudy sweat; 40
I climb'd the Hill, perus'd the Crosse
Hung with my gaine, and his great losse,
Never did tree beare fruit like this,
Balsam of Soules, the bodyes blisse;

---

14. *Doctors:* see Luke 2 : 46.
21. *Sychar:* site of Jacob's well, where Jesus talked with the woman of Samaria (John 4).

But, O his grave! where I saw lent 45
(For he had none,) a Monument,
An undefil'd, and new-heaw'd one,
But there was not the *Corner-stone;*
Sure (then said I,) my Quest is vaine,
Hee'le not be found, where he was slaine, 50
So mild a Lamb can never be
'Midst so much bloud, and Crueltie;
I'le to the Wilderness, and can
Find beasts more mercifull then man,
He liv'd there safe, 'twas his retreat 55
From the fierce *Jew,* and *Herods* heat,
And forty dayes withstood the fell,
And high temptations of hell;
With Seraphins there talked he
His fathers flaming ministrie, 60
He heav'nd their *walks,* and with his eyes
Made those wild shades a Paradise,
Thus was the desert sanctified
To be the refuge of his bride;
I'le thither then; see, It is day, 65
The Sun's broke through to guide my way.
  But as I urg'd thus, and writ down
What pleasures should my Journey crown,
What silent paths, what shades, and Cells,
Faire, virgin-flowers, and hallow'd *Wells* 70
I should rove in, and rest my head
Where my deare Lord did often tread,
Sugring all dangers with successe,
Me thought I heard one singing thus;

1.

Leave, leave, thy gadding thoughts; 75
Who Pores
and spies
Still out of Doores
descries
Within them nought. 80

2.

The skinne, and shell of things
Though faire,
are not
Thy wish, nor pray'r
but got 85
By meer Despair
of wings.

3.

To rack old Elements,
or Dust
and say 90
Sure here he must
needs stay
Is not the way,
nor just.
Search well another world; who studies this, 95
Travels in Clouds, seeks *Manna,* where none is.

Acts Cap. 17. ver. 27, 28.

That they should seek the Lord, if happily they might feel after him, and finde him, though he be not far off from every one of us, for in him we live, and move, and have our being.

The Showre

'Twas so, I saw thy birth: That drowsie Lake
From her faint bosome breath'd thee, the disease
Of her sick waters, and Infectious Ease.
But, now at Even
Too grosse for heaven, 5
Thou fall'st in teares, and weep'st for thy mistake.

2.

Ah! it is so with me; oft have I prest
Heaven with a lazie breath, but fruitles this

Peirc'd not; Love only can with quick accesse
Unlock the way, 10
When all else stray
The smoke, and Exhalations of the brest.

3.

Yet, if as thou doest melt, and with thy traine
Of drops make soft the Earth, my eyes could weep
O're my hard heart, that's bound up, and asleep, 15
Perhaps at last
(Some such showres past,)
My God would give a Sun-shine after raine.

Distraction

O knit me, that am crumbled dust! the heape
Is all dispers'd, and cheape;
Give for a handfull, but a thought
And it is bought;
Hadst thou 5
Made me a starre, a pearle, or a rain-bow,
The beames I then had shot
My light had lessend not,
But now
I find my selfe the lesse, the more I grow; 10
The world
Is full of voices; Man is call'd, and hurl'd
By each, he answers all,
Knows ev'ry note, and call,
Hence, still 15
Fresh dotage tempts, or old usurps his will.
Yet, hadst thou clipt my wings, when Coffin'd in
This quicken'd masse of sinne,
And saved that light, which freely thou
Didst then bestow, 20
I feare
I should have spurn'd, and said thou didst forbeare;

Or that thy store was lesse,
But now since thou didst blesse
So much, 25
I grieve, my God! that thou hast made me such.
I grieve?
O, yes! thou know'st I doe; Come, and releive
And tame, and keepe downe with thy light
Dust that would rise, and dimme my sight, 30
Lest left alone too long
Amidst the noise, and throng,
Oppressed I
Striving to save the whole, by parcells dye.

The Pursuite

Lord! what a busie, restles thing
Hast thou made man?
Each day, and houre he is on wing,
Rests not a span;
Then having lost the Sunne, and light 5
By clouds surpriz'd
He keepes a Commerce in the night
With aire disguis'd;
Hadst thou given to this active dust
A state untir'd, 10
The lost Sonne had not left the huske
Nor home desir'd;
That was thy secret, and it is
Thy mercy too,
For when all failes to bring to blisse, 15
Then, this must doe.
Ah! Lord! and what a Purchase will that be
To take us sick, that sound would not take thee?

Compare the theme of Herbert's *The Pulley.*
11. ***lost Sonne:*** the Prodigal Son.

The Retreate

Happy those early dayes! when I
Shin'd in my Angell-infancy.
Before I understood this place
Appointed for my second race,
Or taught my soul to fancy ought 5
But a white, Celestiall thought,
When yet I had not walkt above
A mile, or two, from my first love,
And looking back (at that short space,)
Could see a glimpse of his bright-face; 10
When on some *gilded Cloud,* or *flowre*
My gazing soul would dwell an houre,
And in those weaker glories spy
Some shadows of eternity;
Before I taught my tongue to wound 15
My Conscience with a sinfull sound,
Or had the black art to dispence
A sev'rall sinne to ev'ry sence,
But felt through all this fleshly dresse
Bright *shootes* of everlastingnesse. 20
O how I long to travell back
And tread again that ancient track!
That I might once more reach that plaine,
Where first I left my glorious traine,
From whence th' Inlightned spirit sees 25
That shady City of Palme trees;
But (ah!) my soul with too much stay
Is drunk, and staggers in the way.
Some men a forward motion love,
But I by backward steps would move, 30
And when this dust falls to the urn
In that state I came return.

Corruption

Sure, It was so. Man in those early days
    Was not all stone, and Earth,
He shin'd a little, and by those weak Rays
    Had some glimpse of his birth.
He saw Heaven o'r his head, and knew from whence   5
    He came (condemned,) hither,
And, as first Love draws strongest, so from hence
    His mind sure progress'd thither.
Things here were strange unto him: Swet, and till
    All was a thorn, or weed,   10
Nor did those last, but (like himself,) dyed still
    As soon as they did *Seed,*
They seem'd to quarrel with him; for that Act
    That fel him, foyl'd them all,
He drew the Curse upon the world, and Crackt   15
    The whole frame with his fall.
This made him long for *home,* as loath to stay
    With murmurers, and foes;
He sigh'd for *Eden,* and would often say
    Ah! what bright days were those?   20
Nor was Heav'n cold unto him; for each day
    The vally, or the Mountain
Afforded visits, and still *Paradise* lay
    In some green shade, or fountain.
Angels lay *Leiger* here; Each Bush, and Cel,   25
    Each Oke, and high-way knew them,
Walk but the fields, or sit down at some *wel,*
    And he was sure to view them.
Almighty *Love*! where art thou now? mad man
    Sits down, and freezeth on,   30
He raves, and swears to stir nor fire, nor fan,
    But bids the thread be spun.
I see, thy Curtains are Close-drawn; Thy bow
    Looks dim too in the Cloud,
Sin triumphs still, and man is sunk below   35

The Center, and his shrowd;
All's in deep sleep, and night; Thick darknes lyes
And hatcheth o'r thy people;
But hark! what trumpets that? what Angel cries
Arise! Thrust in thy sickle. 40

Son-dayes

Bright shadows of true Rest! some shoots of blisse,
Heaven once a week;
The next worlds gladnes prepossest in this;
A day to seek

Eternity in time; the steps by which 5
We Climb above all ages; Lamps that light
Man through his heap of dark days; and the rich,
And full redemption of the whole weeks flight.

2.

The Pulleys unto headlong man; times bower;
The narrow way; 10
Transplanted Paradise; Gods walking houre;
The Cool o'th' day;

The Creatures *Jubile;* Gods parle with dust;
Heaven here; Man on those hills of Myrrh, and flowres;
Angels descending; the Returns of Trust; 15
A Gleam of glory, after six-days-showres.

3.

The Churches love-feasts; Times Prerogative,
And Interest
Deducted from the whole; The Combs, and hive,
And home of rest. 20

The milky way Chalkt out with Suns; a Clue
That guides through erring hours; and in full story

A taste of Heav'n on earth; the pledge, and Cue
Of a full feast; And the Out Courts of glory.

The World

I saw Eternity the other night
Like a great *Ring* of pure and endless light,
All calm, as it was bright,
And round beneath it, Time in hours, days, years
Driv'n by the spheres 5
Like a vast shadow mov'd, In which the world
And all her train were hurl'd;
The doting Lover in his queintest strain
Did their Complain,
Neer him, his Lute, his fancy, and his flights, 10
Wits sour delights,
With gloves, and knots the silly snares of pleasure
Yet his dear Treasure
All scatter'd lay, while he his eys did pour
Upon a flowr. 15

2

The darksome States-man hung with weights and woe
Like a thick midnight-fog mov'd there so slow
He did nor stay, nor go;
Condemning thoughts (like sad Ecclipses) scowl
Upon his soul, 20
And Clouds of crying witnesses without
Pursued him with one shout.
Yet dig'd the Mole, and lest his ways be found
Workt under ground,
Where he did Clutch his prey, but one did see 25
That policie,
Churches and altars fed him, Perjuries
Were gnats and flies,
It rain'd about him bloud and tears, but he
Drank them as free. 30

3

The fearfull miser on a heap of rust
Sate pining all his life there, did scarce trust
    His own hands with the dust,
Yet would not place one peece above, but lives
        In feare of theeves. 35
Thousands there were as frantick as himself
    And hug'd each one his pelf,
The down-right Epicure plac'd heav'n in sense
        And scornd pretence
While others slipt into a wide Excesse 40
        Said little lesse;
The weaker sort slight, triviall wares Inslave
        Who think them brave,
And poor, despised truth sate Counting by
        Their victory. 45

4

Yet some, who all this while did weep and sing,
And sing, and weep, soar'd up into the *Ring,*
    But most would use no wing.
O fools (said I,) thus to prefer dark night
        Before true light, 50
To live in grots, and caves, and hate the day
    Because it shews the way,
The way which from this dead and dark abode
        Leads up to God,
A way where you might tread the Sun, and be 55
        More bright than he.
But as I did their madnes so discusse
        One whisper'd thus,
This Ring the Bride-groome did for none provide
        But for his bride. 60

John Cap. 2. ver. 16, 17.

All that is in the world, the lust of the flesh, the lust of the Eys, and the pride of life, is not of the father, but is of the world.

And the world passeth away, and the lusts thereof, but he that doth the will of God abideth for ever.

They Are All Gone into the World of Light

They are all gone into the world of light!
  And I alone sit lingring here;
Their very memory is fair and bright,
  And my sad thoughts doth clear.

It glows and glitters in my cloudy brest 5
  Like stars upon some gloomy grove,
Or those faint beams in which this hill is drest,
    After the Sun's remove.

I see them walking in an Air of glory,
  Whose light doth trample on my days: 10
My days, which are at best but dull and hoary,
    Meer glimering and decays.

O holy hope! and high humility,
  High as the Heavens above!
These are your walks, and you have shew'd them me 15
    To kindle my cold love,

Dear, beauteous death! the Jewel of the Just,
  Shining nowhere, but in the dark;
What mysteries do lie beyond thy dust;
    Could man outlook that mark! 20

He that hath found some fledg'd birds nest, may know
  At first sight, if the bird be flown;
But what fair Well, or Grove he sings in now,
    That is to him unknown.

And yet, as Angels in some brighter dreams 25
  Call to the soul, when man doth sleep:
So some strange thoughts transcend our wonted theams,
    And into glory peep.

If a star were confin'd into a Tomb
  Her captive flames must needs burn there; 30
But when the hand that lockt her up, gives room,
    She'l shine through all the sphære.

O Father of eternal life, and all
  Created glories under thee!
Resume thy spirit from this world of thrall 35
    Into true liberty.

Either disperse these mists, which blot and fill
  My perspective (still) as they pass,
Or else remove me hence unto that hill,
    Where I shall need no glass. 40

The Timber

Sure thou didst flourish once! and many Springs,
Many bright mornings, much dew, many showers
Past ore thy head: many light *Hearts* and *Wings*
Which now are dead, lodg'd in thy living bowers.

And still a new succession sings and flies; 5
Fresh Groves grow up, and their green branches shoot
Towards the old and still enduring skies,
While the low *Violet* thrives at their root.

But thou beneath the sad and heavy *Line*
Of death, dost waste all senseless, cold and dark; 10
Where not so much as dreams of light may shine,
Nor any thought of greenness, leaf or bark.

And yet (as if some deep hate and dissent,
Bred in thy growth betwixt high winds and thee,
Were still alive) thou dost great storms resent 15
Before they come, and know'st how near they be.

Else all at rest thou lyest, and the fierce breath
Of tempests can no more disturb thy ease;
But this thy strange resentment after death
Means onely those, who broke (in life) thy peace. 20

So murthered man, when lovely life is done,
And his blood freez'd, keeps in the Center still
Some secret sense, which makes the dead blood run
At his approach, that did the body kill.

And is there any murth'rer worse then sin? 25
Or any storms more foul then a lewd life?
Or what *Resentient* can work more within,
Than true remorse, when with past sins at strife?

He that hath left lifes vain joys and vain care,
And truly hates to be detain'd on earth, 30
Hath got an house where many mansions are,
And keeps his soul unto eternal mirth.

But though thus dead unto the world, and ceas'd
From sin, he walks a narrow, private way;
Yet grief and old wounds make him sore displeas'd, 35
And all his life a rainy, weeping day.

For though he should forsake the world, and live
As meer a stranger, as men long since dead;
Yet joy it self will make a right soul grieve
To think, he should be so long vainly lead. 40

But as shades set off light, so tears and grief
(Though of themselves but a sad blubber'd story)
By shewing the sin great, shew the relief
Far greater, and so speak my Saviors glory.

If my way lies through deserts and wilde woods; 45
Where all the Land with scorching heat is curst;
Better, the pools should flow with rain and floods
To fill my bottle, than I die with thirst.

Blest showers they are, and streams sent from above
Begetting *Virgins* where they use to flow; 50
And trees of life no other waters love,
These upper springs and none else make them grow.

But these chaste fountains flow not till we dye;
Some drops may fall before, but a clear spring
And ever running, till we leave to fling 55
Dirt in her way, will keep above the skie.

Rom. Cap. 6. ver. 7.
He that is dead, is freed from sin.

Quickness

False life! a foil and no more, when
Wilt thou be gone?
Thou foul deception of all men
That would not have the true come on.

Thou art a Moon-like toil; a blinde 5
Self-posing state;
A dark contest of waves and winde;
A meer tempestuous debate.

Life is a fix'd, discerning light,
A knowing Joy; 10
No chance, or fit: but ever bright,
And calm and full, yet doth not cloy.

'Tis such a blissful thing, that still
Doth vivifie,
And shine and smile, and hath the skill 15
To please without Eternity.

Thou art a toylsom Mole, or less
A moving mist
But life is, what none can express,
A quickness, which my God hath kist. 20

Thomas Traherne

(1637–1674)

A SHOEMAKER'S SON, a country clergyman, a gentle fanatic on such matters as simplified spelling and the ecstatic life; publisher of a volume rebuking the Roman church, but not of his poems, which he laid aside in notebooks; Traherne is the middle term between the greater seventeenth-century devotional poets, whom he might almost as well not have read, and Blake, who certainly did not read him. He has a body of ejaculatory reflections to communicate

> (How like an Angel came I down!
> How Bright are all Things here!)

and no particular notion of how to go on with a poem except by prolonging the mood in which it is being composed. "Shadows in the Water," for instance, iterates rather than develops its material, dwelling on the childhood experience which we are meant to take as a key to adult felicity in a dual world, until simply by being detained so long with that experience we come to divine what it signifies; but Traherne distrusts, apparently, all attempt to articulate his full meaning. Tenuously linked to Herbert by an uncluttered felicity of diction, he is innocent of Herbert's view, which Herbert owed Donne, that the poem's province is a moving through and scrutiny of its materials. He faces forward to a time when it will be sufficient to testify that one has had an emotional experience; not only is Wordsworth's immortality ode implicit in his work, but also Wordsworth's dealings with daffodils ("I gaz'd, and gaz'd"). It was a taste trained on Wordsworth which in 1903, when his manuscripts had just been discovered, found him incomparably superior to Herbert, Crashaw, and Vaughan "in the most essential qualities of the poet."

TEXT: *Centuries, Poems and Thanksgivings,* ed. H. M. Margoliouth (Oxford, 1958).

The Salutation

1

These little Limmes,
These Eys and Hands which here I find,
These rosie Cheeks wherwith my Life begins,
Where have ye been,? Behind
What Curtain were ye from me hid so long! 5
Where was? in what Abyss, my Speaking Tongue?

2

When silent I,
So many thousand thousand years,
Beneath the Dust did in a Chaos lie,
How could I Smiles or Tears, 10
Or Lips or Hands or Eys or Ears perceiv?
Welcom ye Treasures which I now receiv.

3

I that so long
Was Nothing from Eternitie,
Did little think such Joys as Ear or Tongue, 15
To Celebrat or See:
Such Sounds to hear, such Hands to feel, such Feet,
Beneath the Skies, on such a Ground to meet.

4

New Burnisht Joys!
Which yellow Gold and Pearl excell! 20
Such Sacred Treasures are the Lims in Boys,
In which a Soul doth Dwell;
Their Organized Joynts, and Azure Veins
More Wealth include, than all the World contains.

5

From Dust I rise, 25
And out of Nothing now awake,
These Brighter Regions which salute mine Eys,
A Gift from GOD I take.
The Earth, the Seas, the Light, the Day, the Skies,
The Sun and Stars are mine, if those I prize. 30

6

Long time before
I in my Mothers Womb was born,
A GOD preparing did this Glorious Store,
The World for me adorne.
Into this Eden so Divine and fair, 35
So Wide and Bright, I com his Son and Heir.

7

A Stranger here
Strange Things doth meet, Strange Glories see;
Strange Treasures lodg'd in this fair World appear,
Strange all, and New to me. 40
But that they mine should be, who nothing was,
That Strangest is of all, yet brought to pass.

Wonder

1

How like an Angel came I down!
How Bright are all Things here!
When first among his Works I did appear
O how their GLORY me did Crown?
The World resembled his *Eternitie,* 5
In which my Soul did Walk;
And evry Thing that I did see,
Did with me talk.

2

The Skies in their Magnificence
The Lively, Lovely Air; 10
Oh how Divine, how soft, how Sweet, how fair!
The Stars did entertain my Sence,
And all the Works of GOD so Bright and pure,
So Rich and Great did seem,
As if they ever must endure, 15
In my Esteem.

3

A Native Health and Innocence
Within my Bones did grow,
And while my GOD did all his Glories shew,
I felt a Vigour in my Sence 20
That was all SPIRIT. I within did flow
With Seas of Life, like Wine;
I nothing in the World did know,
But 'twas Divine.

4

Harsh ragged Objects were conceald, 25
Oppressions Tears and Cries,
Sins, Griefs, Complaints, Dissentions, Weeping Eys,
Were hid: and only Things reveald,
Which Heav'nly Spirits, and the Angels prize.
The State of Innocence 30
And Bliss, not Trades and Poverties,
Did fill my Sence.

5

The Streets were pavd with Golden Stones,
The Boys and Girles were mine,
Oh how did all their Lovly faces shine! 35
The Sons of Men were Holy Ones.
Joy, Beauty, Welfare did appear to me,
And evry Thing which here I found,

While like an Angel I did see,
Adornd the Ground. 40

6

Rich Diamond and Pearl and Gold
In evry Place was seen;
Rare Splendors, Yellow, Blew, Red, White and Green,
Mine Eys did evrywhere behold,
Great Wonders clothd with Glory did appear, 45
Amazement was my Bliss.
That and my Wealth was evry where:
No Joy to this!

7

Cursd and Devisd Proprieties,
With Envy, Avarice 50
And Fraud, those Feinds that Spoyl even Paradice,
Fled from the Splendor of mine Eys.
And so did Hedges, Ditches, Limits, Bounds,
I dreamd not ought of those,
But wanderd over all mens Grounds, 55
And found Repose.

8

Proprieties themselvs were mine,
And Hedges Ornaments;
Walls, Boxes, Coffers, and their rich Contents
Did not Divide my Joys, but shine. 60
Clothes, Ribbans, Jewels, Laces, I esteemd
My Joys by others worn;
For me they all to wear them seemd
When I was born.

Shadows in the Water

In unexperienc'd Infancy
Many a sweet Mistake doth ly:

Mistake tho false, intending tru;
A *Seeming* somewhat more than *View;*
    That doth instruct the Mind 5
    In Things that ly behind,
And many Secrets to us show
Which afterwards we com to know.

Thus did I by the Water's brink
Another World beneath me think; 10
And while the lofty spacious Skies
Reversed there abus'd mine Eys,
    I fancy'd other Feet
    Came mine to touch and meet;
As by som Puddle I did play 15
Another World within it lay.

Beneath the Water Peeple drown'd.
Yet with another Hev'n crown'd,
In spacious Regions seem'd to go
Freely moving to and fro: 20
    In bright and open Space
    I saw their very face;
Eys, Hands and Feet they had like mine;
Another Sun did with them shine.

'Twas strange that peeple there should walk 25
And yet I could not hear them talk:
That throu a little watry Chink,
Which one dry Ox or Horse might drink,
    We other Worlds should see,
    Yet not admitted be; 30
And other Confines there behold
Of Light and Darkness, Heat and Cold.

I call'd them oft, but call'd in vain;
No Speeches we could entertain:
Yet did I there expect to find 35
Som other World, to pleas my Mind.
    I plainly saw by these

A new *Antipodes*,
Whom, tho they were so plainly seen,
A Film kept off that stood between. 40

By walking Men's reversed Feet
I chanc'd another World to meet;
Tho it did not to View exceed
A Phantasm, 'tis a World indeed,
Where skies beneath us shine, 45
And Earth by Art divine
Another face presents below,
Where Peeple's feet against Ours go.

Within the Regions of the Air,
Compass'd about with Hev'ns fair, 50
Great Tracts of Land there may be found
Enricht with Fields and fertil Ground;
Where many num'rous Hosts,
In those far distant Coasts,
For other great and glorious Ends, 55
Inhabit, my yet unknown Friends.

O ye that stand upon the Brink,
Whom I so near me, throu the Chink,
With Wonder see: What faces there,
Whose Feet, whose Bodies, do ye wear? 60
I my Companions see
In You, another Me.
They seemed Others, but are We;
Our second Selvs those Shadows be.

Look how far off those lower Skies 65
Extend themselvs! scarce with mine Eys
I can them reach. O ye my Friends,
What *Secret* borders on those Ends?
Are lofty Hevens hurl'd
'Bout your inferior World? 70

Are ye the Representatives
Of other Peopl's distant Lives?

Of all the Play-mates which I knew
That here I do the Image view
In other Selvs; what can it mean? 75
But that below the purling Stream
    Som unknown Joys there be
    Laid up in Store for me;
To which I shall, when that thin Skin
Is broken, be admitted in. 80

A Serious and a Curious Night-Meditation

Here must Wee rest; and where else should wee rest?
Is not a man's owne House, to sleep in, best?
If this bee all our House, They are too blame;
That bragge of the great House, from whence they came:
And evermore their speeches Enterlace; 5
I, and my Fathers House: Alasse! alasse!
What is my Fathers House! and what am I!
My fathers House is Earth; where I must lie:
And I a worme, noe man; that fits noe roome,
Till like a worme, I crawle into my Tombe. 10
The wombe was first my Grave; whence since I Rose,
My body Grave-like doth my Soule Inclose:
This body like a Corp's with sheets o're spread,
Dieing each Night, lies buried in a Bed.
O're which my spreading Tester's large Extent, 15
borne with carv'd Anticks, shewes my Monument.
My close low builded Chamber, where I lie,
shewes like a little Chappel, where I lie:
Whilest at my Window, pretty Birds do Ring,
My Knell; and with their Notes my OBit sing. 20
Thus when the worlds vaine Toyles my soul hath wearied;
I, in my body, Bed and house lie buried.

Then have I little Cause to feare my Tombe;
since this wherein I lie, my Grave's become.

sleep is Cosin-german unto Death:
sleep and Death differ, noe more, then a Carkasse
and a skeleton.

V

THE SURVIVAL

Robert Herrick (1591–1674)

Robert Herrick

(1591–1674)

Though he published his sole book in 1648, when the third-generation metaphysicals, Cowley, Crashaw, even Cleveland, were in print, Herrick was the chronological contemporary of King, Herbert, and Carew, and the poetic contemporary of a still earlier time. He was then 57. Donne was seventeen years dead. The case has been aptly likened by Mr. John Hayward to that of some elderly Georgian poet, making his debut, uninfluenced by Pound and Eliot, not in Rupert Brooke's time but around 1948.

He had been, by then, twenty years a country vicar, only recently ejected from his living because of his obdurate allegiance to King Charles, and living in Westminster on the charity of friends. Almost certainly most of the poems he now prepared for their first publication had been written before his long country sojourn, in the far-off days when he had been intimate in London with Ben Jonson's disciples, and circulated verses in manuscript, and even been esteemed Jonson's equal: and written "Upon Julia's Breasts," and the advice "To live merrily, and to trust to Good Verses," and "His Farewell to Sack," which he likened to

> the warme soft side
> Of the resigning, yet resisting Bride

and the "Welcome to Sack," again, "soule of my life and fame," to which he swore not a second time to turn apostate; and much else on the theme of seizing the flying moment and on the happy smiles of light loves.

The book's title, *Hesperides,* connects the poems' strange bright world of girls and flowers with the land of the golden apples at the western end of the world; and no doubt many of them, and not only the section of divine poems to which he gave the subtitle *Noble Numbers,* were retouched, if not written, in the west country of England where he had had his vicarage. Certainly his artistry is extreme. Over the more than 1400 poems he contrives to cast a look of prolific ease, restated in their profusion, their limpidity, their delicate patterning of sound, their apparent innocence of the stances of artifice. The very errata are prefaced by an easy quatrain, as though verse, like breathing, came more naturally than prose. Yet there is barely a poem without a classical source, or a Latin turn of phrase. He pillaged the ancients as remorselessly as Ben; he pillaged Ben himself. Latterly he even used Burton's *Anatomy of Melancholy* (1621) as a huge commonplace book. "Here again Burton had collected much of the traditional thought and used some of the phrasing which Herrick shapes into a poem": so his editor remarks of the song that begins "Gather ye rosebuds . . .", and proceeds to exhibit five apposite citations, in three languages. He was also the friend of William and Henry Lawes, and in the tireless fitting of words to a musician's needs, in which he can surpass Jonson himself, there is great hidden labor.

But in a time of "ingenuities and 'strong lines'" the 1400 poems seemed old-fashioned. Twenty years later the edition was still not sold out, while Cleveland had been perhaps twenty times reprinted. By then the Rev. Mr. Herrick had long since been restored to his living in Devonshire, where he died full of years in 1674, having outlived his juniors Henry King, George Herbert, Carew, Habington, Milton, Crashaw, Cleveland, Denham, Cowley, Lovelace, and Traherne; Oliver Cromwell and King Charles I; and (by half a century) the vogue of direct easy song.

TEXT: *Poetical Works,* ed. L. C. Martin (Oxford, 1956).

COMMENT: S. Musgrove, *The Universe of Robert Herrick* (Auckland, New Zealand, 1950). Marchette Chute, *Two Gentle Men, the Lives of George Herbert and Robert Herrick* (New York, 1959). William Jay Smith, Introduction to the Laurel *Herrick* (New York, 1962).

HESPERIDES

The Argument of His Book

I sing of *Brooks*, of *Blossomes*, *Birds*, and *Bowers*:
Of *April*, *May*, of *June*, and *July*-Flowers.
I sing of *May-poles*, *Hock-carts*, *Wassails*, *Wakes*,
Of *Bride-grooms*, *Brides*, and of their *Bridall-cakes*.
I write of *Youth*, of *Love*, and have Accesse 5
By these, to sing of cleanly-*Wantonnesse*.
I sing of *Dewes*, of *Raines*, and piece by piece
Of *Balme*, of *Oyle*, of *Spice*, and *Amber-Greece*.
I sing of *Times trans-shifting*; and I write
How *Roses* first came *Red*, and *Lilies White*. 10
I write of *Groves*, of *Twilights*, and I sing
The Court of *Mab*, and of the *Fairie-King*.
I write of *Hell*; I sing (and ever shall)
Of *Heaven*, and hope to have it after all.

To the Soure Reader

If thou dislik'st the Piece thou light'st on first;
Thinke that of All, that I have writ, the worst:
But if thou read'st my Booke unto the end,
And still do'st this, and that verse, reprehend:
O Perverse man! If All disgustfull be, 5
The Extreame Scabbe take thee, and thine, for me.

To *Perilla*

Ah my *Perilla!* do'st thou grieve to see
Me, day by day, to steale away from thee?
Age cals me hence, and my gray haires bid come,
And haste away to mine eternal home;
'Twill not be long (*Perilla*) after this, 5
That I must give thee the *supremest* kisse:
Dead when I am, first cast in salt, and bring
Part of the creame from that *Religious Spring;*
With which (*Perilla*) wash my hands and feet;
That done, then wind me in that very sheet 10
Which wrapt thy smooth limbs (when thou didst implore
The Gods protection, but the night before)
Follow me weeping to my Turfe, and there
Let fall a *Primrose,* and with it a teare:
Then lastly, let some weekly-strewings be 15
Devoted to the memory of me:
Then shall my *Ghost* not walk about, but keep
Still in the coole, and silent shades of sleep.

To His Mistresses

Helpe me! helpe me! now I call
To my pretty *Witchcrafts* all:
Old I am, and cannot do
That, I was accustom'd to.
Bring your *Magicks, Spels, and Charmes,* 5
To enflesh my thighs, and armes:
Is there no way to beget
In my limbs their former heat?
Æson had (as *Poets* faine)
Baths that made him young againe: 10
Find that *Medicine* (if you can)

For your drie-decrepid man:
Who would faine his strength renew,
Were it but to pleasure you.

Cherrie-ripe

Cherrie-Ripe, Ripe, Ripe, I cry,
Full and faire ones; come and buy:
If so be, you ask me where
They doe grow? I answer, There,
Where my *Julia's* lips doe smile; 5
There's the Land, or Cherry-Ile:
Whose Plantations fully show
All the yeere, where Cherries grow.

The Vision to *Electra*

I dream'd we both were in a bed
Of Roses, almost smothered:
The warmth and sweetnes had me there
Made lovingly familiar:
But that I heard thy sweet breath say, 5
Faults done by night, will blush by day:
I kist thee (panting,) and I call
Night to the Record! that was all.
But ah! if empty dreames so please,
Love give me more such nights as these. 10

Upon *Julia's* Voice

So smooth, so sweet, so silv'ry is thy voice,
As, could they hear, the Damn'd would make no noise,
But listen to thee, (walking in thy chamber)
Melting melodious words, to Lutes of Amber.

Againe

When I thy singing next shall heare,
Ile wish I might turne all to eare,
To drink in Notes, and Numbers; such
As blessed soules cann't heare too much:
Then melted down, there let me lye 5
Entranc'd, and lost confusedly:
And by thy Musique strucken mute,
Die, and be turn'd into a Lute.

Upon Roses

Under a Lawne, than skyes more cleare,
Some ruffled Roses nestling were:
And snugging there, they seem'd to lye
As in a flowrie Nunnery:
They blush'd, and look'd more fresh than flowers 5
Quickned of late by Pearly showers;
And all, because they were possest
But of the heat of *Julia's* breast:
Which as a warme, and moistned spring,
Gave them their ever flourishing. 10

Delight in Disorder

A sweet disorder in the dresse
Kindles in cloathes a wantonnesse:
A Lawne about the shoulders thrown
Into a fine distraction:
An erring Lace, which here and there 5

Enthralls the Crimson Stomacher:
A Cuffe neglectfull and thereby
Ribbands to flow confusedly:
A winning wave (deserving Note)
In the tempestuous petticote: 10
A carelesse shooe-string, in whose tye
I see a wilde civility:
Doe more bewitch me, than when Art
Is too precise in every part.

To *Anthea* Lying in Bed

So looks *Anthea,* when in bed she lyes,
Orecome, or halfe betray'd by Tiffanies:
Like to a Twi-light, or that simpring Dawn,
That Roses shew, when misted o're with Lawn.
Twilight is yet, till that her Lawnes give way; 5
Which done, that Dawne, turnes then to perfect day.

A Country Life: To His Brother, *M. Tho: Herrick*

Thrice, and above, blest (my soules halfe) art thou,
In thy both Last, and Better Vow:
Could'st leave the City, for exchange, to see
The Countries sweet simplicity:
And it to know, and practice; with intent 5
To grow the sooner innocent:
By studying to know vertue; and to aime
More at her nature, than her name:
The last is but the least; the first doth tell
Wayes lesse to live, than to live well: 10
And both are knowne to thee, who now can'st live
Led by thy conscience; to give
Justice to soone-pleas'd nature; and to show,
Wisdome and she together goe,

And keep one Centre: This with that conspires, 15
  To teach Man to confine desires:
And know, that Riches have their proper stint,
  In the contented mind, not mint.
And can'st instruct, that those who have the itch
  Of craving more, are never rich. 20
These things thou know'st to'th'height, and dost prevent
  That plague; because thou art content
With that Heav'n gave thee with a warie hand,
  (More blessed in thy Brasse, than Land)
To keep cheap Nature even, and upright; 25
  To coole, not cocker Appetite.
Thus thou can'st tearcely live to satisfie
  The belly chiefly; not the eye:
Keeping the barking stomach wisely quiet,
  Lesse with a neat, than needfull diet. 30
But that which most makes sweet thy country life,
  Is, the fruition of a wife:
Whom (Stars consenting with thy Fate) thou hast
  Got, not so beautifull, as chast:
By whose warme side thou dost securely sleep 35
  (While Love the Centinell doth keep)
With those deeds done by day, which n'er affright
  Thy silken slumbers in the night.
Nor has the darknesse power to usher in
  Feare to those sheets, that know no sin. 40
But still thy wife, by chast intentions led,
  Gives thee each night a Maidenhead.
The Damaskt medowes, and the peebly streames
  Sweeten, and make soft your dreames:
The Purling springs, groves, birds, and well-weav'd Bowrs, 45
  With fields enameled with flowers,
Present their shapes; while fantasie discloses
  Millions of *Lillies* mixt with *Roses*.
Then dream, ye heare the Lamb by many a bleat
  Woo'd to come suck the milkie Teat: 50
While *Faunus* in the Vision comes to keep,
  From rav'ning wolves, the fleecie sheep.
With thousand such enchanting dreams, that meet

To make sleep not so sound, as sweet:
Nor can these figures so thy rest endeare, 55
As not to rise when *Chanticlere*
Warnes the last Watch; but with the Dawne dost rise
To work, but first to sacrifice;
Making thy peace with heav'n, for some late fault,
With Holy-meale, and spirting-salt. 60
Which done, thy painfull Thumb this sentence tells us,
Jove for our labour all things sells us.
Nor are thy daily and devout affaires
Attended with those desp'rate cares,
Th' industrious Merchant has; who for to find 65
Gold, runneth to the Western Inde,
And back again, (tortur'd with fears) doth fly,
Untaught, to suffer Poverty.
But thou at home, blest with securest ease,
Sitt'st, and beleev'st that there be seas, 70
And watrie dangers; while thy whiter hap,
But sees these things within thy Map.
And viewing them with a more safe survey,
Mak'st easie Feare unto thee say,
A heart thrice wall'd with Oke, and Brasse, that man 75
Had, first, durst plow the Ocean.
But thou at home without or tyde or gale,
Canst in thy Map securely saile:
Seeing those painted Countries; and so guesse
By those fine Shades, their Substances: 80
And from thy Compasse taking small advice,
Buy'st Travell at the lowest price.
Nor are thine eares so deafe, but thou canst heare
(Far more with wonder, than with feare)
Fame tell of States, of Countries, Courts, and Kings; 85
And beleeve there be such things:
When of these truths, thy happyer knowledge lyes,
More in thine eares, than in thine eyes.
And when thou hear'st by that too-true-Report,
Vice rules the Most, or All at Court: 90
Thy pious wishes are, (though thou not there)
Vertue had, and mov'd her Sphere.

But thou liv'st fearlesse; and thy face ne'r shewes
  Fortune when she comes, or goes.
But with thy equall thoughts, prepar'd dost stand, 95
  To take her by the either hand:
Nor car'st which comes the first, the foule or faire;
  A wise man ev'ry way lies square.
And like a surly *Oke* with storms perplext;
  Growes still the stronger, strongly vext. 100
Be so, bold spirit; stand Center-like, unmov'd;
  And be not onely thought, but prov'd
To be what I report thee; and inure
  Thy selfe, if want comes to endure:
And so thou dost: for thy desires are 105
  Confin'd to live with private *Larr:*
Not curious whether Appetite be fed,
  Or with the first, or second bread.
Who keep'st no proud mouth for delicious cates:
  Hunger makes coorse meats, delicates. 110
Can'st, and unurg'd, forsake that Larded fare,
  Which Art, not Nature, makes so rare;
To taste boyl'd Nettles, Colworts, Beets, and eate
  These, and sowre herbs, as dainty meat?
While soft Opinion makes thy *Genius* say, 115
  Content makes all Ambrosia.
Nor is it, that thou keep'st this stricter size
  So much for want, as exercise:
To numb the sence of Dearth, which sho'd sinne haste it,
  Thou might'st but onely see't, not taste it. 120
Yet can thy humble roofe maintaine a Quire
  Of singing Crickits by thy fire:
And the brisk Mouse may feast her selfe with crums,
  Till that the green-ey'd Kitling comes.
Then to her Cabbin, blest she can escape 125
  The sudden danger of a Rape.
And thus thy little-well-kept-stock doth prove,
  Wealth cannot make a life, but Love.
Nor art thou so close-handed, but can'st spend
  (Counsell concurring with the end) 130
As well as spare: still conning o'r this Theame,

To shun the first, and last extreame.
Ordaining that thy small stock find no breach,
Or to exceed thy Tether's reach:
But to live round, and close, and wisely true 135
To thine own selfe; and knowne to few.
Thus let thy Rurall Sanctuary be
Elizium to thy wife and thee;
There to disport your selves with golden measure:
For seldome use commends the pleasure. 140
Live, and live blest; thrice happy Paire; Let Breath,
But lost to one, be th' others death.
And as there is one Love, one Faith, one Troth,
Be so one Death, one Grave to both.
Till when, in such assurance live, ye may 145
Nor feare, or wish your dying day.

His Fare-well to Sack

Farewell thou Thing, time-past so knowne, so deare
To me, as blood to life and spirit: Neare,
Nay, thou more neare than kindred, friend, man, wife,
Male to the female, soule to body: Life
To quick action, or the warme soft side 5
Of the resigning, yet resisting Bride.
The kisse of Virgins; First-fruits of the bed;
Soft speech, smooth touch, the lips, the Maiden-head:
These, and a thousand sweets, co'd never be
So neare, or deare, as thou wast once to me. 10
O thou the drink of Gods, and Angels! Wine
That scatter'st Spirit and Lust; whose purest shine,
More radiant than the Summers Sun-beams shows;
Each way illustrious, brave; and like to those
Comets we see by night; whose shagg'd portents 15
Fore-tell the comming of some dire events:
Or some full flame, which with a pride aspires,
Throwing about his wild, and active fires.
'Tis thou, above Nectar, O Divinest soule!

(Eternall in thy self) that canst controule 20
That, which subverts whole nature, grief and care;
Vexation of the mind, and damn'd Despaire.
'Tis thou, alone, who with thy Mistick Fan,
Work'st more than Wisdome, Art, or Nature can,
To rouze the sacred madnesse; and awake 25
The frost-bound-blood, and spirits; and to make
Them frantick with thy raptures, flashing through
The soule, like lightning, and as active too.
'Tis not *Apollo* can, or those thrice three
Castalian Sisters, sing, if wanting thee. 30
Horace, Anacreon both had lost their fame,
Had'st thou not fill'd them with thy fire and flame.
Phœbean splendour! and thou *Thespian* spring!
Of which, sweet Swans must drink, before they sing
Their true-pac'd-Numbers, and their Holy-Layes, 35
Which makes them worthy *Cedar,* and the *Bayes.*
But why? why longer doe I gaze upon
Thee with the eye of admiration?
Since I must leave thee; and enforc'd, must say
To all thy witching beauties, Goe, Away. 40
But if thy whimpring looks doe ask me why?
Then know, that Nature bids thee goe, not I.
'Tis her erroneous self has made a braine
Uncapable of such a Soveraigne,
As is thy powerfull selfe. Prethee not smile; 45
Or smile more inly; lest thy looks beguile
My vowes denounc'd in zeale, which thus much show thee,
That I have sworn, but by thy looks to know thee.
Let others drink thee freely; and desire
Thee and their lips espous'd; while I admire, 50
And love thee; but not taste thee. Let my Muse
Faile of thy former helps; and onely use
Her inadult'rate strength: what's done by me
Hereafter, shall smell of the Lamp, not thee.

The Vision

Sitting alone (as one forsook)
Close by a Silver-shedding Brook;
With hands held up to Love, I wept;
And after sorrowes spent, I slept:
Then in a Vision I did see 5
A glorious forme appeare to me:
A Virgins face she had; her dresse
Was like a sprightly *Spartanesse*.
A silver bow with green silk strung,
Down from her comely shoulders hung: 10
And as she stood, the wanton Aire
Dandled the ringlets of her haire.
Her legs were such *Diana* shows,
When tuckt up she a hunting goes;
With Buskins shortned to descrie 15
The happy dawning of her thigh:
Which when I saw, I made accesse
To kisse that tempting nakednesse:
But she forbad me, with a wand
Of Mirtle she had in her hand: 20
And chiding me, said, Hence, Remove,
Herrick, thou art too coorse to love.

Upon a Virgin Kissing a Rose

'Twas but a single *Rose*,
Till you on it did breathe;
But since (me thinks) it shows
Not so much *Rose*, as Wreathe.

Corinna's Going a Maying

Get up, get up for shame, the Blooming Morne
Upon her wings presents the god unshorne.
  See how *Aurora* throwes her faire
  Fresh-quilted colours through the aire:
  Get up, sweet-Slug-a-bed, and see 5
  The Dew-bespangling Herbe and Tree.
Each Flower has wept, and bow'd toward the East,
Above an houre since; yet you not drest,
  Nay! not so much as out of bed?
  When all the Birds have Mattens seyd, 10
  And sung their thankfull Hymnes: 'tis sin,
  Nay, profanation to keep in,
When as a thousand Virgins on this day,
Spring, sooner than the Lark, to fetch in May.

Rise; and put on your Foliage, and be seene 15
To come forth, like the Spring-time, fresh and greene;
  And sweet as *Flora*. Take no care
  For Jewels for your Gowne, or Haire:
  Feare not; the leaves will strew
  Gemms in abundance upon you: 20
Besides, the childhood of the Day has kept,
Against you come, some *Orient Pearls* unwept:
  Come, and receive them while the light
  Hangs on the Dew-locks of the night:
  And *Titan* on the Eastern hill 25
  Retires himselfe, or else stands still
Till you come forth. Wash, dresse, be briefe in praying:
Few Beads are best, when once we goe a Maying.

Come, my *Corinna,* come; and comming, marke
How each field turns a street; each street a Parke 30
  Made green, and trimm'd with trees: see how
  Devotion gives each House a Bough,

    Or Branch: Each Porch, each doore, ere this,
    An Arke a Tabernacle is
Made up of white-thorn neatly enterwove; 35
As if here were those cooler shades of love.
    Can such delights be in the street,
    And open fields, and we not see't?
    Come, we'll abroad; and let's obay
    The Proclamation made for May: 40
And sin no more, as we have done, by staying;
But my *Corinna,* come, let's goe a Maying.

There's not a budding Boy, or Girle, this day,
But is got up, and gone to bring in May.
    A deale of Youth, ere this, is come 45
    Back, and with *White-thorn* laden home.
    Some have dispatcht their Cakes and Creame,
    Before that we have left to dreame:
And some have wept, and woo'd, and plighted Troth,
And chose their Priest, ere we can cast off sloth: 50
    Many a green-gown has been given;
    Many a kisse, both odde and even:
    Many a glance too has been sent
    From out the eye, Loves Firmament:
Many a jest told of the Keyes betraying 55
This night, and Locks pickt, yet w'are not a Maying.

Come, let us goe, while we are in our prime;
And take the harmlesse follie of the time.
    We shall grow old apace, and die
    Before we know our liberty. 60
    Our life is short; and our dayes run
    As fast away as do's the Sunne:
And as a vapour, or a drop of raine
Once lost, can ne'r be found againe:
    So when or you or I are made 65
    A fable, song, or fleeting shade;
    All love, all liking, all delight
    Lies drown'd with us in endlesse night.

Then while time serves, and we are but decaying;
Come, my *Corinna,* come, let's goe a Maying. 70

The Lilly in a Christal

You have beheld a smiling *Rose*
When Virgins hands have drawn
O'r it a Cobweb-Lawne:
And here, you see, this Lilly shows,
Tomb'd in a *Christal* stone, 5
More faire in this transparent case,
Than when it grew alone;
And had but single grace.

You see how *Creame* but naked is;
Nor daunces in the eye 10
Without a Strawberrie:
Or some fine tincture, like to this,
Which draws the sight thereto,
More by that wantoning with it;
Than when the paler hieu 15
No mixture did admit.

You see how *Amber* through the streams
More gently stroaks the sight,
With some conceal'd delight;
Than when he darts his radiant beams 20
Into the boundlesse aire:
Where either too much light his worth
Doth all at once impaire,
Or set it little forth.

Put Purple Grapes, or Cherries in- 25
To Glasse, and they will send
More beauty to commend
Them, from that cleane and subtile skin,
Than if they naked stood,

And had no other pride at all, 30
But their own flesh and blood,
And tinctures naturall.

Thus Lillie, Rose, Grape, Cherry, Creame,
And Straw-berry do stir
More love, when they transfer 35
A weak, a soft, a broken beame;
Than if they sho'd discover
At full their proper excellence;
Without some Scean cast over,
To juggle with the sense. 40

Thus let this *Christal'd Lillie* be
A Rule, how far to teach,
Your nakednesse must reach:
And that, no further, than we see
Those glaring colours laid 45
By Arts wise hand, but to this end
They sho'd obey a shade;
Lest they too far extend.

So though y'are white as Swan, or Snow,
And have the power to move 50
A world of men to love:
Yet, when your Lawns and Silks shal flow,
And that white cloud divide
Into a doubtful Twi-light; then,
Then will your hidden Pride 55
Raise greater fires in men.

The Welcome to Sack

So soft streams meet, so springs with gladder smiles
Meet after long divorcement by the Iles:
When Love (the child of likenesse) urgeth on
Their Christal natures to an union.

So meet stolne kisses, when the Moonie nights 5
Call forth fierce Lovers to their wisht Delights:
So *Kings* & *Queens* meet, when Desire convinces
All thoughts, but such as aime at getting Princes,
As I meet thee. Soule of my life, and fame!
Eternall Lamp of Love! whose radiant flame 10
Out-glares the Heav'ns **Osiris*; and thy gleams
Out-shine the splendour of his mid-day beams.
Welcome, O welcome my illustrious Spouse;
Welcome as are the ends unto my Vowes:
I! far more welcome than the happy soile, 15
The Sea-scourg'd Merchant, after all his toile,
Salutes with tears of joy; when fires betray
The smoakie chimneys of his *Ithaca*.
Where hast thou been so long from my embraces,
Poore pittyed Exile? Tell me, did thy Graces 20
Flie discontented hence, and for a time
Did rather choose to blesse another clime?
Or went'st thou to this end, the more to move me,
By thy short absence, to desire and love thee?
Why frowns my Sweet? Why won't my Saint confer 25
Favours on me, her fierce Idolater?
Why are Those Looks, Those Looks the which have been
Time-past so fragrant, sickly now drawn in
Like a dull Twi-light? Tell me; and the fault
Ile expiate with Sulphur, Haire, and Salt: 30
And with the Christal humour of the spring,
Purge hence the guilt, and kill this quarrelling.
Wo't thou not smile, or tell me what's amisse?
Have I been cold to hug thee, too remisse,
Too temp'rate in embracing? Tell me, ha's desire 35
To thee-ward dy'd i'th'embers, and no fire
Left in this rak't-up Ash-heap, as a mark
To testifie the glowing of a spark?
Have I divorc't thee onely to combine
In hot Adult'ry with another Wine? 40
True, I confesse I left thee, and appeale
'Twas done by me, more to confirme my zeale,
And double my affection on thee; as doe those,

* The Sun

Whose love growes more enflam'd, by being Foes.
But to forsake thee ever, co'd there be 45
A thought of such like possibilitie?
When thou thy selfe dar'st say, thy Iles shall lack
Grapes, before *Herrick* leaves Canarie Sack.
Thou mak'st me ayrie, active to be born,
Like *Iphyclus,* upon the tops of Corn. 50
Thou mak'st me nimble, as the winged howers,
To dance and caper on the heads of flowers,
And ride the Sun-beams. Can there be a thing
Under the heavenly **Isis,* that can bring — * The Moon
More love unto my life, or can present 55
My *Genius* with a fuller blandishment?
Illustrious Idoll! co'd th'*Ægyptians* seek
Help from the *Garlick, Onyon,* and the *Leek,*
And pay no vowes to thee? who wast their best
God, and far more transcendent than the rest? 60
Had *Cassius,* that weak Water-drinker, known
Thee in thy Vine, or had but tasted one
Small Chalice of thy frantick liquor; He
As the wise *Cato* had approv'd of thee. 64
Had not **Joves* son, that brave *Tyrinthian* Swain, — * Hercules
(Invited to the *Thesbian* banquet) ta'ne
Full goblets of thy gen'rous blood; his spright
Ne'r had kept heat for fifty Maids that night.
Come, come and kisse me; Love and lust commends
Thee, and thy beauties; kisse, we will be friends 70
Too strong for Fate to break us: Look upon
Me, with that full pride of complexion,
As *Queenes,* meet *Queenes;* or come thou unto me,
As *Cleopatra* came to *Anthonie;*
When her high carriage did at once present 75
To the *Triumvir,* Love and Wonderment.
Swell up my nerves with spirit; let my blood
Run through my veines, like to a hasty flood.
Fill each part full of fire, active to doe
What thy commanding soule shall put it to. 80
And till I turne Apostate to thy love,
Which here I vow to serve, doe not remove

Thy Fiers from me; but *Apollo's* curse
Blast these-like actions, or a thing that's worse;
When these Circumstants shall but live to see 85
The time that I prevaricate from thee.
Call me *The sonne of Beere,* and then confine
Me to the Tap, the Tost, the Turfe; Let Wine
Ne'r shine upon me; May my Numbers all
Run to a sudden Death, and Funerall. 90
And last, when thee (deare Spouse) I disavow,
Ne'r may Prophetique *Daphne* crown my Brow.

To Live Merrily, and to Trust to Good Verses

Now is the time for mirth,
Nor cheek, or tongue be dumbe:
For with the flowrie earth,
The golden pomp is come.

The golden Pomp is come; 5
For now each tree do's weare
(Made of her Pap and Gum)
Rich beads of *Amber* here.

Now raignes the *Rose,* and now
Th'*Arabian* Dew besmears 10
My uncontrolled brow,
And my retorted haires.

Homer, this Health to thee,
In Sack of such a kind,
That it wo'd make thee see, 15
Though thou wert ne'r so blind.

Next, *Virgil,* Ile call forth,
To pledge this second Health
In Wine, whose each cup's worth
An Indian Common-wealth. 20

A Goblet next Ile drink
  To *Ovid;* and suppose,
Made he the pledge, he'd think
  The world had all *one Nose.*

Then this immensive cup
  Of *Aromatike* wine,
Catullus, I quaffe up
  To that Terce Muse of thine.

Wild I am now with heat;
  O *Bacchus!* coole thy Raies! 30
Or frantick I shall eate
  Thy *Thyrse,* and bite the *Bayes.*

Round, round, the roof do's run;
  And being ravisht thus,
Come, I will drink a Tun 35
  To my *Propertius.*

Now, to *Tibullus,* next,
  This flood I drink to thee:
But stay; I see a Text,
  That this presents to me. 40

Behold, *Tibullus* lies
  Here burnt, whose smal return
Of ashes, scarce suffice
  To fill a little Urne.

Trust to good Verses then; 45
  They onely will aspire,
When Pyramids, as men,
  Are lost, i'th'funerall fire.

And when all Bodies meet
  In *Lethe* to be drown'd; 50
Then onely Numbers sweet,
  With endless life are crown'd.

To Violets

Welcome Maids of Honour,
You doe bring
In the Spring;
And wait upon her.

She has Virgins many, 5
Fresh and faire;
Yet you are
More sweet than any.

Y'are the Maiden Posies,
And so grac't, 10
To be plac't,
'Fore Damask Roses.

Yet though thus respected,
By and by
Ye doe lie,
Poore Girles, neglected. 15

To the Virgins, to Make Much of Time

Gather ye Rose-buds while ye may,
Old Time is still a flying:
And this same flower that smiles to day,
To morrow will be dying.

The glorious Lamp of Heaven, the Sun, 5
The higher he's a getting;
The sooner will his Race be run,
And neerer he's to Setting.

That Age is best, which is the first,
When Youth and Blood are warmer; 10
But being spent, the worse, and worst
Times, still succeed the former.

Then be not coy, but use your time;
And while ye may, goe marry:
For having lost but once your prime, 15
You may for ever tarry.

His Poetrie His Pillar

Onely a little more
I have to write,
Then Ile give o're,
And bid the world Good-night.

'Tis but a flying minute, 5
That I must stay,
Or linger in it;
And then I must away.

O time that cut'st down all!
And scarce leav'st here 10
Memoriall
Of any men that were.

How many lye forgot
In Vaults beneath?
And piece-meale rot 15
Without a fame in death?

Behold this living stone,
I reare for me,
Ne'r to be thrown
Downe, envious Time by thee. 20

Pillars let some set up,
(If so they please)
Here is my hope,
And my *Pyramides.*

A Meditation for His Mistresse

You are a *Tulip* seen to day,
But (Dearest) of so short a stay;
That where you grew, scarce man can say.

You are a lovely *July-flower,*
Yet one rude wind, or ruffling shower, 5
Will force you hence, (and in an houre.)

You are a sparkling *Rose* i'th'bud,
Yet lost, ere that chast flesh and blood
Can shew where you or grew, or stood.

You are a full-spread faire-set Vine, 10
And can with Tendrills love intwine,
Yet dry'd, ere you distill your Wine.

You are like Balme inclosed (well)
In *Amber,* or some *Chrystall* shell,
Yet lost ere you transfuse your smell. 15

You are a dainty *Violet,*
Yet wither'd, ere you can be set
Within the Virgins Coronet.

You are the *Queen* all flowers among,
But die you must (faire Maid) ere long, 20
As He, the maker of this Song.

To the Rose

SONG

Goe happy Rose, and enterwove
With other Flowers, bind my Love.
  Tell her too, she must not be,
  Longer flowing, longer free,
  That so oft has fetter'd me. 5

Say (if she's fretfull) I have bands
Of Pearle, and Gold, to bind her hands:
  Tell her, if she struggle still,
  I have Mirtle rods, (at will)
  For to tame, though not to kill. 10

Take thou my blessing, thus, and goe,
And tell her this, but doe not so,
  Lest a handsome anger flye,
  Like a Lightning, from her eye,
  And burn thee' up, as well as I. 15

The Hock-Cart, *or* Harvest Home

TO THE RIGHT HONOURABLE, MILDMAY, EARLE OF WESTMORLAND

Come Sons of Summer, by whose toile,
We are the Lords of Wine and Oile:
By whose tough labours, and rough hands,
We rip up first, then reap our lands.
Crown'd with the eares of corne, now come, 5
And, to the Pipe, sing Harvest home.
Come forth, my Lord, and see the Cart
Drest up with all the Country Art.

See, here a *Maukin,* there a sheet,
As spotlesse pure, as it is sweet: 10
The Horses, Mares, and frisking Fillies,
(Clad, all, in Linnen, white as Lillies.)
The Harvest Swaines, and Wenches bound
For joy, to see the *Hock-cart* crown'd.
About the Cart, heare, how the Rout 15
Of Rurall Younglings raise the shout;
Pressing before, some coming after,
Those with a shout, and these with laughter.
Some blesse the Cart; some kisse the sheaves;
Some prank them up with Oaken leaves: 20
Some crosse the Fill-horse; some with great
Devotion, stroak the home-borne wheat:
While other Rusticks, lesse attent
To Prayers, than to Merryment,
Run after with their breeches rent. 25
Well, on, brave boyes, to your Lords Hearth,
Glitt'ring with fire; where, for your mirth,
Ye shall see first the large and cheefe
Foundation of your Feast, Fat Beefe:
With Upper Stories, Mutton, Veale 30
And Bacon, (which makes full the meale)
With sev'rall dishes standing by,
As here a Custard, there a Pie,
And here all tempting Frumentie.
And for to make the merry cheere, 35
If smirking Wine be wanting here,
There's that, which drowns all care, stout Beere;
Which freely drink to your Lords health,
Then to the Plough, (the Common-wealth)
Next to your Flailes, your Fanes, your Fatts; 40
Then to the Maids with Wheaten Hats:
To the rough Sickle, and crookt Sythe,
Drink frollick boyes, till all be blythe.
Feed, and grow fat; and as ye eat,
Be mindfull, that the lab'ring Neat 45

---

21. ***crosse the Fill-horse:*** get astride the shaft horse.

(As you) may have their fill of meat.
And know, besides, ye must revoke
The patient Oxe unto the Yoke,
And all goe back unto the Plough
And Harrow, (though they'r hang'd up now.) 50
And, you must know, your Lords word's true,
Feed him ye must, whose food fils you.
And that this pleasure is like raine,
Not sent ye for to drowne your paine,
But for to make it spring againe. 55

To *Anthea*

WHO MAY COMMAND HIM ANYTHING

Bid me to live, and I will live
Thy Protestant to be:
Or bid me love, and I will give
A loving heart to thee.

A heart as soft, a heart as kind, 5
A heart as sound and free,
As in the whole world thou canst find,
That heart Ile give to thee.

Bid that heart stay, and it will stay,
To honour thy Decree: 10
Or bid it languish quite away,
And't shall doe so for thee.

Bid me to weep, and I will weep,
While I have eyes to see:
And having none, yet I will keep 15
A heart to weep for thee.

Bid me despaire, and Ile despaire,
Under that *Cypresse* tree:

Or bid me die, and I will dare
  E'en Death, to die for thee. 20

Thou art my life, my love, my heart,
  The very eyes of me:
And hast command of every part,
  To live and die for thee.

To Meddowes

Ye have been fresh and green,
  Ye have been fill'd with flowers:
And ye the Walks have been
  Where Maids have spent their houres.

You have beheld, how they 5
  With *Wicker Arks* did come
To kisse, and beare away
  The richer Couslips home.

Y'ave heard them sweetly sing,
  And seen them in a Round: 10
Each Virgin, like a Spring,
  With Hony-succles crown'd.

But now, we see, none here,
  Whose silv'rie feet did tread,
And with dishevell'd Haire, 15
  Adorn'd this smoother Mead.

Like Unthrifts, having spent,
  Your stock, and needy grown,
Y'are left here to lament
  Your poore estates, alone. 20

A Nuptiall Song, or Epithalamie, on Sir *Clipseby Crew* and His Lady

What's that we see from far? the spring of Day
Bloom'd from the East, or faire Injewel'd May
  Blowne out of April; or some New-
  Star fill'd with glory to our view,
    Reaching at heaven, 5
To add a nobler Planet to the seven?
  Say, or doe we not descrie
Some Goddesse, in a cloud of Tiffanie
   To move, or rather the
  Emergent *Venus* from the Sea? 10

'Tis she! 'tis she! or else some more Divine
Enlightned substance; mark how from the Shrine
  Of holy Saints she paces on,
  Treading upon *Vermilion*
    And *Amber;* Spice- 15
ing the Chafte Aire with fumes of Paradise.
  Then come on, come on, and yeeld
A savòur like unto a blessed field,
   When the bedabled Morne
  Washes the golden eares of corne. 20

See where she comes; and smell how all the street
Breathes Vine-yards and Pomgranats: O how sweet!
  As a fir'd Altar, is each stone,
  Perspiring pounded Cynamon.
    The Phenix nest, 25
Built up of odours, burneth in her breast.
  Who therein wo'd not consume
His soule to Ash-heaps in that rich perfume?
   Bestroaking Fate the while
  He burnes to Embers on the Pile. 30

Himen, O Himen! Tread the sacred ground;
Shew thy white feet, and head with Marjoram crown'd:
Mount up thy flames, and let thy Torch
Display the Bridegroom in the porch,
In his desires 35
More towring, more disparkling than thy fires:
Shew her how his eyes do turne
And roule about, and in their motions burne
Their balls to Cindars: haste,
Or else to ashes he will waste. 40

Glide by the banks of Virgins then, and passe
The Shewers of Roses, lucky-foure-leav'd grasse:
The while the cloud of younglings sing,
And drown yee with a flowrie Spring:
While some repeat 45
Your praise, and bless you, sprinkling you with Wheat:
While that others doe divine;
Blest is the Bride, on whom the Sun doth shine;
And thousands gladly wish
You multiply, as doth a Fish. 50

And beautious Bride we do confess y'are wise,
In dealing forth these bashfull jealousies:
In Lov's name do so; and a price
Set on your selfe, by being nice:
But yet take heed; 55
What now you seem, be not the same indeed,
And turne *Apostate:* Love will
Part of the way be met; or sit stone-still.
On then, and though you slow-
ly go, yet, howsoever, go. 60

And now y'are enter'd; see the Codled Cook
Runs from his *Torrid Zone,* to prie, and look,
And blesse his dainty Mistresse: see,
The Aged point out, This is she,

---

54. *nice:* reticent

Who now must sway 65
The House (Love shield her) with her Yea and Nay:
And the smirk Butler thinks it
Sin, in's Nap'rie, not to express his wit;
Each striving to devise
Some gin, wherewith to catch your eyes. 70

To bed, to bed, kind Turtles, now, and write
This the short'st day, and this the longest night;
But yet too short for you: 'tis we,
Who count this night as long as three,
Lying alone, 75
Telling the Clock strike Ten, Eleven, Twelve, One.
Quickly, quickly then prepare;
And let the Young-men and the Bride-maids share
Your Garters; and their joynts
Encircle with the Bride-grooms Points. 80

By the Brides eyes, and the teeming life
Of her green hopes, we charge ye, that no strife,
(Farther than Gentlenes tends) gets place
Among ye, striving for her lace:
O doe not fall 85
Foule in these noble pastimes, lest ye call
Discord in, and so divide
The youthfull Bride-groom, and the fragrant Bride:
Which Love fore-fend; but spoken,
Be't to your praise, no peace was broken. 90

Strip her of Spring-time, tender-whimpring-maids,
Now *Autumne's* come, when all those flowrie aids
Of her Delayes must end; Dispose
That *Lady-smock*, that *Pansie*, and that *Rose*
Neatly apart; 95
But for *Prick-madam*, and for *Gentle-heart;*
And soft-*Maidens-blush*, the Bride
Makes holy these, all others lay aside:
Then strip her, or unto her
Let him come, who dares undo her. 100

And to enchant yee more, see every where
About the Roofe a *Syren* in a Sphere;
(As we think) singing to the dinne
Of many a warbling *Cherubin:*
O marke yee how 105
The soule of Nature melts in numbers: now
See, a thousand *Cupids* flye,
To light their Tapers at the Brides bright eye.
To Bed; or her they'l tire,
Were she an Element of fire. 110

And to your more bewitching, see, the proud
Plumpe Bed beare up, and swelling like a cloud,
Tempting the two too modest; can
Yee see it brusle like a Swan,
And you be cold 115
To meet it, when it woo's and seemes to fold
The Armes to hugge it? throw, throw
Your selves into the mighty over-flow
Of that white Pride, and Drowne
The night, with you, in floods of Downe. 120

The bed is ready, and the maze of Love
Lookes for the treaders; every where is wove
Wit and new misterie; read, and
Put in practise, to understand
And know each wile, 125
Each hieroglyphick of a kisse or smile;
And do it to the full; reach
High in your own conceipt, and some way teach
Nature and Art, one more
Play, than they ever knew before. 130

If needs we must for Ceremonies-sake,
Blesse a *Sack-posset;* Luck go with it; take
The Night-Charme quickly; you have spells,
And magicks for to end, and hells,
To passe; but such 135
And of such Torture as no one would grutch

To live therein for ever: Frie
And consume, and grow again to die,
And live, and in that case,
Love the confusion of the place. 140

But since It must be done, dispatch, and sowe
Up in a sheet your Bride, and what if so
It be with Rock, or walles of Brasse,
Ye Towre her up, as *Danae* was;
Thinke you that this, 145
Or hell it selfe a powerfull Bulwarke is?
I tell yee no; but like a
Bold bolt of thunder he will make his way,
And rend the cloud, and throw
The sheet about, like flakes of snow. 150

All now is husht in silence; *Midwife-moone,*
With all her *Owle-ey'd* issue begs a boon
Which you must grant; that's entrance; with
Which extract, all we can call pith
And quintiscence 155
Of Planetary bodies; so commence
All faire *Constellations*
Looking upon yee, that two Nations
Springing from two such Fires,
May blaze the vertue of their Sires. 160

To Daffadills

Faire Daffadills, we weep to see
You haste away so soone:
As yet the early-rising Sun
Has not attain'd his Noone.
Stay, stay, 5
Untill the hasting day
Has run
But to the Even-song;

And, having pray'd together, we
Will goe with you along. 10

We have short time to stay, as you,
We have as short a Spring;
As quick a growth to meet Decay,
As you, or any thing.
We die, 15
As your hours doe, and drie
Away,
Like to the Summers raine;
Or as the pearles of Mornings dew
Ne'r to be found againe. 20

His Age

Dedicated to His Peculiar Friend, M. JOHN WICKES,
under the Name of POSTHUMUS

Ah *Posthumus!* Our yeares hence flye,
And leave no sound; nor piety,
Or prayers, or vow
Can keepe the wrinkle from the brow:
But we must on, 5
As Fate do's lead or draw us; none,
None, *Posthumus,* co'd ere decline
The doome of cruell *Proserpine.*

The pleasing wife, the house, the ground
Must all be left, no one plant found 10
To follow thee,
Save only the *Curst-Cipresse* tree:
A merry mind
Looks forward, scornes what's left behind:
Let's live, my *Wickes,* then, while we may, 15
And here enjoy our Holiday.

W'ave seen the past-best Times, and these
Will nere return, we see the Seas,
    And Moons to wain;
But they fill up their Ebbs again: 20
    But vanisht man,
Like to a Lilly-lost, nere can,
Nere can repullulate, or bring
His dayes to see a second Spring.

But on we must, and thither tend, 25
Where *Anchus* and rich *Tullus* blend
    Their sacred seed:
Thus has *Infernall Love* decreed;
    We must be made,
Ere long, a song, ere long, a shade. 30
Why then, since life to us is short,
Lets make it full up, by our sport.

Crown we our Heads with Roses then,
And 'noint with *Tirian Balme*; for when
    We two are dead, 35
The world with us is buried.
    Then live we free,
As is the Air, and let us be
Our own fair wind, and mark each one
Day with the white and Luckie stone. 40

We are not poore; although we have
No roofs of Cedar, nor our brave
    Baiæ, nor keep
Account of such a flock of sheep;
    Nor Bullocks fed 45
To lard the shambles: Barbels bred
To kisse our hands, nor do we wish
For *Pollio's* Lampries in our dish.

If we can meet, and so conferre,
Both by a shining Salt-seller; 50

And have our Roofe,
Although nor archt, yet weather proofe,
And seeling free,
From that cheape *Candle baudery*:
We'le eate our Beane with that full mirth, 55
As we were Lords of all the earth.

Well then, on what Seas we are tost,
Our comfort is, we can't be lost.
Let the winds drive
Our Barke; yet she will keepe alive 60
Amidst the deepes;
'Tis constancy (my *Wickes*) which keepes
The Pinnace up; which though she erres
I'th' Seas, she saves her passengers.

Say, we must part (sweet mercy blesse 65
Us both i'th' Sea, Camp, Wildernesse)
Can we so farre
Stray, to become lesse circular,
Than we are now?
No, no, that selfe same heart, that vow, 70
Which made us one, shall ne'r undoe;
Or ravell so, to make us two.

Live in thy peace; as for my selfe,
When I am bruised on the Shelfe
Of Time, and show 75
My locks behung with frost and snow:
When with the reume,
The cough, the ptisick, I consume
Unto an almost nothing; then,
The Ages fled, Ile call agen: 80

And with a teare compare these last
Lame, and bad times, with those are past,
While *Baucis* by,
My old leane wife, shall kisse it dry:
And so we'l sit 85

By'th'fire, foretelling snow and slit,
And weather by our aches, grown
Now old enough to be our own

True Calenders, as Pusses eare
Washt ore 's to tell what change is neare: 90
Then to asswage
The gripings of the chine by age,
I'le call my young
Iülus to sing such a song
I made upon my *Julia's* brest; 95
And of her blush at such a feast.

Then shall he read that flowre of mine
Enclos'd within a christall shrine:
A Primrose next;
A piece, then of a higher text: **100**
For to beget
In me a more transcendant heate,
Than that insinuating fire,
Which crept into each aged Sire

When the faire *Hellen,* from her eyes, **105**
Shot forth her loving Sorceries:
At which I'le reare
Mine aged limbs above my chaire:
And hearing it,
Flutter and crow, as in a fit **110**
Of fresh concupiscence, and cry,
No lust theres like to Poetry.

Thus frantick crazie man (God wot)
Ile call to mind things half forgot:
And oft between, **115**
Repeat the Times that I have seen!
Thus ripe with tears,
And twisting my *Iülus* hairs;
Doting, Ile weep and say (In Truth)
Baucis, these were my sins of youth. **120**

Then next Ile cause my hopefull Lad
(If a wild Apple can be had)
To crown the Hearth,
(*Larr* thus conspiring with our mirth)
Then to infuse 125
Our browner Ale into the cruse:
Which sweetly spic't, we'l first carouse
Unto the *Genius* of the house.

Then the next health to friends of mine
(Loving the brave *Burgundian wine*) 130
High sons of Pith,
Whose fortunes I have frolickt with:
Such as co'd well
Bear up the Magick bough, and spel:
And dancing 'bout the Mystick *Thyrse,* 135
Give up the just applause to verse:

To those, and then agen to thee
We'l drink, my *Wickes,* untill we be
Plump as the cherry,
Though not so fresh, yet full as merry 140
As the crickit;
The untam'd Heifer, or the Pricket,
Untill our tongues shall tell our ears,
W'are younger by a score of years.

Thus, till we see the fire lesse shine 145
From th' embers, than the kitlings eyne,
We'l still sit up,
Sphering about the wassail cup,
To all those times,
Which gave me honour for my Rhimes, 150
The cole once spent, we'l then to bed,
Farre more than night bewearied.

In this touching fantasy of a man never wed, Herrick plays at being Philemon, whose marriage with Baucis was a prototype of uneventful devotion; also Horace, the friend of Posthumus, and Aeneas, father of Iulus. In lines 95–99 he presumably nominates his favorites among his more than 1400 compositions.

To Blossoms

Faire pledges of a fruitfull Tree,
Why do yee fall so fast?
Your date is not so past;
But you may stay yet here a while,
To blush and gently smile; 5
And go at last.

What, were yee borne to be
An houre or half's delight;
And so to bid goodnight?
'Twas pitie Nature brought yee forth 10
Meerly to shew your worth,
And lose you quite.

But you are lovely Leaves, where we
May read how soon things have
Their end, though ne'r so brave: 15
And after they have shown their pride,
Like you a while: They glide
Into the Grave.

The Apparition of His Mistresse Calling Him to *Elizium*

Desunt nonnulla

Come then, and like two Doves with silv'rie wings,
Let our soules flie to' th' shades, where ever springs
Sit smiling in the Meads; where Balme and Oile,
Roses and Cassia crown the untill'd soyle.
Where no disease raignes, or infection comes 5

To blast the Aires, but *Amber-greece* and *Gums.*
This, that, and ev'ry Thicket doth transpire
More sweet, than *Storax* from the hallowed fire:
Where ev'ry tree a wealthy issue beares
Of fragrant Apples, blushing Plums, or Peares: 10
And all the shrubs, with sparkling spangles, shew
Like Morning-Sun-shine tinsilling the dew.
Here in green Meddowes sits eternall May,
Purfling the Margents, while perpetual Day
So double gilds the Aire, as that no night 15
Can ever rust th'Enamel of the light.
Here, naked Younglings, handsome Striplings run
Their Goales for Virgins kisses; which when done,
Then unto Dancing forth the learned Round
Commixt they meet, with endlesse Roses crown'd. 20
And here we'll sit on Primrose-banks, and see
Love's *Chorus* led by *Cupid;* and we'l be
Two loving followers too unto the Grove,
Where Poets sing the stories of our love.
There thou shalt hear Divine *Musæus* sing 25
Of *Hero,* and *Leander;* then Ile bring
Thee to the Stand, where honour'd *Homer* reades
His *Odisees,* and his high *Iliades.*
Àbout whose Throne the crowd of Poets throng
To heare the incantation of his tongue: 30
To *Linus,* then to *Pindar;* and that done,
Ile bring thee *Herrick* to *Anacreon,*
Quaffing his full-crown'd bowles of burning Wine,
And in his Raptures speaking Lines of Thine,
Like to His subject; and as his Frantick- 35
Looks, shew him truly *Bacchanalian* like,
Besmear'd with Grapes; welcome he shall thee thither,
Where both may rage, both drink and dance together.
Then stately *Virgil,* witty *Ovid,* by
Whom faire *Corinna* sits, and doth comply 40
With Yvorie wrists, his Laureat head, and steeps
His eye in dew of kisses, while he sleeps.
Then soft *Catullus,* sharp-fang'd *Martial*
And towring *Lucan, Horace, Juvenal,*

And Snakie *Perseus,* these, and those, whom Rage 45
(Dropt from the jarres of heaven) fill'd t'engage
All times unto their frenzies; Thou shalt there
Behold them in a spacious Theater.
Among which glories, (crown'd with sacred Bayes,
And flatt'ring Ivie) Two recite their Plaies, 50
Beumont and *Fletcher,* Swans, to whom all eares
Listen, while they (like Syrens in their Spheres)
Sing their *Evadne;* and still more for thee
There yet remaines to know, than thou can'st see
By glim'ring of a fancie: Doe but come, 55
And there Ile shew thee that capacious roome
In which thye Father *Johnson* now is plac't,
As in a Globe of Radiant fire, and grac't
To be in that Orbe crown'd (that doth include
Those Prophets of the former Magnitude) 60
And be our chiefe; But harke, I heare the Cock,
(The Bell-man of the night) proclaime the clock
Of late struck one; and now I see the prime
Of Day break from the pregnant East, 'tis time
I vanish; more I had to say; 65
But Night determines here, Away.

The Night-piece, to *Julia*

Her Eyes the Glow-worme lend thee,
The Shooting Starres attend thee;
And the Elves also,
Whose little eyes glow,
Like the sparks of fire, befriend thee. 5

No *Will-o'-th'-Wispe* mis-light thee;
Nor Snake, or Slow-worme bite thee:
But on, on thy way
Not making a stay,
Since Ghost ther's none to affright thee. 10

Let not the darke thee cumber;
What though the Moon do's slumber?
The Starres of the night
Will lend thee their light,
Like Tapers cleare without number. 15

Then *Julia* let me wooe thee,
Thus, thus to come unto me:
And when I shall meet
Thy silv'ry feet,
My soule Ile poure into thee. 20

To His Lovely Mistresses

One night i' th' yeare, my dearest Beauties, come
And bring those *dew-drink-offerings* to my Tomb.
When thence ye see my reverend Ghost to rise,
And there to lick th' effused sacrifice:
Though palenes be the Livery that I weare, 5
Looke ye not wan, or colourlesse for feare.
Trust mee I will not hurt ye; or once shew
The least grim looke, or cast a frown on you:
Nor shall the Tapers when I'm there, burn blew.
This I may do (perhaps) as I glide by, 10
Cast on my Girles a glance, and loving eye:
Or fold mine armes, and sigh, because I've lost
The world so soon, and in it, you the most.
Than these, no feares more on your Fancies fall,
Though then I smile, and speake no words at all. 15

Upon *Julia's* Clothes

When as in silks my *Julia* goes,
Then, then (me thinks) how sweetly flowes
That liquefaction of her clothes.

Next, when I cast mine eyes and see
That brave Vibration each way free; 5
O how that glittering taketh me!

An Ode for [Ben Jonson]

Ah *Ben!*
Say how, or when
Shall we thy Guests
Meet at those *Lyrick* Feasts,
Made at the *Sun,* 5
The *Dog,* the triple *Tunne*?
Where we such clusters had,
As made us nobly wild, not mad;
And yet each Verse of thine
Out-did the meate, out-did the frolick wine. 10

My *Ben*
Or come agen:
Or send to us,
Thy wits great over-plus;
But teach us yet 15
Wisely to husband it;
Let we that Tallent spend:
And having once brought to an end
That precious stock; the store
Of such a wit the world sho'd have no more. 20

On Himselfe

The worke is done: young men, and maidens set
Upon my curles the *Mirtle Coronet,*
Washt with sweet ointments; Thus at last I come
To suffer in the Muses *Martyrdome:*

But with this comfort, if my blood be shed, 5
The Muses will weare blackes, when I am dead.

The Pillar of Fame

Fames pillar here, at last, we set,
Out-during *Marble, Brasse,* or *Jet,*
Charm'd and enchanted so,
As to withstand the blow
Of overthrow: 5
Nor shall the seas,
Or OUTRAGES
Of storms orebear
What we up-rear,
Tho Kingdoms fal, 10
This pillar never shall
Decline or waste at all;
But stand for ever by his owne
Firme and well fixt foundation.

To his Book's end this last line he'd have plac't, 15
Jocond his Muse was; but his Life was chast.

Finis.

NOBLE NUMBERS

A Thanksgiving to God, for His House

Lord, Thou hast given me a cell
Wherein to dwell;

And little house, whose humble Roof
Is weather-proof;
Under the sparres of which I lie 5
Both soft, and drie;
Where Thou my chamber for to ward
Hast set a Guard
Of harmlesse thoughts, to watch and keep
Me, while I sleep. 10
Low is my porch, as is my Fate,
Both void of state;
And yet the threshold of my doore
Is worn by'th poore,
Who thither come, and freely get 15
Good words, or meat:
Like as my Parlour, so my Hall
And Kitchin's small:
A little Butterie, and therein
A little Byn, 20
Which keeps my little loafe of Bread
Unchipt, unflead:
Some brittle sticks of Thorne or Briar
Make me a fire,
Close by whose living coale I sit, 25
And glow like it.
Lord, I confesse too, when I dine,
The Pulse is Thine,
And all those other Bits, that bee
There plac'd by Thee; 30
The Worts, the Purslain, and the Messe
Of Water-cresse,
Which of Thy kindnesse Thou hast sent;
And my content
Makes those, and my beloved Beet, 35
To be more sweet.
'Tis Thou that crown'st my glittering Hearth
With guiltlesse mirth;
And giv'st me Wassaile Bowles to drink,
Spic'd to the brink. 40
Lord, 'tis thy plenty-dropping hand,

That soiles my land;
And giv'st me, for my Bushell sowne,
Twice ten for one:
Thou mak'st my teeming Hen to lay 45
Her egg each day:
Besides my healthfull Ewes to beare
Me twins each yeare:
The while the conduits of my Kine
Run Creame, (for Wine.) 50
All these, and better Thou dost send
Me, to this end,
That I should render, for my part,
A thankfull heart;
Which, fir'd with incense, I resigne, 55
As wholly Thine;
But the acceptance, that must be,
My Christ, by Thee.

To His Saviour, a Child; a Present, by a Child

Go prettie child and beare this Flower
Unto thy little Saviour;
And tell Him, by that Bud now blown,
He is the *Rose of Sharon* known:
When thou hast said so, stick it there 5
Upon his Bibb, or Stomacher:
And tell Him, (for good handsell too)
That thou has brought a Whistle new,
Made of a clean strait oaten reed,
To charme his cries, (at time of need:) 10
Tell Him, for Corall, thou hast none;
But if thou hadst, He sho'd have one;
But poore thou art, and knowne to be
Even as monilesse, as He.
Lastly, if thou canst win a kisse 15
From those mellifluous lips of his;
Then never take a second on,
To spoile the first impression.

VI

COURTLY WITS

Thomas Carew (1595–1640)
Sir John Suckling (1609–1642)
William Habington (1605–1654)
Richard Lovelace (1618–1657)

Habington is an anomaly, a Catholic in belief but a Puritan reactionary in verse. The other three are primarily Jonsonians, though it is as true of them as of the other Jonsonian, Herrick, that nobody quite escaped Donne's influence.

Thomas Carew

(1595–1640)

Izaak Walton recalled him as "m^{r} Thomas cary a poet of note and a great libertine in his life and talke"; Clarendon adverted to a life "spent with less Severity or Exactness than it ought to have been"; his elderly father wrote of being "at my wittes end and know not what to do with hym"; yet he was known (Clarendon again) as

> a Person of a pleasant and facetious Wit, and made many Poems (especially in the amorous Way) which for the Sharpness of the Fancy, and the Elegancy of the Language, in which that Fancy was spread, were at least equal, if not superior to any of that Time.

He was the despair of his father's old age. Sir Matthew Carew's fortunes having collapsed shortly after the son came down from Oxford, it was incumbent on Thomas to fend for himself, and the theme of his life, or at least of the phases of it recoverable from the letters his kinfolk wrote to and fro, is the poet's inability to take this obligation seriously. He fiddled at the study of law but liked frivolity better; he went to Italy and Holland as secretary to the ambassador, but was sent home apparently for writing a lampoon on his patron; he spent an unnoticed year in France among some hundred persons attending on Sir Edward Herbert; he finally wrangled an ornamental appointment at the court of Charles I.

Readers of poetry need find none of this wasted: not Oxford, not law, not Italy nor Paris, where he found out what the continental poets were doing; not the elegant idleness he filled with verses. Court life then still touched the life of the mind: he knew Townshend, heard Donne preach, dined with Jonson. And he is to

Jonson what Herbert is to Donne, the most deeply original of disciples.

He learned from Jonson how to labor at a poem, how to sharpen its argument, infold its details, and leave no inert expression. One version of the famous "Aske me no more . . ." makes the rose "damaske," another "flaming"; both epithets are pretty enough, but when he arrives, in at least the third draft, at "fading," he has hit upon the way of filling up those two syllables that will also richly enforce the stanza's theme:

> Aske me no more where Jove bestowes,
> When June is past, the fading rose:
> For in your beauties orient deepe,
> These flowers as in their causes, sleepe.

The third and fourth lines, similarly, did not always murmur their gravely learned echo of the Final Cause; at first they read,

> For on yor Cheekes and lips they bee
> Fresher than on anie tree,

and even when he first arrived at that final image, he did not have the flowers "sleepe" in their causes but "meete" there.

He learned also a more elusive lesson, Jonson's way of commanding a compendious indebtedness to the classics, a skill Carew also applied to contemporary French and Italian poetry. He borrows freely from Propertius and Catullus, from Ronsard, from Giambattista Marino, whom he perhaps knew in Paris. If Donne presides over the economy of his conceits, he was always clear that his purposes were never Donne's, and Marino seems to have taught him how to weave conceits into a context of easy hyperbole.

He never gathered nor edited his poems, and has been overshadowed in conventional esteem by Lovelace, who did. Lovelace, moreover, gives no scandal, disturbs fewer meditative echoes, and is content to play the tuneful gallant as though he had been invented by Sir Walter Scott. But it was Waller, the third of the easy Caroline song-writers, whose reputation survived the Stuart dynasty and the revolution in taste presided over by Dryden; Pope was one day to speak shortly of Carew as "a lesser Waller." That these three poets were to enjoy a staying power in precise inverse proportion to their nutritive content may be ascribed to several middle-class criteria:

respectability, common sense, preference for the undemanding, but chiefly perhaps to the fact that mannerisms of Waller's were readily detachable by later writers for very different purposes. Carew's intelligence, Carew's poise and strength, can scarcely be inspected in isolation from his own tautly imagined celebrations of pleasurable transiency, which common sense does not like to think about.

TEXT: *Poems,* ed. Rhodes Dunlap (Oxford, 1949).

COMMENT: F. R. Leavis, "The Line of Wit," in *Revaluation* (Chatto and Windus, 1936).

To A. L.

PERSWASIONS TO LOVE

Thinke not cause men flatt'ring say,
Y' are fresh as Aprill, sweet as May,
Bright as is the morning starre,
That you are so, or though you are
Be not therefore proud, and deeme 5
All men unworthy your esteeme.
For being so, you loose the pleasure
Of being faire, since that rich treasure
Of rare beauty, and sweet feature
Was bestow'd on you by nature 10
To be enjoy'd, and 'twere a sinne,
There to be scarce, where shee hath bin
So prodigall of her best graces;
Thus common beauties, and meane faces
Shall have more pastime, and enjoy 15
The sport you loose by being coy.
Did the thing for which I sue
Onely concerne my selfe not you,
Were men so fram'd as they alone
Reap'd all the pleasure, women none, 20
Then had you reason to be scant;

But 'twere a madnesse not to grant
That which affords (if you consent)
To you the giver, more content
Than me the beggar; Oh then bee 25
Kinde to your selfe if not to mee;
Starve not your selfe, because you may
Thereby make me pine away;
Nor let brittle beautie make
You your wiser thoughts forsake: 30
For that lovely face will faile,
Beautie's sweet, but beautie's fraile;
'Tis sooner past, 'tis sooner done
Then Summers raine, or winters Sun:
Most fleeting when it is most deare, 35
'Tis gone while wee but say 'tis here.
These curious locks so aptly twind,
Whose every haire a soule doth bind,
Will change their abroun hue, and grow
White, and cold as winters snow. 40
That eye which now is *Cupids* nest
Will prove his grave, and all the rest
Will follow; in the cheeke, chin, nose
Nor lilly shall be found nor rose.
And what will then become of all 45
Those, whom now you servants call?
Like swallowes when your summers done,
They'le flye and seeke some warmer Sun.
Then wisely chuse one to your friend,
Whose love may, when your beauties end, 50
Remaine still firme: be provident
And thinke before the summers spent
Of following winter; like the Ant
In plenty hoord for time of scant.
Cull out amongst the multitude 55
Of lovers, that seeke to intrude
Into your favour, one that may
Love for an age, not for a day;

26. Carew seems to have ended his poem here, and later extended it with a free translation (lines 29–84) of a *canzone* by G. B. Marino (1569–1625).

One that will quench your youthfull fires,
And feed in age your hot desires. 60
For when the stormes of time have mov'd
Waves on that cheeke which was belov'd,
When a faire Ladies face is pin'd
And yellow spred, where red once shin'd,
When beauty, youth, and all sweets leave her, 65
Love may returne, but lover never:
And old folkes say there are no paynes
Like itch of love in aged vaines.
Oh love me then, and now begin it,
Let us not loose this present minute: 70
For time and age will worke that wrack
Which time or age shall ne're call backe.
The snake each yeare fresh skin resumes,
And Eagles change their aged plumes;
The faded Rose each spring, receives 75
A fresh red tincture on her leaves:
But if your beauties once decay,
You never know a second *May*.
Oh, then be wise, and whilst your season
Affords you dayes for sport, doe reason; 80
Spend not in vaine your lives short houre,
But crop in time your beauties flower:
Which will away, and doth together
Both bud, and fade, both blow and wither.

Song

MURDRING BEAUTIE.

Ile gaze no more on her bewitching face,
Since ruine harbours there in every place:
For my enchanted soule alike shee drownes
With calmes and tempests of her smiles and frownes.
I'le love no more those cruell eyes of hers, 5
Which pleas'd or anger'd still are murderers:

For if she dart (like lightning) through the ayre
Her beames of wrath, she kils me with despaire.
If shee behold me with a pleasing eye,
I surfet with excesse of joy, and dye. 10

Secresie Protested

Feare not (deare Love) that I'le reveale
Those houres of pleasure we two steale;
No eye shall see, nor yet the Sun
Descry, what thou and I have done;
No eare shall heare our love, but wee 5
Silent as the night will bee.
The God of love himselfe (whose dart
Did first wound mine, and then thy heart)
Shall never know, that we can tell
What sweets in stolne embraces dwell. 10
This only meanes may find it out,
If when I dye, Physicians doubt
What caus'd my death, and there to view
Of all their judgements which was true,
Rip up my heart, Oh then I feare 15
The world will see thy picture there.

12–16. See Donne, "The Dampe," lines 1–4.

SONG

To My Inconstant Mistris

When thou, poore excommunicate
  From all the joyes of love, shalt see
The full reward, and glorious fate,
  Which my strong faith shall purchase me,
  Then curse thine owne inconstancie. 5

A fayrer hand than thine, shall cure
  That heart, which thy false oathes did wound;
And to my soule, a soule more pure
  Than thine, shall by Loves hand be bound,
  And both with equall glory crown'd. 10

Then shalt thou weepe, entreat, complaine
  To Love, as I did once to thee;
When all thy teares shall be as vaine
  As mine were then, for thou shalt bee
  Damn'd for thy false Apostasie. 15

SONG

Perswasions To Enjoy

If the quick spirits in your eye
  Now languish, and anon must dye;
If every sweet, and every grace,
Must fly from that forsaken face:
  Then (*Celia*) let us reape our joyes, 5
  E're time such goodly fruit destroyes.

Or, if that golden fleece must grow
For ever, free from aged snow;
If those bright Suns must know no shade,
Nor your fresh beauties ever fade: 10
Then feare not (*Celia*) to bestow,
What still being gather'd, still must grow.
  Thus, either *Time* his Sickle brings
  In vaine, or else in vaine his wings.

Ingratefull Beauty Threatned

Know *Celia,* (since thou art so proud,)
'Twas I that gave thee thy renowne:
Thou hadst, in the forgotten crowd
Of common beauties, liv'd unknowne,
Had not my verse exhal'd thy name, 5
And with it, ympt the wings of fame.

That killing power is none of thine,
I gave it to thy voyce, and eyes:
Thy sweets, thy graces, all are mine;
Thou art my starre, shin'st in my skies; 10
Then dart not from thy borrowed sphere
Lightning on him, that fixt thee there.

Tempt me with such affrights no more,
Lest what I made, I uncreate;
Let fooles thy mystique formes adore, 15
I'le know thee in thy mortall state:
Wise Poets that wrap't Truth in tales,
Knew her themselves, through all her vailes.

6. *ympt:* word used by falconers, of repairing a wing with other feathers.

Celia Bleeding, to the Surgeon

Fond man, that canst beleeve her blood
Will from those purple chanels flow;
Or that the pure untainted flood
Can any foule distemper know;
Or that thy weake steele can incize 5
The Crystall case, wherein it lyes.

Know; her quick blood, proud of his seat,
  Runs dauncing through her azure veines;
Whose harmony no cold, nor heat
  Disturbs, whose hue no tincture staines; 10
And the hard rock wherein it dwells,
The keenest darts of Love repels.

But thou reply'st, behold she bleeds;
  Foole, thou'rt deceivd; and dost not know
The mystique knot whence this proceeds, 15
  How Lovers in each other grow;
Thou struckst her arme, but 'twas my heart
Shed all the blood, felt all the smart.

SONG

To My Mistris, I Burning in Love

I Burne, and cruell you, in vaine
Hope to quench me with disdaine;
If from your eyes, those sparkles came,
That have kindled all this flame,
What bootes it me, though now you shrowde 5
Those fierce Comets in a cloude?
Since all the flames that I have felt,
Could your snow yet never melt,
Nor, can your snow (though you should take
Alpes into your bosome) slake 10
The heate of my enamour'd heart;
But with wonder learne Loves art!
No seaes of yce can coole desire,
Equall flames must quench Loves fire:
Then thinke not that my heat can dye, 15
Till you burne aswell as I.

SONG

To Her Againe, She Burning in a Feaver

Now she burnes as well as I,
Yet my heat can never dye;
She burnes that never knew desire,
She that was yce, she now is fire,
Shee whose cold heart, chaste thoughts did arme 5
So, as Loves flames could never warme
The frozen bosome where it dwelt,
She burnes, and all her beauties melt;
She burnes, and cryes, Loves fires are milde;
Feavers are Gods, and He's a childe. 10
Love; let her know the difference
Twixt the heat of soule, and sence.
Touch her with thy flames divine,
So shalt thou quench her fire, and mine.

SONG

To One That Desired To Know My Mistris

Seeke not to know my love, for shee
Hath vow'd her constant faith to me;
Her milde aspects are mine, and thou
Shalt only find a stormy brow:
For if her beautie stirre desire 5
In me, her kisses quench the fire.
Or, I can to Love's fountaine goe,
Or dwell upon her hills of snow;
But when thou burn'st, she shall not spare
One gentle breath to coole the ayre; 10
Thou shalt not climbe those *Alpes,* nor spye

Where the sweet springs of *Venus* lye.
Search hidden Nature, and there find
A treasure to inrich thy mind;
Discover Arts not yet reveal'd, 15
But let my Mistris live conceal'd;
Though men by knowledge wiser grow,
Yet here 'tis wisdome not to know.

A Pastorall Dialogue

SHEPHERD NYMPH CHORUS

Shepherd This mossie bank they prest. *Nymph* That aged Oak
Did canopie the happy payre
All night from the dampe ayre.
Chorus Here let us sit and sing the words they spoke,
Till the day breaking, their embraces broke. 5

Shepherd See love, the blushes of the morne appeare,
And now she hangs her pearlie store
(Rob'd from the Easterne shore)
I'th' Couslips bell, and Roses eare:
Sweet, I must stay no longer here. 10

Nymph Those streakes of doubtfull light, usher not day,
But shew my sunne must set; no Morne
Shall shine till thou returne,
The yellow Planets, and the gray
Dawne, shall attend thee on thy way. 15

Shepherd If thine eyes guild my pathes, they may forbeare
Their uselesse shine. *Nymph* My teares will quite
Extinguish their faint light.
Shepherd Those drops will make their beames more cleare,
Loves flames will shine in every teare. 20

Chorus They kist, and wept, and from their lips, and eyes,
In a mixt dew, of brinie sweet,

Their joyes, and sorrowes meet,
But she cryes out. *Nymph* Shepherd arise,
The Sun betrayes us else to spies. 25

Shepherd The winged houres flye fast, whilst we embrace,
But when we want their help to meet,
They move with leaden feet.
Nymph Then let us pinion *Time,* and chase
The day for ever from this place. 30

Shepherd Harke! *Nymph* Aye me stay! *Shepherd* For ever.
Nymph No, arise,
Wee must be gone. *Shepherd* My nest of spice.
Nymph My soule. *Shepherd* My Paradise.
Chorus Neither could say farewell, but through their eyes
Griefe, interrupted speach with teares supplyes. 35

To My Cousin (*C. R.*) Marrying My Lady (*A.*)

Happy Youth, that shalt possesse
Such a spring-tyde of delight,
As the sated Appetite
Shall enjoying such excesse,
Wish the flood of pleasure lesse: 5
When the Hymeneall Rite
Is perform'd, invoke the night,
That it may in shadowes dresse
Thy too reall happinesse;
Else (as *Semele*) the bright 10
Deitie in her full might,
May thy feeble soule oppresse.
Strong perfumes, and glaring light,
Oft destroy both smell, and sight.

C. R. was Carew Raleigh (1605–1666), Sir Walter Raleigh's second son and a remote connection of Carew's. He married Sir Anthony Ashley's widow some time after 1627.

10. *Semele:* a woman visited by Zeus and consumed to ashes by the experience.

A Rapture

I will enjoy thee now my *Celia,* come
And flye with me to Loves Elizium:
The Gyant, Honour, that keepes cowards out,
Is but a Masquer, and the servile rout
Of baser subjects onely, bend in vaine 5
To the vast Idoll, whilst the nobler traine
Of valiant Lovers, daily sayle betweene
The huge Collosses legs, and passe unseene
Unto the blissfull shore; be bold, and wise,
And we shall enter, the grim Swisse denies 10
Only tame fooles a passage, that not know
He is but forme, and onely frights in show
The duller eyes that looke from farre; draw neere,
And thou shalt scorne, what we were wont to feare.
We shall see how the stalking Pageant goes 15
With borrowed legs, a heavie load to those
That made, and beare him; not as we once thought
The seed of Gods, but a weake modell wrought
By greedy men, that seeke to enclose the common,
And within private armes empale free woman. 20
Come then, and mounted on the wings of love
Wee'le cut the flitting ayre, and sore above
The Monsters head, and in the noblest seates
Of those blest shades, quench, and renew our heates.
There, shall the Queene of Love, and Innocence, 25
Beautie and Nature, banish all offence
From our close Ivy twines, there I'le behold
Thy bared snow, and thy unbraded gold.
There, my enfranchiz'd hand, on every side
Shall o're thy naked polish'd Ivory slide. 30
No curtaine there, though of transparant lawne,
Shall be before thy virgin-treasure drawne;

15. *Pageant:* here, a stage giant.

But the rich Mine, to the enquiring eye
Expos'd, shall ready still for mintage lye,
And we will coyne young *Cupids*. There, a bed 35
Of Roses, and fresh Myrtles, shall be spread
Under the cooler shade of Cypresse groves:
Our pillowes, of the downe of *Venus* Doves,
Whereon our panting lims wee'le gently lay
In the faint respites of our active play; 40
That so our slumbers, may in dreames have leisure,
To tell the nimble fancie our past pleasure;
And so our soules that cannot be embrac'd,
Shall the embraces of our bodyes taste.
Meane while the bubbling streame shall court the shore, 45
Th'enamoured chirping Wood-quire shall adore
In varied tunes the Deitie of Love;
The gentle blasts of Westerne winds, shall move
The trembling leaves, & through their close bows breath
Still Musick, whilst we rest our selves beneath 50
Their dancing shade; till a soft murmure, sent
From soules entranc'd in amorous languishment
Rowze us, and shoot into our veines fresh fire,
Till we, in their sweet extasie expire.
Then, as the empty Bee, that lately bore, 55
Into the common treasure, all her store,
Flyes 'bout the painted field with nimble wing,
Deflowring the fresh virgins of the Spring;
So will I rifle all the sweets, that dwell
In my delicious Paradise, and swell 60
My bagge with honey, drawne forth by the power
Of fervent kisses, from each spicie flower.
I'le seize the Rose-buds in their perfum'd bed,
The Violet knots, like curious Mazes spread
O're all the Garden, taste the ripned Cherry, 65
The warme, firme Apple, tipt with corall berry:
Then will I visit, with a wandring kisse,
The vale of Lillies, and the Bower of blisse:
And where the beauteous Region doth divide
Into two milkie wayes, my lips shall slide 70
Downe those smooth Allies, wearing as I goe

A tract for lovers on the printed snow;
Thence climbing o're the swelling *Appenine,*
Retire into thy grove of Eglantine;
Where I will all those ravisht sweets distill 75
Through Loves Alimbique, and with Chimmique skill
From the mixt masse, one soveraigne Balme derive,
Then bring that great *Elixar* to thy hive.
  Now in more subtile wreathes I will entwine
My sinowie thighes, my legs and armes with thine; 80
Thou like a sea of milke shalt lye display'd,
Whilst I the smooth, calme Ocean, invade
With such a tempest, as when *Jove* of old
Fell downe on *Danae* in a storme of gold:
Yet my tall Pine, shall in the *Cyprian* straight 85
Ride safe at Anchor, and unlade her fraight:
My Rudder, with thy bold hand, like a tryde,
And skilfull Pilot, thou shalt steere, and guide
My Bark into Loves channell, where it shall
Dance, as the bounding waves doe rise or fall: 90
Then shall thy circling armes, embrace and clip
My willing bodie, and thy balmie lip
Bathe me in juyce of kisses, whose perfume
Like a religious incense shall consume,
And send up holy vapours, to those powres 95
That blesse our loves, and crowne our sportfull houres,
That with such Halcion calmenesse, fix our soules
In steadfast peace, as no affright controules.
There, no rude sounds shake us with sudden starts,
No jealous eares, when we unrip our hearts 100
Sucke our discourse in, no observing spies
This blush, that glance traduce; no envious eyes
Watch our close meetings, nor are we betrayd
To Rivals, by the bribed chamber-maid.
No wedlock bonds unwreathe our twisted loves; 105
We seeke no midnight Arbor, no darke groves
To hide our kisses, there, the hated name
Of husband, wife, lust, modest, chaste, or shame,
Are vaine and empty words, whose very sound
Was never heard in the Elizian ground. 110

All things are lawfull there, that may delight
Nature, or unrestrained Appetite;
Like, and enjoy, to will, and act, is one,
We only sinne when Loves rites are not done.
  The Roman *Lucrece* there, reades the divine 115
Lectures of Loves great master, *Aretine,*
And knowes as well as *Lais,* how to move
Her plyant body in the act of love.
To quench the burning Ravisher, she hurles
Her limbs into a thousand winding curles, 120
And studies artfull postures, such as be
Carv'd on the barke of every neighbouring tree
By learned hands, that so adorn'd the rinde
Of those faire Plants, which as they lay entwinde,
Have fann'd their glowing fires. The Grecian Dame, 125
That in her endlesse webb, toyl'd for a name
As fruitlesse as her worke, doth there display
Her selfe before the Youth of *Ithaca,*
And th'amorous sport of gamesome nights prefer,
Before dull dreames of the lost Traveller. 130
Daphne hath broke her barke, and that swift foot,
Which th'angry Gods had fastned with a root
To the fixt earth, doth now unfetter'd run,
To meet th'embraces of the youthfull Sun:
She hangs upon him, like his Delphique Lyre, 135
Her kisses blow the old, and breath new fire:
Full of her God, she sings inspired Layes,
Sweet Odes of love, such as deserve the Bayes,
Which she her selfe was. Next her, *Laura* lyes
In *Petrarchs* learned armes, drying those eyes 140
That did in such sweet smooth-pac'd numbers flow,
As made the world enamour'd of his woe.

---

115. *Lucrece:* Roman matron, celebrated because rape drove her to suicide.
116. *Aretine:* Pietro Aretino (1492–1556), author of licentious sonnets.
117. *Lais:* Corinthian courtesan.
125. *Grecian Dame:* Penelope, who resisted the Ithacan suitors.
131. *Daphne* fled from Apollo's embrace and was turned into a bay tree.
139. *Laura:* according to Petrarch's sonnets, a married woman who rejected his intimacies.

These, and ten thousand Beauties more, that dy'de
Slave to the Tyrant, now enlarg'd, deride
His cancell'd lawes, and for their time mispent, 145
Pay into Loves Exchequer double rent.
  Come then my *Celia,* wee'le no more forbeare
To taste our joyes, struck with a Pannique feare,
But will depose from his imperious sway
This proud *Usurper* and walke free, as they 150
With necks unyoak'd; nor is it just that Hee
Should fetter your soft sex with Chastitie,
Which Nature made unapt for abstinence;
When yet this false Impostor can dispence
With humane Justice, and with sacred right, 155
And maugre both their lawes command me fight
With Rivals, or with emulous Loves, that dare
Equall with thine, their Mistresse eyes, or haire:
If thou complaine of wrong, and call my sword
To carve out thy revenge, upon that word 160
He bids me fight and kill, or else he brands
With markes of infamie my coward hands,
And yet religion bids from blood-shed flye,
And damns me for that Act. Then tell me why
This Goblin Honour which the world adores, 165
Should make men Atheists, and not women Whores.

---

156. ***maugre:*** despite.

An Other

[EPITAPH ON THE LADY MARY VILLERS]

This little Vault, this narrow roome,
Of Love, and Beautie is the tombe;
The dawning beame that 'gan to cleare
Our clouded skie, lyes darkned here,

If scholarship has correctly identified her, she died at the age of two and a half. Her parents were Carew's patrons.

For ever set to us, by death 5
Sent to enflame the world beneath;
'Twas but a bud, yet did containe
More sweetnesse than shall spring againe,
A budding starre that might have growne
Into a Sun, when it had blowne. 10
This hopefull beautie, did create
New life in Loves declining state;
But now his Empire ends, and we
From fire, and wounding darts are free:
His brand, his bow, let no man feare, 15
The flames, the arrowes, all lye here.

An Hymeneall Dialogue

BRIDE AND GROOME

Groome Tell me (my love) since Hymen ty'de
The holy knot, hast thou not felt
A new infused spirit slide
Into thy brest, whilst thine did melt?

Bride First tell me (sweet) whose words were those? 5
For though your voyce the ayre did breake,
Yet did my soule the sence compose,
And through your lips my heart did speake.

Groome Then I perceive, when from the flame
Of love, my scorch'd soule did retire, 10
Your frozen heart in her place came,
And sweetly melted in that fire.

Bride 'Tis true, for when that mutuall change
Of soules, was made with equall gaine,
I straight might feele diffus'd a strange, 15
But gentle heat through every veine.

Chorus Oh blest dis-union, that doth so
Our bodyes from our soules divide,
As two doe one, and one foure grow,
Each by contraction multiply'de. 20

Bride Thy bosome then I'le make my nest,
Since there my willing soule doth pearch.
Groome And for my heart in thy chast brest,
I'le make an everlasting search.

Chorus Oh blest disunion, &c. 25

An Elegie upon the Death of the Deane of Pauls, Dr. John Donne

Can we not force from Widdowed Poetry,
Now thou art dead (Great DONNE) one Elegie
To crowne thy Hearse? Why yet dare we not trust
Though with unkneaded dowe-bak't prose thy dust,
Such as the uncisor'd Churchman from the flower 5
Of fading Rhetorique, short liv'd as his houre,
Dry as the sand that measures it, should lay
Upon thy Ashes, on the funerall day?
Have we no voice, no tune? Did'st thou dispense
Through all our language, both the words and sense? 10
'Tis a sad truth; The Pulpit may her plaine,
And sober Christian precepts still retaine,
Doctrines it may, and wholesome Uses frame,
Grave Homilies, and Lectures, But the flame
Of thy brave Soule, (that shot such heat and light, 15
As burnt our earth, and made our darknesse bright,
Committed holy Rapes upon our Will,
Did through the eye the melting heart distill;
And the deepe knowledge of darke truths so teach,

---

5. *uncisor'd:* unshorn, as a sign of mourning.

As sense might judge, what phansie could not reach;) 20
Must be desir'd for ever. So the fire,
That fills with spirit and heat the Delphique quire,
Which kindled first by thy Promethean breath,
Glow'd here a while, lies quench't now in thy death;
The Muses garden with Pedantique weedes 25
O'rspred, was purg'd by thee; The lazie seeds
Of servile imitation throwne away;
And fresh invention planted, Thou didst pay
The debts of our penurious bankrupt age;
Licentious thefts, that make poëtique rage 30
A Mimique fury, when our soules must bee
Possest, or with Anacreons Extasie,
Or Pindars, not their owne; The subtle cheat
Of slie Exchanges, and the jugling feat
Of two-edg'd words, or whatsoever wrong 35
By ours was done the Greeke, or Latine tongue,
Thou hast redeem'd, and open'd Us a Mine
Of rich and pregnant phansie, drawne a line
Of masculine expression, which had good
Old Orpheus seene, Or all the ancient Brood 40
Our superstitious fooles admire, and hold
Their lead more precious, then thy burnish't Gold,
Thou hadst beene their Exchequer, and no more
They each in others dust, had rak'd for Ore.
Thou shalt yield no precedence, but of time, 45
And the blinde fate of language, whose tun'd chime
More charmes the outward sense; Yet thou maist claime
From so great disadvantage greater fame,
Since to the awe of thy imperious wit
Our stubborne language bends, made only fit 50
With her tough-thick-rib'd hoopes to gird about
Thy Giant phansie, which had prov'd too stout
For their soft melting Phrases. As in time
They had the start, so did they cull the prime

32-33. *Anacreon, Pindar:* Greek poets on whom Carew represents Donne's uncreative contemporaries as depending.

Buds of invention many a hundred yeare, 55
And left the rifled fields, besides the feare
To touch their Harvest, yet from those bare lands
Of what is purely thine, thy only hands
(And that thy smallest worke) have gleaned more
Then all those times, and tongues could reape before; 60
But thou art gone, and thy strict lawes will be
Too hard for Libertines in Poetrie.
They will repeale the goodly exil'd traine
Of gods and goddesses, which in thy just raigne
Were banish'd nobler Poems, now, with these 65
The silenc'd tales o'th' Metamorphoses
Shall stuffe their lines, and swell the windy Page,
Till Verse refin'd by thee, in this last Age
Turne ballad rime, Or those old Idolls bee
Ador'd againe, with new apostasie; 70
Oh, pardon mee, that breake with untun'd verse
The reverend silence that attends thy herse,
Whose awfull solemne murmures were to thee
More than these faint lines, A loud Elegie,
That did proclaime in a dumbe eloquence 75
The death of all the Arts, whose influence
Growne feeble, in these panting numbers lies
Gasping short winded Accents, and so dies:
So doth the swiftly turning wheele not stand
In th'instant we withdraw the moving hand, 80
But some small time maintaine a faint weake course
By vertue of the first impulsive force:
And so whil'st I cast on thy funerall pile
Thy crowne of Bayes, Oh, let it crack a while,
And spit disdaine, till the devouring flashes 85
Suck all the moysture up, then turne to ashes.
I will not draw the envy to engrosse
All thy perfections, or weepe all our losse;
Those are too numerous for an Elegie,
And this too great, to be express'd by mee. 90
Though every pen should share a distinct part,
Yet art thou Theme enough to tyre all Art;

Let others carve the rest, it shall suffice
I on thy Tombe this Epitaph incise.

Here lies a King, that rul'd as hee thought fit 95
The universall Monarchy of wit;
Here lie two Flamens, and both those, the best,
Apollo's first, at last, the true Gods Priest.

A Song

Aske me no more where *Jove* bestowes,
When *June* is past, the fading rose:
For in your beauties orient deepe,
These flowers as in their causes, sleepe.

Aske me no more whither doth stray, 5
The golden Atomes of the day:
For in pure love heaven did prepare
Those powders to inrich your haire.

Aske me no more whither doth hast,
The Nightingale when May is past: 10
For in your sweet dividing throat,
She winters and keepes warme her note.

Aske me no more where those starres light,
That downewards fall in dead of night:
For in your eyes they sit, and there, 15
Fixed become as in their sphere.

Aske me no more if East or West,
The Phenix builds her spicy nest:
For unto you at last shee flies,
And in your fragrant bosome dyes. 20

An Excuse of Absence

You'le aske perhaps wherefore I stay,
Loving so much, so long away,
O doe not thinke t'was I did part,
It was my body, not my hearte,
For like a Compasse in your love, 5
One foote is fix'd and cannot moove,
The other may follow her blinde guide
Of giddy fortune, but not slide
Beyound your service, nor dares venture
To wander farre from you the Center. 10

Not imitated from Donne, but translated, compass and all, from the 96th madrigal (pub. 1598) of G. B. Guarini (1538–1612).

Sir John Suckling

(1609–1642)

THE VERY PARADIGM of a Caroline courtly poet, Suckling at eighteen inherited the ample properties of his father, who had been secretary of state, promptly went abroad for a two years' grand tour, was knighted on his return, set out again for two years' adventuring in the Thirty Years' War, and on finally settling in England in 1632 proceeded to frequent the court, fill ceremonial posts, and run up a reputation as "the greatest gallant of his time, and the greatest gamester, both for bowling and cards, so that no shopkeeper would trust him for 6 d." There is no evidence that this characterization is exaggerated, though the scandal-loving John Aubrey set it down. But at last recalcitrant Parliament darkened the world, and by 1641 his theatrically promonarchist activities had made it urgent for him to flee to France, where he soon died miserably, Aubrey says by his own hand.

He differed from his friend Carew chiefly in possessing ample means and less talent. They shared a Jonsonian allegiance which for Suckling meant confident amusement with lovesickness. Though his tone accommodates borrowings from Donne, it is the Jonson of "In the Person of Womankind" and "In defence of their inconstancie," not the Donne of "Goe, and catche a falling starre," who stands behind the easy aristocratic railleries of Suckling's songs and sonnets, or the crisply affectionate folk-mimicry of his "Ballad upon a Wedding."

TEXT: In the absence of a suitable edition, these selections depend on Professor Bald's transcriptions.

Song

Why so pale and wan fond Lover?
prethee why so pale?
Will, when looking well can't move her,
looking ill prevail?
prethee why so pale? 5

Why so dull and mute young sinner,
prethee why so mute?
Will when speaking well can't win her,
saying nothing doe't?
prethee why so mute? 10

Quit, quit for shame, this will not move,
this cannot take her;
If of her self she will not love,
nothing can make her:
the divel take her. 15

Sonnet. II

Of thee (kind boy) I ask no red and white
to make up my delight,
no odd becomming graces,
Black eyes, or little know-not-whats, in faces;
Make me but mad enough, give me good store 5
Of Love, for her I Court
I ask no more,
'Tis love in love that makes the sport.

There's no such thing as that we beauty call,
it is meer cousenage all; 10
for though some long ago

Like't certain colours mingled so and so,
That doth not tie me now from chusing new,
If I a fancy take
    To black and blue, 15
That fancy doth it beauty make.

'Tis not the meat; but 'tis the appetite
  makes eating a delight,
  and if I like one dish
More than another, that a Pheasant is; 20
What in our watches, that in us is found,
So to the height and nick
    We up be wound,
No matter by what hand or trick.

Sonnet. III

Oh! for some honest Lovers ghost,
    Some kind unbodied post
    Sent from the shades below.
    I strangely long to know
Whether the nobler Chaplets wear, 5
Those that their mistrisse scorn did bear,
    Or those that were us'd kindly.

For what-so-e're they tell us here
    To make those sufferings dear,
    'Twill there I fear be found, 10
    That to the being crown'd,
T'have lov'd alone will not suffice,
Unlesse we also have been wise,
    And have our Loves enjoy'd.

What posture can we think him in, 15
    That here unlov'd agen
    Departs, and's thither gone

Where each sits by his own?
Or how can that *Elizium* be
Where I my Mistresse still must see 20
Circled in others Armes?

For there the Judges all are just,
And *Sophonisba* must
Be his whom she held dear;
Not his who lov'd her here: 25
The sweet *Philoclea* since she dy'de
Lies by her *Pirocles* his side,
Not by *Amphialus*.

Some Bayes (perchance) or Myrtle bough
For difference crowns the brow 30
Of those kind souls that were
The noble Martyrs here;
And if that be the onely odds
(As who can tell) ye kinder Gods,
Give me the Woman here. 35

23. *Sophonisba:* a historical Carthaginian lady. It is sufficient to know that she and Philoclea (line 26), a character in Sidney's *Arcadia*, get into the poem because each loved one man but was subjected to the importunities of another.

[Song]

Out upon it, I have lov'd
Three whole days together;
And am like to love three more,
If it prove fair weather.

Time shall moult away his wings 5
Ere he shall discover
In the whole wide world agen
Such a constant Lover.

But the spite on't is, no praise
Is due at all to me: 10
Love with me had made no staies,
Had it any been but she.

Had it any been but she
And that very Face,
There had been at least ere this 15
A dozen dozen in her place.

[The Siege]

'Tis now since I sate down before
That foolish Fort, a heart;
(Time strangely spent) a Year, and more,
And still I did my part:

Made my approaches, from her hand 5
Unto her lip did rise,
And did already understand
The language of her eyes.

Proceeded on with no lesse Art,
My Tongue was Enginer; 10
I thought to undermine the heart
By whispering in the ear.

When this did nothing, I brought down
Great Canon-oaths and shot
A thousand thousand to the Town, 15
And still it yeelded not.

I then resolv'd to starve the place
By cutting off all kisses,

1. *sate down:* encamped. Not Suckling's expression but the normal technical term.

Praysing and gazing on her face,
  And all such little blisses. 20

To draw her out, and from her strength,
  I drew all batteries in:
And brought my self to lie at length
  As if no siege had been.

When I had done what man could do, 25
  And thought the place mine owne,
The Enemy lay quiet too,
  And smil'd at all was done.

I sent to know from whence and where,
  These hopes, and this relief? 30
A Spie inform'd, Honour was there,
  And did command in chief.

March, march (quoth I) the word straight give,
  Lets lose no time, but leave her:
That Giant upon ayre will live, 35
  And hold it out for ever.

To such a place our Camp remove
  As will no siege abide;
I hate a fool that starves her Love
  Onely to feed her pride. 40

A Ballade. Upon a Wedding

I tell the *Dick* where I have been,
Where I the rarest things have seen;
    Oh things beyond compare!
Such sights again cannot be found

It was the wedding of the Earl of Suffolk's daughter to Baron Broghill. *Dick* (line 1) is Suckling's fellow-courtier Richard Lovelace. He is amusing himself with the pretense that they both took in the wedding as goggle-eyed rustics.

In any place on English ground, 5
Be it at Wake, or Fair.

At Charing Crosse, hard by the way
Where we (thou know'st) do sell our Hay,
There is a house with stairs;
And there did I see comming down 10
Such folk as are not in our Town,
Vorty at least, in Pairs.

Amongst the rest, one Pest'lent fine,
(His beard no bigger though than thine)
Walks on before the rest: 15
Our Landlord looks like nothing to him;
The King (God blesse him) 'twould undo him:
Should he go still so drest.

At Course-a-Park, without all doubt,
He should have first been taken out. 20
By all the Maids i'th'Town:
Though lusty *Roger* there had been,
Or little *George* upon the Green,
Or *Vincent* of the Crown.

But wot you what? the youth was going 25
To make an end of all his wooing;
The Parson for him staid:
Yet by his leave (for all his haste)
He did not so much wish all past,
(Perchance) as did the maid. 30

The maid (and thereby hangs a tale)
For such a maid no Whitson-ale
Could ever yet produce:
No grape that's kindly ripe, could be

---

19. *Course-a-Park:* a round game involving kissing.
32. *Whitson-ale:* a rustic festival.
34. *kindly:* by natural process.

So round, so plump, so soft as she, 35
    Nor half so full of Juyce.

Her finger was so small, the Ring
Would not stay on which he did bring,
    It was too wide a Peck:
And to say truth (for out it must) 40
It lookt like the great Collar (just)
    About our young Colts neck.

Her feet beneath her Petticoat,
Like little mice stole in and out,
    As if they fear'd the light: 45
But *Dick* she dances such a way!
No sun upon an Easter day
    Is half so fine a sight.

He would have kist her once or twice,
But she would not, she was nice, 50
    She would not do't in sight,
And then she lookt as who should say
I will do what I list to day;
    And you shall do't at night.

Her Cheeks so rare a white was on, 55
No Dazy makes comparison,
    (Who sees them is undone)
For streaks of red were mingled there,
Such as are on a Katherne Pear,
    (The side that's next the Sun.) 60

Her lips were red, and one was thin,
Compar'd to that was next her chin;
    (Some Bee had stung it newly.)
But (*Dick*) her eyes so guard her face,
I durst no more upon them gaze, 65
    Than on the Sun in July.

---

50. *nice:* punctilious.

Her mouth so small when she does speak,
Thou'dst swear her teeth her words did break,
    That they might passage get,
But she so handled still the matter, 70
They came as good as ours, or better,
    And are not spent a whit.

If wishing should be any sin,
The Parson himself had guilty bin,
    (She lookt that day so purely;) 75
And did the youth so oft the feat
At night, as some did in conceit,
    It would have spoil'd him, surely.

Passion o'me! how I run on!
There's that that would be thought upon, 80
    (I trow) besides the Bride.
The bus'nesse of the Kitchin's great,
For it is fit that men should eat;
    Nor was it there deni'd.

Just in the nick the Cook knockt thrice, 85
And all the waiters in a trice
    His summons did obey,
Each serving-man with dish in hand,
Marcht boldly up, like our Train'd Band,
    Presented and away. 90

When all the meat was on the Table,
What man of knife, or teeth, was able
    To stay to be intreated?
And this the very reason was,
Before the Parson could say Grace, 95
    The company was seated.

Now hatts fly off, and youths carouse;
Healths first go round, and then the house,
    The Brides came thick and thick;
And when 'twas nam'd anothers health, 100

---

89. *Trained Band:* militia.

Perhaps he made it hers by stealth,
(And who could help it? *Dick*)

C'th'sodain up they rise and dance;
Then sit again and sigh, and glance:
Then dance again and kisse: 105
Thus sev'rall waies the time did passe,
Whil'st ev'ry Woman wisht her place,
And ev'ry Man wisht his.

By this time all were stoln aside
To counsel and undresse the Bride; 110
But that he must not know:
But yet 'twas thought he ghest her mind,
And did not mean to stay behind
Above an hour or so.

When in he came (*Dick*) there she lay 115
Like new-faln snow melting away,
('Twas time I trow to part)
Kisses were now the onely stay,
Which soon she gave, as who should say,
God B'w'y'! with all my heart. 120

But just as heav'ns would have to crosse it,
In came the Bride-maids with the Posset.
The Bridegroom eat in spight;
For had he left the Women to't
It would have cost two hours to do't, 125
Which were too much that night.

At length the candles out, and now,
All that they had not done, they doe:
What that is, who can tell?
But I believe it was no more 130
Then thou and I have done before
With *Bridget*, and with *Nell*.

---

122. *Posset:* it was customary to offer this spiced drink to newlyweds. When educated men still thought in Latin, they would scarcely have been unconscious of a double-entendre in the name.

William Habington

(1605–1654)

HABINGTON was born the day before that fifth of November made infamous by Guy Fawkes' plot, in connection with which his father was nearly executed. This lesson was not lost on the poet, whose life was appropriately circumspect. He received a Jesuit education abroad, moved near the court when the court countenanced Catholic courtiers, paid suit to a lady whose father would have preferred a better match and married her perhaps secretly, exercised in her honor the courtier's normal knack for versifying, and published the poems in the year of their marriage, anonymously. The book, largely a sonnet sequence, was called *Castara* (chaste altar); the author figures in it as Araphil (altar lover), and its every sentiment is certified as to sanctity. Both of them, according to repeated assurances, kept chaste. Such a man as Carew, Habington's contemporary at court, did not, and Habington's prefatory attack on "loose copies of lust happily exprest" decries, with probably such poems as Carew's in mind, what he took to be the prevailing fashion in verse, as surely as does his selection of the forty-year-old *Astrophel and Stella* for model. Neither the School of Donne nor the Tribe of Ben suited his purposes, nor, probably, his talents. He was the perpetual tertiary writer who always prefers a mode sufficiently worn to be safe and pat.

Yet he had read Donne, if only to rebut him, and Donne's ghost walks his pages. Habington's *Memento Mori* speaks, he would hardly have known why, in rhythms that echo disquietingly something closer to the sinews of speech than Sidney's sonnet sequence:

> *Castara*, see that dust, the sportive wind
> So wantons with. 'Tis happ'ly all you'le finde

Left of some beauty: and how still it flies,
To trouble, as it did in life, our eyes.

If he cannot sustain that timbre, he can illustrate its ventriloqual pervasiveness, as in four or five poems a voice more cogent, urgent than his own, or for a line or two at a time a wit more daring, animates his protestingly decorous pages, and solicits, at such moments, our attention. There were augmented editions, no longer anonymous, of *Castara,* in 1635 and 1640. In the latter year Parliament was summoned for the first time in eleven years, Catholics were less tolerated, and Habington fell silent. The Civil War broke out, and he kept clear of it, to die under the Protectorate of Oliver Cromwell, neither persecuted nor noticed.

TEXT: *Poems,* ed. Kenneth Allott (London, 1948).

To a Wanton

In vaine faire sorceresse, thy eyes speake charmes,
In vaine thou mak'st loose circles with thy armes.
I'me 'bove thy spels. No magicke him can move,
In whom *Castara* hath inspir'd her love.
As she, keepe thou strict cent'nell o're thy eare, 5
Lest it the whispers of soft Courtiers heare;
Reade not his raptures, whose invention must
Write journey worke, both for his Patrons lust,
And his owne plush: let no admirer feast
His eye oth' naked banquet of thy brest. 10
If this faire president, nor yet my want
Of love, to answer thine, make thee recant
Thy sorc'ries; Pity shall to justice turne,
And judge thee, witch, in thy owne flames to burne.

---

11. *president:* precedent?

To *Castara*

UPON BEAUTIE

Castara, see that dust, the sportive wind
So wantons with. 'Tis happ'ly all you'le finde
Left of some beauty: and how still it flies,
To trouble, as it did in life, our eyes.
O empty boast of flesh? Though our heires gild 5
The farre fetch Phrigian marble, which shall build
A burthen to our ashes, yet will death
Betray them to the sport of every breath.
Dost thou, poor relique of our frailty, still
Swell up with glory? Or is it thy skill, 10
To mocke weake man, whom every wind of praise
Into the aire, doth 'bove his center raise.
If so, mocke on: And tell him that his lust
To beauty's, madnesse. For it courts but dust.

Against Them Who Lay Unchastity to the Sex of Women

They meet but with unwholesome Springs,
And Summers which infectious are:
They heare but when the Meremaid sings,
And onely see the falling starre:
Who ever dare, 5
Affirme no woman chaste and faire.

Goe cure your feavers: and you'le say
The Dog-dayes scorch not all the yeare:

3–4. See Donne's "Goe, and catche a falling starre," to which Habington evidently intends a rejoinder. Donne's poems were published in 1633, this poem in 1635.

In Copper Mines no longer stay,
But travell to the West, and there 10
The right ones see:
And grant all gold's not Alchimie.

What mad man 'cause the glow-wormes flame
Is cold, sweares there's no warmth in fire?
'Cause some make forfeit of their name, 15
And slave themselves to mans desire;
Shall the sex free
From guilt, damn'd to the bondage be?

Not grieve *Castara,* though 'twere fraile,
Thy Vertue then would brighter shine, 20
When thy example should prevaile,
And every womans faith be thine,
And were there none;
'Tis Majesty to rule alone.

To Roses in the Bosome of *Castara*

Yee blushing Virgins happie are
In the chaste Nunn'ry of her brests,
For hee'd prophane so chaste a faire,
Who ere should call them *Cupids* nests.

Transplanted thus how bright yee grow, 5
How rich a perfume doe yee yeeld?
In some close garden, Cowslips so
Are sweeter than ith' open field.

In those white Cloysters live secure
From the rude blasts of wanton breath, 10
Each houre more innocent and pure,
Till you shall wither into death.

Then that which living gave you roome,
Your glorious sepulcher shall be.
There wants no marble for a tombe, 15
Whose brest hath marble beene to me.

To the Right Honourable the Countesse of *C.*

Madam,

Should the cold *Muscovit,* whose furre and stove
Can scarse prepare him heate enough for love,
But view the wonder of your presence, he
Would scorne his winters sharpest injury:
And trace the naked groves, till he found bayse 5
To write the beautious triumphs of your prayse.
As a dull Poet even he would say,
Th' unclouded Sun had never showne them day
Till that bright minute; that he now admires
No more why the coy Spring so soone retires 10
From their unhappy clyme; It doth pursue
The Sun, and he derives his light from you.
Hee'd tell you how the fetter'd Baltick Sea
Is set at freedome, while the yce away
Doth melt at your approach; how by so faire 15
Harmonious beauty, their rude manners are
Reduc't to order; how to them you bring
The wealthiest mines below, above the Spring.
Thus would his wonder speake. For he would want
Religion to beleeve, there were a Saint 20
Within, and all he saw was but the shrine.
But I here pay my vowes to the devine
Pure essence there inclos'd, which if it were
Not hid in a faire cloud, but might appeare
In its full lustre, would make Nature live 25
In a state equall to her primitive.
But sweetly thats obscur'd. Yet though our eye
Cannot the splendor of your soule descry
In true perfection, by a glimmering light,

Your language yeelds us, we can guesse how bright 30
The Sunne within you shines, and curse th' unkind
Eclipse, or else our selves for being blinde.
How hastily doth Nature build up man
To leave him so imperfect? For he can
See nought beyond his sence; she doth controule 35
So farre his sight he nere discern'd a soule.
For had yours beene the object of his eye;
It had turn'd wonder to Idolatry.

Richard Lovelace

(1618–1657)

Lovelace at Oxford was "the most amiable and beautiful Person that ever Eye beheld, a Person also of innate modesty, virtue and courtly deportment, which made him then, but especially after, when he retired to the great City, much admired and adored by the Female Sex." He so caught the eye of Charles I on a 1636 visit to the University that the degree of M.A. was promptly conferred on him by the king's special request. Alas, Charles I was doomed, and the beautiful courtier with him; his loyalty earned him two spells in prison, during the second of which (1648–1649) he prepared *Lucasta* for the press. After the king's execution he dwelt obscurely in London, and did not outlive the Commonwealth. He probably knew Carew and certainly Marvell, whose commendatory poem to *Lucasta* (1649) contrasts the world of gallant play in which his friend was at home—

> Who best could prayse, had then the greatest prayse,
> Twas more esteemd to give, than weare the Bayes:
> Modest ambition studi'd only then,
> To honour not her selfe, but worthy men.

to that of the Commonwealth's "Word-peckers, Paper-rats, Book-scorpions," when

> The barbed Censurers begin to looke
> Like the grim consistory on thy Booke;
> And on each line cast a reforming eye,
> Severer than the yong Presbytery.
> Till when in vaine they have thee all perus'd,
> You shall for being faultlesse be accus'd.

For he was fated, in the commissars' view, to be the very epitome of social uselessness.

His songs for music, about love and parting, articulate with enviable finesse a gallantry wholly free from melodrama; though all is convention, it never occurs to him that he need strike a pose. He takes, and is right to take, vast satisfaction from the ease of his own performance. He can develop compliments with dazzling insouciance; he can moralize the death of a fly caught in a cobweb without a minatory tone transgressing on his gaiety; he never forgets that the beauty is but a woman, the fly but a fly, and the poem (in his hands) but an effort of agreeable exuberance. Men would be the poorer had they nothing to say about the doom of flies, and Lovelace's real subject is the human glory of his own loquacious wit, neither teaching nor moving but simply, on each amenable occasion, distinguishing by speech men from the brutes.

TEXT: *Poems,* ed. G. H. Wilkinson (Oxford, 1930).

SONG SET BY MR. HENRY LAWES

To *Lucasta,* Going beyond the Seas

I

If to be absent were to be
Away from thee;
Or that when I am gone,
You or I were alone;
Then my *Lucasta* might I crave 5
Pity from blustring winde, or swallowing wave.

II

But I'le not sigh one blast or gale
To swell my saile,
Or pay a teare to swage

The foaming blew-Gods rage; 10
For whether he will let me passe
Or no, I'm still as happy as I was.

III

Though Seas and Land betwixt us both,
Our Faith and Troth,
Like separated soules, 15
All time and space controules:
Above the highest sphere wee meet
Unseene, unknowne, and greet as Angels greet.

IV

So then we doe anticipate
Our after-fate, 20
And are alive i' th' skies,
If thus our lips and eyes
Can speake like spirits unconfin'd
In Heav'n, their earthy bodies left behind.

---

10. ***blew-God:*** either Neptune (who is blue) or Aeolus (who blows).

SONG SET BY MR. JOHN LANIERE

To *Lucasta,* Going to the Warres

I

Tell me not (Sweet) I am unkinde,
That from the Nunnerie
Of thy chaste breast, and quiet minde,
To Warre and Armes I flie.

II

True; a new Mistresse now I chase, 5
The first Foe in the Field;
And with a stronger Faith imbrace
A Sword, a Horse, a Shield.

III

Yet this Inconstancy is such,
As you too shall adore; 10
I could not love thee (Deare) so much,
Lov'd I not Honour more.

SONG SET BY MR. HENRY LAWES

To *Amarantha,* That She Would Dishevell Her Haire

I

Amarantha sweet and faire,
Ah brade no more that shining haire!
As my curious hand or eye,
Hovering round thee let it flye.

II

Let it flye as unconfin'd 5
As it's calme Ravisher, the winde;
Who hath left his darling th' East,
To wanton o're that spicie Neast.

III

Ev'ry Tresse must be confest
But neatly tangled at the best; 10
Like a Clue of golden thread,
Most excellently ravelled.

IV

Doe not then winde up that light
In Ribands, and o're-cloud in Night;
Like the Sun in's early ray, 15
But shake your head and scatter day.

V

See 'tis broke! Within this Grove
The Bower, and the walkes of Love,
Weary lye we downe and rest,
And fanne each others panting breast. 20

VI

Heere wee'l strippe and coole our fire
In Creame below, in milke-baths higher:
And when all Well's are drawne dry,
I'le drink a teare out of thine eye.

VII

Which our very Joyes shall leave 25
That sorrowes thus we can deceive;
Or our very sorrowes weepe,
That joyes so ripe, so little keepe.

The Scrutinie

SONG SET BY MR. THOMAS CHARLES

I

Why should you sweare I am forsworn,
Since thine I vow'd to be?
Lady it is already Morn,
And 'twas last night I swore to thee
That fond impossibility. 5

II

Have I not lov'd thee much and long,
A tedious twelve houres space?
I must all other Beauties wrong,
And rob thee of a new imbrace;
Could I still dote upon thy Face. 10

III

Not, but all joy in thy browne haire,
By others may be found;
But I must search the black and faire
Like skillfull Minerallist's that sound
For Treasure in un-plow'd-up ground. 15

IV

Then, if when I have lov'd my round,
Thou prov'st the pleasant she;
With spoyles of meaner Beauties crown'd,
I laden will returne to thee,
Ev'n sated with Varietie. 20

To *Althea,* from Prison

SONG SET BY DR. JOHN WILSON

I

When Love with unconfined wings
Hovers within my Gates;
And my divine *Althea* brings
To whisper at the Grates:
When I lye tangled in her haire, 5
And fetterd to her eye;
The *Gods* that wanton in the Aire,
Know no such Liberty.

II

When flowing Cups run swiftly round
With no allaying *Thames,* 10
Our carelesse heads with Roses bound,
Our hearts with Loyall Flames;
When thirsty griefe in Wine we steepe,
When Healths and draughts go free,

Fishes that tipple in the Deepe, 15
Know no such Libertie.

III

When (like committed Linnets) I
With shriller throat shall sing
The sweetnes, Mercy, Majesty,
And glories of my KING; 20
When I shall voyce aloud, how Good
He is, how Great should be;
Inlarged Winds that curle the Flood,
Know no such Liberty.

IV

Stone Walls doe not a Prison make, 25
Nor I'ron bars a Cage;
Mindes innocent and quiet take
That for an Hermitage;
If I have freedome in my Love,
And in my soule am free; 30
Angels alone that sore above,
Injoy such Liberty.

Lucasta's World

EPODE

I

Cold as the breath of winds that blow
To silver shot descending snow
LUCASTA sight; when she did close
The World in frosty chaines!
And then a frowne to Rubies frose 5
The blood boyl'd in our veines:
Yet cooled not the heat her Sphere
Of Beauties, first had kindled there.

II

Then mov'd, and with a suddaine Flame
Impatient to melt all againe, 10
Straight from her eyes she lightning hurl'd,
And Earth in ashes mournes;
The Sun his blaze denies the world,
And in her luster burnes:
Yet warmed not the hearts, her nice 15
Disdaine had first congeal'd to Ice.

III

And now her teares nor griev'd desire
Can quench this raging, pleasing fire;
Fate but one way allowes; behold
Her smiles Divinity! 20
They fann'd this heat, and thaw'd that cold,
So fram'd up a new sky.
Thus Earth from flames and Ice repreev'd,
E're since hath in her Sun-shine liv'd.

Valiant Love

I

Now fie upon that everlasting Life, I Dye!
She hates! Ah me! It makes me mad;
As if Love fir'd his Torch at a moist Eye,
Or with his Joyes e're Crown'd the sad?
Oh let me live and shout when I fall on! 5
Let me ev'n Triumph in the first attempt!
Loves Duellist from Conquest's not exempt
When his fair Murdresse shall not gain one groan,
And He expire ev'n in Ovation.

II

Let me make my approach when I lye downe 10
With counter-wrought and Travers Eyes;

With Peals of Confidence Batter the Towne:
   Had ever Beggar yet the Keyes?
No, I will vary stormes with Sun and Winde;
   Be rough, and offer Calme Condition, 15
   March in (and pray't) or starve the Garrison.
Let her make sallies hourely, yet I'le find
(Though all beat of) shee's to be undermin'd.

III

Then may it please your *Little Excellence*
   Of Hearts, t' ordaine by sound of Lips, 20
That henceforth none in Tears dare Love comence
   (Her thoughts ith' full, his in th' Eclipse)
On paine of having's Launce broke on her Bed,
   That he be branded all Free Beauties slave,
   And his own hollow eyes be domb'd his grave: 25
Since in your Hoast that Coward nere was fed
Who to his Prostrate ere was Prostrated.

La Bella Bona Roba

I

I cannot tell who loves the Skeleton
Of a poor Marmoset, nought but boan, boan.
Give me a nakednesse with her cloath's on.

II

Such whose white-sattin upper coat of skin,
Cut upon Velvet rich Incarnadin, 5
Ha's yet a Body (and of Flesh) within.

III

Sure it is meant good Husbandry in men,
Who do incorporate with Aëry leane,
T' repair their sides, and get their Ribb agen.

2. *Marmoset:* this word, like "Bona Roba," was a seventeenth-century euphemism for "prostitute." "Clothes" was slang for "skin."

IV

Hard hap unto that Huntsman that Decrees 10
Fat joys for all his swet, when as he sees,
After his 'Say, nought but his Keepers Fees.

V

Then Love I beg, when next thou tak'st thy Bow,
Thy angry shafts, and dost Heart-chasing go,
Passe *Rascall Deare,* strike me the largest Doe. 15

---

12. *'Say:* essay, attempt.
14. *Heart:* also hart.
15. *Rascall Deare:* the lean or inferior deer of the herd.

A Black Patch on *Lucasta's* Face

Dull as I was, to think that a Court Fly,
Presum'd so neer her Eye;
When 'twas th'industrious Bee
Mistook her glorious Face for Paradise,
To summe up all his Chymistry of Spice; 5
With a brave pride and honour led,
Neer both her Suns he makes his bed;
And though a Spark struggles to rise as red:
Then Æmulates the gay
Daughter of Day, 10
Acts the *Romantick Phœnix* fate:
When now with all his Sweets lay'd out in state,
Lucasta scatters but one Heat,
And all the Aromatick pills do sweat,
And Gums calcin'd, themselves to powder beat; 15
Which a fresh gale of Air
Conveys into her Hair;
Then chast he's set on fire,
And in these holy flames doth glad expire;
And that black marble Tablet there 20

So neer her either Sphere,
Was plac'd; nor foyl, nor Ornament,
But the sweet little Bees large Monument.

Another

1

As I beheld a Winters Evening Air,
Curl'd in her court false locks of living hair,
Butter'd with Jessamine the Sun left there,

2

Galliard and clinquant she appear'd to give,
A Serenade or Ball to us that grieve, 5
And teach us *A la mode* more gently live.

3

But as a *Moor,* who to her Cheeks prefers
White Spots t'allure her black Idolaters,
Me thought she look'd all ore bepatch'd with Stars;

4

Like the dark front of some *Ethiopian* Queen, 10
Vailed all ore with Gems of Red, Blew, Green;
Whose ugly Night seem'd masked with days Skreen;

5

Whilst the fond people offer'd Sacrifice
To Saphyrs 'stead of Veins and Arteries,
And bow'd unto the Diamonds, not her Eyes. 15

6

Behold *Lucasta's* Face, how't glows like Noon!
A Sun intire is her complexion,
And form'd of one whole Constellation.

7

So gently shining, so serene, so cleer,
Her look doth Universal Nature cheer; 20
Only a cloud or two hangs here and there.

Love Made in the First Age

TO CHLORIS

1

In the Nativity of time,
Chloris! it was not thought a Crime
In direct *Hebrew* for to woe.
Now wee make Love, as all on fire,
Ring Retrograde our lowd Desire, 5
And Court in *English* Backward too.

2

Thrice happy was that golden Age,
When Complement was constru'd Rage,
And fine words in the Center hid;
When cursed *No* stain'd no Maids Blisse, 10
And all discourse was summ'd in *Yes,*
And Nought forbad, but to forbid.

3

Love then unstinted, Love did sip,
And Cherries pluck'd fresh from the Lip,
On Cheeks and Roses free he fed; 15
Lasses like *Autumne* Plums did drop,
And Lads, indifferently did crop
A Flower, and a Maiden-head.

3. ***Hebrew:*** by one tradition, the language of Eden. Unlike English (line 6), it is written from right to left.

4

Then unconfined each did Tipple
Wine from the Bunch, Milk from the Nipple, 20
  Paps tractable as Udders were;
Then equally the wholsome Jellies,
Were squeez'd from Olive-Trees, and Bellies,
  Nor Suits of Trespasse did they fear.

5

A fragrant Bank of Straw-berries, 25
Diaper'd with Violets Eyes,
  Was Table, Table-cloth, and Fare;
No Pallace to the Clouds did swell,
Each humble Princesse then did dwell
  In the *Piazza* of her Hair. 30

6

Both broken Faith, and th' cause of it,
All damning Gold was damm'd to th' Pit;
  Their Troth seal'd with a Clasp and Kisse,
Lasted untill that extreem day,
In which they smil'd their Souls away, 35
  And in each other breath'd new blisse.

7

Because no fault, there was no tear;
No grone did grate the granting Ear;
  No false foul breath their Del'cat smell:
No Serpent kiss poyson'd the Tast, 40
Each touch was naturally Chast,
  And their mere Sense a Miracle.

8

Naked as their own innocence,
And unimbroyder'd from Offence
  They went, above poor Riches, gay; 45
On softer than the Cignets Down,

In beds they tumbled of their own;
  For each within the other lay.

9

Thus did they live: Thus did they love,
Repeating only joyes Above; 50
  And Angels were, but with Cloaths on,
Which they would put off cheerfully,
To bathe them in the *Galaxie,*
  Then gird them with the Heavenly Zone.

10

Now, *CHLORIS!* miserably crave, 55
The offer'd blisse you would not have;
  Which evermore I must deny,
Whilst ravish'd with these Noble Dreams,
And crowned with mine own soft Beams,
  Injoying of my self I lye. 60

A Fly Caught in a Cobweb

Small type of great ones, that do hum,
Within this whole World's narrow Room,
That with a busie hollow Noise
Catch at the people's vainer Voice,
And with spread Sails play with their breath, 5
Whose very Hails new christen Death.
Poor Fly caught in an airy net,
Thy Wings have fetter'd now thy feet;
Where like a *Lyon* in a Toyl,
Howere, thou keep'st a noble Coyl, 10
And beat'st thy gen'rous breast, that ore
The plains thy fatal buzzes rore,
Till thy al-belly'd foe (round Elf)
Hath quarter'd thee within himself.
  Was it not better once to play 15
I' th' light of a Majestick Ray?

Where though too neer and bold, the fire
Might sindge thy upper down attire,
And thou ith' storm to loose an Eye,
A Wing, or a self-trapping Thigh; 20
Yet hadst thou faln like him, whose Coil
Made Fishes in the Sea to broyl;
When now th' ast scap'd the noble Flame,
Trapp'd basely in a slimy frame;
And free of Air, thou art become 25
Slave to the spawn of Mud and Lome.
Nor is't enough thy self do'st dresse
To thy swoln Lord a num'rous messe,
And by degrees thy thin Veins bleed,
And piece-meal dost his poyson feed; 30
But now devour'd, art like to be
A Net spun for thy Familie,
And straight expanded in the Air
Hang'st for thy issue too a snare.
Strange witty Death, and cruel ill, 35
That killing thee, thou thine dost kill!
Like Pies in whose intombed ark,
All Fowl crowd downward to a Lark;
Thou art thine En'mies Sepulcher,
And in thee buriest too thine heir. 40
Yet Fates a glory have reserv'd
For one so highly hath deserv'd;
As the *Rhinoceros* doth dy
Under his Castle-Enemy,
As through the *Cranes* trunk Throat doth speed, 45
The *Aspe* doth on his feeder feed;
Fall yet triumphant in thy woe,
Bound with the entrails of thy foe.

---

21. ***him:*** Phaethon, who borrowed the chariot of the sun and drove it recklessly.

VII

MEN OF SENSE AND MEN OF WIT

Edmund Waller (1606–1687)
John Denham (1615–1669)
John Cleveland (1613–1658)
Abraham Cowley (1618–1667)

Waller and Denham came to be numbered among the founding fathers of Augustan poetry, and Restoration judgment hailed Cowley as a learned wit. Cleveland's vogue was briefer but intense; he was probably the most popular poet of the century's middle years.

Edmund Waller

(1606–1687)

Lucidity and ease were Waller's specialties; he seems to have been born with them, and the Augustans thought he had invented them. Dryden was to state that "well-placing of words, for the sweetness of pronunciation, was not known till Mr. Waller introduced it." His name and Denham's are coupled throughout so much Augustan literary theorizing, so many eighteenth-century *obiter dicta* on the brief history of enlightened versification, that it is difficult to remember that he was born before Shakespeare had written *Coriolanus*.

His poems have two salient qualities only; a readily paraphrasable argument, developed in easy steps, and a knack for fitting sentences which never arrest the mind to cadences which never impede the tongue. Both qualities recommended him to an age which strove toward other criteria than these, but judged these indispensable. Whatever he says, he says twice at least, but each time gracefully.

> When Architects have done their Part
> The Matter may betray their Art;
> Time, if we use ill-chosen Stone,
> Soon brings a well-built Palace down.

"Done their part" has the flaccid ease of a colloquialism: the word "part" invites no special attention. Yet its vowel not only rhymes with that of "art" but repeats that of "architects," and this bridge of assonance that spans the first line has its miniature fellow in the heart of the second: "m*ay* betr*ay*." These are items of detachable technique that can be isolated, admired, and imitated, their ingenious grace independent of what is being said. What is being said, in turn, attempts no great urgency. The argument of the poem we are quoting ("Of English Verse") is simply this, that English verse, though carved in sand (unlike Latin) and hence mutable, can last quite long enough to sway a living beauty. My mind is not on fame, it is on your favors. This air of chivalrous naughtiness was to be much liked: it made the poet no more than the Restoration wits were to think he ought to be, a salon entertainer. "Go, lovely Rose," his finest achievement, is once more an achievement of rhymes and cadences; orderly prose would be adequate to its argument, yet reduced to prose it would argue its way through a piece of graceful trifling.

Waller married a rich heiress at twenty-five, buried her at twenty-eight, courted other beauties, was involved, not to his credit, in the Civil War, seven years of which he spent abroad under sentence of banishment for double dealing; sat in Parliament again after the Restoration; and having joined the Royal Society on its incorporation was much pointed to, along with Denham and Dryden, as proof that the society commanded poetical as well as methodical intelligences.

TEXT: There has been no modern edition of Waller's works since 1893. The present text comes from a late seventeenth-century printing.

Of Loving at First Sight

Not caring to observe the Wind,
Or the new Sea explore,
Snatch'd from my self, how far behind
Already I behold the Shore!

May not a thousand Dangers sleep 5
In the smooth Bosom of this Deep?
No: 'Tis so Rockless and so Clear,
That the rich Bottom does appear
Pav'd all with precious things, not torn
From shipwrack'd Vessels, but there Born. 10

Sweetness, Truth, and ev'ry Grace,
Which Time and Use are wont to teach,

The Eye may in a Moment reach,
And read distinctly in her Face.

Some other Nymphs, with Colours faint, 15
And Pencil slow, may *Cupid* paint,
And a weak Heart in time destroy;
She has a Stamp and Prints the Boy,
Can with a single Look inflame
The coldest Breast, the rudest Tame. 20

Song

Go lovely Rose,
Tell her that wastes her time and me,
That now she knows,
When I resemble her to thee,
How sweet and fair she seems to be. 5

Tell her that's Young,
And shuns to have her Graces spy'd,
That hadst thou sprung
In Desarts, where no Men abide,
Thou must have uncommended dy'd. 10

Small is the worth
Of Beauty from the Light retir'd;
Bid her come forth,
Suffer her self to be desir'd,
And not blush so to be admir'd. 15

Then Die, that she
The common Fate of all things rare
May read in thee:
How small a part of time they share,
That are so wondrous Sweet and Fair. 20

To *Phillis*

Phillis, why shou'd we delay
Pleasures shorter than the Day?
Cou'd we (which we never can)
Stretch our Lives beyond their Span;
Beauty like a Shadow flies, 5
And our Youth before us dies.
Or wou'd Youth and Beauty stay,
Love hath Wings, and will away.
Love hath swifter Wings than Time;
Change in Love to Heav'n does climb; 10
Gods that never change their State,
Vary oft their Love and Hate.
Phillis, to this Truth we owe
All the Love betwixt us two:
Let not you and I inquire, 15
What has been our past Desire;
On what Shepherds you have smil'd,
Or what Nymphs I have beguil'd;
Leave it to the Planets too,
What we shall hereafter do; 20
For the Joys we now may prove,
Take advice of present Love.

Song

Stay *Phœbus,* stay,
The World to which you fly so fast,
Conveying Day
From us to them, can pay your Haste
With no such Object, nor salute your Rise 5
With no such Wonder, as *de Mornay's* Eyes.

Well do's this prove
The Error of those antique Books,
Which made you move
About the World; her charming Looks 10
Wou'd fix your Beams, and make it ever Day,
Did not the rowling Earth snatch her away.

On My Lady *Isabella* Playing on the Lute

Such moving sounds, from such a careless touch,
So unconcern'd her self, and we so much!
What Art is this, that with so little Pains
Transports us thus, and o'er our Spirits reigns!
The trembling Strings about her Fingers crowd, 5
And tell their Joy for ev'ry Kiss aloud:
Small Force there needs to make them tremble so;
Touch'd by that Hand who wou'd not tremble too?
Here Love takes stand, and while she charms the Ear,
Empties his Quiver on the list'ning Deer; 10
Musick so softens and disarms the Mind,
That not an Arrow does Resistance find.
Thus the fair Tyrant Celebrates the Prize,
And acts her self the Triumph of her Eyes.
So *Nero* once, with Harp in hand, survey'd 15
His Flaming *Rome,* and as it Burnt he Play'd.

To a Very Young Lady

Why came I so untimely forth
Into a World which wanting thee,
Cou'd entertain us with no worth
Or shadow of Felicity?
That Time shou'd me so far remove 5
From that which I was born to Love!

Yet, fairest Blossom, do not slight
  That Age which you may know so soon;
The Rosie Morn resigns her Light,
  And milder Glory, to the Noon: 10
And then what Wonders shall you do,
Whose dawning Beauty warms us so?

Hope waits upon the flowry Prime,
  And Summer, though it be less gay,
Yet is not look'd on as a time 15
  Of Declination or Decay.
For, with a full Hand, that does bring
All that was promis'd by the Spring.

To the Mutable Fair

  Here, *Cælia,* for thy sake I part
With all that grew so near my Heart;
The Passion that I had for thee,
The Faith, the Love, the Constancy,
And, that I may successful prove, 5
Transform my self to what you Love.
  For that I was so much to prize
Those simple Virtues you despise,
Fool that with such dull Arrows strove,
Or hop'd to reach a flying Dove; 10
For you, that are in Motion still,
Decline our Force, and mock our Skill.
Who like *Don Quixot* do advance
Against a Wind-mill our vain Lance.
  Now will I wander thro' the Air, 15
Mount, make a stop at ev'ry Fair,
And, with a Fancy unconfin'd
(As lawless as the Sea or Wind)
Pursue you wheresoe'er you fly,
And with your various Thoughts comply. 20
  The formal Stars do travel so,

As we their Names and Courses know,
And he that on their Changes looks,
Wou'd think them govern'd by our Books,
But never were the Clouds reduc'd 25
To any Art; the Motion us'd
By those free Vapours are so light,
So frequent, that the Conquer'd Sight
Despairs to find the Rules that guide
Those gilded Shadows as they slide. 30
And therefore of the spacious Air
Jove's Royal Consort had the Care:
And by that Pow'r did once escape,
Declining bold *Ixion*'s Rape;
She, with her own Resemblance, grac'd 35
A shining Cloud, which he embrac'd.
  Such was that Image, so it smil'd
With seeming Kindness, which beguil'd
Your *Thirsis* lately, when he thought
He had his fleeting *Cælia* caught. 40
'Twas shap'd like her, but for the Fair
He fill'd his Arms with yielding Air:
  A Fate for which he grieves the less,
Because the Gods had like Success.
For in their Story one, we see, 45
Pursue a Nymph, and takes a Tree:
A second, with a Lover's haste,
Soon overtakes whom he had chac'd;
But she that did a Virgin seem,
Possest appears a wandring Stream: 50
For his supposed Love a third
Lays greedy hold upon a Bird;
And stands amaz'd to find his Dear
A wild Inhabitant of th' Air.
  To these old Tales such Nymphs as you 55
Give Credit, and still make them new;
The Am'rous now like Wonders find,
In the swift Changes of your Mind.
  But, *Cælia,* if you apprehend
The Muse of your incensed Friend; 60

Nor wou'd that he record your Blame,
And make it live, repeat the same,
Again deceive him, and again,
And then he swears he'll not complain.
For still to be deluded so, 65
Is all the Pleasure Lovers know,
Who, like good Faulkners, take delight,
Not in the Quarry, but the Flight.

To One Married to an Old Man

Since thou wou'dst needs, bewitcht with some ill Charms,
Be bury'd in those Monumental Arms:
All we can wish, is, May that Earth lie light
Upon thy tender Limbs, and so good Night.

To Mr. *Henry Lawes*

WHO HAD THEN NEWLY SET A SONG OF A MINE IN THE YEAR 1635

Verse makes *Heroick* Virtue live,
But you can Life to Verses give:
As when in open Air we blow,
The Breath (tho' strain'd) sounds flat and low:
But if a Trumpet take the Blast, 5
It lifts it high, and makes it last;
So in your Ayrs our Numbers drest
Make a shrill Sally from the Breast
Of Nymphs, who Singing what we Pen'd,
Our Passions to themselves commend, 10
While Love, Victorious with thy Art,
Governs at once their Voice and Heart;
You, by the help of Tune and Time,
Can make that Song which was but Rhime.

Noy pleading, no Man doubts the Cause, 15
Or questions Verses set by *Lawes.*
As a Church-window, thick with Paint,
Lets in a Light but dim and faint;
So others, with Division, hide
The Light of Sense, the Poets Pride; 20
But you alone may truly boast
That not a Syllable is lost;
The Writer's, and the Setter's, Skill
At once the Ravish'd Ears do fill.
Let those which only warble long, 25
And gargle in their Throats a Song,
Content themselves with *UT, RE, MI;*
Let Words and Sense be set by thee.

Of English Verse

Poets may boast [as safely-vain]
Their Work shall with the World remain:
Both bound together, Live, or Die,
The Verses and the Prophecy.

But who can hope his Lines shou'd long 5
Last, in a daily changing Tongue?
While they are new, Envy prevails,
And as that dies, our Language fails.

When Architects have done their Part,
The Matter may betray their Art; 10
Time, if we use ill-chosen Stone,
Soon brings a well-built Palace down.

Poets that lasting Marble seek,
Must Carve in *Latin,* or in *Greek;*
We write in Sand, our Language grows, 15
And like our Tide ours overflows.

Chaucer his Sense can only boast,
The Glory of his Numbers lost;
Years have defac'd his matchles Strain,
And yet he did not Sing in vain. 20

The Beauties which adorn'd that Age,
The shining Subjects of his Rage,
Hoping they shou'd Immortal prove,
Rewarded with Success his Love.

This was the gen'rous Poet's scope, 25
And all an *English* Pen can hope
To make the Fair approve his Flame,
That can so far extend their Fame.

Verse thus design'd has no ill Fate,
If it arrive but at the Date 30
Of fading Beauty, if it prove
But as long-liv'd as present Love.

Of the Last Verses in the Book

When we for Age cou'd neither Read nor Write,
The Subject made us able to indite.
The Soul with Nobler Resolutions deckt,
The Body stooping, does her self erect:
No Mortal Parts are requisite to raise 5
Her, that Unbody'd can her Maker praise.
The Seas are quiet, when the Winds give o'er;
So calm are we, when Passions are no more:
For then we know how vain it was to boast
Of fleeting Things, so certain to be lost. 10
Clouds of Affection from our younger Eyes
Conceal that emptiness, which Age decries.
The Soul's dark Cottage, batter'd and decay'd,
Let's in new Light thrô chinks that time has made:

Stronger by weakness, wiser Men become 15
As they draw near to their Eternal home:
Leaving the Old, both Worlds at once they view,
That stand upon the Threshold of the New.

Sir John Denham

(1615–1669)

THOUGH HIS MIND measured against Marvell's or even Cowley's seems utterly commonplace, the Augustans a century later were to find Denham the most congenial of the Caroline poets: pioneer of the closed couplet and the moralized song, sharing with Waller credit for establishing modes of verse whose weight could sustain, it seemed, the interest of an at last cohesive civilization.

Cooper's Hill, which was repeatedly imitated for nearly two centuries, notably by the young Pope in *Windsor Forest,* inaugurated, in Dr. Johnson's words,

> a species of composition that may be denominated *local poetry,* of which the fundamental subject is some particular landscape, to be poetically described, with the addition of such embellishments as may be supplied by historical retrospection, or incidental meditation.

To account for Johnson's omission of Ben Jonson's "To Penshurst" or Marvell's "Upon Appleton House," we should consider how congenial to the eighteenth century is the special sense *Cooper's Hill* gives to the terms "meditation" and "retrospection." An age which, encouraged by new definitions of "common sense," liked to feel sure how to distinguish between the poem's public materials and the poet's contributions, felt that it knew where it was with a poet who took up his station on a hill on the right bank of the river near his home at Egham in Surrey, picked out the dome of old St. Paul's to the east, pondered this, swung round toward Windsor three miles north-north-west, then dropped his gaze to the Thames and Runneymede meadow below him, accompanying these acts with the appropriate reflections.

Four lines in particular of *Cooper's Hill* (189–192) were singled out by Dryden for their "sweetness" and subsequently became securely lodged in the eighteenth century's stock of quotations, theme for a continuous tradition of allusion, parody, and commendation. "So much meaning is comprised in so few words," wrote Johnson,

> the particulars of resemblance are so perspicaciously collected, and every mode of excellence separated from its adjacent fault by so nice a line of limitation; the different parts of the sentence are so accurately adjusted; and the flow of the last couplet is so smooth and sweet; that the passage, however celebrated, has not been praised above its merit.

And Pope, pretending to commend a bad poet, wrote

> Flow, Welsted, flow! like thine inspirer, beer,
> Tho' stale, not ripe, tho' thin, yet never clear;
> So sweetly mawkish, and so smoothly dull;
> Heady, not strong; o'erflowing, tho' not full.

The celebrated lines are not to be found in the pirated 1642 edition of *Cooper's Hill,* nor in the four reprints of that piracy. It was in revising the poem for the first authorized edition (1655) that Denham, replacing four inferior lines with eight better ones, achieved the quatrain on which his fame rests.

TEXT: from the final form of the poem in Denham's Collected Edition of 1668, as given in *The Poetical Works of Sir John Denham,* ed. Theodore Howard Banks, Jr. (New Haven, Conn., 1928).

CRITICISM: Samuel Johnson, "Life of Denham" (*Lives of the Poets*). Banks' edition of the *Works* contains a generous sampling of other comments from Dryden to Gosse.

Cooper's Hill

Sure there are Poets which did never dream
Upon *Parnassus,* nor did tast the stream
Of *Helicon,* we therefore may suppose
Those made not Poets, but the Poets those.
And as Courts make not Kings, but Kings the Court, 5

So where the Muses & their train resort,
Parnassus stands; if I can be to thee
A Poet, thou *Parnassus* art to me.
Nor wonder, if (advantag'd in my flight,
By taking wing from thy auspicious height) 10
Through untrac't ways, and aery paths I fly,
More boundless in my Fancy than my eie:
My eye, which swift as thought contracts the space
That lies between, the first salutes the place
Crown'd with that sacred pile, so vast, so high, 15
That whether 'tis a part of Earth, or sky,
Uncertain seems, and may be thought a proud
Aspiring mountain, or descending cloud,
Pauls, the late theme of such a Muse whose flight
Has bravely reach't and soar'd above thy height: 20
Now shalt thou stand though sword, or time, or fire,
Or zeal more fierce than they, thy fall conspire,
Secure, whilst thee the best of Poets sings,
Preserv'd from ruine by the best of Kings.
Under his proud survey the City lies, 25
And like a mist beneath a hill doth rise;
Whose state and wealth the business and the crowd,
Seems at this distance but a darker cloud:
And is to him who rightly things esteems,
No other in effect than what it seems: 30
Where, with like hast, though several ways, they run
Some to undo, and some to be undone;
While luxury, and wealth, like war and peace,
Are each the others ruine, and increase;
As Rivers lost in Seas some secret vein 35
Thence reconveighs, there to be lost again.
Oh happiness of sweet retir'd content!
To be at once secure, and innocent.
Windsor the next (where *Mars* with *Venus* dwells,
Beauty with strength) above the Valley swells 40

15. ***that sacred pile:*** St. Paul's Cathedral (which was, despite the prediction in line 21, subsequently destroyed in the Great Fire of 1666).

19. ***such a Muse:*** Waller's, in his poem "Upon His Majesty's Repairing of Paul's."

Into my eye, and doth it self present
With such an easie and unforc't ascent,
That no stupendious precipice denies
Access, no horror turns away our eyes:
But such a Rise, as doth at once invite 45
A pleasure, and a reverence from the sight.
Thy mighty Masters Embleme, in whose face
Sate meekness, heightned with Majestick Grace
Such seems thy gentle height, made only proud
To be the basis of that pompous load, 50
Than which, a nobler weight no Mountain bears,
But *Atlas* only that supports the Sphears.
When Natures hand this ground did thus advance,
'Twas guided by a wiser power than Chance;
Mark't out for such a use, as if 'twere meant 55
T' invite the builder, and his choice prevent.
Nor can we call it choice, when what we chuse,
Folly, or blindness only could refuse.
A Crown of such Majestick towrs doth Grace
The Gods great Mother, when her heavenly race 60
Do homage to her, yet she cannot boast
Amongst that numerous, and Celestial host,
More *Hero's* than can *Windsor,* nor doth Fames
Immortal book record more noble names.
Not to look back so far, to whom this Isle 65
Owes the first Glory of so brave a pile,
Whether to *Cæsar, Albanact,* or *Brute,*
The Brittish *Arthur,* or the Danish *Knute,*
(Though this of old no less contest did move,
Than when for *Homers* birth seven Cities strove) 70
(Like him in birth, thou should'st be like in fame,
As thine his fate, if mine had been his Flame)
But whosoere it was, Nature design'd

---

50. *that pompous load:* Windsor Castle.
56. *prevent:* anticipate.
60. *The Gods great Mother:* the Roman goddess Cybele; Denham in the 1642 version of the poem had referred to her by name.
67. *Brute:* Brut, the grandson of Aeneas and legendary founder of London. *Albanact* was his son.

First a brave place, and then as brave a mind.
Not to recount those several Kings, to whom 75
It gave a Cradle, or to whom a Tombe,
But thee (great *Edward*) and thy greater son,
(The lillies which his Father wore, he won)
And thy *Bellona,* who the Consort came
Not only to thy Bed, but to thy Fame, 80
She to thy Triumph led one Captive King,
And brought that son, which did the second bring.
Then didst thou found that Order (whither love
Or victory thy Royal thoughts did move)
Each was a noble cause, and nothing less, 85
Than the design, has been the great success:
Which forraign Kings, and Emperors esteem
The second honour to their Diadem.
Had thy great Destiny but given thee skill,
To know as well, as power to act her will, 90
That from those Kings, who then thy captives were,
In after-times should spring a Royal pair
Who should possess all that thy mighty power,
Or thy desires more mighty, did devour;
To whom their better Fate reserves what ere 95
The Victor hopes for, or the Vanquisht fear;
That bloud, which thou and thy great Grandsire shed,
And all that since these sister Nations bled,
Had been unspilt, had happy *Edward* known
That all the bloud he spilt, had been his own. 100
When he that Patron chose, in whom are joyn'd
Souldier and Martyr, and his arms confin'd

---

77. *great Edward:* Edward III; his son was the storied Black Prince.
79. *Bellona:* the Roman war goddess. The reference is to Edward III's queen Phillippa.
81. *one Captive King:* King David II of Scotland, captured in battle, 1346.
82. *the second:* King John II of France whom the Black Prince captured at Poitiers, 1356.
83. *that Order:* the Order of the Garter.
92. *a Royal pair:* Charles I and his consort Henrietta Maria.
101. *that Patron:* St. George.

Within the Azure Circle, he did seem
But to foretell, and prophesie of him,
Who to his Realms that Azure round hath joyn'd, 105
Which Nature for their bound at first design'd.
That bound, which to the Worlds extreamest ends,
Endless it self, its liquid arms extends;
Nor doth he need those Emblemes which we paint,
But is himself the Souldier and the Saint. 110
Here should my wonder dwell, & here my praise,
But my fixt thoughts my wandring eye betrays,
Viewing a neighbouring hill, whose top of late
A Chappel crown'd, till in the Common Fate,
The adjoyning Abby fell: (may no such storm 115
Fall on our times, where ruine must reform.)
Tell me (my Muse) what monstrous dire offence,
What crime could any Christian King incense
To such a rage? Was't Luxury, or Lust?
Was he so temperate, so chast, so just? 120
Were these their crimes? They were his own much more:
But wealth is Crime enough to him that's poor,
Who having spent the Treasures of his Crown,
Condemns their Luxury to feed his own.
And yet this Act, to varnish o're the shame 125
Of sacriledge, must bear devotions name.
No Crime so bold, but would be understood
A real, or at least a seeming good.
Who fears not to do ill, yet fears the Name,
And free from Conscience, is a slave to Fame. 130
Thus he the Church at once protects, & spoils:
But Princes swords are sharper than their stiles.
And thus to th' ages past he makes amends,

103. *Azure Circle:* the blue garter which encircles the red cross of St. George on the star worn by Knights of the Garter.

105–106. When the crowns of England and Scotland were united, the one king's realm was for the first time completely surrounded by the sea.

113. *a neighbouring hill:* St. Anne's hill.

115. *Abby:* Chertsey Abbey, despoiled by Henry VIII.

131. *protects:* by writing a book against Luther, Henry VIII won from the Pope the title of "Defender of the Faith."

Their Charity destroys, their Faith defends.
Then did Religion in a lazy Cell, 135
In empty, airy contemplations dwell;
And like the block, unmoved lay: but ours,
As much too active, like the stork devours.
Is there no temperate Region can be known,
Betwixt their Frigid, and our Torrid Zone? 140
Could we not wake from that Lethargick dream,
But to be restless in a worse extream?
And for that Lethargy was there no cure,
But to be cast into a Calenture?
Can knowledge have no bound, but must advance 145
So far, to make us wish for ignorance?
And rather in the dark to grope our way,
Than led by a false guide to erre by day?
Who sees these dismal heaps, but would demand
What barbarous Invader sackt the land? 150
But when he hears, no Goth, no Turk did bring
This desolation, but a Christian King;
When nothing, but the Name of Zeal, appears
'Twixt our best actions and the worst of theirs,
What does he think our Sacriledge would spare, 155
When such th' effects of our devotions are?
Parting from thence 'twixt anger, shame, & fear,
Those for whats past, & this for whats too near:
My eye descending from the Hill, surveys
Where *Thames* amongst the wanton vallies strays. 160
Thames, the most lov'd of all the Oceans sons,
By his old Sire to his embraces runs,
Hasting to pay his tribute to the Sea,
Like mortal life to meet Eternity.
Though with those streams he no resemblance hold, 165
Whose foam is Amber, and their Gravel Gold;
His genuine, and less guilty wealth t' explore,
Search not his bottom, but survey his shore;
Ore which he kindly spreads his spacious wing,
And hatches plenty for th' ensuing Spring. 170

---

144. *Calenture:* fever.

Nor then destroys it with too fond a stay,
Like Mothers which their Infants overlay.
Nor with a sudden and impetuous wave,
Like profuse Kings, resumes the wealth he gave.
No unexpected inundations spoyl 175
The mowers hopes, nor mock the plowmans toyl:
But God-like his unwearied Bounty flows;
First loves to do, then loves the Good he does.
Nor are his Blessings to his banks confin'd,
But free, and common, as the Sea or Wind; 180
When he to boast, or to disperse his stores
Full of the tributes of his grateful shores,
Visits the world, and in his flying towers
Brings home to us, and makes both *Indies* ours;
Finds wealth where 'tis, bestows it where it wants 185
Cities in deserts, woods in Cities plants.
So that to us no thing, no place is strange,
While his fair bosom is the worlds exchange.
O could I flow like thee, and make thy stream
My great example, as it is my theme! 190
Though deep, yet clear, though gentle, yet not dull,
Strong without rage, without ore-flowing full.
Heaven her *Eridanus* no more shall boast,
Whose Fame in thine, like lesser Currents lost,
Thy Nobler streams shall visit *Jove's* aboads, 195
To shine amongst the Stars, and bath the Gods.
Here Nature, whether more intent to please
Us or her self, with strange varieties,
(For things of wonder give no less delight
To the wise Maker's, than beholders sight. 200
Though these delights from several causes move
For so our children, thus our friends we love)
Wisely she knew, the harmony of things,
As well as that of sounds, from discords springs.
Such was the discord, which did first disperse 205
Form, order, beauty through the Universe;
While driness moysture, coldness heat resists,

183. *his flying towers:* the trade ships.
193. *Eridanus:* a constellation, popularly called "The River."

All that we have, and that we are, subsists.
While the steep horrid roughness of the Wood
Strives with the gentle calmness of the flood. 210
Such huge extreams when Nature doth unite,
Wonder from thence results, from thence delight.
The stream is so transparent, pure, and clear,
That had the self-enamour'd youth gaz'd here,
So fatally deceiv'd he had not been, 215
While he the bottom, not his face had seen.
But his proud head the aery Mountain hides
Among the Clouds; his shoulders, and his sides
A shady mantle cloaths; his curled brows
Frown on the gentle stream, which calmly flows, 220
While winds and storms his lofty forehead beat:
The common fate of all that's high or great.
Low at his foot a spacious plain is plac't,
Between the mountain and the stream embrac't:
Which shade and shelter from the Hill derives, 225
While the kind river wealth and beauty gives;
And in the mixture of all these appears
Variety, which all the rest indears.
This scene had some bold Greek, or Brittish Bard
Beheld of old, what stories had we heard, 230
Of Fairies, Satyrs, and the Nymphs their Dames,
Their feasts, their revels, & their amorous flames:
'Tis still the same, although their aery shape
All but a quick Poetick sight escape.
There *Faunus* and *Sylvanus* keep their Courts, 235
And thither all the horned hoast resorts,
To graze the ranker mead, that noble heard
On whose sublime and shady fronts is rear'd
Natures great Master-piece; to shew how soon
Great things are made, but sooner are undone. 240
Here have I seen the King, when great affairs
Give leave to slacken, and unbend his cares,
Attended to the Chase by all the flower

---

214. *the self-enamour'd youth:* Narcissus.

Of youth, whose hopes a Nobler prey devour:
Pleasure with Praise, & danger, they would buy, 245
And wish a foe that would not only fly.
The stagg now conscious of his fatal Growth,
At once indulgent to his fear and sloth,
To some dark covert his retreat had made,
Where nor mans eye, nor heavens should invade 250
His soft repose; when th' unexpected sound
Of dogs, and men, his wakeful ear doth wound.
Rouz'd with the noise, he scarce believes his ear,
Willing to think th' illusions of his fear
Had given this false Alarm, but straight his view 255
Confirms, that more than all he fears is true.
Betray'd in all his strengths, the wood beset,
All instruments, all Arts of ruine met;
He calls to mind his strength, and then his speed,
His winged heels, and then his armed head; 260
With these t' avoid, with that his Fate to meet:
But fear prevails, and bids him trust his feet.
So fast he flyes, that his reviewing eye
Has lost the chasers, and his ear the cry;
Exulting, till he finds, their Nobler sense 265
Their disproportion'd speed does recompense.
Then curses his conspiring feet, whose scent
Betrays that safety which their swiftness lent.
Then tries his friends, among the baser herd,
Where he so lately was obey'd, and fear'd, 270
His safety seeks: the herd, unkindly wise,
Or chases him from thence, or from him flies.
Like a declining States-man, left forlorn
To his friends pity, and pursuers scorn,
With shame remembers, while himself was one 275
Of the same herd, himself the same had done.
Thence to the coverts, & the conscious Groves,
The scenes of his past triumphs, and his loves;
Sadly surveying where he rang'd alone
Prince of the soyl, and all the herd his own; 280
And like a bold Knight Errant did proclaim

Combat to all, and bore away the Dame;
And taught the woods to eccho to the stream
His dreadful challenge, and his clashing beam.
Yet faintly now declines the fatal strife; 285
So much his love was dearer than his life.
Now every leaf, and every moving breath
Presents a foe, and every foe a death.
Wearied, forsaken, and pursu'd, at last
All safety in despair of safety plac'd, 290
Courage he thence resumes, resolv'd to bear
All their assaults, since 'tis in vain to fear.
And now too late he wishes for the fight
That strength he wasted in Ignoble flight:
But when he sees the eager chase renew'd, 295
Himself by dogs, the dogs by men pursu'd:
He straight revokes his bold resolve, and more
Repents his courage, than his fear before;
Finds that uncertain waies unsafest are,
And Doubt a greater mischief than Despair. 300
Then to the stream, when neither friends, nor force,
Nor speed, nor Art avail, he shapes his course;
Thinks not their rage so desperate t' assay
An Element more merciless than they.
But fearless they pursue, nor can the floud 305
Quench their dire thirst; alas, they thirst for bloud.
So towards a Ship the oarefin'd Gallies ply,
Which wanting Sea to ride, or wind to fly,
Stands but to fall reveng'd on those that dare
Tempt the last fury of extream despair. 310
So fares the Stagg among th' enraged Hounds,
Repels their force, and wounds returns for wounds.
And as a Hero, whom his baser foes
In troops surround, now these assails, now those,
Though prodigal of life, disdains to die 315
By common hands; but if he can descry
Some nobler foes approach, to him he calls,
And begs his Fate, and then contented falls.
So when the King a mortal shaft lets fly

From his unerring hand, then glad to dy, 320
Proud of the wound, to it resigns his bloud,
And stains the Crystal with a Purple floud.
This a more Innocent, and happy chase,
Than when of old, but in the self-same place,
Fair liberty pursu'd, and meant a Prey 325
To lawless power, here turn'd, and stood at bay.
When in that remedy all hope was plac't
Which was, or should have been at least, the last.
Here was that Charter seal'd, wherein the Crown
All marks of Arbitrary power lays down: 330
Tyrant and slave, those names of hate and fear,
The happier stile of King and Subject bear:
Happy, when both to the same Center move,
When Kings give liberty, and Subjects love.
Therefore not long in force this Charter stood; 335
Wanting that seal, it must be seal'd in bloud.
The Subjects arm'd, the more their Princes gave,
Th' advantage only took the more to crave.
Till Kings by giving, give themselves away,
And even that power, that should deny, betray. 340
"Who gives constrain'd, but his own fear reviles
"Not thank't, but scorn'd; nor are they gifts, but spoils.
Thus Kings, by grasping more than they could hold,
First made their Subjects by oppression bold:
And popular sway, by forcing Kings to give 345
More than was fit for Subjects to receive,
Ran to the same extreams; and one excess
Made both, by striving to be greater, less.
When a calm River rais'd with sudden rains,
Or Snows dissolv'd, oreflows th' adjoyning Plains, 350
The Husbandmen with high-rais'd banks secure
Their greedy hopes, and this he can endure.
But if with Bays and Dams they strive to force
His channel to a new, or narrow course;

---

324. *the self-same place:* Runnymede, where King John was compelled to sign the Magna Carta.

No longer then within his banks he dwells, 355
First to a Torrent, then a Deluge swells:
Stronger, and fiercer by restraint he roars,
And knows no bound, but makes his power his shores.

John Cleveland

(1613–1658)

"CLEVELANDISM," wrote Dryden, ". . . wresting and torturing a word into another meaning." Thus "a Royaller Exchange" is a transformation richer than the Royal Exchange in London, "exchange" having lost its monetary sense, and "royal," its regal. Shakespeare's

> Full fadom five thy Father lies,
> Of his bones are Corall made:
> Those are pearles that were his eies,
> Nothing of him that doth fade,
> But doth suffer a Sea-change
> Into something rich, & strange:

presumably lies behind six lines of Cleveland's elegy on the drowned Edward King; but Cleveland found it necessary to make every line the focus of ingenious attention:

> We'l dive no more for pearls, the hope to see
> Thy sacred relikes of Mortality
> Shall welcome storms, and make the sea-man prize
> His shipwrack now more than his Merchandize.
> He shall embrace the waves, and to thy tomb
> As to a *Royaller Exchange* shall come.

The trick is as easy to diagnose as it is tortuous to execute: unflagging hyperbole, and whenever possible a tight knot of epigrammatic opportunism. It would deserve no notice had it not been so immensely popular: some twenty editions made Cleveland the most purchased and most imitated poet of the midcentury. This sort of disorganized cleverness was to pass, within thirty years of the publication of Donne's poems, for poetry in the manner of Donne. And it was no isolated freak: it attracted disciples. For a determining number of technically literate people (chiefly university people) the operation of wit had become a game of words, cleverer because more flashily complicated, and easier because disengaged from sustained emotional discipline, than anything of Donne's generation.

Cleveland was a Cambridge man, a satirical propagandist for the king's side, and for a time a political prisoner. He died two years before the Restoration.

TEXT: There is an unsatisfactory edition by J. Berdan (New Haven, Conn., 1911). The following selections are from *Poems, 1651* as transcribed by R. C. Bald, and *Poems, 1653,* as transcribed by Helen Gardner.

Mark Anthony

When as the Nightingale chanted her Vespers,
And the wild Forrester couch'd on the ground,
Venus invited me in the evening whispers,
Unto a fragrant field with Roses crown'd;
  Where she before had sent 5
  My wishes complement,
  Unto my hearts content,
  Playd with me on the Green.
    Never Mark Anthony
    Dallied more wantonly 10
    With the fair Egyptian Queen.

First on her cherry cheeks I mine eys feasted;
Thence fear of surfeiting made me retire:
Next on her warm lips, which when I tasted,
My duller spirits made active as fire. 15
  Then we began to dart
  Each at anothers heart,
  Arrows that knew no smart;
  Sweet lips and smiles between.
    Never Mark, &c. 20

Wanting a glasse to plate her amber tresses,
Which like a bracelet rich decked mine arm,

Gaudier than *Juno* wears when as she graces
Jove with embraces more stately than warm.
  Then did she peep in mine 25
  Eys humour Christalline;
  I in her eys was seen,
  As if we one had been.
    Never Mark, &c.

Mistical Grammer of amorous glances, 30
Feeling of Pulses the Physick of Love,
Rhetoricall courtings, and Musicall dances;
Numbring of kisses Arithmetic prove.
  Eys like Astronomy,
  Streight limb'd Geometry: 35
  In her hearts ingeny
  Our wits are sharp and keen.
    Never Mark, &c.

This most anthologized of Cleveland poems is very possibly not his at all.

On the Memory of Mr. Edward King, Drown'd in the Irish Seas

I like not tears in tune, nor do I prize
His artificial grief who scans his eys,
Mine weep down pious beads, but why should I
Confine them to the Muses Rosary?
I am no Poet here; my pen's the spout 5
Where the Rain-water of mine eys runs out
In pity of that Name, whose fate we see
Thus copi'd out in griefs Hydrography:
The Muses are not Mair-maids, though upon
His death the Ocean might turn *Helicon*. 10

Cleveland's contribution to the occasion for which Milton wrote *Lycidas*.

The Sea's too rough for verse; who rimes upon't
With *Xerxes* strives to fetter the *Hellespont.*
My tears will keep no channell, know no laws
To guide their streams; but (like the waves their cause)
Run with disturbance, till they swallow me 15
As a description of his misery.
But can his spacious vertue find a grave
Within th'imposthum'd bubble of a wave?
Whose learning if we sound, we must confesse
The sea but shallow, and him bottomlesse. 20
Could not the winds to counter-mand thy death,
With their whole card of lungs redeem thy breath?
Or some new Island in thy rescue peep,
To heave thy resurrection from the deep?
That so the world might see thy safety wrought, 25
With no lesse wonder than thy self was thought.
The famous *Stagirite,* who in his life
Had nature as familiar as his wife,
Bequeath'd his Widow to survive with thee,
Queen Dowager of all Phylosophy: 30
An ominous Legacy, that did portend
Thy fate and Predecessors second end:
Some have affirm'd, that what on earth we find,
The sea can parallel in shape, and kind:
Books, arts, and tongues were wanting, but in thee 35
Neptune hath got an University.
We'l dive no more for pearls, the hope to see
Thy sacred relikes of Mortality
Shall welcome storms, and make the sea-man prize
His shipwrack now more than his Merchandize. 40
He shall embrace the waves, and to thy tomb
As to a *Royaller Exchange* shall come.
What can we now expect? water, and fire;
Both elements our ruine do conspire:

---

12. Xerxes, when the Hellespont had displeased him, gave it 300 lashes and had a pair of fetters cast into it (Herodotus, vii, 35).
22. *card:* the compass, epitomizing every direction from which wind can blow.
27. *Stagirite:* Aristotle.

And that dissolves us, which doth us compound. 45
One *Vatican* was burnt, another drown'd.
We of the Gown our Libraries must tosse,
To understand the greatnesse of our losse,
Be pupills to our grief, and so much grow
In learning, as our sorrows overflow. 50
When we have fil'd the Rundlets of our eys,
We'l issue't forth, and vent such Elegies,
As that our tears shal seem the *Irish* seas,
We floting Islands, living *Hebrides.*

---

46. *Vatican:* here, a synecdoche for a vast library. One such burned at Alexandria, another went to the bottom of the Irish Sea in the person of King.

The Antiplatonick

For shame, thou everlasting Wooer,
Still saying grace, and never falling to her!
Love that's in contemplation plac't,
Is *Venus* drawn but to the wast.
Unlesse your flame confesse its gender, 5
And your Parley cause surrender
Y'are Salamanders of a cold desire
That live untoucht amid the hottest fire.

What though she be a Dame of stone
The Widow of *Pigmalion;* 10
As hard and un-relenting she,
As the new-crusted *Niobe;*
Or what doth more of statue carry,
A Nunne of the Platonick Quarry!
Love melts the rigour which the rocks have bred, 15
A flint will break upon a Feather-bed.

For shame you pretty Female Elves

---

12. *Niobe:* she wept for her fourteen children until she turned to stone.

Cease for to candy up your selves:
No more, you sectaries of the Game,
No more of your calcining flame. 20
Women commence by *Cupids* Dart
As a King hunting dubs a Hart,
Loves votaries inthrall each others soul,
Till both of them live but upon Parole.

Vertue's no more in Woman-kind 25
But the green sicknesse of the mind.
Philosophy, their new delight,
A kind of Char-coal appetite.
There's no Sophistry prevails
Where all-convincing love assails; 30
But the disputing petticoat will warp
As skillfull gamesters are to seeke at sharp.

The souldier, that man of iron,
Whom ribs of Horror all inviron;
That's strung with Wire, instead of Veins, 35
In whose embraces you're in chains,
Let a Magnetick girl appear,
Straight he turns *Cupids* Cuirasseer,
Love storms his lips, and takes the Fortresse in,
For all the Bristled Turn-pikes of his chin. 40

Since Loves Artillery then checks
The brest-works of the firmest sex,
Come let us in affections riot,
Th'are sickly pleasures keep a Diet:
Give me a lover bold and free, 45
Not Eunucht with formality;
Like an Ambassadour that beds a Queen
With the nice Caution of a sword between.

---

18. *candy:* crystallize.
21. *commence:* graduate.
22. *dubs:* ennobles.
32. *gamesters:* fencers.
to seeke at sharp: unskillful at sword play (as distinguished from fencing with foils).

Abraham Cowley

(1618–1667)

It was in the course of a biographical introduction to the works of Abraham Cowley that Dr. Johnson encapsulated, for a subsequent century's derision, "a race of writers that may be termed 'the metaphysical poets.'" "Their thoughts are often new, but seldom natural; . . . the most heterogeneous ideas are yoked by violence together; nature and art are ransacked for illustrations, comparisons, and allusions. . . ." These remarks bring Johnson's system of judgment to bear on a tradition which in health and degeneracy alike had become radically unsympathetic; and Cowley, not Cleveland nor for that matter Donne, was their occasion simply because by 1779 he was the only "metaphysical" still sufficiently current to be included in a shrewd publishers' standard issue of The English Poets.* His style, for one thing, was not like Donne's or Marvell's intimate, but like Dryden's public; he is moved not to meditate on an occasion but to adorn it. His conceits do not develop an argument but illustrate, as from the platform, a proposition, and a proposition first clearly stated:

> In a true piece of *Wit* all things must be,
> Yet all things there *agree*.

His procedures are public also in being susceptible to justification from precedent. It was he who detached the tradition of "strong lines" from Donne's dialectical urgency and yoked it instead to the unchallengeable authority of Pindar, and in so doing inaugurated the dreary series of Odes on which, for the next hundred years, the

* The first edition of Donne's poems was in 1633, the seventh in 1669, but the eighth not until 1719; after that he vanishes for some two centuries into the limbo of multivolume anthologies.

poets who still sought effects of electrifying concentration were to waste their labor. The one man who had the genius to do something viable with an innovation of Cowley's was W. B. Yeats, who took from the poem "On the Death of Mr. William Hervey" the noble stanza and the tone of intimate yet public grief with which he built his celebration of the memory of Major Robert Gregory.

Cowley at fifteen published his first volume of verse, at eighteen entered Cambridge (where he knew Crashaw), and after graduation took up a minor academic career from which, in 1644, his royalist allegiance got him expelled. He spent ten years in exile with the queen, but returned to England before the Commonwealth had run its course to resume a savant's life, joining poetry with work toward the degree of M.D. He became, in due course, a Fellow of the Royal Society, and wrote "A Proposition for the Advancement of Experimental Philosophy," and the society's historian, Bishop Sprat, was his executor and biographer. Sprat said that he had "a firmness and strength of mind that was proof against the Art of Poetry itself," meaning by the art of poetry something giddy; and did not hesitate to commend the affinity of his irregular lines with the movement of prose, "which is certainly the most Useful kind of Writing of all others: for it is the style of all business and conversation:" propositions in which one may now discern unintended ironies.

TEXT: *Poems,* ed. A. R. Waller (Cambridge, 1905).

COMMENT: A. Alvarez, *The School of Donne,* Chap. 7.
Samuel Johnson, "Life of Cowley" (*Lives of the Poets*).

The Motto

Tentanda via est, &c

What shall I do to be for ever known,
And make the *Age to come* my own?

Tentanda via est: beginning of the long passage in Virgil's *Georgics* (III-8ff.) which provided Cowley's precedent, "I must find a way to rise from the ground, and soar in triumph over the heads of men. . . ."

I shall like *Beasts* or *Common People* dy,
  Unless you write my *Elegy;*
Whilst others *Great,* by being *Born* are grown, 5
  Their *Mothers Labour,* not their own.
In this Scale *Gold,* in th'other *Fame* does ly,
  The *weight* of *that,* mounts this so *high.*
These men are *Fortunes Jewels,* moulded bright;
  Brought forth with their own fire and light. 10
If I, her *vulgar stone* for either look;
  Out of *my self* it must be *strook.*
Yet I must on; what sound is't strikes mine ear?
  Sure I *Fames Trumpet* hear.
It sounds like the *last Trumpet;* for it can 15
  Raise up the *bur'ied Man.*
Unpast *Alpes* stop me, but I'll cut through all,
  And march, the *Muses Hannibal.*
Hence all the *flattering vanities* that lay
  Nets of *Roses* in the way. 20
Hence the desire of *Honors,* or *Estate;*
  And all, that is not above *Fate.*
Hence *Love* himself, that *Tyrant* of my days,
  Which intercepts my coming praise.
Come my best *Friends,* my *Books,* and lead me on; 25
  'Tis time that I were gon.
Welcome, great *Stagirite,* and teach me now
  All I was born to know.
Thy *Scholars* vict'ries thou dost far out-do;
  He conquer'd th' *Earth,* the whole *World you.* 30
Welcome learn'd *Cicero,* whose blest *Tongue* and *Wit*
  Preserves *Romes greatness yet.*
Thou art the *first* of *Ora'tors;* only he
  Who best can *praise Thee, next* must be.
Welcome the *Mantu'an Swan, Virgil* the *Wise,* 35
  Whose verse *walks highest,* but not flies.
Who brought green *Poesie* to her perfect Age;
  And made that *Art* which was a *Rage.*
Tell me, ye mighty *Three,* what shall I do

27. *Stagirite:* Aristotle.
29. *Thy Scholar:* Alexander the Great, who had Aristotle for tutor.

To be like one of you. 40
But you have climb'd the *Mountains* top, there sit
On the calm flour'ishing head of it,
And whilst with wearied steps we upward go,
See *Us,* and *Clouds* below.

Ode. of Wit

Tell me, O tell, what kind of thing is *Wit,*
Thou who *Master* art of it.
For the *First matter* loves *Variety* less;
Less *Women* lov't, either in *Love* or *Dress.*
A thousand different shapes it bears, 5
Comely in thousand shapes appears.
Yonder we saw it plain; and here 'tis now,
Like *Spirits* in *a Place,* we know not *How.*

London that vents of *false Ware* so much store,
In no *Ware* deceives us more. 10
For men led by the *Colour,* and the *Shape,*
Like *Zeuxes Birds* fly to the painted *Grape*;
Some things do through our Judgment pass
As through a *Multiplying Glass.*
And sometimes, if the *Object* be too far, 15
We take a *Falling Meteor* for a *Star.*

Hence 'tis a *Wit* that greatest *word* of *Fame*
Grows such a common Name,
And *Wits* by our *Creation* they become,
Just so, as *Tit'lar Bishops* made at *Rome.* 20
'Tis not a *Tale,* 'tis not a *Jest*
Admir'd with *Laughter* at a feast,

---

2. *Thou:* the addressee's identity is not known.
3. *First matter:* scholastic term for that from which everything else was made.
12. *Zeuxis* painted grapes so realistically that passing birds pecked at them.
14. *Multiplying:* magnifying.
20. Titular bishops have rank but no see.

Nor florid *Talk* which can that *Title* gain;
The *Proofs* of *Wit* for ever must remain.

'Tis not to force some lifeless *Verses* meet 25
With their five gowty feet.
All ev'ry where, like *Mans*, must be the *Soul*,
And *Reason* the *Inferior Powers* controul.
Such were the *Numbers* which could call
The *Stones* into the *Theban* wall. 30
Such *Miracles* are ceast; and now we see
No *Towns* or *Houses* rais'd by *Poetrie*.

Yet 'tis not to adorn, and gild each part;
That shows more *Cost*, than *Art*.
Jewels at *Nose* and *Lips* but ill appear; 35
Rather than *all things Wit*, let *none* be there.
Several *Lights* will not be seen,
If there be nothing else between.
Men doubt, because they stand so thick i'th'skie,
If those be *Stars* which paint the *Galaxie*. 40

'Tis not when two like words make up one noise;
Jests for *Dutch Men*, and *English Boys*.
In which who finds out *Wit*, the same may see
In *An'grams* and *Acrostiques Poetrie*.
Much less can that have any place 45
At which a *Virgin* hides her face,
Such *Dross* and *Fire* must purge away; 'tis just
The *Author blush*, there where the *Reader* must.

'Tis not such *Lines* as almost crack the *Stage*
When *Bajazet* begins to rage. 50
Nor a tall *Meta'phor* in the *Bombast way*,
Nor the dry chips of short lung'd *Seneca*.
Nor upon all things to obtrude,
And force some odd *Similitude*.

29–30. Amphion built Thebes with music.
50. Bajazet: ranting conqueror in Marlowe's *Tamburlaine*.

What is it then, which like the *Power Divine* 55
We only can by *Negatives* define?

In a true piece of *Wit* all things must be,
Yet all things there *agree*.
As in the *Ark*, joyn'd without force or strife,
All *Creatures* dwelt; all *Creatures* that had *Life*. 60
Or as the *Primitive Forms* of all
(If we compare great things with small)
Which without *Discord* or *Confusion* lie,
In that strange *Mirror* of the *Deitie*.

But *Love* that moulds *One Man* up out of *Two*, 65
Makes me forget and injure you.
I took *you* for *my self* sure when I thought
That you in any thing were to be *Taught*.
Correct my error with thy Pen;
And if any ask me then, 70
What thing right *Wit*, and height of *Genius* is,
I'll onely shew your *Lines*, and says, *'Tis This*.

On the Death of Mr. William Hervey

Immodicis brevis est aetas, et rara Senectus. Mart.

It was a dismal, and a fearful night,
Scarce could the Morn drive on th'unwilling Light,
When *Sleep, Deaths Image*, left my troubled brest,
By something *liker Death* possest.
My eyes with Tears did uncommanded flow, 5
And on my Soul hung the dull weight
Of some *Intolerable Fate*.
What Bell was that? Ah me! Too much I know.

My sweet *Companion*, and my gentle *Peere*,
Why hast thou left me thus unkindly here, 10

Hervey, Cowley's college friend, died in 1642.

Thy *end* for ever, and my *Life* to moan;
  O thou hast left me all alone!
Thy *Soul and Body* when *Deaths Agonie*
  Besieg'd around thy noble heart,
  Did not with more reluctance part 15
Then *I*, my dearest *Friend*, do part from *Thee*.

My dearest *Friend*, would I had dy'd for thee!
Life and this *World* henceforth will tedious bee.
Nor shall I know hereafter what to do
  If once my *Griefs* prove *tedious* too. 20
Silent and sad I walk about all day,
  As sullen *Ghosts* stalk speechless by
  Where their hid *Treasures* ly;
Alas, my *Treasure's* gone, why do I stay?

He was my *Friend*, the truest *Friend* on earth; 25
A strong and mighty *Influence* joyn'd our *Birth*.
Nor did we envy the most sounding *Name*
  By *Friendship* giv'n of old to *Fame*.
None but his *Brethren* he, and *Sisters* knew,
  Whom the kind youth preferr'd to Me; 30
  And ev'n in that we did agree,
For much above my self I lov'd them too.

Say, for you saw us, ye immortal *Lights*,
How oft unweari'd have we spent the Nights?
Till the *Ledæan Stars* so fam'd for *Love*, 35
  Wondred at us from above.
We spent them not in toys, in lusts, or wine;
  But search of deep *Philosophy*.
  Wit, *Eloquence*, and *Poetry*,
Arts which I lov'd, for they, my *Friend*, were *Thine*. 40

Ye fields of *Cambridge*, our dear *Cambridge*, say,
Have ye not seen us walking every day?
Was there a *Tree* about which did not know
  The *Love* betwixt us two?

35. *Ledaean stars:* Leda's sons, the twins Castor and Pollux.

Henceforth, ye gentle *Trees,* for ever fade; 45
  Or your sad branches thicker joyn,
  And into darksome shades combine,
Dark as the *Grave* wherein my *Friend* is laid.

Henceforth no learned *Youths* beneath you sing,
Till all the tuneful *Birds* to'your boughs they bring; 50
No tuneful *Birds* play with their wonted chear,
  And call the learned *Youths* to hear,
No whistling *Winds* through the glad branches fly,
  But all with sad solemnitie,
  Mute and unmoved be, 55
Mute as the *Grave* wherein my *Friend* does ly.

To him my *Muse* made haste with every strain
Whilst it was new, and *warm* yet from the *Brain.*
He lov'd my worthless *Rhimes,* and like a Friend
  Would find out something to *commend.* 60
Hence now, my *Muse,* thou canst not me delight;
  Be this my latest verse
  With which I now adorn his *Herse,*
And this my *Grief,* without *thy* help shall write.

Had I a wreath of *Bays* about my brow, 65
I should contemn that flourishing honor now,
Condemn it to the *Fire,* and joy to hear
  It rage and crackle there.
Instead of *Bays,* crown with sad *Cypress* me;
  Cypress which *Tombs* does beautifie; 70
  Not *Phœbus* griev'd so much as I
For him, who first was made that mournful *Tree.*

Large was his *Soul;* as large a *Soul* as ere
Submitted to *inform* a *Body* here.
High as the Place 'twas shortly'in *Heav'n* to have, 75
  But low, and humble as his *Grave.*
So *high* that all the *Virtues* there did come

---

72. ***him:*** Cyparissus, whom Apollo loved. He was turned into a cypress.

As to their chiefest seat
Conspicuous, and great;
So *low* that for *Me* too it made a room. 80

He scorn'd this busie world below, and all
That we, *Mistaken Mortals,* Pleasure call;
Was fill'd with inn'ocent *Gallantry* and *Truth,*
Triumphant ore the sins of *Youth.*
He like the *Stars,* to which he now is gone, 85
That shine with beams like *Flame,*
Yet burn not with the same,
Had all the *Light* of *Youth,* of the *Fire* none.

Knowledge he only sought, and so soon caught,
As if for him *Knowledge* had rather *sought.* 90
Nor did more *Learning* ever crowded lie
In such a short *Mortalitie.*
When ere the skilful *Youth* discourst or writ,
Still did the *Notions* throng
About his eloquent Tongue, 95
Nor could his *Ink* flow faster than his *Wit.*

So strong a *Wit* did *Nature* to him frame,
As all things but his *Judgement* overcame;
His *Judgement* like the heav'nly *Moon* did show,
Temp'ring that mighty *Sea* below. 100
Oh had he liv'd in *Learnings World,* what bound
Would have been able to controul
His over-powering Soul?
We'have lost in him *Arts* that not yet are *found.*

His *Mirth* was the pure *Spirits* of various Wit, 105
Yet never did his *God* or *Friends* forget.
And when deep talk and wisdom came in view,
Retir'd and gave to them their due:
For the rich help of *Books* he always took,
Though his own searching mind before 110
Was so with *Notions* written ore
As if wise *Nature* had made that her *Book.*

So many *Virtues* joyn'd in him, as we
Can scarce pick here and there in *Historie.*
More than old *Writers Practice* ere could reach, 115
  As much as they could ever *teach.*
These did *Religion, Queen* of Virtues sway,
  And all their sacred *Motions* steare,
  Just like the First and *Highest Sphere*
Which wheels about, and turns all *Heav'n* one way. 120

With as much Zeal, Devotion, Pietie,
He always *Liv'd,* as other Saints do *Dye.*
Still with his soul severe account he kept,
  Weeping all *Debts* out ere he slept.
Then down in peace and innocence he lay, 125
  Like the *Suns* laborious light,
  Which still in *Water* sets at Night,
Unsullied with his *Journey* of the *Day.*

Wondrous young Man, why wert thou made so good,
To be snatcht hence ere better *understood?* 130
Snatcht before half of thee enough was seen!
  Thou Ripe, and yet thy *Life* but *Green!*
Nor could thy Friends take their last sad Farewel,
  But Danger and *Infectious Death*
  Malitiously seiz'd on that Breath 135
Where *Life, Spirit, Pleasure* always us'd to dwell.

But happy Thou, ta'ne from this frantick age,
Where *Igno'rance* and *Hypocrisie* does rage!
A fitter *time* for Heav'n no soul ere chose,
  The place now onely free from those. 140
There 'mong the *Blest* thou dost for ever shine,
  And wheresoere thou casts thy view
  Upon that white and radiant crew,
See'st not a *Soul* cloath'd with more *Light* than *Thine.*

And if the glorious *Saints* cease not to know 145
Their wretched Friends who *fight* with *Life* below;
The Flame to *Me* does still the same abide,

Onely more pure and rarifi'd.
There whilst immortal Hymns thou dost reherse,
Thou dost with holy pity see 150
Our dull and earthly *Poesie,*
Where *Grief* and *Mis'ery* can be join'd with *Verse.*

On the Death of Mr. *Crashaw*

Poet and *Saint!* to thee alone are given
The two most sacred *Names* of *Earth* and *Heaven.*
The hard and rarest *Union* which can be
Next that of *Godhead* with *Humanitie.*
Long did the *Muses* banisht *Slaves* abide, 5
And built vain *Pyramids* to mortal pride;
Like *Moses* Thou (though Spells and Charms withstand)
Hast brought them nobly home back to their *Holy Land.*
Ah wretched *We, Poets* of *Earth!* but *Thou*
Wert *Living* the same *Poet* which thou'rt *Now.* 10
Whilst *Angels* sing to thee their ayres divine,
And joy in an applause so great as *thine.*
Equal society with them to hold,
Thou need'st not make *new Songs,* but say the *Old.*
And they (kind Spirits!) shall all rejoyce to see 15
How little less than *They, Exalted Man* may be.
Still the old *Heathen Gods* in *Numbers* dwell,
The *Heav'enliest* thing on Earth still keeps up *Hell.*
Nor have we yet quite purg'd the *Christian Land;*
Still *Idols* here, like *Calves* at *Bethel* stand. 20
And though *Pans Death* long since all *Oracles* broke,
Yet still in Rhyme the *Fiend Apollo* spoke:
Nay with the worst of Heathen dotage We
(Vain men!) the *Monster Woman Deifie;*
Find *Stars,* and tye our *Fates* there in a *Face,* 25
And *Paradise* in them by whom we *lost* it, place.
What different faults corrupt our *Muses* thus?
Wanton as *Girles,* as *old Wives, Fabulous!*
Thy spotless *Muse,* like *Mary,* did contain

The boundless *Godhead;* she did well disdain 30
That her *eternal Verse* employ'd should be
On a less subject than *Eternitie;*
And for a sacred *Mistress* scorn'd to take,
But her whom *God* himself scorn'd not his *Spouse* to make.
It (in a kind) *her Miracle* did do; 35
A fruitful *Mother* was, and *Virgin* too.
  * How well (blest Swan) did Fate contrive thy death;
And made thee render up thy tuneful breath
In thy great *Mistress* Arms? thou most divine
And richest *Off'ering* of *Loretto's Shrine!* 40
Where like some holy *Sacrifice* t'expire,
A *Fever* burns thee, and *Love* lights the *Fire.*
Angels (they say) brought the fam'ed *Chappel* there,
And bore the sacred Load in Triumph through the air.
'Tis surer much they brought thee there, and *They,* 45
And *Thou,* their charge, went *singing* all the way.
  Pardon, my *Mother Church,* if I consent
That *Angels* led him when from thee he went,
For even in *Error* sure no *Danger* is
When joyn'd with so much *Piety* as *His.* 50
Ah, mighty *God,* with shame I speak't, and grief;
Ah that our greatest *Faults* were in *Belief!*
And our weak *Reason* were ev'en weaker yet,
Rather than thus our *Wills* too strong for it.
His *Faith* perhaps in some nice Tenents might 55
Be wrong; his *Life,* I'm sure, was *in the right.*
And I my self a *Catholick* will be,
So far at least, great *Saint,* to *Pray* to thee.
  Hail, *Bard Triumphant!* and some care bestow
On *us,* the *Poets Militant* Below! 60
Oppos'ed by our old En'emy, adverse *Chance,*
Attacqu'ed by *Envy,* and by *Ignorance,*
Enchain'd by *Beauty,* tortur'd by *Desires,*

---

* M. *Crashaw* died of a Fever at *Loretto,* being newly chosen Canon of that Church. [Cowley's note]

55. *nice:* finicky. *Tenents:* tenets.

59–60. The language is that of the church militant (the living) invoking the aid of the church triumphant (the sainted dead).

Expos'd by *Tyrant-Love* to savage *Beasts* and *Fires.*
Thou from low earth in nobler *Flames* didst rise, 65
And like *Elijah,* mount *Alive* the skies.
Elisha-like (but with a wish much less,
More fit thy *Greatness,* and my *Littleness*)
Lo here I beg (I whom thou once didst prove
So humble to *Esteem,* so Good to *Love*) 70
Not that thy *Spirit* might on me *Doubled* be,
I ask but *Half* thy mighty *Spirit* for Me.
And when my *Muse* soars with so strong a Wing,
'Twill learn of things *Divine,* and first of *Thee* to sing.

Drinking

The thirsty *Earth* soaks up the *Rain,*
And drinks, and gapes for drink again.
The *Plants* suck in the *Earth,* and are
With constant drinking fresh and fair.
The *Sea* it self, which one would think 5
Should have but little need of *Drink,*
Drinks ten thousand *Rivers* up,
So fill'd that they or'eflow the *Cup.*
The busie *Sun* (and one would guess
By's drunken fiery face no less) 10
Drinks up the *Sea,* and when h'as done,
The *Moon* and *Stars* drink up the *Sun.*
They drink and dance by their own light,
They drink and revel all the night.
Nothing in *Nature*'s *Sober* found, 15
But an eternal *Health* goes round.
Fill up the *Bowl* then, fill it high,
Fill all the *Glasses* there, for why
Should every creature drink but *I,*
Why, *Man* of *Morals,* tell me why? 20

This and the next two poems are imitated from Anacreon.

The Epicure

Fill the *Bowl* with rosie Wine,
Around our temples *Roses* twine.
And let us chearfully awhile,
Like the *Wine* and *Roses* smile.
Crown'd with Roses we contemn 5
Gyge's wealthy *Diadem*.
To day is *Ours;* what do we fear?
To day is *Ours;* we have it here.
Let's treat it kindly, that it may
Wish, at least, with us to stay. 10
Let's banish *Business,* banish *Sorrow;*
To the *Gods* belongs *To morrow*.

Another

Underneath this Myrtle shade,
On flowry beds supinely laid,
With od'orous Oyls my head o're-flowing,
And around it Roses growing,
What should I do but drink away 5
The *Heat,* and *troubles* of the Day?
In this more than *Kingly* state,
Love himself shall on me wait.
Fill to me, *Love,* nay fill it up;
And mingled cast into the Cup, 10
Wit, and *Mirth,* and noble *Fires,*
Vigorous *Health,* and gay *Desires*.
The *Wheel* of Life no less will stay
In a *smooth* than *Rugged* way.
Since it equally does flee, 15
Let the *Motion* pleasant be.

Why do we precious *Oyntments* shower,
Nobler *wines* why do we pour,
Beauteous *Flowers* why do we spread,
Upon the Mon'uments of the *Dead?* 20
Nothing they but *Dust* can show,
Or *Bones* that hasten to be so.
Crown me with *Roses* whilst I *Live,*
Now your *Wines* and *Oyntments* give.
After *Death* I nothing crave, 25
Let me *Alive* my pleasures have,
All are *Stoicks* in the *Grave.*

Written in Juice of Lemmon

1

Whilst what I write I do not see,
I dare thus, even to *you,* write *Poetry.*
Ah foolish Muse, which do'st so high aspire,
And know'st her judgment well
How much it does thy power excel, 5
Yet dar'st be read by, thy just doom, the *Fire.*

2

Alas, thou think'st thy self secure,
Because thy form is *Innocent* and *Pure:*
Like *Hypocrites,* which seem unspotted here;
But when they sadly come to dye, 10
And the last *Fire* their Truth must try,
Scrauld o're like thee, and *blotted* they appear.

3

Go then, but reverently go,
And, since thou needs must *sin, confess* it too:
Confess't, and with humility clothe thy shame; 15

Lemon-juice writing becomes visible when it is heated.

For thou, who else must burned be
An *Heretick*, if she pardon thee,
May'st like a *Martyr* then *enjoy* the *Flame*.

4

But if her *wisdom* grow severe,
And suffer not her *goodness* to be there; 20
If her large mercies cruelly it restrain;
Be not discourag'd, but require
A more gentle *Ordeal Fire*,
And bid her by *Loves-Flames* read it again.

5

Strange power of heat, thou yet dost show 25
Like winter earth, *naked*, or *cloath'd* with *Snow*,
But, as the quickning *Sun* approaching near,
The *Plants* arise up by degrees,
A sudden paint adorns the trees,
And all kind *Natures Characters* appear. 30

6

So, nothing yet in Thee is seen,
But when a *Genial heat* warms thee within,
A new-born *Wood* of various Lines there grows;
Here buds an A, and there a B,
Here sprouts a V, and there a T, 35
And all the flourishing *Letters* stand in *Rows*.

7

Still, silly *Paper*, thou wilt think
That all this might as well be writ with *Ink*.
Oh no; there's sense in this, and *Mysterie*;
Thou now maist change thy *Authors* name, 40
And to her *Hand* lay noble claim;
For as *She Reads*, she *Makes* the words in Thee.

8

Yet if thine own unworthiness
Will still, that thou art mine, not Hers, confess;

Consume thy self with Fire before her Eyes, 45
And so her *Grace* or *Pity* move:
The *Gods,* though *Beasts* they do not Love,
Yet like them when they'r burnt in *Sacrifice.*

The Change

1

Love in her Sunny Eyes does basking play;
Love walks the pleasant Mazes of her Hair;
Love does on both her Lips for ever stray;
And *sows* and *reaps* a thousand *kisses* there.
In all her outward parts *Love*'s always seen; 5
But, oh, He never went within.

2

Within *Love*'s foes, his greatest foes abide,
Malice, Inconstancy, and Pride.
So the Earths face, Trees, Herbs, and Flowers do dress,
With other beauties numberless: 10
But at the *Center, Darkness* is, and *Hell;*
There wicked *Spirits,* and there the *Damned* dwell.

3

With me alas, quite contrary it fares;
Darkness and *Death* lies in my weeping eyes,
Despair and Paleness in my face appears, 15
And Grief, and Fear, Love's greatest Enemies;
But, like the *Persian-Tyrant, Love* within
Keeps his proud *Court,* and ne're is seen.

4

Oh take *my Heart,* and by that means you'll prove
Within, too stor'd enough of *Love:* 20
Give me but Yours, I'll by that change so thrive,
That *Love* in all my parts shall live.

So powerful is this change, it render can,
My *outside Woman,* and your *inside Man.*

The Extasie

1

I leave *Mortality,* and things below;
I have no time in *Complements* to wast,
Farewel to'ye all in hast,
For I am *call'd* to go.
A *Whirlwind* bears up my dull Feet, 5
Th'officious *Clouds* beneath them meet.
And (Lo!) I *mount,* and (Lo!)
How small the biggest Parts of *Earths* proud *Tittle* show!

2

Where shall I find the noble *Brittish* Land?
Lo, I at last a *Northern Spec* espie, 10
Which in the *Sea* does lie,
And seems a *Grain* o'th' *Sand!*
For this will any *sin,* or *Bleed?*
Of *Civil Wars* is this the *Meed?*
And is it this, alas, which we 15
(Oh *Irony* of *Words!*) do call *Great Britanie?*

3

I pass by th'arched *Magazins,* which hold
Th' eternal stores of *Frost,* and *Rain,* and *Snow;*
Dry, and *secure* I go,
Nor shake with *Fear,* or *Cold.* 20
Without *affright* or *wonder*
I meet *Clouds* charg'd with *Thunder,*
And *Lightnings* in my way
Like harmless *Lambent Fiers* about my Temples play.

4

Now into'a gentle *Sea* of rowling *Flame* 25
I'm *plung'ed,* and still mount higher there,
As *Flames* mount up through *aire.*
So perfect, yet so tame,
So great, so pure, so bright a fire
Was that unfortunate desire, 30
My faithful *Breast* did cover,
Then, when I was of late a wretched *Mortal Lover.*

5

Through several *Orbs* which one fair *Planet* bear,
Where I behold distinctly as I pass
The *Hints* of *Galilæos Glass,* 35
I touch at last the spangled *Sphære.*
Here all th'extended *Skie*
Is but one *Galaxie,*
'Tis all so bright and gay,
And the *joynt Eyes* of *Night* make up a perfect *Day.* 40

6

Where am I now? *Angels* and *God* is here;
An unexhausted *Ocean* of *delight*
Swallows my *senses* quite,
And drowns all *What,* or *How,* or *Where.*
Not *Paul,* who first did thither pass, 45
And this great *Worlds Columbus* was,
The *tyrannous pleasure* could express.
Oh 'tis *too much* for *Man!* but let it ne're be *less.*

7

The mighty' *Elijah* mounted so on high,
That second Man, who *leapt* the *Ditch* where all 50
The rest of Mankind *fall,*
And went not *downwards* to the *skie.*
With much of pomp and show

(As Conquering *Kings* in *Triumph* go)
Did he to *Heav'en* approach, 55
And wondrous was his *Way,* and wondrous was his *Coach.*

8

'Twas gawdy all, and rich in every part,
Of *Essences* of *Gems,* and *Spirit* of *Gold*
Was its *substantial mold;*
Drawn forth by *Chymique Angels* art. 60
Here with *Moon-beams* 'twas *silver'd* bright,
There double-*gilt* with the *Suns* light
And mystique Shapes cut round in it,
Figures that did transcend a *Vulgar Angels* wit.

9

The *Horses* were of temper'd *Lightning* made, 65
Of all that in *Heav'ens* beauteous *Pastures* feed,
The noblest, sprightfulst breed,
And *flaming Mains* their *Necks* array'd.
They all were shod with *Diamond,*
Not such as *here* are found, 70
But such *light solid* ones as shine
On the *Transparent Rocks* o'th' *Heaven Chrystalline.*

10

Thus mounted the great *Prophet* to the skies:
Astonisht Men who oft had seen *Stars fall,*
Or that which so they call, 75
Wondred from hence to see one *rise.*
The soft *Clouds* melted him a way,
The *Snow* and *Frosts* which in it lay
A while the sacred *footsteps* bore,
The *Wheels* and *Horses Hoofs* hizz'd as they past them ore. 80

11

He past by th' *Moon* and *Planets,* and did fright
All the *Worlds* there which at this *Meteor* gaz'ed,
And their *Astrologers* amaz'd
With th'unexampled sight.

But where he stopt will ne're be known, 85
Till *Phœnix Nature* aged grown
To'a better *Being* do aspire,
And mount ***herself***, like ***Him***, to' ***Eternitie*** in ***Fire***.

The Country Mouse

A PARAPHRASE UPON HORACE 2 BOOK, SATYR. 6

At the large foot of a fair hollow tree,
Close to plow'd ground, seated commodiously,
His antient and Hereditary House,
There dwelt a good substantial Country-Mouse:
Frugal, and grave, and careful of the main, 5
Yet, one, who once did nobly entertain
A City Mouse well coated, sleek, and gay,
A Mouse of high degree, which lost his way,
Wantonly walking forth to take the Air,
And arriv'd early, and belighted there, 10
For a days lodging: the good hearty Hoast,
(The antient plenty of his hall to boast)
Did all the stores produce, that might excite,
With various tasts, the Courtiers appetite.
Fitches and Beans, Peason, and Oats, and Wheat, 15
And a large Chestnut, the delicious meat
Which *Jove* himself, were he a Mouse, would eat.
And for a *Haut goust* there was mixt with these
The swerd of Bacon, and the coat of Cheese.
The precious Reliques, which at Harvest, he 20
Had gather'd from the Reapers luxurie.
Freely (said he) fall on and never spare,
The bounteous Gods will for to morrow care.
And thus at ease on beds of straw they lay,
And to their Genius sacrific'd the day. 25
Yet the nice guest's Epicurean mind,
(Though breeding made him civil seem and kind)
Despis'd this Country feast, and still his thought

Upon the Cakes and Pies of *London* wrought.
Your bounty and civility (said he) 30
Which I'm surpriz'd in these rude parts to see,
Shews that the Gods have given you a mind,
Too noble for the fate which here you find.
Why should a Soul, so virtuous and so great,
Lose it self thus in an Obscure retreat? 35
Let savage Beasts lodg in a Country Den,
You should see Towns, and Manners know, and men:
And taste the generous Lux'ury of the Court,
Where all the Mice of quality resort;
Where thousand beauteous shees about you move, 40
And by high fare, are plyant made to love.
We all e're long must render up our breath,
No cave or hole can shelter us from death.
Since Life is so uncertain, and so short,
Let's spend it all in feasting and in sport. 45
Come, worthy Sir, come with me, and partake,
All the great things that mortals happy make.
Alas, what virtue hath sufficient Arms,
T'oppose bright Honour, and soft Pleasures charms?
What wisdom can their magick force repel? 50
It draws this reverend Hermit from his Cel.
It was the time, when witty Poets tell,
That Phœbus *into* Thetis *bosom fell:*
She blusht at first, and then put out the light,
And drew the modest Curtains of the night. 55
Plainly, the troth to tell, the Sun was set,
When to the Town our wearied Travellers get,
To a Lords house, as Lordly as can be
Made for the use of Pride and Luxury,
They come; the gentle Courtier at the door 60
Stops and will hardly enter in before.
But 'tis, Sir, your command, and being so,
I'm sworn t' obedience, and so in they go.
Behind a hanging in a spacious room,
(The richest work of *Mortclakes* noble Loom) 65
They wait awhile their wearied limbs to rest,
Till silence should invite them to their feast.

About the hour that Cynthia's *Silver light,*
Had touch'd the pale Meridies of the night;
At last the various Supper being done, 70
It happened that the Company was gone,
Into a room remote, Servants and all,
To please their nobles fancies with a Ball.
Our host leads forth his stranger, and do's find,
All fitted to the bounties of his mind. 75
Still on the Table half fill'd dishes stood,
And with delicious bits the floor was strow'd.
The courteous mouse presents him with the best,
And both with fat varieties are blest,
Th' industrious Peasant every where does range, 80
And thanks the gods for his Life's happy change.
Loe, in the midst of a well fraited Pye,
They both at last glutted and wanton lye.
When see the sad Reverse of prosperous fate,
And what fierce storms on mortal glories wait. 85
With hideous noise, down the rude servants come,
Six dogs before run barking into th' room;
The wretched gluttons fly with wild affright,
And hate the fulness which retards their flight.
Our trembling Peasant wishes now in vain, 90
That Rocks and Mountains cover'd him again.
Oh how the change of his poor life he curst!
This, of all lives (said he) is sure the worst.
Give me again, *ye gods,* my Cave and wood;
With peace, let tares and acorns be my food. 95

VIII

LUCID RETROSPECT

Andrew Marvell (1621–1678)

Andrew Marvell

(1621–1678)

THE MOST COOLLY ELUSIVE of poets was a minister's son from Yorkshire, educated at Cambridge, where he may or may not have been briefly a Catholic convert. The Civil War began when he was twenty-one, and all his grown life was spent in its shadow. Unlike Carew and Lovelace, courtiers, or King and Herrick, ecclesiastics, he had no essential royalist attachment; unlike Milton, thirty-four and opinionated, no ideological commitment; so we need not be surprised that the future tutor of Cromwell's son-in-law spent the first five years of the war touring the continent (Holland, Switzerland, France, Italy, Spain), or in a preface to Lovelace's *Lucasta* (1649) scorned the Commonwealth censors ("envious caterpillars"), or addressed to Cromwell (1650) a Horatian ode far from uncommitted but nobly judicious, having for its most moving lines a celebration of Charles I's manner of meeting his death. His fine mind, working upon ideas, assessed always in their light the actual. His examination of the great myth of retirement, which brings within his scope so many pastoral themes, focused, in "Upon Appleton House" and its distilled afterpiece "The Garden," upon the abstention from active life of Cromwell's general, the great Lord Fairfax, who broke with his chief in 1650 and took Marvell into his establishment as tutor to his daughter Maria. Yet by 1655 he was a dedicated supporter of Cromwell; by 1657, Latin secretary (assistant to the secretary of state); from 1659 until his death, member of Parliament for Hull and author of the counter-monarchist satires on which, though he did not sign them, his contemporary reputation was based.

He was no more attached to poetic than to political parties; he saw the limits, and the potential use, of everything. Donne's material, Donne's way of arguing, informs "The Definition of Love" and

"To His Coy Mistress," but not Donne's intensity of the grasped occasion. Marvell's are ideal and summarizing poems; we do not think at once of a lady swayed by them; he writes as though to show what a tradition can do. Clevelandisms abound in "Upon Appleton House," but Clevelandisms put to their appropriate use, which Marvell discerned to be not trenchant but playful. Denham and Waller enter his amalgam when he needs them; so do Carew, Townshend, Herbert, Crashaw. He can summarize a mode, and the pressure behind that mode, and the thrust of a long civilization behind that pressure; and then turn his attention to another mode.

That the School of Donne should have culminated in so urbane a summarizer was perhaps to be expected; inventors are commonly succeeded by enthusiasts, and they by masters. But that the master should have been capable of so detached yet so discerning and impassioned a celebration of the intelligence was a boon which, if literature were all, would nearly excuse the Civil War, because it lent him pressure and focus. If he has anything of his own to say it is this, that one does not ever know securely which side to take, all sides excluding what wants to be conserved; but that one holds, being civilized, all urgencies in balance, and makes, from time to time, pragmatic commitments. The urgencies, here and now in one man's life, animate the forms of style, the decorums of a long civilization, Greek, Roman, and native, with whose aid one seeks to judge them; and one's final commitment is to that civilization. Civilization fused with local urgency is at its rare best the formula for poise; and Marvell, never betraying such an insight, is the greatest minor poet in the English language.

TEXT: *Poems and Letters,* ed. H. M. Margoliouth (Oxford, 1952).

COMMENT: A. Alvarez, *The School of Donne* (New York, 1951), Chap. V. T. S. Eliot, "Andrew Marvell," *Selected Essays* (New York, 1950).

A Dialogue

BETWEEN *the Resolved Soul, and Created Pleasure*

Courage my Soul, now learn to wield
The weight of thine immortal Shield.
Close on thy Head thy Helmet bright.
Ballance thy Sword against the Fight.
See where an Army, strong as fair, 5
With silken Banners spreads the air.
Now, if thou bee'st that thing Divine,
In this day's Combat let it shine:
And shew that Nature wants an Art
To conquer one resolved Heart. 10
Pleasure Welcome the Creations Guest,
Lord of Earth, and Heaven Heir.
Lay aside that Warlike Crest,
And of Nature's banquet share:
Where the Souls of fruits and flow'rs 15
Stand prepar'd to heighten yours.
Soul I sup above, and cannot stay
To bait so long upon the way.
Pleasure On these downy Pillows lye,
Whose soft Plumes will thither fly: 20
On these Roses strow'd so plain
Lest one Leaf thy Side should strain.
Soul My gentler Rest is on a Thought,
Conscious of doing what I ought.
Pleasure If thou bee'st with Perfumes pleas'd, 25
Such as oft the Gods appeas'd,
Thou in fragrant Clouds shalt show
Like another God below.
Soul A Soul that knowes not to presume
Is Heaven's and its own perfume. 30
Pleasure Every thing does seem to vie

---

18. *bait:* stop for food.

Which should first attract thine Eye:
But since none deserves that grace,
In this Crystal view *thy* face.
Soul When the Creator's skill is priz'd, 35
The rest is all but Earth disguis'd.
Pleasure Heark how Musick then prepares
For thy Stay these charming Aires;
Which the posting Winds recall,
And suspend the Rivers Fall. 40
Soul Had I but any time to lose,
On this I would it all dispose.
Cease Tempter. None can chain a mind
Whom this sweet Chordage cannot bind.

Chorus

Earth cannot shew so brave a Sight 45
As when a single Soul does fence
The Batteries of alluring Sense,
And Heaven views it with delight.
Then persevere: for still new Charges sound:
And if thou overcom'st thou shalt be crown'd. 50
Pleasure All this fair, and soft, and sweet,
Which scatteringly doth shine,
Shall within one Beauty meet,
And she be only thine.
Soul If things of Sight such Heavens be, 55
What Heavens are those we cannot see?
Pleasure Where so e're thy Foot shall go
The minted Gold shall lie;
Till thou purchase all below,
And want new Worlds to buy. 60
Soul Wer't not a price who'ld value Gold?
And that's worth nought that can be sold.
Pleasure Wilt thou all the Glory have
That War or Peace commend?

---

44. *Chordage:* this and the word "Resolved" in the title are plays on musical terms.
46. *fence:* ward off.

Half the World shall be thy Slave 65
  The other half thy Friend.
Soul What Friends, if to my self untrue?
What Slaves, unless I captive you?
Pleasure Thou shalt know each hidden Cause;
  And see the future Time: 70
Try what depth the Centre draws;
  And then to Heaven climb.
Soul None thither mounts by the degree
Of Knowledge, but Humility.

Chorus

Triumph, triumph, victorious Soul; 75
The World has not one Pleasure more:
The rest does lie beyond the Pole,
And is thine everlasting Store.

On a Drop of Dew

See how the Orient Dew,
Shed from the Bosom of the Morn
  Into the blowing Roses,
Yet careless of its Mansion new;
For the clear Region where 'twas born 5
  Round in its self incloses:
  And in its little Globes Extent,
Frames as it can its native Element.
  How it the purple flow'r does slight,
    Scarce touching where it lyes, 10
  But gazing back upon the Skies,
    Shines with a mournful Light;
      Like its own Tear,
Because so long divided from the Sphear.
  Restless it roules and unsecure, 15
    Trembling lest it grow impure:
  Till the warm Sun pitty it's Pain,

---

5. *For:* because of.

And to the Skies exhale it back again.
So the Soul, that Drop, that Ray
Of the clear Fountain of Eternal Day, 20
Could it within the humane flow'r be seen,
Remembring still its former height,
Shuns the sweat leaves and blossoms green;
And, recollecting its own Light,
Does, in its pure and circling thoughts, express 25
The greater Heaven in an Heaven less.
In how coy a Figure wound,
Every way it turns away:
So the World excluding round,
Yet receiving in the Day. 30
Dark beneath, but bright above:
Here disdaining, there in Love.
How loose and easie hence to go:
How girt and ready to ascend.
Moving but on a point below, 35
It all about does upwards bend.
Such did the Manna's sacred Dew destil;
White, and intire, though congeal'd and chill.
Congeal'd on Earth: but does, dissolving, run
Into the Glories of th' Almighty Sun. 40

37–40. See Exod. 16 : 14–21.

Bermudas

Where the remote *Bermudas* ride
In th' Oceans bosome unespy'd,
From a small Boat, that row'd along,
The listning Winds receiv'd this Song.
What should we do but sing his Praise 5
That led us through the watry Maze,
Unto an Isle so long unknown,
And yet far kinder than our own?
Where he the huge Sea-Monsters wracks,

That lift the Deep upon their Backs. 10
He lands us on a grassy Stage;
Safe from the Storms, and Prelat's rage.
He gave us this eternal Spring,
Which here enamells every thing;
And sends the Fowl's to us in care, 15
On daily Visits through the Air.
He hangs in shades the Orange bright,
Like golden Lamps in a green Night.
And does in the Pomgranates close,
Jewels more rich than *Ormus* show's. 20
He makes the Figs our mouths to meet;
And throws the Melons at our feet.
But Apples plants of such a price,
No Tree could ever bear them twice.
With Cedars, chosen by his hand, 25
From *Lebanon,* he stores the Land.
And makes the hollow Seas, that roar,
Proclaime the Ambergris on shoar.
He cast (of which we rather boast)
The Gospels Pearl upon our Coast. 30
And in these Rocks for us did frame
A Temple, where to sound his Name.
Oh let our Voice his Praise exalt,
Till it arrive at Heavens Vault.
Which thence (perhaps) rebounding, may 35
Eccho beyond the *Mexique Bay.*
Thus sung they, in the *English* boat,
An holy and a chearful Note,
And all the way, to guide their Chime,
With falling Oars they kept the time. 40

---

20. *Ormus:* city of luxury at the entrance to the Persian Gulf.
23. *Apples:* pineapples.

Clorinda and Damon

C *Damon* come drive thy flocks this way.
D No: 'tis too late they went astray.

C I have a grassy Scutcheon spy'd,
Where *Flora* blazons all her pride.
The Grass I aim to feast thy Sheep: 5
The Flow'rs I for thy Temples keep.
D Grass withers; and the Flow'rs too fade.
C Seize the short Joyes then, ere they vade.
Seest thou that unfrequented Cave?
D That den? *C* Loves Shrine. *D* But Virtue's Grave. 10
C In whose cool bosome we may lye
Safe from the Sun. *D* not Heaven's Eye.
C Near this, a Fountaines liquid Bell
Tinkles within the concave Shell.
D Might a Soul bath there and be clean, 15
Or slake its Drought? *C* What is't you mean?
D These once had been enticing things,
Clorinda, Pastures, Caves, and Springs.
C And what late change? *D* The other day
Pan met me. *C* What did great *Pan* say? 20
D Words that transcend poor Shepherds skill,
But He ere since my Songs does fill:
And his Name swells my slender Oate.
C Sweet must *Pan* sound in *Damons* Note.
D *Clorinda's* voice might make it sweet. 25
C Who would not in *Pan's* Praises meet?

Chorus

Of *Pan* the flowry Pastures sing,
Caves eccho, and the Fountains ring.
Sing then while he doth us inspire;
For all the World is our *Pan's* Quire. 30

A Dialogue between *Thyrsis* and *Dorinda*

Dorinda When Death, shall part us from these Kids,
And shut up our divided Lids,
Tell me *Thyrsis,* prethee do,
Whither thou and I must go.

Thyrsis	To the Elizium: (*Dorinda*) oh where i'st?	5
Thyrsis	A Chast Soul, can never mis't.	
Dorinda	I know no way, but one, our home;	
	Is our cell Elizium?	
Thyrsis	Turn thine Eye to yonder Skie,	
	There the milky way doth lye;	10
	'Tis a sure but rugged way,	
	That leads to Everlasting day.	
Dorinda	There Birds may nest, but how can I,	
	That have no wings and cannot fly?	
Thyrsis	Do not sigh (fair Nimph) for fire	15
	Hath no wings, yet doth aspire	
	Till it hit, against the pole,	
	Heaven's the Center of the Soul.	
Dorinda	But in Elizium how do they	
	Pass Eternity away?	20
Thyrsis	Oh, ther's, neither hope nor fear	
	Ther's no Wolf, no Fox, nor Bear.	
	No need of Dog to fetch our stray,	
	Our Lightfoot we may give away;	
	No Oat-pipe's needfull, there thine Ears	25
	May feast with Musick of the Spheres.	
Dorinda	Oh sweet! oh sweet! How I my future state	
	By silent thinking, Antidate:	
	I prethee let us spend our time to come	
	In talking of *Elizium*.	30
Thyrsis	Then I'le go on: There, sheep are full	
	Of sweetest grass, and softest wooll;	
	There, birds sing Consorts, garlands grow,	
	Cool winds do whisper, springs do flow.	
	There, alwayes is, a rising Sun,	35
	And day is ever, but begun.	
	Shepheards there, bear equal sway,	
	And every Nimph's a Queen of *May*.	

18. The soul tends naturally toward heaven, as the body toward earth's center.

Dorinda Ah me, ah me. (*Thyrsis*) *Dorinda,* why do 'st cry?

Dorinda I'm sick, I'm sick, and fain would dye: 40
Convince me now, that this is true;
By bidding, with mee, all adieu.

Thyrsis I cannot live, without thee, I
Will for thee, much more with thee dye.

Chorus Then let us give *Carillo* charge o'th Sheep, 45
And thou and I'le pick poppies and them steep
In wine, and drink on't even till we weep,
So shall we smoothly pass away in sleep.

A Dialogue
between the Soul and Body

Soul O who shall, from this Dungeon, raise
A Soul inslav'd so many wayes?
With bolts of Bones, that fetter'd stands
In Feet; and manacled in Hands.
Here blinded with an Eye; and there 5
Deaf with the drumming of an Ear.
A Soul hung up, as 'twere, in Chains
Of Nerves, and Arteries, and Veins.
Tortur'd, besides each other part,
In a vain Head, and double Heart. 10

Body O who shall me deliver whole,
From bonds of this Tyrannic Soul?
Which, stretcht upright, impales me so,
That mine own Precipice I go;
And warms and moves this needless Frame: 15
(A Fever could but do the same.)
And, wanting where its spight to try,
Has made me live to let me dye.

---

15. *needless*: free from needs.

A Body that could never rest,
Since this ill Spirit it possest. 20

Soul What Magick could me thus confine
Within anothers Grief to pine?
Where whatsoever it complain,
I feel, that cannot feel, the pain.
And all my Care its self employes, 25
That to preserve, which me destroys:
Constrain'd not only to indure
Diseases, but, whats worse, the Cure:
And ready oft the Port to gain,
Am Shipwrackt into Health again. 30

Body But Physick yet could never reach
The Maladies Thou me dost teach;
Whom first the Cramp of Hope does Tear:
And then the Palsie Shakes of Fear.
The Pestilence of Love does heat: 35
Or Hatred's hidden Ulcer eat.
Joy's chearful Madness does perplex:
Or Sorrow's other Madness vex.
Which Knowledge forces me to know;
And Memory will not foregoe. 40
What but a Soul could have the wit
To build me up for Sin so fit?
So Architects do square and hew,
Green Trees that in the Forest grew.

The Nymph Complaining for the Death of her *Faun*

The wanton Troopers riding by
Have shot my Faun and it will dye.
Ungentle men! They cannot thrive
To kill thee. Thou neer didst alive
Them any harm: alas nor cou'd 5
Thy death yet do them any good.

I'me sure I never wisht them ill;
Nor do I for all this; nor will:
But, if my simple Pray'rs may yet
Prevail with Heaven to forget 10
Thy murder, I will Joyn my Tears
Rather than fail. But, O my fears!
It cannot dye so. Heavens King
Keeps register of every thing:
And nothing may we use in vain. 15
Ev'n Beasts must be with justice slain;
Else Men are made their *Deodands*.
Though they should wash their guilty hands
In this warm life-blood, which doth part
From thine, and wound me to the Heart, 20
Yet could they not be clean: their Stain
Is dy'd in such a Purple Grain.
There is not such another in
The World, to offer for their Sin.
Unconstant *Sylvio*, when yet 25
I had not found him counterfeit,
One morning (I remember well)
Ty'd in this silver Chain and Bell,
Gave it to me: nay and I know
What he said then; I'me sure I do. 30
Said He, look how your Huntsman here
Hath taught a Faun to hunt his *Dear*.
But *Sylvio* soon had me beguil'd.
This waxed tame, while he grew wild,
And quite regardless of my Smart, 35
Left me his Faun, but took his Heart.
Thenceforth I set my self to play
My solitary time away,
With this: and very well content,
Could so mine idle Life have spent. 40
For it was full of sport; and light
Of foot, and heart; and did invite,

---

17. *Deodand:* something which, having caused a person's death, was confiscated by the crown for pious uses. This law stood until 1846.

Me to its game: it seem'd to bless
Its self in me. How could I less
Than love it? O I cannot be 45
Unkind, t' a Beast that loveth me.
  Had it liv'd long, I do not know
Whether it too might have done so
As *Sylvio* did: his Gifts might be
Perhaps as false or more than he. 50
But I am sure, for ought that I
Could in so short a time espie,
Thy Love was far more better then
The love of false and cruel men.
  With sweetest milk, and sugar, first 55
I it at mine own fingers nurst.
And as it grew, so every day
It wax'd more white and sweet than they.
It had so sweet a Breath! And oft
I blusht to see its foot more soft, 60
And white, (shall I say than my hand?)
NAY any Ladies of the Land.
  It is a wond'rous thing, how fleet
'Twas on those little silver feet.
With what a pretty skipping grace, 65
It oft would challenge me the Race:
And when 'thad left me far away,
'Twould stay, and run again, and stay.
For it was nimbler much than Hindes;
And trod, as on the four Winds. 70
  I have a Garden of my own,
But so with Roses over grown,
And Lillies, that you would it guess
To be a little Wilderness.
And all the Spring time of the year 75
It onely loved to be there.
Among the beds of Lillyes, I
Have sought it oft, where it should lye;
Yet could not, till it self would rise,
Find it, although before mine Eyes. 80

For, in the flaxen Lillies shade,
It like a bank of Lillies laid.
Upon the Roses it would feed,
Until its Lips ev'n seem'd to bleed:
And then to me 'twould boldly trip, 85
And print those Roses on my Lip.
But all its chief delight was still
On Roses thus its self to fill:
And its pure virgin Limbs to fold
In whitest sheets of Lillies cold. 90
Had it liv'd long, it would have been
Lillies without, Roses within.
  O help! O help! I see it faint:
And dye as calmely as a Saint.
See how it weeps. The Tears do come 95
Sad, slowly dropping like a Gumme.
So weeps the wounded Balsome: so
The holy Frankincense doth flow.
The brotherless *Heliades*
Melt in such Amber Tears as these. 100
  I in a golden Vial will
Keep these two crystal Tears; and fill
It till it do o'reflow with mine;
Then place it in *Diana's* Shrine.
  Now my Sweet Faun is vanish'd to 105
Whither the Swans and Turtles go:
In fair *Elizium* to endure,
With milk-white Lambs, and Ermins pure.
O do not run too fast: for I
Will but bespeak thy Grave, and dye. 110
  First my unhappy Statue shall
Be cut in Marble; and withal,
Let it be weeping too: but there
Th' Engraver sure his Art may spare;
For I so truly thee bemoane, 115
That I shall weep though I be Stone:

---

99. *Heliades:* the daughters of Helios, the sun, who wept for their foolhardy brother Phaethon. They were changed into trees, and the sun hardened their tears into amber.

Until my Tears, still dropping, wear
My breast, themselves engraving there.
There at my feet shalt thou be laid,
Of purest Alabaster made: 120
For I would have thine Image be
White as I can, though not as Thee.

To His Coy Mistress

Had we but World enough, and Time,
This coyness Lady were no crime.
We would sit down, and think which way
To walk, and pass our long Loves Day.
Thou by the *Indian Ganges* side 5
Should'st Rubies find: I by the Tide
Of *Humber* would complain. I would
Love you ten years before the Flood:
And you should if you please refuse
Till the Conversion of the *Jews*. 10
My vegetable Love should grow
Vaster than Empires, and more slow.
An hundred years should go to praise
Thine Eyes, and on thy Forehead Gaze.
Two hundred to adore each Breast: 15
But thirty thousand to the rest.
An Age at least to every part,
And the last Age should show your Heart.
For Lady you deserve this State;
Nor would I love at lower rate. 20
 But at my back I alwaies hear
Times winged Charriot hurrying near:
And yonder all before us lye
Desarts of vast Eternity.
Thy Beauty shall no more be found; 25
Nor, in thy marble Vault, shall sound

11. The only powers of the vegetable soul were growth and reproduction.

My ecchoing Song: then Worms shall try
That long preserv'd Virginity:
And your quaint Honour turn to dust;
And into ashes all my Lúst. 30
The Grave's a fine and private place,
But none I think do there embrace.
  Now therefore, while the youthful hew
Sits on thy skin like morning dew,
And while thy willing Soul transpires 35
At every pore with instant Fires,
Now let us sport us while we may;
And now, like am'rous birds of prey,
Rather at once our Time devour,
Than languish in his slow-chapt pow'r. 40
Let us roll all our Strength, and all
Our sweetness, up into one Ball:
And tear our Pleasures with rough strife,
Thorough the Iron gates of Life.
Thus, though we cannot make our Sun 45
Stand still, yet we will make him run.

Mourning

I

You, that decipher out the Fate
Of humane Off-springs from the Skies,
What mean these Infants which of late
Spring from the Starrs of *Chlora's* Eyes?

II

Her Eyes confus'd, and doubled ore, 5
With Tears suspended ere they flow;
Seem bending upwards, to restore
To Heaven, whence it came, their Woe.

III

When, molding of the watry Spheärs,
Slow drops unty themselves away; 10
As if she, with those precious Tears,
Would strow the ground where *Strephon* lay.

IV

Yet some affirm, pretending Art,
Her Eyes have so her Bosome drown'd,
Only to soften near her Heart 15
A place to fix another Wound.

V

And, while vain Pomp does her restrain
Within her solitary Bowr,
She courts her self in am'rous Rain;
Her self both *Danae* and the Showr. 20

VI

Nay others, bolder, hence esteem
Joy now so much her Master grown,
That whatsoever does but seem
Like Grief, is from her Windows thrown.

VII

Nor that she payes, while she survives, 25
To her dead Love this Tribute due;
But casts abroad these Donatives,
At the installing of a new.

VIII

How wide they dream! The *Indian* Slaves
That sink for Pearl through Seas profound, 30
Would find her Tears yet deeper Waves
And not of one the bottom sound.

---

20. *Danae:* imprisoned princess whom the enamored Zeus visited as a golden shower.

IX

I yet my silent Judgment keep,
Disputing not what they believe
But sure as oft as Women weep, 35
It is to be suppos'd they grieve.

The Definition of Love

I

My Love is of a birth as rare
As 'tis for object strange and high:
It was begotten by despair
Upon Impossibility.

II

Magnanimous Despair alone 5
Could show me so divine a thing,
Where feeble Hope could ne'r have flown
But vainly flapt its Tinsel Wing.

III

And yet I quickly might arrive
Where my extended Soul is fixt, 10
But Fate does Iron wedges drive,
And alwaies crouds it self betwixt.

IV

For Fate with jealous Eye does see
Two perfect Loves; nor lets them close:
Their union would her ruine be, 15
And her Tyrannick pow'r depose.

V

And therefore her Decrees of Steel
Us as the distant Poles have plac'd,

---

18. *Poles:* the celestial poles around which the heavens appear to revolve.

(Though Loves whole World on us doth wheel)
Not by themselves to be embrac'd. 20

VI

Unless the giddy Heaven fall,
And Earth some new Convulsion tear;
And, us to joyn, the World should all
Be cramp'd into a *Planisphere.*

VII

As Lines so Loves *oblique* may well 25
Themselves in every Angle greet:
But ours so truly *Paralel,*
Though infinite can never meet.

VIII

Therefore the Love which us doth bind.
But Fate so enviously debarrs, 30
Is the Conjunction of the Mind,
And Opposition of the Stars.

---

24. *Planisphere:* a flat representation of a sphere. If it used both sides of a sheet for the two hemispheres, the poles would be brought together.
31–32. *Conjunction, Opposition:* technical terms from astrology.

The Picture of Little *T. C.* in a Prospect of Flowers

I

See with what simplicity
This Nimph begins her golden daies!
In the green Grass she loves to lie,
And there with her fair Aspect tames
The Wilder flow'rs, and gives them names: 5
But only with the Roses playes;
And them does tell
What Colour best becomes them, and what Smell.

II

Who can foretel for what high cause
This Darling of the Gods was born! 10
Yet this is She whose chaster Laws
The wanton Love shall one day fear,
And, under her command severe,
See his Bow broke and Ensigns torn.
Happy, who can 15
Appease this virtuous Enemy of Man!

III

O then let me in time compound,
And parly with those conquering Eyes;
Ere they have try'd their force to wound,
Ere, with their glancing wheels, they drive 20
In Triumph over Hearts that strive,
And them that yield but more despise.
Let me be laid,
Where I may see thy Glories from some shade.

IV

Mean time, whilst every verdant thing 25
It self does at thy Beauty charm,
Reform the errours of the Spring;
Make that the Tulips may have share
Of sweetness, seeing they are fair;
And Roses of their thorns disarm: 30
But most procure
That Violets may a longer Age endure.

V

But O young beauty of the Woods,
Whom Nature courts with fruits and flow'rs,
Gather the Flow'rs, but spare the Buds; 35

---

10. Little T. C. was Theophila Cornewall (born 1644); "Theophila" means "darling of the gods." The proverb says that their darlings die young, and T. C.'s elder sister of the same name had died two days after baptism.

Lest *Flora* angry at thy crime,
To kill her Infants in their prime,
Do quickly make th' Example Yours;
  And, ere we see,
Nip in the blossome all our hopes and Thee. 40

The Mower to the Glo-Worms

I

Ye living Lamps, by whose dear light
The Nightingale does sit so late,
And studying all the Summer-night,
Her matchless Songs does meditate;

II

Ye Country Comets, that portend 5
No War, nor Princes funeral,
Shining unto no higher end
Then to presage the Grasses fall;

III

Ye Glo-worms, whose officious Flame
To wandring Mowers shows the way, 10
That in the Night have lost their aim,
And after foolish Fires do stray;

IV

Your courteous Lights in vain you wast,
Since *Juliana* here is come,
For She my Mind hath so displac'd 15
That I shall never find my home.

The Mower's Song

I

My Mind was once the true survey
Of all these Medows fresh and gay;
And in the greenness of the Grass
Did see its Hopes as in a Glass;
When *Juliana* came, and She 5
What I do to the Grass, does to my Thoughts and Me.

II

But these, while I with Sorrow pine,
Grew more luxuriant still and fine;
That not one Blade of Grass you spy'd,
But had a Flower on either side; 10
When *Juliana* came, and She
What I do to the Grass, does to my Thoughts and Me.

III

Unthankful Medows, could you so
A fellowship so true forego,
And in your gawdy May-games meet, 15
While I lay trodden under feet?
When *Juliana* came, and She
What I do to the Grass, does to my Thoughts and Me.

IV

But what you in Compassion ought,
Shall now by my Revenge be wrought: 20
And Flow'rs, and Grass, and I and all,
Will in one common Ruine fall.
For *Juliana* comes, and She
What I do to the Grass, does to my Thoughts and Me.

V

And thus, ye Meadows, which have been 25
Companions of my thoughts more green,
Shall now the Heraldry become
With which I shall adorn my Tomb;
For *Juliana* comes, and She
What I do to the Grass, does to my Thoughts and Me. 30

Ametas and *Thestylis* Making Hay-Ropes

I

Ametas Think'st Thou that this Love can stand,
Whilst Thou still dost say me nay?
Love unpaid does soon disband:
Love binds Love as Hay binds Hay.

II

Thestylis Think'st Thou that this Rope would twine 5
If we both should turn one way?
Where both parties so combine,
Neither Love will twist nor Hay.

III

Ametas Thus you vain Excuses find,
Which your selve and us delay: 10
And Love tyes a Womans Mind
Looser than with Ropes of Hay.

IV

Thestylis What you cannot constant hope
Must be taken as you may.

V

Ametas Then let's both lay by our Rope, 15
And go kiss within the Hay.

The Garden

I

How vainly men themselves amaze
To win the Palm, the Oke, or Bayes;
And their uncessant Labours see
Crown'd from some single Herb or Tree.
Whose short and narrow verged Shade 5
Does prudently their Toyles upbraid;
While all Flow'rs and all Trees do close
To weave the Garlands of repose.

II

Fair quiet, have I found thee here,
And Innocence thy Sister dear! 10
Mistaken long, I sought you then
In busie Companies of Men.
Your sacred Plants, if here below,
Only among the Plants will grow.
Society is all but rude, 15
To this delicious Solitude.

III

No white nor red was ever seen
So am'rous as this lovely green.
Fond Lovers, cruel as their Flame,
Cut in these Trees their Mistress name. 20
Little, Alas, they know, or heed,
How far these Beauties Hers exceed!

---

2. *the Palm, the Oke, or Bayes:* chaplets woven for victors.

Fair Trees! where s'eer your barkes I wound,
No Name shall but your own be found.

IV

When we have run our Passions heat, 25
Love hither makes his best retreat.
The *Gods,* that mortal Beauty chase,
Still in a Tree did end their race.
Apollo hunted *Daphne* so,
Only that She might Laurel grow. 30
And *Pan* did after *Syrinx* speed,
Not as a Nymph, but for a Reed.

V

What wond'rous Life in this I lead!
Ripe Apples drop about my head:
The Luscious Clusters of the Vine 35
Upon my Mouth do crush their Wine;
The Nectaren, and curious Peach,
Into my hands themselves do reach;
Stumbling on Melons, as I pass,
Insnar'd with Flow'rs, I fall on Grass. 40

VI

Mean while the Mind, from pleasure less,
Withdraws into its happiness:
The Mind, that Ocean where each kind
Does streight its own resemblance find:
Yet it creates, transcending these, 45
Far other Worlds, and other Seas;
Annihilating all that's made
To a green Thought in a green Shade.

VII

Here at the Fountains sliding foot,
Or at some Fruit-trees mossy root, 50

29–32. *Daphne* and *Syrinx* turned into trees when their pursuers got too close. The laurel then became sacred to Apollo, and so the leaf of poets' crowns, and Pan plays reeds.

Casting the Bodies Vest aside,
My Soul into the boughs does glide:
There like a Bird it sits, and sings,
Then whets, and combs its silver Wings;
And, till prepar'd for longer flight, 55
Waves in its Plumes the various Light.

VIII

Such was that happy Garden-state,
While Man there walk'd without a Mate:
After a Place so pure, and sweet,
What other Help could yet be meet! 60
But 'twas beyond a Mortal's share
To wander solitary there:
Two Paradises 'twere in one
To live in Paradise alone.

IX

How well the skilful Gardner drew 65
Of flow'rs and herbes this Dial new;
Where from above the milder Sun
Does through a fragrant Zodiack run;
And, as it works, th' industrious Bee
Computes its time as well as we. 70
How could such sweet and wholsome Hours
Be reckon'd but with herbs and flow'rs!

Upon Appleton House, to My Lord *Fairfax*

I

Within this sober Frame expect
Work of no Forrain *Architect;*
That unto Caves the Quarries drew,

Lord Fairfax (1612–1671), Parliamentary general during the Civil War, retired to his Yorkshire seat, Nun Appleton, in 1650. Marvell spent two years there as language teacher to Lord Fairfax's daughter Mary.

And Forrests did to Pastures hew;
Who of his great Design in pain 5
Did for a Model vault his Brain,
Whose Columnes should so high be rais'd
To arch the Brows that on them gaz'd.

II

Why should of all things Man unrul'd
Such unproportion'd dwellings build? 10
The Beasts are by their Denns exprest:
And Birds contrive an equal Nest;
The low roof'd tortoises do dwell
In cases fit of Tortoise-shell:
No Creature loves an empty space; 15
Their Bodies measure out their Place.

III

But He, superfluously spread,
Demands more room alive than dead.
And in his hollow Palace goes
Where Winds as he themselves may lose. 20
What need of all this Marble Crust
T'impark the wanton Mote of Dust,
That thinks by Breadth the World t'unite
Though the first Builders fail'd in Height?

IV

But all things are composed here 25
Like Nature, orderly and near:
In which we the Dimensions find
Of that more sober Age and Mind,
When larger sized Men did stoop
To enter at a narrow loop; 30
As practising, in doors so strait,
To strain themselves through *Heavens Gate*.

---

24. *first Builders:* the workmen of the tower of Babel, which was meant to reach heaven.

V

And surely when the after Age
Shall hither come in *Pilgrimage,*
These sacred Places to adore, 35
By *Vere* and *Fairfax* trod before,
Men will dispute how their Extent
Within such dwarfish Confines went:
And some will smile at this, as well
As *Romulus* his Bee-like Cell. 40

VI

Humility alone designs
Those short but admirable Lines,
By which, ungirt and unconstrain'd,
Things greater are in less contain'd.
Let others vainly strive t'immure 45
The *Circle* in the *Quadrature!*
These *holy Mathematicks* can
In ev'ry Figure equal Man.

VII

Yet thus the laden House does sweat,
And scarce indures the *Master* great: 50
But where he comes the swelling Hall
Stirs, and the *Square* grows *Spherical;*
More by his *Magnitude* distrest,
Then he is by its straitness prest:
And too officiously it slights 55
That in it self which him delights.

VIII

So Honour better Lowness bears,
Then That unwonted Greatness wears.
Height with a certain Grace does bend,

---

40. *Romulus:* the founder of Rome, whose hive-shaped hut was preserved in the imperial city.
52. The roof of the hall was in fact domed.

But low Things clownishly ascend. 60
And yet what needs there here Excuse,
Where ev'ry Thing does answer Use?
Where neatness nothing can condemn,
Nor Pride invent what to contemn?

IX

A Stately *Frontispice of Poor* 65
Adorns without the open Door:
Nor less the Rooms within commends
Daily new *Furniture of Friends.*
The House was built upon the Place
Only as for *a Mark of Grace;* 70
And for an *Inn* to entertain
Its *Lord* a while, but not remain.

X

Him *Bishops-Hill,* or *Denton* may,
Or *Bilbrough,* better hold than they:
But Nature here hath been so free 75
As if she said leave this to me.
Art would more neatly have defac'd
What she had laid so sweetly wast;
In fragrant Gardens, shaddy Woods,
Deep Meadows, and transparent Floods. 80

XI

While with slow Eyes we these survey,
And on each pleasant footstep stay,
We opportunly may relate
The Progress of this Houses Fate.
A *Nunnery* first gave it birth. 85
For *Virgin Buildings* oft brought forth.
And all that Neighbour-Ruine shows
The Quarries whence this dwelling rose.

---

65. *frontispice:* decorated entrance: but here the decorations, like the "furniture" of line 68, are human beings.

XII

Near to this gloomy Cloysters Gates
There dwelt the blooming Virgin *Thwates;* 90
Fair beyond measure, and an Heir
Which might Deformity make fair.
And oft She spent the Summer Suns
Discoursing with the *Suttle Nunns.*
Whence in these Words one to her weav'd, 95
(As 'twere by Chance) Thoughts long conceiv'd.

XIII

'Within this holy leisure we
'Live innocently as you see.
'These Walls restrain the World without,
'But hedge our Liberty about. 100
'These Bars inclose that wider Den
'Of those wild Creatures, called Men.
'The Cloyster outward shuts its Gates,
'And, from us, locks on them the Grates.

XIV

'Here we, in shining Armour white, 105
'Like *Virgin Amazons* do fight.
'And our chast *Lamps* we hourly trim,
'Lest the great *Bridegroom* find them dim.
'Our *Orient* Breaths perfumed are
'With insense of incessant Pray'r. 110
'And Holy-water of our Tears
'Most strangly our Complexion clears.

---

90. *Thwates:* Isabel Thwaites, who was courted by William Fairfax of Steeton, Marvell's patron's great-great-grandfather. Her guardian, the prioress of Nun Appleton, shut her away, but she was later released by force and married Fairfax in 1518.

107–108. see Matt. 25 : 1–13.

109. *Orient:* literally "rising"; and Marvell would have remembered the Latin *orans,* "praying."

XV

'Not Tears of Grief; but such as those
'With which calm Pleasure overflows;
'Or Pity, when we look on you 115
'That live without this happy Vow.
'How should we grieve that must be seen
'Each one a *Spouse*, and each a *Queen;*
'And can in *Heaven* hence behold
'Our brighter Robes and Crowns of Gold? 120

XVI

'When we have prayed all our Beads,
'Some One the holy *Legend* reads;
'While all the rest with Needles paint
'The Face and Graces of the *Saint.*
'But what the Linnen can't receive 125
'They in their Lives do interweave.
'This Work the *Saints* best represents;
'That serves for *Altar's Ornaments.*

XVII

'But much it to our work would add
'If here your hand, your Face we had: 130
'By it we would *our Lady* touch;
'Yet thus She you resembles much.
'Some of your Features, as we sow'd,
'Through ev'ry *Shrine* should be bestow'd.
'And in one Beauty we would take 135
'Enough a thousand *Saints* to make.

XVIII

'And (for I dare not quench the Fire
'That me does for your good inspire)
' 'Twere Sacriledge a Man t'admit
'To holy things, for *Heaven* fit. 140
'I see the *Angels* in a Crown
'On you the Lillies show'ring down:

'And round about you Glory breaks,
'That something more than humane speaks.

XIX

'All Beauty, when at such a height, 145
'Is so already consecrate.
'*Fairfax* I know; and long ere this
'Have mark'd the Youth, and what he is.
'But can he such a *Rival* seem
'For whom you *Heav'n* should disesteem? 150
'Ah, no! and 'twould more Honour prove
'He your *Devoto* were, than *Love*.

XX

'Here live beloved, and obey'd:
'Each one your Sister, each your Maid.
'And, if our Rule seem strictly pend, 155
'The Rule it self to you shall bend.
'Our *Abbess* too, now far in Age,
'Doth your succession near presage.
'How soft the yoke on us would lye,
'Might such fair Hands as yours it tye! 160

XXI

'Your voice, the sweetest of the Quire,
'Shall draw *Heav'n* nearer, raise us higher.
'And your Example, if our Head,
'Will soon us to perfection lead.
'Those Virtues to us all so dear, 165
'Will straight grow Sanctity when here:
'And that, once sprung, increase so fast
'Till Miracles it work at last.

XXII

'Nor is our *Order* yet so nice,
'Delight to banish as a Vice. 170
'Here Pleasure Piety doth meet;

---

169. *nice:* scrupulous.

'One perfecting the other Sweet.
'So through the mortal fruit we boyl
'The Sugars uncorrupting Oyl:
'And that which perisht while we pull, 175
'Is thus preserved clear and full.

XXIII

'For such indeed are all our Arts;
'Still handling Natures finest Parts.
'Flow'rs dress the Altars; for the Clothes,
'The Sea-born Amber we compose; 180
'Balms for the griv'd we draw; and Pasts
'We mold, as Baits for curious tasts.
'What need is here of Man? unless
'These as sweet Sins we should confess.

XXIV

'Each Night among us to your side 185
'Appoint a fresh and Virgin Bride;
'Whom if *our Lord* at midnight find,
'Yet Neither should be left behind.
'Where you may lye as chast in Bed,
'As Pearls together billeted. 190
'All Night embracing Arm in Arm,
'Like Chrystal pure with Cotton warm.

XXV

'But what is this to all the store
'Of Joys you see, and may make more!
'Try but a while, if you be wise: 195
'The Tryal neither Costs, nor Tyes.
Now *Fairfax* seek her promis'd faith:
Religion that dispensed hath;
Which She hence forward does begin;
The *Nuns* smooth Tongue has suckt her in. 200

---

180. *Sea-born Amber:* ambergris, for the altar cloths.
181. *Pasts:* pastries.
197–199. The antecedent of "which" is "religion."

XXVI

Oft, though he knew it was in vain,
Yet would he valiantly complain.
'Is this that *Sanctity* so great,
'An Art by which you finly'r cheat?
'Hypocrite Witches, hence *avant,* 205
'Who though in prison yet inchant!
'Death only can such Theeves make fast,
'As rob though in the Dungeon cast.

XXVII

'Were there but, when this House was made,
'One Stone that a just Hand had laid, 210
'It must have fall'n upon her Head
'Who first Thee from thy Faith misled.
'And yet, how well soever ment,
'With them 'twould soon grow fraudulent:
'For like themselves they alter all, 215
'And vice infects the very Wall.

XXVIII

'But sure those Buildings last not long,
'Founded by Folly, kept by Wrong.
'I know what Fruit their Gardens yield,
'When they it think by Night conceal'd. 220
'Fly from their Vices. 'Tis thy state,
'Not Thee, that they would consecrate.
'Fly from their Ruine. How I fear
'Though guiltless lest thou perish there.

XXIX

What should he do? He would respect 225
Religion, but not Right neglect:
For first Religion taught him Right,
And dazled not but clear'd his sight.
Sometimes resolv'd his Sword he draws,

---

221. *state:* estate.

But reverenceth then the Laws: 230
For Justice still that Courage led;
First from a Judge, then Souldier bred.

XXX

Small Honour would be in the Storm.
The *Court* him grants the lawful Form;
Which licens'd either Peace or Force, 235
To hinder the unjust Divorce.
Yet still the *Nuns* his Right debar'd,
Standing upon their holy Guard.
Ill-counsell'd Women, do you know
Whom you resist, or what you do? 240

XXXI

Is not this he whose Offspring fierce
Shall fight through all the *Universe;*
And with successive Valour try
France, Poland, either *Germany;*
Till one, as long since prophecy'd, 245
His Horse through conquer'd *Britain* ride?
Yet, against Fate, his Spouse they kept;
And the great Race would intercept.

XXXII

Some to the Breach against their Foes
Their *Wooden Saints* in vain oppose. 250
Another bolder stands at push
With their old *Holy-Water Brush.*
While the disjointed *Abbess* threads
The gingling Chain-shot of her *Beads.*
But their lowd'st Cannon were their Lungs; 255
And sharpest Weapons were their Tongues.

XXXIII

But, waving these aside like Flyes,
Young *Fairfax* through the Wall does rise.
Then th' unfrequented Vault appear'd,

And superstitions vainly fear'd. 260
The *Relicks false* were set to view;
Only the Jewels there were true.
But truly bright and holy *Thwaites*
That weeping at the *Altar* waites.

XXXIV

But the glad Youth away her bears, 265
And to the *Nuns* bequeaths her Tears:
Who guiltily their Prize bemoan,
Like Gipsies that a Child hath stoln.
Thenceforth (as when th'Inchantment ends
The Castle vanishes or rends) 270
The wasting Cloister with the rest
Was in one instant dispossest.

XXXV

At the demolishing, this Seat
To *Fairfax* fell as by Escheat.
And what both *Nuns* and *Founders* will'd 275
'Tis likely better thus fulfill'd.
For if the *Virgin* prov'd not theirs,
The *Cloyster* yet remained hers.
Though many a *Nun* there made her Vow,
'Twas no *Religious House* till now. 280

XXXVI

From that blest Bed the *Heroe* came,
Whom *France* and *Poland* yet does fame:
Who, when retired here to Peace,
His warlike Studies could not cease;
But laid these Gardens out in sport 285
In the just Figure of a Fort;
And with five Bastions it did fence,
As aiming one for ev'ry Sense.

XXXVII

When in the *East* the Morning Ray
Hangs out the Colours of the Day, 290

The Bee through these known Allies hums,
Beating the Dian with its *Drumms.*
Then Flow'rs their drowsie Eylids raise,
Their Silken Ensigns each displayes,
And dries its Pan yet dank with Dew, 295
And fills its Flask with Odours new.

XXXVIII

These, as their *Governour* goes by,
In fragrant Vollyes they let fly;
And to salute their *Governess*
Again as great a charge they press: 300
None for the *Virgin Nymph;* for She
Seems with the Flow'rs a Flow'r to be.
And think so still! though not compare
With Breath so sweet, or Cheek so faire.

XXXIX

Well shot ye Firemen! Oh how sweet, 305
And round your equal Fires do meet;
Whose shrill report no Ear can tell,
But Ecchoes to the Eye and smell.
See how the Flow'rs, as at *Parade,*
Under their *Colours* stand displaid: 310
Each *Regiment* in order grows,
That of the Tulip Pinke and Rose.

XL

But when the vigilant *Patroul*
Of Stars walks round about the *Pole,*
Their Leaves, that to the stalks are curl'd, 315
Seem to their Staves the *Ensigns* furl'd.
Then in some Flow'rs beloved Hut
Each Bee as Sentinel is shut;

---

292. *Dian:* reveille.
295. *Pan:* the part of the musket lock which held the priming. "Flasks" (l. 296) thus suggests the powder flask.

And sleeps so too: but, if once stir'd,
She runs you through, or askes *the Word*. 320

XLI

Oh Thou, that dear and happy Isle
The Garden of the World ere while,
Thou *Paradise* of four Seas,
Which *Heaven* planted us to please,
But, to exclude the World, did guard 325
With watry if not flaming Sword;
What luckless Apple did we tast,
To make us Mortal, and The Wast?

XLII

Unhappy! shall we never more
That sweet *Militia* restore, 330
When Gardens only had their Towrs,
And all the Garrisons were Flowrs,
When Roses only Arms might bear,
And Men did rosie Garlands wear?
Tulips, in several Colours barr'd, 335
Were then the *Switzers* of our *Guard*.

XLIII

The *Gardiner* had the *Souldiers* place,
And his more gentle Forts did trace.
The Nursery of all things green
Was then the only *Magazeen*. 340
The *Winter Quarters* were the Stoves,
Where he the tender Plants removes.
But War all this doth overgrow:
We Ord'nance Plant and Powder sow.

XLIV

And yet their walks one on the Sod 345
Who, had it pleased him and *God*,
Might once have made our Gardens spring

---

328. *The:* thee.

Fresh as his own and flourishing.
But he preferr'd to the *Cinque Ports*
These five imaginary Forts: 350
And, in those half-dry Trenches, spann'd
Pow'r which the Ocean might command.

XLV

For he did, with his utmost Skill,
Ambition weed, but *Conscience* till.
Conscience, that Heaven-nursed Plant, 355
Which most our Earthly Gardens want.
A prickling leaf it bears, and such
As that which shrinks at ev'ry touch;
But Flowrs eternal, and divine,
That in the Crowns of Saints do shine. 360

XLVI

The sight does from these *Bastions* ply,
Th' invisible *Artilery;*
And at proud *Cawood Castle* seems
To point the *Battery* of its Beams.
As if it quarrell'd in the Seat 365
Th' Ambition of its *Prelate* great.
But ore the Meads below it plays,
Or innocently seems to gaze.

XLVII

And now to the Abbyss I pass
Of that unfathomable Grass, 370
Where Men like Grashoppers appear,
But Grashoppers are Gyants there:
They, in there squeking Laugh, contemn
Us as we walk more low than them:

---

349. *Cinque Ports:* the five Channel towns, Hastings, Romney, Hythe, Dover, and Sandwich. Fairfax as commander-in-chief was responsible for their defense.

363. *Cawood Castle,* two miles southeast of Nun Appleton, was a seat of the Archbishop of York.

And, from the Precipices tall 375
Of the green spir's, to us do call.

XLVIII

To see Men through this Meadow Dive,
We wonder how they rise alive.
As, under Water, none does know
Whether he fall through it or go. 380
But, as the Marriners that sound,
And show upon their Lead the Ground,
They bring up Flow'rs so to be seen,
And prove they've at the Bottom been.

XLIX

No Scene that turns with Engines strange 385
Does oftner than these Meadows change.
For when the Sun the Grass hath vext,
The tawny Mowers enter next;
Who seem like *Israalites* to be,
Walking on foot through a green Sea. 390
To them the Grassy Deeps divide,
And crowd a Lane to either Side.

L

With whistling Sithe, and Elbow strong,
These Massacre the Grass along:
While one, unknowing, carves the *Rail,* 395
Whose yet unfeather'd Quils her fail.
The Edge all bloody from its Breast
He draws, and does his stroke detest;
Fearing the Flesh untimely mow'd
To him a Fate as black forebode. 400

LI

But bloody *Thestylis,* that waites
To bring the mowing Camp their Cates,

---

385. *Engines:* the machines used to work the scenic effects at court masques.
395. *Rail:* the corn crake, which nests in meadows.
401. *Thestylis:* the reapers' cook in Virgil's second Eclogue.

Greedy as Kites has trust it up,
And forthwith means on it to sup:
When on another quick She lights, 405
And cryes, he call'd us *Israelites;*
But now, to make his saying true,
Rails rain for Quails, for Manna Dew.

LII

Unhappy Birds! what does it boot
To build below the Grasses Root; 410
When Lowness is unsafe as Hight,
And Chance o'retakes what scapeth spight?
And now your Orphan Parents Call
Sounds your untimely Funeral.
Death-Trumpets creak in such a Note, 415
And 'tis the *Sourdine* in their Throat.

LIII

Or sooner hatch or higher build:
The Mower now commands the Field;
In whose new Traverse seemeth wrought
A Camp of Battail newly fought: 420
Where, as the Meads with Hay, the Plain
Lyes quilted ore with Bodies slain:
The Women that with forks it fling,
Do represent the Pillaging.

LIV

And now the careless Victors play, 425
Dancing the Triumphs of the Hay;
Where every Mowers wholesome Heat
Smells like an *Alexanders sweat.*
Their Females fragrant as the Mead
Which they in *Fairy Circles* tread: 430
When at their Dances End they kiss,
Their new-made Hay not sweeter is.

---

416. *Sourdine:* a low-register trumpet.
428. Legend made Alexander the Great a sweet-smelling monarch.

LV

When after this 'tis pil'd in Cocks,
Like a calm Sea it shews the Rocks:
We wondring in the River near 435
How Boats among them safely steer.
Or, like the *Desert Memphis Sand,*
Short *Pyramids* of Hay do stand.
And such the *Roman Camps* do rise
In Hills for Soldiers Obsequies. 440

LVI

This *Scene* again withdrawing brings
A new and empty Face of things;
A levell'd space, as smooth and plain,
As Clothes for *Lilly* strecht to stain.
The World when first created sure 445
Was such a Table rase and pure.
Or rather such is the *Toril*
Ere the Bulls enter at Madril.

LVII

For to this naked equal Flat,
Which *Levellers* take Pattern at, 450
The Villagers in common chase
Their Cattle, which it closer rase;
And what below the Sith increast
Is pincht yet nearer by the Beast.
Such, in the painted World, appear'd 455
Davenant with th' Universal Heard.

LVIII

They seem within the polisht Grass
A Landskip drawen in Looking-Glass.

---

444. *Lilly:* Sir Peter Lely, the painter, who came to England in 1641. The cloths are his canvases.

456. *Universal Heard:* quoted from the description in Davenant's *Gondibert* of a painting of the Six Days of Creation. On the sixth day, ". . . strait an universal Herd appears." The "table rase" of line 446 is a blank canvas.

And shrunk in the huge Pasture show
As Spots, so shap'd, on Faces do. 460
Such Fleas, ere they approach the Eye,
In Multiplying Glasses lye.
They feed so wide, so slowly move,
As *Constellations* do above.

LIX

Then, to conclude these pleasant Acts, 465
Denton sets ope its *Cataracts;*
And makes the Meadow truly be
(What it but seem'd before) a Sea.
For, jealous of its *Lords* long stay,
It try's t'invite him thus away. 470
The River in it self is drown'd,
And Isl's th' astonish'd Cattle round.

LX

Let others tell the *Paradox*
How Eels now bellow in the Ox;
How Horses at their Tails do kick, 475
Turn'd as they hang to Leeches quick;
How Boats can over Bridges sail;
And Fishes do the Stables scale.
How *Salmons* trespassing are found;
And Pikes are taken in the Pound. 480

LXI

But I, retiring from the Flood,
Take Sanctuary in the Wood;
And, while it lasts, my self imbark
In this yet green, yet growing Ark;
Where the first Carpenter might best 485
Fit Timber for his Keel have Prest.
And where all Creatures might have shares,
Although in Armies, not in Paires.

---

466. *Denton:* a town thirty miles upstream, to which Marvell here imputes cataclysmic powers.

LXII

The double Wood of ancient Stocks
Link'd in so thick, an Union locks, 490
It like two *Pedigrees* appears,
On one hand *Fairfax,* th' other *Veres:*
Of whom though many fell in War,
Yet more to Heaven shooting are:
And, as they Natures Cradle deckt, 495
Will in green Age her Hearse expect.

LXIII

When first the Eye this Forrest sees
It seems indeed as *Wood* not *Trees:*
As if their Neighbourhood so old
To one great Trunk them all did mold 500
There the huge Bulk takes place, as ment
To thrust up a *Fifth Element;*
And stretches still so closely wedg'd
As if the Night within were hedg'd.

LXIV

Dark all without it knits; within 505
It opens passable and thin;
And in as loose an order grows,
As the *Corinthean Porticoes.*
The arching Boughs unite between
The Columnes of the Temple green; 510
And underneath the winged Quires
Echo about their tuned Fires.

LXV

The *Nightingale* does here make choice
To sing the Tryals of her Voice.
Low Shrubs she sits in, and adorns 515
With Musick high the squatted Thorns.
But highest Oakes stoop down to hear,

---

492. *Vere:* family name of the wife of Marvell's patron and mother of his pupil.

And listning Elders prick the Ear.
The Thorn, lest it should hurt her, draws
Within the Skin its shrunken claws. 520

LXVI

But I have for my Musick found
A Sadder, yet more pleasing Sound:
The *Stock-doves,* whose fair necks are grac'd
With Nuptial Rings their Ensigns chast;
Yet always, for some Cause unknown, 525
Sad pair unto the Elms they moan.
O why should such a Couple mourn,
That in so equal Flames do burn!

LXVII

Then as I carless on the Bed
Of gelid *Straw-berryes* do tread, 530
And through the Hazles thick espy
The hatching *Thrastles* shining Eye,
The *Heron* from the Ashes top,
The eldest of its young lets drop,
As if it Stork-like did pretend 535
That *Tribute* to *its Lord* to send.

LXVIII

But most the *Hewel's* wonders are,
Who here has the *Holt-felsters* care.
He walks still upright from the Root,
Meas'ring the Timber with his Foot; 540
And all the way, to keep it clean,
Doth from the Bark the Wood-moths glean.
He, with his Beak, examines well
Which fit to stand and which to fell.

---

535. *Stork-like:* the stork was supposed to leave one of her young behind for the owner of the house where she had nested.
537. *Hewel:* woodpecker.
538. *Holt-felsters:* the woodcutters.

LXIX

The good he numbers up, and hacks; 545
As if he mark'd them with the Ax.
But where he, tinkling with his Beak,
Does find the hollow Oak to speak,
That for his building he designs,
And through the tainted Side he mines. 550
Who could have thought the *tallest Oak*
Should fall by such a *feeble Strok'!*

LXX

Nor would it, had the Tree not fed
A *Traitor-worm,* within it bred.
(As first our *Flesh* corrupt within 555
Tempts impotent and bashful *Sin.*
And yet that *Worm* triumphs not long,
But serves to feed the *Hewels young.*
While the Oake seems to fall content,
Viewing the Treason's Punishment. 560

LXXI

Thus I, *easie Philosopher,*
Among the *Birds* and *Trees* confer:
And little now to make me, wants
Or of the *Fowles,* or of the *Plants.*
Give me but Wings as they, and I 565
Streight floting on the Air shall fly:
Or turn me but, and you shall see
I was but an inverted Tree.

LXXII

Already I begin to call
In their most learned Original: 570
And where I Language want, my Signs
The Bird upon the Bough divines;
And more attentive there doth sit
Than if She were with Lime-twigs knit.

No Leaf does tremble in the Wind 575
Which I returning cannot find.

LXXIII

Out of these scatter'd *Sibyls* Leaves
Strange *Prophecies* my Phancy weaves:
And in one History consumes,
Like *Mexique Paintings,* all the *Plumes.* 580
What *Rome, Greece, Palestine,* ere said
I in this light *Mosaick* read.
Thrice happy he who, not mistook,
Hath read in *Natures mystick Book.*

LXXIV

And see how Chance's better Wit 585
Could with a Mask my studies hit!
The Oak-Leaves me embroyder all,
Between which Caterpillars crawl:
And Ivy, with familiar trails,
Me licks, and clasps, and curles, and hales. 590
Under this *antick Cope* I move
Like some great *Prelate of the Grove,*

LXXV

Then, languishing with ease, I toss
On Pallets swoln of Velvet Moss;
While the Wind, cooling through the Boughs, 595
Flatters with Air my panting Brows.
Thanks for my Rest ye *Mossy Banks,*
And unto you *cool Zephyr's* Thanks,
Who, as my Hair, my Thoughts too shed,
And winnow from the Chaff my Head. 600

LXXVI

How safe, methinks, and strong, behind
These Trees have I incamp'd my Mind;

---

586. *Mask:* emblematic costume. *hit:* suit.
599. *shed:* part.

Where Beauty, aiming at the Heart,
Bends in some Tree its useless Dart;
And where the World no certain Shot 605
Can make, or me it toucheth not.
But I on it securely play,
And gaul its Horsemen all the Day.

LXXVII

Bind me ye *Woodbines* in your 'twines,
Curle me about ye gadding *Vines,* 610
And Oh so close your Circles lace,
That I may never leave this Place:
But, lest your Fetters prove too weak,
Ere I your Silken Bondage break,
Do you, *O Brambles,* chain me too, 615
And courteous *Briars* nail me through.

LXXVIII

Here in the Morning tye my Chain,
Where the two Woods have made a Lane;
While, like a *Guard* on either side,
The Trees before their *Lord* divide; 620
This, like a long and equal Thread,
Betwixt two *Labyrinths* does lead.
But, where the Floods did lately drown,
There at the Ev'ning stake me down.

LXXIX

For now the Waves are fal'n and dry'd, 625
And now the Meadows fresher dy'd;
Whose Grass, with moister colour dasht,
Seems as green Silks but newly washt.
No *Serpent* new nor *Crocodile*
Remains behind our little *Nile;* 630
Unless it self you will mistake,
Among these Meads the only Snake.

LXXX

See in what wanton harmless folds
It ev'ry where the Meadow holds;

And its yet muddy back doth lick, 635
Till as a *Chrystal Mirrour* slick;
Where all things gaze themselves, and doubt
If they be in it or without.
And for his shade which therein shines,
Narcissus like, the *Sun* too pines. 640

LXXXI

Oh what a Pleasure 'tis to hedge
My Temples here with heavy sedge;
Abandoning my lazy Side,
Stretcht as a Bank unto the Tide;
Or to suspend my sliding Foot 645
On the Osiers undermined Root,
And in its Branches tough to hang,
While at my Lines the Fishes twang!

LXXXII

But now away my Hooks, my Quills,
And Angles, idle Utensils. 650
The *young Maria* walks to night:
Hide trifling Youth thy Pleasures slight.
'Twere shame that such judicious Eyes
Should with such Toyes a Man surprize;
She that already is the *Law* 655
Of all her *Sex*, her *Ages Aw*.

LXXXIII

See how loose Nature, in respect
To her, it self doth recollect;
And every thing so whisht and fine,
Starts forth with to its *Bonne Mine*. 660
The *Sun* himself, of *Her* aware,
Seems to descend with greater Care;
And lest *She* see him go to Bed;
In blushing Clouds conceales his Head.

651: *Maria:* Fairfax's daughter and Marvell's pupil.
660. Puts on its best appearance. *Bonne* has two syllables.

LXXXIV

So when the Shadows laid asleep 665
From underneath these Banks do creep,
And on the River as it flows
With *Eben Shuts* begin to close;
The modest *Halcyon* comes in sight,
Flying betwixt the Day and Night; 670
And such an horror calm and dumb,
Admiring Nature does benum.

LXXXV

The viscous Air, wheres'ere She fly,
Follows and sucks her Azure dy;
The gellying Stream compacts below, 675
If it might fix her shadow so;
The stupid Fishes hang, as plain
As *Flies* in *Chrystal* overt'ane;
And Men the silent *Scene* assist,
Charm'd with the *Saphir-winged Mist.* 680

LXXXVI

Maria such, and so doth hush
The *World,* and through the *Ev'ning* rush.
No new-born *Comet* such a Train
Draws through the Skie, nor Star new-slain.
For streight those giddy Rockets fail, 685
Which from the putrid Earth exhale,
But by her *Flames,* in *Heaven* try'd,
Nature is wholly *vitrifi'd.*

LXXXVII

'Tis *She* that to these Gardens gave
That wondrous Beauty which they have; 690
She streightness on the Woods bestows;
To *Her* the Meadow sweetness owes;
Nothing could make the River be
So Chrystal-pure but only *She;*

She yet more Pure, Sweet, Streight, and Fair, 695
Than Gardens, Woods, Meads, Rivers are.

LXXXVIII

Therefore what first *She* on them spent,
They gratefully again present.
The Meadow Carpets where to tread;
The Garden Flow'rs to Crown *Her* Head; 700
And for a Glass the limpid Brook,
Where *She* may all *her* Beautyes look;
But, since *She* would not have them seen,
The Wood about *her* draws a Skreen.

LXXXIX

For *She,* to higher Beauties rais'd, 705
Disdains to be for lesser prais'd.
She counts her Beauty to converse
In all the Languages as *hers;*
Nor yet in those *her self* imployes
But for the *Wisdome,* not the *Noyse;* 710
Nor yet that *Wisdome* would affect,
But as 'tis *Heavens Dialect.*

LXXXX

Blest Nymph! that couldst so soon prevent
Those *Trains* by Youth against thee meant;
Tears (watry Shot that pierce the Mind;) 715
And *Sighs* (Loves Cannon charg'd with Wind;)
True Praise (That breaks through all defence;)
And *feign'd complying Innocence;*
But knowing where this *Ambush* lay,
She scap'd the safe, but roughest Way. 720

LXXXXI

This 'tis to have been from the first
In a *Domestick Heaven* nurst,
Under the *Discipline* severe
Of *Fairfax,* and the starry *Vere;*
Where not one object can come nigh 725

But pure, and spotless as the Eye;
And *Goodness* doth it self intail
On *Females,* if there want a *Male.*

LXXXXII

Go now fond Sex that on your Face
Do all your useless Study place, 730
Nor once at Vice your Brows dare knit
Lest the smooth Forehead wrinkled sit:
Yet your own Face shall at you grin,
Thorough the Black-bag of your Skin;
When *knowledge* only could have fill'd 735
And *Virtue* all those *Furrows till'd.*

LXXXXIII

Hence *She* with Graces more divine
Supplies beyond her *Sex* the *Line;*
And, like a *sprig of Misleto,*
On the *Fairfacian Oak* does grow; 740
Whence, for some universal good,
The *Priest* shall cut the sacred Bud;
While her *glad Parents* most rejoice,
And make their *Destiny* their *Choice.*

LXXXXIV

Mean time ye Fields, Springs, Bushes, Flow'rs, 745
Where yet She leads her studious Hours,
(Till Fate her worthily translates,
And find a *Fairfax* for our *Thwaites*)
Employ the means you have by Her,
And in your kind your selves preferr; 750
That, as all *Virgins* She preceds,
So you all *Woods, Streams, Gardens, Meads.*

LXXXXV

For you *Thessalian Tempe's Seat*
Shall now be scorn'd as obsolete;
Aranjuez, as less, disdain'd; 755
The *Bel-Retiro* as constrain'd;

But name not the *Idalian Grove,*
For 'twas the Seat of wanton Love;
Much less the Dead's *Elysian Fields,*
Yet nor to them your Beauty yields. 760

LXXXXVI

'Tis not, what once it was, the *World;*
But a rude heap together hurl'd;
All negligently overthrown,
Gulfes, Deserts, Precipices, Stone.
Your lesser *World* contains the same. 765
But in more decent Order tame;
You Heaven's Center, Nature's Lap.
And Paradice's only Map.

LXXXXVII

But now the *Salmon-Fishers* moist
Their *Leathern Boats* begin to hoist; 770
And, like *Antipodes* in Shoes,
Have shod their *Heads* in their *Canoos.*
How *Tortoise like,* but not so slow,
These rational *Amphibii* go?
Let 's in: for the dark *Hemisphere* 775
Does now like one of them appear.

753–757. The vale of *Tempe* was sacred to Apollo. *Aranjuez* and *Bel-Retiro* were Spanish royal residences. The *Idalian Grove* was a haunt of Venus'.

An *Horatian* Ode upon *Cromwel's* Return from *Ireland*

The forward Youth that would appear
Must now forsake his *Muses* dear,
  Nor in the Shadows sing
  His Numbers languishing.
'Tis time to leave the Books in dust, 5

Cromwell returned from a military expedition against Ireland in May 1650, sixteen months after the execution of Charles I.

And oyl th' unused Armours rust:
  Removing from the Wall
  The Corslet of the Hall.
So restless *Cromwel* could not cease
In the inglorious Arts of Peace, 10
  But through adventrous War
  Urged his active Star.
And, like the three-fork'd Lightning, first
Breaking the Clouds where it was nurst,
  Did thorough his own Side 15
  His fiery way divide.
For 'tis all one to Courage high
The Emulous or Enemy;
  And with such to inclose
  Is more than to oppose. 20
Then burning through the Air he went,
And Pallaces and Temples rent:
  And *Cæsars* head at last
  Did through his Laurels blast.
'Tis Madness to resist or blame 25
The force of angry Heavens flame:
  And, if we would speak true,
  Much to the Man is due.
Who, from his private Gardens, where
He liv'd reserved and austere, 30
  As if his highest plot
  To plant the Bergamot,
Could by industrious Valour climbe
To ruine the great Work of Time,
  And cast the Kingdome old 35
  Into another Mold.
Though Justice against Fate complain,
And plead the antient Rights in vain:
  But those do hold or break
  As Men are strong or weak. 40
Nature that hateth emptiness,
Allows of penetration less:

24. The laurel was supposed to ward off lightning.

And therefore must make room
Where greater Spirits come.
What Field of all the Civil Wars 45
Where his were not the deepest Scars?
And *Hampton* shows what part
He had of wiser Art.
Where, twining subtile fears with hope,
He wove a Net of such a scope, 50
That *Charles* himself might chase
To *Caresbrooks* narrow case.
That thence the *Royal Actor* born
The *Tragick Scaffold* might adorn:
While round the armed Bands 55
Did clap their bloody hands.
He nothing common did or mean
Upon that memorable Scene:
But with his keener Eye
The Axes edge did try: 60
Nor call'd the *Gods* with vulgar spight
To vindicate his helpless Right,
But bow'd his comely Head,
Down as upon a Bed.
This was that memorable Hour 65
Which first assur'd the forced Pow'r.
So when they did design
The *Capitols* first Line,
A bleeding Head where they begun,
Did fright the Architects to run; 70
And yet in that the *State*
Foresaw it's happy Fate.
And now the *Irish* are asham'd
To see themselves in one Year tam'd:
So much one Man can do, 75

---

47. *Hampton:* Charles I fled from Hampton Court to Carisbrooke (line 52), a fatal step widely attributed to Cromwell's guile.

61. By contrast with Cromwell, who claimed to be the instrument of divine destiny in ordering the king's execution: compare lines 25–26.

67–72. This happened when the foundations of the Temple of Jupiter were being dug at Rome. The head (*caput*) gave the capitol its name.

That does both act and know.
They can affirm his Praises best,
And have, though overcome, confest
How good he is, how just,
And fit for highest Trust: 80
Nor yet grown stiffer with Command,
But still in the *Republick's* hand:
How fit he is to sway
That can so well obey.
He to the *Commons Feet* presents 85
A *Kingdome,* for his first years rents:
And, what he may, forbears
His Fame to make it theirs:
And has his Sword and Spoyls ungirt,
To lay them at the *Publick's* skirt. 90
So when the Falcon high
Falls heavy from the Sky,
She, having kill'd, no more does search,
But on the next green Bow to pearch;
Where, when he first does lure, 95
The Falckner has her sure.
What may not then our *Isle* presume
While Victory his Crest does plume!
What may not others fear
If thus he crown each Year! 100
A *Cæsar* he ere long to *Gaul,*
To *Italy* an *Hannibal,*
And to all States not free
Shall *Clymacterick* be.
The *Pict* no shelter now shall find 105
Within his party-colour'd Mind;
But from this Valour sad
Shrink underneath the Plad:
Happy if in the tufted brake
The *English Hunter* him mistake; 110

---

104. *Clymacterick:* a critical or decisive period.
105. *Pict:* Scot. The word's supposed derivation from *pingere,* to paint, was used to support charges of unreliability.
107. *sad:* steadfast.

Nor lay his Hounds in near
The *Caledonian* Deer.
But thou the Wars and Fortunes Son
March indefatigably on;
And for the last effect 115
Still keep thy Sword erect:
Besides the force it has to fright
The Spirits of the shady Night,
The same *Arts* that did *gain*
A *Pow'r* must it *maintain*. 120

117–118. The sword's power against spirits was derived from its cruciform shape.

Index

Authors, Titles, and First Lines

Rinehart Editions

Hawthorne, SELECTED TALES AND SKETCHES 3 ed., 33
Hesse, THE GLASS BEAD GAME 138
Hesse, STEPPENWOLF 122
Howe, E. W., THE STORY OF A COUNTRY TOWN 127
Howells, THE RISE OF SILAS LAPHAM 19
Ibsen, FOUR PLAYS: Ghosts, Enemy of the People, Wild Duck, Hedda Gabler 4
Irving, SELECTED PROSE 41
James, Henry, THE AMBASSADORS 104
James, Henry, THE AMERICAN 16
James, Henry, SELECTED SHORT STORIES 31
Johnson, RASSELAS, POEMS & SELECTED PROSE 3 ed., 57
Jonson, SELECTED WORKS 152
Keats, SELECTED POETRY AND LETTERS 2 ed., 50
Lincoln, SELECTED SPEECHES, MESSAGES, AND LETTERS 82
LITERATURE OF THE EARLY REPUBLIC 2 ed., 44
London, MARTIN EDEN 80
Mailer, THE NAKED AND THE DEAD 134
MASTERPIECES OF THE SPANISH GOLDEN AGE 93
Melville, MOBY DICK 6
Melville, SEL'D TALES AND POEMS 36
Melville, THE CONFIDENCE-MAN 126
Melville, REDBURN 149
Melville, WHITE-JACKET 132
Meredith, THE ORDEAL OF RICHARD FEVEREL, 123
Milton, PARADISE LOST AND SELECTED POETRY AND PROSE 35
MODERN AMERICAN LITERATURE 53
Newman, THE IDEA OF A UNIVERSITY 102
Norris, Frank, MC TEAGUE 40
Parkman, THE DISCOVERY OF THE GREAT WEST: LA SALLE 77
Peacock, NIGHTMARE ABBEY, THE MISFORTUNES OF ELPHIN, CROTCHET CASTLE 148
PLUTARCH—EIGHT GREAT LIVES 105
Poe, SELECTED PROSE, POETRY, AND Eureka rev. 42
POETRY OF THE NEW ENGLAND RENAISSANCE, 1790–1890 38
Pope, SELECTED POETRY AND PROSE 2 ed., 46
Richardson, CLARISSA 128
RINEHART BOOK OF SHORT STORIES 59
RINEHART BOOK OF SHORT STORIES, alt. ed., 129
RINEHART BOOK OF VERSE 58
Robinson, E. A., SEL. EARLY POEMS AND LETTERS 107
Roosevelt, F. D., SPEECHES, MESSAGES, PRESS CONFERENCES, & LETTERS 83
Scott, THE HEART OF MIDLOTHIAN 14
SELECTED AMERICAN PROSE, 1841–1900 94
SELECTIONS FROM GREEK AND ROMAN HISTORIANS 88
SEVENTEENTH CENTURY POETRY 124
SEVENTEENTH CENTURY PROSE 125
Shakespeare, FIVE PLAYS: Hamlet; King Lear; Henry IV, Part I; Much Ado about Nothing; The Tempest 51
Shakespeare, AS YOU LIKE IT, JULIUS CAESAR, MACBETH 91
Shakespeare, TWELFTH NIGHT, OTHELLO 92
Shaw, SELECTED PLAYS AND OTHER WRITINGS 81
Shelley, SELECTED POETRY AND PROSE 49
Sidney, SELECTED PROSE AND POETRY 137
SIR GAWAIN AND THE GREEN KNIGHT 97
Smollet, HUMPHREY CLINKER 48
SOUTHERN STORIES 106
Spenser, SELECTED POETRY 73
Sterne, TRISTRAM SHANDY 37
Stevenson, MASTER OF BALLANTRAE 67
Strindberg, SELECTED PLAYS AND PROSE 130
Swift, GULLIVER'S TRAVELS 10
Swift, SELECTED PROSE AND POETRY 78
Tennyson, SELECTED POETRY 69
Thackeray, HENRY ESMOND 116
Thackeray, VANITY FAIR 76
THE THEORY OF THE AMERICAN NOVEL 143
Thoreau, WALDEN, ON THE DUTY OF CIVIL DISOBEDIENCE 8
THREE SENTIMENTAL NOVELS, 139
Thoreau, A WEEK ON THE CONCORD AND MERRIMACK RIVERS 118
Tolstoy, THREE SHORT WORKS 131
Trollope, BARCHESTER TOWERS 21
Turgenev, FATHERS AND CHILDREN 17
Twain, THE ADVENTURES OF HUCKLEBERRY FINN 11
Twain, ROUGHING IT 61
Vergil, THE AENEID rev. ed., 63
VICTORIAN POETRY: Clough to Kipling 96
Wharton, HOUSE OF MIRTH 113
Whitman, LEAVES OF GRASS AND SELECTED PROSE 28
Wordsworth, THE PRELUDE, SEL'D SONNETS & MINOR POEMS, rev. & enl. 3